GAMECUBE™

EVERYONE

AVATAR: THE LAST AIRBENDER

BRATZ: FOREVER DIAMONDZ

BRATZ: ROCK ANGELZ

BUST-A-MOVE 3000

CARS

CHICKEN LITTLE

CURIOUS GEORGE

DONKEY KONGA

FAIRLY ODDPARENTS: BREAKIN' DA RULES

FIFA STREET 2

FROGGER: ANCIENT SHADOW

GROOVERIDER SLOT CAR THUNDER

ICE AGE 2: THE MELTDOWN

THE INCREDIBLES: RISE OF THE UNDERMINER

JIMMY NEUTRON BOY GENIUS

JIMMY NEUTRON JET FUSION

LEGO STAR WARS: THE VIDEO GAME

LEGO STAR WARS II: THE ORIGINAL TRILOGY

MADDEN NFL 06

MADDEN NFL 07

MAJOR LEAGUE BASEBALL 2K6

MARIO GOLF: TOADSTOOL TOUR

MARIO POWER TENNIS

MARIO SUPERSTAR BASEBALL

MEGA MAN X COLLECTION

MIDWAY ARCADE TREASURES 3

MONSTER HOUSE

MVP BASEBALL 2005

NASCAR 2005: CHASE FOR THE CUP

NBA LIVE 2005

NBA LIVE 06

NCAA FOOTBALL 2005

NEED FOR SPEED CARBON

NEED FOR SPEED UNDERGROUND 2

NFL STREET 2

OVER THE HEDGE

PAC-MAN WORLD 3

PIKMIN 2

RAMPAGE: TOTAL DESTRUCTION

RAVE MASTER

ROBOTS

SCALER

SHREK SUPERSLAM

SONIC ADVENTURE DX DIRECTOR'S CUT

SONIC GEMS COLLECTION

SONIC HEROES

SPONGEBOB SQUAREPANTS: BATTLE FOR BIKINI BOTTOM

SPONGEBOB SQUAREPANTS: CREATURE FROM THE KRUSTY KRAB

SPONGEBOB SQUAREPANTS: LIGHTS, CAMERA, PANTS!

SSX ON TOUR

TAK: THE GREAT JUJU CHALLENGE

TEENAGE MUTANT NINJA TURTLES 3: MUTANT NIGHTMARE

TIGER WOODS PGA TOUR 06

TY THE TASMANIAN TIGER 3: NIGHT OF THE QUINKAN

YU-GI-OH: FALSEBOUND KINGDOM

ZAPPER

TEEN

ALIEN HOMINID

THE CHRONICLES OF NARNIA: THE LION, THE WITCH AND THE WARDROBE

DRAGON BALL Z: SAGAS

FANTASTIC 4

FIRE EMBLEM: PATH OF RADIANCE

FUTURE TACTICS: THE UPRISING

F-ZERO GX

THE HAUNTED MANSION

THE INCREDIBLE HULK: ULTIMATE DESTRUCTION

MARVEL NEMESIS: RISE OF THE IMPERFECTS

NEED FOR SPEED MOST WANTED

PETER JACKSON'S KING KONG: THE OFFICIAL GAME OF THE MOVIE

RAVE MASTER

THE SIMS : BUSTIN' OUT

THE SIMS 2: PETS

SPIDER-MAN 2

STAR WARS ROGUE SQUADRON III: REBEL STRIKE

TONY HAWK'S AMERICAN WASTELAND

TONY HAWK'S UNDERGROUND 2

ULTIMATE SPIDER-MAN

X-MEN LEGENDS II: RISE OF APOCALYPSE

X-MEN: THE OFFICIAL GAME

ZOIDS: BATTLE LEGENDS

GAMECUBE™

GameCube™ Table of Contents

ALIEN HOMINID

ALL LEVELS, MINI-GAMES, AND HATS
Select Player 1 Setup or Player 2 Setup and change the name to **ROYGBIV**.

HATS FOR 2-PLAYER GAME
Go to the Options screen and rename your alien one of the following:

PLAYER	HAT	NUMBER
ABE	Top Hat	#11
APRIL	Blond Wig	#4
BEHEMOTH	Red Cap	#24
CLETUS	Hunting Hat	#3
DANDY	Flower Petal Hat	#13

PLAYER	HAT	NUMBER
GOODMAN	Black Curly Hair	#7
GRRL	Flowers	#10
PRINCESS	Tiara	#12
SUPERFLY	Afro	#6
TOMFULP	Brown Messy Hair	#2

AVATAR: THE LAST AIRBENDER

ALL TREASURE MAPS
Select Code Entry from Extras and enter 37437.

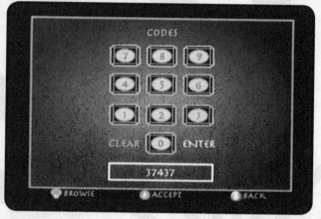

1 HIT DISHONOR
Select Code Entry from Extras and enter 54641.

DOUBLE DAMAGE
Select Code Entry from Extras and enter 34743.

UNLIMITED COPPER
Select Code Entry from Extras and enter 23637.

UNLIMITED CHI
Select Code Entry from Extras and enter 24463.

UNLIMITED HEALTH
Select Code Entry from Extras and enter 94677.

NEVERENDING STEALTH
Select Code Entry from Extras and enter 53467.

CHARACTER CONCEPT ART GALLERY
Select Code Entry from Extras and enter 97831.

BRATZ: FOREVER DIAMONDZ

1000 BLINGZ
While in the Bratz Office, use the Cheat computer to enter SIZZLN.

2000 BLINGZ
While in the Bratz Office, use the Cheat computer to enter FLAUNT.

PET TREATS
While in the Bratz Office, use the Cheat computer to enter TREATZ.

GIFT SET A
While in the Bratz Office, use the Cheat computer to enter STYLIN.

GIFT SET B
While in the Bratz Office, use the Cheat computer to enter SKATIN.

GIFT SET C
While in the Bratz Office, use the Cheat computer to enter JEWELZ.

GIFT SET E
While in the Bratz Office, use the Cheat computer to enter DIMNDZ.

BRATZ: ROCK ANGELZ

CAMERON CHANGED
While in the Bratz Office, use the Cheat computer to enter **STYLIN**.

CHLOE CHANGED
While in the Bratz Office, use the Cheat computer to enter **SPARKLE, FASHION, STRUT** or **FLAIR**.

DYLAN CHANGED
While in the Bratz Office, use the Cheat computer to enter **MEYGEN**.

JADE CHANGED
While in the Bratz Office, use the Cheat computer to enter **FUNKALISH, SLAMMIN** or **HOT**.

LONDON BOY CHANGED
While in the Bratz Office, use the Cheat computer to enter **BLINGZ**.

PARIS BOY CHANGED
While in the Bratz Office, use the Cheat computer to enter **ROCKIN**.

SASHA CHANGED
While in the Bratz Office, use the Cheat computer to enter **FUNKY, SCORCHIN, PRETTY** or **MODEL**.

YASMIN CHANGED
While in the Bratz Office, use the Cheat computer to enter **COOL, CRAZY** or **SASSY**.

RECEIVE 1000 BLINGZ
While in the Bratz Office, use the Cheat computer to enter **YASMIN**.

RECEIVE 2000 BLINGZ
While in the Bratz Office, use the Cheat computer to enter **PHOEBE**.

RECEIVE 2100 BLINGZ
While in the Bratz Office, use the Cheat computer to enter **DANCIN**.

RECEIVE 3000 BLINGZ
While in the Bratz Office, use the Cheat computer to enter **WAYFAB**.

RECEIVE 6000 BLINGZ
While in the Bratz Office, use the Cheat computer to enter **HOTTIE**.

UNLOCKED RINGTONE 12
While in the Bratz Office, use the Cheat computer to enter **BLAZIN**.

UNLOCKED RINGTONE 15
While in the Bratz Office, use the Cheat computer to enter **FIANNA**.

UNLOCKED RINGTONE 16
While in the Bratz Office, use the Cheat computer to enter **ANGELZ**.

BUST-A-MOVE 3000

ANOTHER WORLD
At the title screen, press Y, Left, Right, Y.

FUNGILA AND KATZE
At the title screen, press Y, Right, Left, Y.

CARS

UNLOCK EVERYTHING
Select Cheat Codes from the Options and enter IF900HP.

ALL CHARACTERS
Select Cheat Codes from the Options and enter YAYCARS.

ALL CHARACTER SKINS
Select Cheat Codes from the Options and enter R4MONE.

ALL MINI-GAMES AND COURSES
Select Cheat Codes from the Options and enter MATTL66.

MATER'S COUNTDOWN CLEAN-UP MINI-GAME AND MATER'S SPEEDY CIRCUIT
Select Cheat Codes from the Options and enter TRGTEXC.

FAST START
Select Cheat Codes from the Options and enter IMSPEED.

INFINITE BOOST
Select Cheat Codes from the Options and enter VROOOOM.

ART
Select Cheat Codes from the Options and enter CONC3PT.

VIDEOS
Select Cheat Codes from the Options and enter WATCHIT.

CHICKEN LITTLE

INVINCIBILITY
Select Cheat Codes from the Extras menu and enter Baseball, Baseball, Baseball, Shirt.

BIG FEET
Select Cheat Codes from the Extras menu and enter Hat, Glove, Glove, Hat.

BIG HAIR
Select Cheat Codes from the Extras menu and enter Baseball, Bat, Bat, Baseball.

BIG HEAD
Select Cheat Codes from the Extras menu and enter Hat, Helmet, Helmet, Hat.

PAPER PANTS
Select Cheat Codes from the Extras menu and enter Bat, Bat, Hat, Hat.

SUNGLASSES
Select Cheat Codes from the Extras menu and enter Glove, Glove, Helmet, Helmet.

UNDERWEAR
Select Cheat Codes from the Extras menu and enter Hat, Hat, Shirt, Shirt.

THE CHRONICLES OF NARNIA: THE LION, THE WITCH AND THE WARDROBE

ENABLE CHEATS
At the Title screen, press A then hold L + R and press Down, Down, Right, Up. The text should turn green when the code is entered correctly. Now you can enter the following:

LEVEL SELECT
At the wardrobe, hold L and press Up, Up, Right, Right, Up, Right, Down.

ALL BONUS LEVELS
At the Bonus Drawer, hold L and press Down, Down, Right, Right, Down, Right, Up.

LEVEL SKIP
During gameplay, hold L and press Down, Left, Down, Left, Down, Right, Down, Right, Up.

INVINCIBILITY
During gameplay, hold L and press Down, Up, Down, Right, Right.

RESTORE HEALTH
During gameplay, hold L and press Down, Left, Left, Right.

10,000 COINS
During gameplay, hold L and press Down, Left, Right, Down, Down.

ALL ABILITIES
During gameplay, hold L and press Down, Left, Right, Left, Up.

FILL COMBO METER
During gameplay, hold L and press Up, Up, Right, Up.

CURIOUS GEORGE

CURIOUS GEORGE GOES APE
Pause the game, hold Z and press B, B, A, Y, B.

UNLIMITED BANANAS
Pause the game, hold Z and press A, X, X, Y, A.

ROLLERSKATES AND FEZ HAT
Pause the game, hold Z and press X, A, A, A, B.

UPSIDE DOWN GRAVITY MODE
Pause the game, hold Z and press Y, Y, B, A, A.

DONKEY KONGA

100M VINE CLIMB (1 OR 2 PLAYERS)
Collect 4800 coins to unlock this mini-game for purchase at DK Town.

BANANA JUGGLE (1 OR 2 PLAYERS)
Collect 5800 coins to unlock this mini-game for purchase at DK Town.

BASH K. ROOL (1 PLAYER)
Collect 5800 coins to unlock this mini-game for purchase at DK Town.

DRAGON BALL Z: SAGAS

ALL UPGRADES
Pause the game, select Controller and press Up, Left, Down, Right, Start, Start, Y, A, X, B.

INVINCIBILITY
Pause the game, select Controller and press Down, A, Up, Y, Start, Start, Right, Left, X, B.

PENDULUM MODE
Complete the game.

FAIRLY ODDPARENTS: BREAKIN' DA RULES

PASSWORDS

LEVEL	PASSWORD
2	Wanda, Vicky, Country Boy, Cosmo, Bronze Knee Cap
3	Wanda, Country Boy, Wanda, Crimson Chin, Crimson Chin
4	Bronze Knee Cap, Wanda, Country Boy, Bronze Knee Cap, Spatula Lady
5	Crimson Chin, Country Boy, Country Boy, Crimson Chin, Cosmo

FANTASTIC 4

BARGE ARENA AND STAN LEE INTERVIEW #1
At the Main menu, press B, X, B, Down, Down, X, Up.

INFINITE COSMIC POWER
At the Main menu, press Up, B, B, B, Left, Right, X.

BONUS LEVEL
At the Main menu, press Right, Right, B, X, Left, Up, Down.

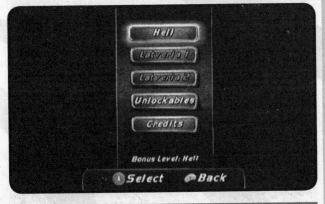

FIFA STREET 2

ALL STAGES
At the Main menu, hold L + Y and press Left, Up, Up, Right, Down, Down, Right, Down.

FIRE EMBLEM: PATH OF RADIANCE

FIRE EMBLEM: PATH OF RADIANCE ART
Complete the game.

FIRE EMBLEM ART
Connect a GBA to the GameCube with the Fire Emblem game.

FE: THE SACRED STONES ART
Connect a GBA to the GameCube with the Fire Emblem: The Sacred Stones game.

FROGGER: ANCIENT SHADOW

UNLOCK LEVELS
Select the Secret Code option and enter the following to unlock various levels in the game.

LEVEL	ENTER
Dr. Wani's Mansion Level 1 with Berry	Berry, Lily, Lumpy, Lily
Dr. Wani's Mansion Level 2 with Berry	Finnius, Frogger, Frogger, Wani
Elder Ruins Level 1 with Berry	Lily, Lily, Wani, Wani
Elder Ruins Level 2 with Berry	Frogger, Berry, Finnius, Frogger
Doom's Temple Level 1 with Berry	Lily, Wani, Lily, Wani
Doom's Temple Level 2 with Berry	Frogger, Lily, Lily, Lily
Doom's Temple Level 3 with Berry	Frogger, Frogger, Frogger, Berry
Sealed Heart Level 1 with Berry	Lily, Lily, Wani, Lumpy
Sealed Heart Level 2 with Berry	Lily, Frogger, Frogger, Lumpy

UNLOCK LETTERS
Select the Secret Code option and enter the following to unlock various letters in the game.

LETTER	ENTER
WHCinc Letter with Hyacinth Flower Seed	Lumpy, Frogger, Frogger, Berry
Opart's Letter with Cosmos Flower Seed	Berry, Lumpy, Frogger, Lumpy
Secret Admirer Letter with Rose Flower Seed	Wani, Lily, Wani, Frogger
Dr. Wani's Letter with Pansy Flower Seed	Lumpy, Berry, Lumpy, Finnius

UNLOCK WIGS
Select the Secret Code option and enter the following to unlock various wigs in the game.

WIG	ENTER
Lobster Wig	Finnius, Wani, Lumpy, Frogger
Bird Nest Wig	Lily, Lily, Lily, Lily
Masted Ship Wig	Lumpy, Lumpy, Lumpy, Lumpy
Skull Wig	Frogger, Lumpy, Lily, Frogger

UNLOCK ARTWORK
Select the Secret Code option and enter the following to unlock various artwork pieces from the game.

ARTWORK	ENTER
Developer Picture 1	Wani, Frogger, Wani, Frogger
Developer Picture 2	Berry, Berry, Berry, Wani
Programmer Art 1	Wani, Wani, Wani, Wani
Programmer Art 2	Lumpy, Frogger, Berry, Lily
Programmer Art 3	Wani, Frogger, Lily, Finnius
Additional Art 1	Frogger, Frogger, Frogger, Frogger
Additional Art 2	Finnius, Finnius, Finnius, Finnius
Additional Art 3	Berry, Berry, Berry, Berry

GROOVERIDER SLOT CAR THUNDER

UNLOCK EVERYTHING
Select Time Trial and enter MARK as your name. Return to the main menu to find the Cheats option.

CREDITS
Select Time Trial and enter BGM as your name. Return to the main menu to find the Cheats option.

THE HAUNTED MANSION

SKELETON ZEKE
At the Legal screen, hold A + B + X + Y. Release the buttons at the Title screen.

LEVEL SELECT
During a game, hold Right and press X, X, B, Y, Y, B, X, A.

INVINCIBILITY
During a game, hold Right and press B, X (x3), B, X, Y, A.

WEAPON UPGRADE
During a game, hold Right and press B, B, Y, Y, X (x3), A.

ICE AGE 2: THE MELTDOWN

ALL BONUSES
Pause the game and press Down, Left, Up, Down, Down, Left, Right, Right.

LEVEL SELECT
Pause the game and press Up, Right, Right, Left, Right, Right, Down, Down.

UNLIMITED PEBBLES
Pause the game and press Down, Down, Left, Up, Up, Right, Up, Down.

INFINITE ENERGY
Pause the game and press Down, Left, Right, Down, Down, Right, Left, Down.

INFINITE HEALTH
Pause the game and press Up, Right, Down, Up, Left, Down, Right, Left.

THE INCREDIBLE HULK: ULTIMATE DESTRUCTION

You must collect a specific comic in the game to activate each code. After collecting the appropriate comic, you can enter the following codes. If you don't have the comic and enter the code, you receive a message "That code cannot be activated... yet". Enter the cheats at the Code Input screen.

UNLOCKED: CABS GALORE
Select Code Input from the Extras menu and enter **CABBIES**.

UNLOCKED: GORILLA INVASION
Select Code Input from the Extras menu and enter **kingkng**.

UNLOCKED: MASS TRANSIT
Select Code Input from the Extras menu and enter **TRANSIT**.

UNLOCKED: 5000 SMASH POINTS
Select Code Input from the Extras menu and enter **SMASH5**.

UNLOCKED: 10000 SMASH POINTS
Select Code Input from the Extras menu and enter **SMASH10**.

UNLOCKED: 15000 SMASH POINTS
Select Code Input from the Extras menu and enter **SMASH15**.

UNLOCKED: AMERICAN FLAG SHORTS
Select Code Input from the Extras menu and enter **AMERICA**.

UNLOCKED: CANADIAN FLAG SHORTS
Select Code Input from the Extras menu and enter **OCANADA**.

UNLOCKED: FRENCH FLAG SHORTS
Select Code Input from the Extras menu and enter **Drapeau**.

UNLOCKED: GERMAN FLAG SHORTS
Select Code Input from the Extras menu and enter **DEUTSCH**.

UNLOCKED: ITALIAN FLAG SHORTS
Select Code Input from the Extras menu and enter **MUTANDA**.

UNLOCKED: JAPANESE FLAG SHORTS
Select Code Input from the Extras menu and enter **FURAGGU**.

UNLOCKED: SPANISH FLAG SHORTS
Select Code Input from the Extras menu and enter **BANDERA**.

UNLOCKED: UK FLAG SHORTS
Select Code Input from the Extras menu and enter **FSHNCHP**.

UNLOCKED: COW MISSILES
Select Code Input from the Extras menu and enter **CHZGUN**.

UNLOCKED: DOUBLE HULK'S DAMAGE
Select Code Input from the Extras menu and enter **DESTROY**.

UNLOCKED: DOUBLE POWER COLLECTABLES
Select Code Input from the Extras menu and enter **BRINGIT**.

UNLOCKED: BLACK AND WHITE
Select Code Input from the Extras menu and enter **RETRO**.

UNLOCKED: SEPIA
Select Code Input from the Extras menu and enter **HISTORY**.

UNLOCKED: ABOMINATION
Select Code Input from the Extras menu and enter **VILLAIN**.

UNLOCKED: GRAY HULK
Select Code Input from the Extras menu and enter **CLASSIC**.

UNLOCKED: JOE FIXIT SKIN
Select Code Input from the Extras menu and enter **SUITFIT**.

UNLOCKED: WILD TRAFFIC
Select Code Input from the Extras menu and enter **FROGGIE**.

UNLOCKED: LOW GRAVITY
Select Code Input from the Extras menu and enter **PILLOWS**.

THE INCREDIBLES: RISE OF THE UNDERMINER

BIG HEADS
Pause the game and access the menu. Choose the Secrets option and enter **EGOPROBLEM**. Re-enter the code to disable it.

MR. INCREDIBLE GAINS 1000 EXPERIENCE POINTS
Pause the game and access the menu. Choose the Secrets option and enter **MRIPROF**.

FROZONE 1000 GAINS EXPERIENCE POINTS
Pause the game and access the menu. Choose the Secrets option and enter **FROZPROF**.

MR. INCREDIBLE GAINS A SUPER-MOVE
Pause the game and access the menu. Choose the Secrets option and enter **MRIBOOM**.

FROZONE GAINS A SUPER-MOVE
Pause the game and access the menu. Choose the Secrets option and enter **FROZBOOM**.\

SHOWS THE GAME CREDITS
Pause the game and access the menu. Choose the Secrets option and enter **ROLLCALL**.

TOUGHER GAME
Pause the game and access the menu. Choose the Secrets option and enter **THISISTOOEASY**. This code cuts damage caused to enemies in half, doubles damage inflicted to the Supers, allows no health recovery, and Experience Points are halved!

EASIER GAME
Pause the game and access the menu. Choose the Secrets option and enter **THISISTOOHARD**. This code doubles damage caused to enemies, halves damage inflicted to the Supers, and doubles the amount of health recovery and Experience Points!

ALL GALLERY ITEMS
Pause the game and access the menu. Choose the Secrets option and enter **SHOWME**.

DOUBLE EXPERIENCE POINTS
Pause the game and access the menu. Choose the Secrets option and enter **MAXIMILLION**.

JIMMY NEUTRON BOY GENIUS

ALL KEY ITEMS
During a game, press R, R, L, A, B, B, A, R, L, R, Start, Down, A, Down.

JIMMY NEUTRON: JET FUSION

ALL MOVIES
During a game, press Z, L, R, R, B, X, X, B, R, R, L, L.

4-HIT COMBO
Pause the game, hold L + R and press A, B, A, Up.

LEGO STAR WARS: THE VIDEO GAME

Extras
Pause the game and select Extras to toggle these cheats on and off.

INVINCIBILITY
At Dexter's Diner, select Enter Code and enter 4PR28U.

BIG BLASTERS
At Dexter's Diner, select Enter Code and enter IG72X4.

CLASSIC BLASTERS
At Dexter's Diner, select Enter Code and enter L449HD.

SILLY BLASTERS
At Dexter's Diner, select Enter Code and enter NR37W1.

BRUSHES
At Dexter's Diner, select Enter Code and enter SHRUB1.

TEA CUPS
At Dexter's Diner, select Enter Code and enter PUCEAT.

MINIKIT DETECTOR
At Dexter's Diner, select Enter Code and enter LD116B.

MOUSTACHES
At Dexter's Diner, select Enter Code and enter RP924W.

PURPLE
At Depxter's Diner, select Enter Code and enter YD77GC.

SILHOUETTES

At Dexter's Diner, select Enter Code and enter MS999Q.

Characters

These codes make each character available for purchase from Dexter's Diner.

BATTLE DROID

At Dexter's Diner, select Enter Code and enter 987UYR.

BATTLE DROID (COMMANDER)

At Dexter's Diner, select Enter Code and enter EN11K5.

BATTLE DROID (GEONOSIS)

At Dexter's Diner, select Enter Code and enter LK42U6.

BATTLE DROID (SECURITY)

At Dexter's Diner, select Enter Code and enter KF999A.

BOBA FETT

At Dexter's Diner, select Enter Code and enter LA811Y.

CLONE

At Dexter's Diner, select Enter Code and enter F8B4L6.

CLONE (EPISODE III)

At Dexter's Diner, select Enter Code and enter ER33JN.

CLONE (EPISODE III, PILOT)

At Dexter's Diner, select Enter Code and enter BHU72T.

CLONE (EPISODE III, SWAMP)

At Dexter's Diner, select Enter Code and enter N3T6P8.

CLONE (EPISODE III, WALKER)

At Dexter's Diner, select Enter Code and enter RS6E25.

COUNT DOOKU

At Dexter's Diner, select Enter Code and enter 14PGMN.

DARTH MAUL

At Dexter's Diner, select Enter Code and enter H35TUX.

DARTH SIDIOUS

At Dexter's Diner, select Enter Code and enter A32CAM.

DISGUISED CLONE

At Dexter's Diner, select Enter Code and enter VR832U.

DROIDEKA

At Dexter's Diner, select Enter Code and enter DH382U.

GENERAL GRIEVOUS

At Dexter's Diner, select Enter Code and enter SF321Y.

GEONOSIAN

At Dexter's Diner, select Enter Code and enter 19D7NB.

GRIEVOUS' BODYGUARD

At Dexter's Diner, select Enter Code and enter ZTY392.

GONK DROID

At Dexter's Diner, select Enter Code and enter U63B2A.

JANGO FETT

At Dexter's Diner, select Enter Code and enter PL47NH.

KI-ADI MUNDI

At Dexter's Diner, select Enter Code and enter DP55MV.

KIT FISTO

At Dexter's Diner, select Enter Code and enter CBR954.

LUMINARA

At Dexter's Diner, select Enter Code and enter A725X4.

MACE WINDU (EPISODE III)

At Dexter's Diner, select Enter Code and enter MS952L.

PADMÉ

At Dexter's Diner, select Enter Code and enter 92UJ7D.

PK DROID

At Dexter's Diner, select Enter Code and enter R840JU.

PRINCESS LEIA

At Dexter's Diner, select Enter Code and enter BEQ82H.

REBEL TROOPER

At Dexter's Diner, select Enter Code and enter L54YUK.

ROYAL GUARD

At Dexter's Diner, select Enter Code and enter PP43JX.

SHAAK TI

At Dexter's Diner, select Enter Code and enter EUW862.

SUPER BATTLE DROID

At Dexter's Diner, select Enter Code and enter XZNR21.

LEGO STAR WARS II: THE ORIGINAL TRILOGY

BEACH TROOPER

At Mos Eisley Canteena, select Enter Code and enter UCK868. You still need to select Characters and purchase this character for 20,000 studs.

BEN KENOBI (GHOST)

At Mos Eisley Canteena, select Enter Code and enter BEN917. You still need to select Characters and purchase this character for 1,100,000 studs.

BESPIN GUARD

At Mos Eisley Canteena, select Enter Code and enter VHY832. You still need to select Characters and purchase this character for 15,000 studs.

BIB FORTUNA

At Mos Eisley Canteena, select Enter Code and enter WTY721. You still need to select Characters and purchase this character for 16,000 studs.

BOBA FETT

At Mos Eisley Canteena, select Enter Code and enter HLP221. You still need to select Characters and purchase this character for 175,000 studs.

DEATH STAR TROOPER

At Mos Eisley Canteena, select Enter Code and enter BNC332. You still need to select Characters and purchase this character for 19,000 studs.

EWOK

At Mos Eisley Canteena, select Enter Code and enter TTT289. You still need to select Characters and purchase this character for 34,000 studs.

GAMORREAN GUARD

At Mos Eisley Canteena, select Enter Code and enter YZF999. You still need to select Characters and purchase this character for 40,000 studs.

GONK DROID

At Mos Eisley Canteena, select Enter Code and enter NFX582. You still need to select Characters and purchase this character for 1,550 studs.

GRAND MOFF TARKIN

At Mos Eisley Canteena, select Enter Code and enter SMG219. You still need to select Characters and purchase this character for 38,000 studs.

GREEDO

At Mos Eisley Canteena, select Enter Code and enter NAH118. You still need to select Characters and purchase this character for 60,000 studs.

HAN SOLO (HOOD)

At Mos Eisley Canteena, select Enter Code and enter YWM840. You still need to select Characters and purchase this character for 20,000 studs.

IG-88

At Mos Eisley Canteena, select Enter Code and enter NXL973. You still need to select Characters and purchase this character for 30,000 studs.

IMPERIAL GUARD

At Mos Eisley Canteena, select Enter Code and enter MMM111. You still need to select Characters and purchase this character for 45,000 studs.

IMPERIAL OFFICER

At Mos Eisley Canteena, select Enter Code and enter BBV889. You still need to select Characters and purchase this character for 28,000 studs.

IMPERIAL SHUTTLE PILOT

At Mos Eisley Canteena, select Enter Code and enter VAP664. You still need to select Characters and purchase this character for 29,000 studs.

IMPERIAL SPY

At Mos Eisley Canteena, select Enter Code and enter CVT125. You still need to select Characters and purchase this character for 13,500 studs.

JAWA

At Mos Eisley Canteena, select Enter Code and enter JAW499. You still need to select Characters and purchase this character for 24,000 studs.

LOBOT

At Mos Eisley Canteena, select Enter Code and enter UUB319. You still need to select Characters and purchase this character for 11,000 studs.

PALACE GUARD

At Mos Eisley Canteena, select Enter Code and enter SGE549. You still need to select Characters and purchase this character for 14,000 studs.

REBEL PILOT

At Mos Eisley Canteena, select Enter Code and enter CYG336. You still need to select Characters and purchase this character for 15,000 studs.

REBEL TROOPER (HOTH)
At Mos Eisley Canteena, select Enter Code and enter EKU849. You still need to select Characters and purchase this character for 16,000 studs.

SANDTROOPER
At Mos Eisley Canteena, select Enter Code and enter YDV451. You still need to select Characters and purchase this character for 14,000 studs.

SKIFF GUARD
At Mos Eisley Canteena, select Enter Code and enter GBU888. You still need to select Characters and purchase this character for 12,000 studs.

SNOWTROOPER
At Mos Eisley Canteena, select Enter Code and enter NYU989. You still need to select Characters and purchase this character for 16,000 studs.

STROMTROOPER
At Mos Eisley Canteena, select Enter Code and enter PTR345. You still need to select Characters and purchase this character for 10,000 studs.

THE EMPEROR
At Mos Eisley Canteena, select Enter Code and enter HHY382. You still need to select Characters and purchase this character for 275,000 studs.

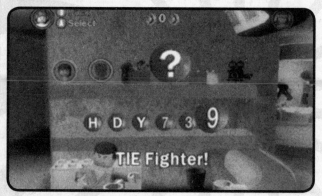

TIE FIGHTER
At Mos Eisley Canteena, select Enter Code and enter HDY739. You still need to select Characters and purchase this character for 60,000 studs.

TIE FIGHTER PILOT
At Mos Eisley Canteena, select Enter Code and enter NNZ316. You still need to select Characters and purchase this character for 21,000 studs.

TIE INTERCEPTOR
At Mos Eisley Canteena, select Enter Code and enter QYA828. You still need to select Characters and purchase this character for 40,000 studs.

TUSKEN RAIDER
At Mos Eisley Canteena, select Enter Code and enter PEJ821. You still need to select Characters and purchase this character for 23,000 studs.

UGNAUGHT
At Mos Eisley Canteena, select Enter Code and enter UGN694. You still need to select Characters and purchase this character for 36,000 studs.

MADDEN NFL 06

Select Madden Cards from My Madden. Then select Madden Codes and enter the following:

PASSWORD	CARD
6W5J6Z	#1 Rex Grossman Gold
6X7W2O	#2 Thomas Jones Gold
6Y5Z6H	#3 Brian Urlacher Gold
6Z9X5Y	#4 Olin Kreutz Gold
7A7Z2G	#5 Tommie Harris Gold
7C6U4H	#6 Carson Palmer Gold
7D1B2H	#7 Chad Johnson Gold
7D1X8K	#8 Rudi Johnson Gold
7D5W8J	#9 Brian Simmons Gold
7D8S6J	#10 J.P. Losman Gold
7E3G7Y	#11 Willis McGahee Gold
7F5B2Y	#12 Eric Moulds Gold
7H3B2Y	#13 Takeo Spikes Gold
7H9E8L	#14 Lawyer Milloy Gold
7J3Y7F	#15 Jake Plummer Gold
7J8F4J	#16 Ashley Lelie Gold
7K5C8V	#17 Al Wilson Gold
7L8C2W	#18 Champ Bailey Gold
1A2D9F	#19 John Lynch Gold
701J3F	#20 D.J. Williams Gold
7P5G3N	#21 Lee Suggs Gold
7Q2E45	#22 Kellen Winslow Jr. Gold
7Q6F4G	#23 Simeon Rice Gold
7Q6X4L	#24 Derrick Brooks Gold
7R7V2E	#25 Ronde Barber Gold
7S4C4D	#26 Anthony McFarland Gold
7T1G2Y	#27 Michael Clayton Gold
7T3V5K	#28 Anquan Boldin Gold
7T6B5N	#29 Larry Fitzgerald Gold
7U4M9B	#30 Bertrand Berry Gold
7U6B3L	#31 LaDainian Tomlinson Gold
8Q2J2R	#55 Donovan McNabb Bronze
8Q2J2X	#55 Donovan McNabb Gold
8V9Y3X	#62 Michael Vick Gold
8X2Y9G	#64 Alge Crumpler Gold
2W4P9T	#188 First and Fifteen Bronze
2W4P9G	#188 First and Fifteen Silver
2Y7L8B	#189 First and Five Bronze
2Z2F4H	#190 Unforced Errors Bronze
2Z2F4G	#190 Unforced Errors Silver
3D3Q3P	#191 Extra Credit Bronze
3D8X6Z	#191 Extra Credit Gold
3D8X6T	#192 Tight Fit Bronze
3E9R4V	#193 5th Down Bronze
3E9R4I	#193 5th Down Silver
3F9G4J	#194 3rd Down Bronze
3F9G4O	#194 3rd Down Silver
3H3U7T	#194 3rd Down Gold
3H3U7F	#195 Human Plow Bronze

PASSWORD	CARD
3H8M5U	#196 Super Dive Bronze
3J3S9Y	#197 Da Boot Bronze
3J3S9E	#197 Da Boot Silver
3T4E3Y	#208 Pocket Protectors Gold
3X1V2H	#210 QB on Target Gold
4D1V2Y	#217 Ouch Gold
4F9D2B	#220 Super Bowl XL Gold
4F9D2H	#221 Super Bowl XLI Gold
4I1V6T	#222 Super Bowl XLII Gold
4F3D7E	#223 Super Bowl XLIII Gold
4I1V6K	#224 Aloha Stadium Gold

MADDEN NFL 07

#199 GOLD LAME DUCK CHEAT CARD
In My Madden, select Madden Codes from Madden Cards. Enter 5LAW00.

#200 GOLD MISTAKE FREE CHEAT CARD
In My Madden, select Madden Codes from Madden Cards. Enter XL7SP1.

#210 GOLD QB ON TARGET CHEAT CARD
In My Madden, select Madden Codes from Madden Cards. Enter WROAOR.

MAJOR LEAGUE BASEBALL 2K6

UNLOCK EVERYTHING
Select Enter Cheat Code from the My 2K6 menu and enter **Derek Jeter**.

TOPPS 2K STARS
Select Enter Cheat Code from the My 2K6 menu and enter **Dream Team**.

SUPER WALL CLIMB
Select Enter Cheat Code from the My 2K6 menu and enter **Last Chance**. Enable the cheats by selecting My Cheats or selecting Cheat Codes from the Options screen in-game.

SUPER PITCHES
Select Enter Cheat Code from the My 2K6 menu and enter **Unhittable**. Enable the cheats by selecting My Cheats or selecting Cheat Codes from the Options screen in-game.

ROCKET ARMS
Select Enter Cheat Code from the My 2K6 menu and enter **Gotcha**. Enable the cheats by selecting My Cheats or selecting Cheat Codes from the Options screen in-game.

BOUNCY BALL
Select Enter Cheat Code from the My 2K6 menu and enter **Crazy Hops**. Enable the cheats by selecting My Cheats or selecting Cheat Codes from the Options screen in-game.

MARIO SUPERSTAR BASEBALL

STAR DASH MINI GAME
Complete Star difficulty on all mini-games.

BABY LUIGI
Complete Challenge Mode with Yoshi.

DIXIE KONG
Complete Challenge Mode with Donkey Kong.

HAMMER BRO
Complete Challenge Mode with Bowser.

MONTY MOLE
Complete Challenge Mode with Mario.

PETEY PIRANHA
Complete Challenge Mode with Wario.

TOADETTE
Complete Challenge Mode with Peach.

KOOPA CASTLE STADIUM
Complete Challenge Mode.

MARVEL NEMESIS: RISE OF THE IMPERFECTS

ALL FANTASTIC FOUR COMICS
Select Cheats from the Options screen and enter **SAVAGELAND**.

ALL TOMORROW PEOPLE COMICS
Select Cheats from the Options screen and enter **NZONE**.

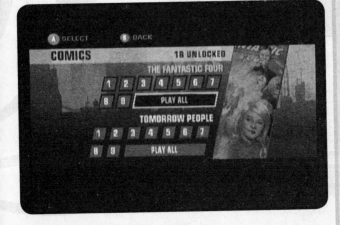

MEGA MAN X COLLECTION

Mega Man X4

BLACK ZERO
At the Character Select screen, highlight Zero and hold R and press Right (x6). Release R, hold X and press Start. Continue holding X until the game starts.

ULTIMATE ARMOR FOR MEGA MAN X
At the Character Select screen, highlight Mega Man X and press X, X, Left (x6). Then hold L + Z and press Start. Continue holding L + Z until the game starts. Complete the level, then find the Leg power-up in the Jungle.

Mega Man X5

BLACK ZERO
At the Character Select screen, highlight Zero and press Down, Down, Up (x9).

ULTIMATE ARMOR FOR MEGA MAN X
At the Character Select screen, highlight Mega Man X and press Up, Up, Down (x9).

Mega Man X6

BLACK ZERO
At the Main menu, highlight Game Start and press L, L, L, R.

ULTIMATE ARMOR FOR MEGA MAN X
At the Main menu, highlight Game Start and press Left, Left, Left, Right.

MIDWAY ARCADE TREASURES 3

HYDRO THUNDER

ALL TRACKS AND BOATS
Get a high score and enter ?PB as your initials.

Offroad Thunder

CLIFFHANGER TRACK
Select Rally and press Right at the Choose Track screen press Right to bring up the Secret Code option. Press Right, Up, Left, to unlock the Cliffhanger track.

CHIEFTAIN & GENERAL VEHICLES
Select Rally and press Right at the Choose Machine screen press Right to bring up the Secret Code option. Press Left (x3) to unlock Chieftain. Press Left (x3) again to unlock General.

DUST DEVIL & SILVER STREAK VEHICLES
Select Rally and press Right at the Choose Machine screen press Right to bring up the Secret Code option. Press Left, Up, Right to unlock Dust Devil. Press Left, Up, Right again to unlock Silver Streak.

HYENA & BAD OMEN VEHICLES
Select Rally and press Right at the Choose Machine screen press Right to bring up the Secret Code option. Press Right (x3) to unlock Hyena. Press Right (x3) again to unlock Bad Omen.

WILDCAT & THRASHER VEHICLES
Select Rally and press Right at the Choose Machine screen press Right to bring up the Secret Code option. Press Up (x3) to unlock Wildcat. Press Up (x3) again to unlock Thrasher.

SAN FRANCISCO: RUSH 2049

ACTIVATE CHEAT MENU
At the Main menu, highlight Options and press L + R + Y + X. Now you can enter the following cheats.

ALL CARS
At the Cheat Menu, highlight All Cars and press A, A, X, X, L, L. Hold R and press Y. Release R, hold L and press A.

ALL TRACKS
At the Cheat Menu, highlight All Tracks, hold A + Y and press R. Release A and Y. Hold Y + X and press L. Release Y and X. Press A, A, X, X, hold L + R and press Y.

ALL PARTS
At the Cheat Menu, highlight All Parts, hold Y and press X, A, L, R. Release Y, hold X and press A. Release X and press Y, Y.

RESURRECT IN PLACE
At the Cheat Menu, highlight Resurrect in Place and press R, R, L, L, A, Y, X.

FRAME SCALE
At the Cheat Menu, highlight Frame Scale hold L and press A, A, X. Release L, hold R and press A, A, X.

TIRE SCALING
At the Cheat Menu, highlight Tire Scaling press and press Y, X, A, Y, X, A. Hold R and press A.

FOG COLOR
At the Cheat Menu, highlight Fog Color hold L and press Y, release L, hold A and press Y, release A, hold X and press Y, release X, hold R and press Y.

CAR COLLISIONS
At the Cheat Menu, highlight Car Collisions hold L + R and press Y, X, A. Release L and R and press Y, X, A.

CONE MINES
At the Cheat Menu, highlight Cone Mines hold X and press R, L. Release X and press Y. Hold A and press Y. Release A and press Y.

CAR MINES
At the Cheat Menu, highlight Car Mines, hold L + R + Y and press A, X. Release L, R and Y. Press A, X.

TRACK ORIENTATION
At the Cheat Menu, highlight Track Orientation hold L + R and press Y. Release L and R and press A, Y, X. Hold L + R and press Y.

AUTO ABORT
At the Cheat Menu, highlight Auto Abort and press A, L, Y, R, X. Hold L + R and press A, Y.

SUPER SPEED
At the Cheat Menu, highlight Super Speed hold X + R and press L. Release X and R. Hold A and press Y. Release A and press A, A, A.

INVINCIBLE
At the Cheat Menu, highlight Invincible hold L + Y and press X, A. Release L + Y. Hold R and press A, Y, X.

INVISIBLE CAR
At the Cheat Menu, highlight Invisible Car hold L and press Y. Release L. Hold R and press X. Release R and press A. Hold L + R and press Y. Release L and R and press X, X, X.

INVISIBLE TRACK
At the Cheat Menu, highlight Invisible Track press R, L, X, Y, A, A, Y, X. Hold L + R and press A.

BRAKES
At the Cheat Menu, highlight Brakes press X, X, X. Hold L + Y + A and press R.

SUPER TIRES
At the Cheat Menu, highlight Super Tires hold R and press Y, Y, Y. Release R. Hold L and press A, A, X.

MASS
At the Cheat Menu, highlight Mass hold A and press Y, Y, X. Release A and press L, R.

SUICIDE MODE
At the Cheat Menu, highlight Suicide Mode hold X and press R, L, R, L. Release X. Hold Y and press R, L, R, L.

BATTLE PAINT SHOP
At the Cheat Menu, highlight Battle Paint Shop hold A and press L, R, L, R. Release A and press Y, Y, Y.

DEMOLITION BATTLE
At the Cheat Menu, highlight Demolition Battle hold L + A and press X, Y. Release L and A. Hold R + A and press X, Y.

RANDOM WEAPONS
At the Cheat Menu, highlight Random Weapons hold L + A and press Y, X. Release L and A. Hold R + A and press Y, X.

MONSTER HOUSE

FULL HEALTH
During a game, hold L + R and press A, A, A, Y.

REFILL SECONDARY WEAPON AMMO
During a game, hold L + R and press Y, Y, A, A.

ALL TOY MONKEYS AND ART GALLERY
During a game, hold L + R and press Y, X, Y, X, B, B, B, A.

MVP BASEBALL 2005

ALL STADIUMS, PLAYERS, UNIFORMS, AND REWARDS
Create a player named **Katie Roy**.

RED SOX ST. PATRICK'S DAY UNIFORM
Create a player named **Neverlose Sight**.

BAD HITTER WITH THIN BAT
Create a player named **Erik Kiss**.

GOOD HITTER WITH BIG BAT
Create a player named **Isaiah Paterson**, **Jacob Paterson** or **Keegan Paterson**.

BIGGER BODY
Create a player named **Kenny Lee**.

NASCAR 2005: CHASE FOR THE CUP

ALL BONUSES
At the Edit Driver screen, enter **Open Sesame** as your name.

DALE EARNHARDT
At the Edit Driver screen, enter **The Intimidator** as your name.

$10,000,000
At the Edit Driver screen, enter **Walmart NASCAR** as your name.

LAKESHORE DRIVE TRACK
At the Edit Driver screen, enter **Walmart Exclusive** as your name.

DODGE EVENTS
At the Edit Driver screen, enter **Dodge Stadium** as your name.

MR CLEAN DRIVERS
At the Edit Driver screen, enter **Mr.Clean Racing** as your name.

MR. CLEAN PIT CREW
At the Edit Driver screen, enter **Clean Crew** as your name.

2,000,000 PRESTIGE POINTS/LEVEL 10 IN FIGHT TO THE TOP MODE
At the Edit Driver screen, enter **You TheMan** as your name.

NBA LIVE 2005

50,000 DYNASTY POINTS
Enter **YISS55CZ0E** as an NBA Live Code.

ALL CLASSICS HARDWOOD JERSEYS
Enter **PRYI234N0B** as an NBA Live Code.

ALL TEAM GEAR
Enter **1NVDR89ER2** as an NBA Live Code.

ALL SHOES
Enter **FHM389HU80** as an NBA Live Code.

AIR UNLIMITED SHOES
Enter **XVLJD9895V** as an NBA Live Code.

HUARACHE 2K4 SHOES
Enter **VNBA60230T** as an NBA Live Code.

NIKE BG ROLLOUT SHOES
Enter **0984ADF90P** as an NBA Live Code.

NIKE SHOX ELITE SHOES
Enter **2388HDFCBJ** as an NBA Live Code.

ZOOM GENERATION LOW SHOES
Enter **234SDJF9W4** as an NBA Live Code.

ZOOM LEBRON JAMES II SHOES
Enter **1KENZO23XZ** as an NBA Live Code.

ATLANTA HAWKS ALTERNATE UNIFORM
Enter **HDI834NN9N** as an NBA Live Code.

BOSTON CELTICS ALTERNATE UNIFORM
Enter **XCV43MGMDS** as an NBA Live Code.

DALLAS MAVERICKS ALTERNATE UNIFORM
Enter **AAPSEUD09U** as an NBA Live Code.

NEW ORLEANS HORNETS ALTERNATE UNIFORM
Enter **JRE7H4D90F** as a NBA Live Code.

NEW ORLEANS HORNETS ALTERNATE UNIFORM 2
Enter **JRE7H4D9WH** as a NBA Live Code.

SEATTLE SONICS ALTERNATE UNIFORM
Enter **BHD87YY27Q** as a NBA Live Code.

GOLDEN STATE WARRIORS ALTERNATE UNIFORM
Enter **NAVNY29548** as an NBA Live Code.

NBA LIVE 06

EASTERN ALL-STARS 2005-06 AWAY JERSEYS
Select NBA Codes from My NBA Live and enter **XCVB5387EQ**.

EASTERN ALL-STARS 2005-06 HOME JERSEY
Select NBA Codes from My NBA Live and enter **234SDFGHMO**.

WESTERN ALL-STARS 2005-06 AWAY JERSEY
Select NBA Codes from My NBA Live and enter **39N56B679J**.

WESTERN ALL-STARS 2005-06 HOME JERSEY
Select NBA Codes from My NBA Live and enter **2J9UWABNP1**.

BOSTON CELTICS 2005-06 ALTERNATE JERSEY
Select NBA Codes from My NBA Live and enter **193KSHU88J**.

CLEVELAND CAVALIERS 2005-06 ALTERNATE JERSEY
Select NBA Codes from My NBA Live and enter **9922NVDKVT**.

DENVER NUGGETS 2005-06 ALTERNATE JERSEYS
Select NBA Codes from My NBA Live and enter **XWETJK72FC**.

DETROIT PISTONS 2005-06 ALTERNATE JERSEY
Select NBA Codes from My NBA Live and enter **JANTWIKBS6**.

INDIANA PACERS 2005-06 ALTERNATE AWAY JERSEY
Select NBA Codes from My NBA Live and enter **PSDF90PPJN**.

INDIANA PACERS 2005-06 ALTERNATE HOME JERSEY
Select NBA Codes from My NBA Live and enter **SDF786WSHW**.

SACRAMENTO KINGS 2005-06 ALTERNATE JERSEY
Select NBA Codes from My NBA Live and enter **654NNBFDWA**.

A3 GARNETT 3
Select NBA Codes from My NBA Live and enter **DRI239CZ49**.

JORDAN MELO V.5 WHITE & BLUE
Select NBA Codes from My NBA Live and enter **5223WERPII**.

JORDAN MELO V.5 WHITE & YELLOW
Select NBA Codes from My NBA Live and enter **ZXDR7362Q1**.

JORDAN XIV BLACK & RED
Select NBA Codes from My NBA Live and enter **144FVNHM35**.

JORDAN XIV WHITE & GREEN
Select NBA Codes from My NBA Live and enter
67YFH9839F.

JORDAN XIV WHITE & RED
Select NBA Codes from My NBA Live and enter
743HFDRAU8.

S. CARTER III LE
Select NBA Codes from My NBA Live and enter
JZ3SCARTVY.

T-MAC 5 BLACK
Select NBA Codes from My NBA Live and enter **258SHQW95B**.

T-MAC 5 WHITE
Select NBA Codes from My NBA Live and enter **HGS83KP234P**.

ANSWER DMX 10
Select NBA Codes from My NBA Live and enter
RBKAIUSAB7.

ANSWER IX AND THE RBK
ANSWER IX VIDEO
Select NBA Codes from My NBA Live and enter
AI9BUBBA7T.

THE QUESTION AND THE
MESSAGE FROM ALLEN
IVERSON VIDEO
Select NBA Codes from My NBA Live and enter **HOYAS3AI6L**.

NCAA FOOTBALL 2005

PENNANT CODES

Select My NCAA, then choose Pennant Collection. Now you can enter the following Pennant Codes:

ENTER	CODE	ENTER	CODE
Cuffed Cheat	EA Sports	Badgers All-time	U Rah Rah
1st and 15	Thanks	Florida All-time	Great To Be
Baylor power-up	Sic Em	Florida All-time	Great To Be
Blink (ball spotted short)	For	Florida State All-time	Uprising
Boing (dropped passes)	Registering	Georgia All-time	Hunker Down
Crossed the Line	Tiburon	Iowa All-time	On Iowa
Illinois Team Boost	Oskee Wow	LSU All-time	Geaux Tigers
Jumbalaya	Hike	Notre Dame All-time	Golden Domer
Molasses Cheat	Home Field	Oklahoma All-time	Boomer
QB Dud	Elite 11	Oklahoma State All-time	Go Pokes
Stiffed	NCAA	Pittsburgh All-time	Lets Go Pitt
Take Your Time	Football	Purdue All-time	Boiler Up
Texas Tech Team Boost	Fight	Syracuse All-time	Orange Crush
Thread the Needle	2005	Tennessee All-time	Big Orange
Virginia Tech Team Boost	Tech Triumph	Texas A&M All-time	Gig Em
What a Hit	Blitz	Texas All-time	Hook Em
2003 All-Americans	Fumble	UCLA All-time	Mighty
Alabama All-time	Roll Tide	Ohio State All-time	Killer Bucks
Miami All-time	Raising Cane	Ohio State All-time	Killer Nuts
Michigan All-time	Go Blue	Virginia All-time	Wahoos
Mississippi State All-time	Hail State	Georgia Tech Mascot Team	Ramblinwreck
Nebraska All-time	Go Big Red	Iowa St. Mascot Team	Red And Gold
North Carolina All-time	Rah Rah	Kansas Mascot Team	Rock Chalk
Penn State All-time	We Are	Kentucky Mascot Team	On On UK
Clemson All-time	Death Valley	Michigan State Mascot Team	Go Green
Colorado All-time	Glory	Minnesota Mascot Team	Rah Rah Rah
Kansas State All-time	Victory	Missouri Mascot Team	Mizzou Rah
Oregon All-time	Quack Attack	NC State Mascot Team	Go Pack
USC All-time	Fight On	NU Mascot Team	Go Cats
Washington All-time	Bow Down	Ole Miss Mascot Team	Hotty Totty
Arizona mascot team	Bear Down	West Virginia Mascot Team	Hail WV
Arkansas All-time	WooPigSooie	Wake Forest Mascot Team	Go Deacs Go
Auburn All-time	War Eagle	WSU Mascot Team	All Hail

NEED FOR SPEED CARBON

CASTROL CASH
At the main menu, press Down, Up, Left, Down, Right, Up, X, B. This will give you 10,000 extra cash.

INFINITE CREW CHARGE
At the main menu, press Down, Up, Up, Right, Left, Left, Right, X.

INFINITE NITROUS
At the main menu, press Left, Up, Left, Down, Left, Down, Right, X.

INFINITE SPEEDBREAKER
At the main menu, press Down, Right, Right, Left, Right, Up, Down, X.

NEED FOR SPEED CARBON LOGO VINYLS
At the main menu, press Right, Up, Down, Up, Down, Left, Right, X.

NEED FOR SPEED CARBON SPECIAL LOGO VINYLS
At the main menu, press Up, Up, Down, Down, Down, Down, Up, X.

NEED FOR SPEED MOST WANTED

BURGER KING CHALLENGE
At the Title screen, press Up, Down, Up, Down, Left, Right, Left, Right.

CASTROL SYNTEC VERSION OF FORD GT
At the Title screen, press Left, Right, Left, Right, Up, Down, Up, Down.

MARKER IN BACKROOM OF ONE-STOP SHOP
At the Title screen, press Up, Up, Down, Down, Left, Right, Up, Down.

NEED FOR SPEED UNDERGROUND 2

$200 IN CAREER MODE
At the Title screen, press Up, Up, Up, Left, R, R, R, Down.

$1000 IN CAREER MODE
At the Title screen, press Left, Left, Right, X, X, Right, L, R.

HUMMER H2 CAPONE
At the Title screen, press Up, Left, Up, Up, Down, Left, Down, Left.

BEST BUY VINYL
At the Title screen, press Up, Down, Up, Down, Down, Up, Right, Left.

BURGER KING VINYL
At the Title screen, press Up, Up, Up, Up, Down, Up, Up, Left.

PERFORMANCE LEVEL 1
At the Title screen, press L, R, L, R, Left, Left, Right, Up.

PERFORMANCE LEVEL 2
At the Title screen, press R, R, L, R, Left, Right, Up, Down.

VISUAL LEVEL 1
At the Title screen, press R, R, Up, Down, L, L, Up, Down.

VISUAL LEVEL 2
At the Title screen, press L, R, Up, Down, L, Up, Up, Down.

NFL STREET 2

Select Cheats from the Options screen and enter the following:

FUMBLE MODE
Enter **GreasedPig** as a code.

MAX CATCHING
Enter **MagnetHands** as a code.

NO FIRST DOWNS
Enter **NoChains** as a code.

NO FUMBLES MODE
Enter **GlueHands** as a code.

UNLIMITED TURBO
Enter **NozBoost** as a code.

EA FIELD
Enter **EAField** as a code.

GRIDIRON PARK
Enter **GRIDIRONPRK** as a code.

AFC EAST ALL-STARS
Enter **EAASFSCT** as a code.

AFC NORTH ALL-STARS
Enter **NAOFRCTH** as a code.

AFC SOUTH ALL-STARS
Enter **SAOFUCTH** as a code.

AFC WEST ALL-STARS
Enter **WAEFSCT** as a code.

NFC EAST ALL-STARS
Enter **NNOFRCTH** as a code.

NFC NORTH ALL-STARS
Enter **NNAS66784** as a code.

NFC SOUTH ALL-STARS
Enter **SNOFUCTH** as a code.

NFC WEST ALL STARS
Enter **ENASFSCT** as a code.

REEBOK TEAM
Enter **Reebo** as a code.

TEAM XZIBIT
Enter **TeamXzibit** as a code.

OVER THE HEDGE

COMPLETE LEVELS
Pause the game, hold L + R and press Y, X, Y, X, X, B.

ALL MINIGAMES
Pause the game, hold L + R and press Y, X, Y, Y, B, B.

ALL MOVES
Pause the game, hold L + R and press Y, X, Y, B, B, X.

EXTRA DAMAGE
Pause the game, hold L + R and press Y, X, Y, X, Y, B.

MORE HP FROM FOOD
Pause the game, hold L + R and press Y, X, Y, X, B, Y.

ALWAYS POWER PROJECTILE
Pause the game, hold L + R and press Y, X, Y, X, B, X.

BONUS COMIC 14
Pause the game, hold L + R and press Y, X, B, B, X, Y.

BONUS COMIC 15
Pause the game, hold L + R and press Y, Y, B, X, B, X.

PAC-MAN WORLD 3

ALL LEVELS AND MAZE GAMES
At the main menu, press Left, Right, Left, Right, X, Up at the main menu to unlock all levels and 3D maze mini-games.

PETER JACKSON'S KING KONG: THE OFFICIAL GAME OF THE MOVIE

At the Main menu, hold L + R and press Down, X, Up, Y, Down, Down, Up, Up. Release L + R to access the Cheat option. The Cheat option is also available on the pause menu.

GOD MODE
Select Cheat and enter **8wonder**

ALL CHAPTERS
Select Cheat and enter **KKst0ry**.

AMMO 999
Select Cheat and enter **KK 999 mun**.

MACHINE GUN
Select Cheat and enter **KKcapone**.

REVOLVER
Select Cheat and enter **KKtigun**.

SNIPER RIFLE
Select Cheat and enter **KKsn1per**.

INFINITE SPEARS
Select Cheat and enter **lance 1nf**.

ONE-HIT KILLS
Select Cheat and enter **GrosBras**.

EXTRAS
Select Cheat and enter **KKmuseum**.

PIKMIN 2

TITLE SCREEN
At the Title screen, press the following for a variety of options:

Press R to make the Pikmin form NINTENDO.
Press L to go back to PIKMIN 2.
Press X to get a beetle.
Use the C-Stick to move it around.
Press L to dispose of the Beetle.

Press Y to get a Chappie.
Use the C-Stick to move it around.
Press Z to eat the Pikmin.
Press L to dispose of Chappie.

RAMPAGE: TOTAL DESTRUCTION

ALL MONSTERS AND CITIES
At the Main menu, press R + L to access the Cheat menu and enter **141421**.

ALL LEVELS
At the Main menu, press R + L to access the Cheat menu and enter **271828**.

INVULNERABLE TO ATTACKS
At the Main menu, press R + L to access the Cheat menu and enter **986960**.

ALL SPECIAL ABILITIES
At the Main menu, press R + L to access the Cheat menu and enter **011235**.

CPU VS CPU DEMO
At the Main menu, press R + L to access the Cheat menu and enter **082864**. This unlocks all of the monsters.

FAST CPU VS CPU DEMO
At the Main menu, press R + L to access the Cheat menu and enter **874098**. This unlocks all of the monsters.

ONE-HIT DESTROYS BUILDINGS
At the Main menu, press R + L to access the Cheat menu and enter **071767**.

OPENING MOVIE
At the Main menu, press R + L to access the Cheat menu and enter **667300**.

ENDING MOVIE
At the Main menu, press R + L to access the Cheat menu and enter **667301**.

CREDITS
At the Main menu, press R + L to access the Cheat menu and enter **667302**.

VERSION INFORMATION
At the Main menu, press R + L to access the Cheat menu and enter **314159**.

DISABLE CHEATS
At the Main menu, press R + L to access the Cheat menu and enter **000000**.

RAVE MASTER

REINA
At the Title screen, press Up, Up, Down, Down, Left, Right, Left, Right, B, A.

ROBOTS

BIG HEAD
Pause the game and press Up, Down, Down, Up, Right, Right, Left, Right.

INVINCIBLE
Pause the game and press Up, Right, Down, Up, Left, Down, Right, Left.

UNLIMITED SCRAP
Pause the game and press Down, Down, Left, Up, Up, Right, Up, Down.

SCALER

FULL HEALTH
Pause the game, select audio from the options and press R, L, R, L, Y, Y, X, X, R, X.

200,000 KLOKKIES
Pause the game, select audio from the options and press L, L, R, R, Y, X, Y.

INFINITE ELECTRIC BOMBS
Pause the game, select audio from the options and press R, R, L, L, Y, Y, X.

SHREK SUPERSLAM

ALL CHARACTERS AND LEVELS
At the Title screen, press L, R, X, B.

ALL CHALLENGES
At the Title screen, press Y, Y, Y, X, X, X, Y, B, X, B, B, B, Up, Down, Left, Right, L, R.

ALL STORY MODE CHAPTERS
At the Title screen, press Y, B, R, X.

ALL MEDALS AND TROPHIES
At the Title screen, press R, L, Y, B.

SUPER SPEED MODIFIER
At the Title screen, press L, L, R, R, L, R, L, R, B, X, Y, Y.

PIZZA ONE
At the Title screen, press Up, Up, Y, Y, Right, Right, X, X, Down, Down, L, R, Left, Left, B, B, L, R.

PIZZA TWO
At the Title screen, press X, X, B, B, R, R, Left, Left, L, L.

PIZZA THREE
At the Title screen, press Down, Down, Right, X, Up, Y, Left, B, L, L.

SLAMMAGEDDON
At the Title screen, press Up, Up, Down, Down, Left, Right, Left, Right, Y, B, B, L, R.

THE SIMS 2: PETS

CHEAT GNOME
During a game, press L, L, R, A, A, Up.

CAT AND DOG CODES
Select New Key from Game Options and enter the following codes for the corresponding cat or dog.

PET	CODE
Bandit Mask Cats	EEGJ2YRQZZAIZ9QHA64
Bandit Mask Dogs	EEGJ2YRQZQARQ9QHA64
Black Dot Cats	EEGJ2YRZQQ1IQ9QHA64
Black Dot Dogs	EEGJ2YRQZZ1IQ9QHA64
Black Smiley Cats	EEGJ2YRQQZ1RQ9QHA64
Black Smiley Dogs	EEGJ2YRQQQARQ9QHA64
Blue Bones Cats	EEGJ2YRQZZARQ9QHA64
Blue Bones Dogs	EEGJ2YRZZZ1IZ9QHA64
Blue Camouflage Cats	EEGJ2YRZZQ1IQ9QHA64
Blue Camouflage Dogs	EEGJ2YRZZZ1RQ9QHA64
Blue Cats	EEGJ2YRQZZAIQ9QHA64
Blue Dogs	EEGJ2YRQQQ1IZ9QHA64
Blue Star Cats	EEGJ2YRQQZ1IZ9QHA64
Blue Star Dogs	EEGJ2YRZQ1IQ9QHA64
Deep Red Cats	EEGJ2YRQQQAIQ9QHA64
Deep Red Dogs	EEGJ2YRQZQ1RQ9QHA64
Goofy Cats	EEGJ2YRQZQ1IZ9QHA64
Goofy Dogs	EEGJ2YRZZZARQ9QHA64
Green Cats	EEGJ2YRZQQAIZ9QHA64
Green Dogs	EEGJ2YRZQZAIQ9QHA64
Green Flower Cats	EEGJ2YRZQZAIQ9QHA64
Green Flower Dogs	EEGJ2YRZQZ1RQ9QHA64
Light Green Cats	EEGJ2YRZZZ1RQ9QHA64
Light Green Dogs	EEGJ2YRZQQ1RQ9QHA64
Navy Hearts Cats	EEGJ2YRQZ1IQ9QHA64
Navy Hearts Dogs	EEGJ2YRQQZ1IQ9QHA64
Neon Green Cats	EEGJ2YRZZQAIQ9QHA64
Neon Green Dogs	EEGJ2YRZQQAIQ9QHA64
Neon Yellow Cats	EEGJ2YRZZQARQ9QHA64
Neon Yellow Dogs	EEGJ2YRQQQAIZ9QHA64
Orange Diagonal Cats	EEGJ2YRQQZAIQ9QHA64
Orange Diagonal Dogs	EEGJ2YRZQZ1IZ9QHA64
Panda Cats	EEGJ2YRQZQAIZ9QHA6

PET	CODE
Pink Cats	EEGJ2YRQZZ1IZ9QHA64
Pink Dogs	EEGJ2YRZQZ1RQ9QHA64
Pink Vertical Strip Cats	EEGJ2YRQQQARQ9QHA6
Pink Vertical Strip Dogs	EEGJ2YRZZZAIQ9QHA64
Purple Cats	EEGJ2YRQQZARQ9QHA64
Purple Dogs	EEGJ2YRQQZAIZ9QHA64
Star Cats	EEGJ2YRZQZARQ9QHA6
Star Dogs	EEGJ2YRZQZAIZ9QHA64
White Paws Cats	EEGJ2YRQQQ1RQ9QHA64
White Paws Dogs	EEGJ2YRZQQ1IZ9QHA64
White Zebra Stripe Cats	EEGJ2YRZZZQ1IZ9QHA6
White Zebra Stripe Dogs	EEGJ2YRZZZ1IQ9QHA64
Zebra Stripes Dogs	EEGJ2YRZZQAIZ9QHA64

THE SIMS: BUSTIN' OUT

Pause the game to enter the following codes. You must enter the Enable Cheats code first. After entering another code, select the gnome to access it.

ENABLE CHEATS
Press Down, L, Z, R, Left, X. When entered correctly, A gnome appears in front of your house.

FILL ALL MOTIVES
Press L, R, Y, Down, Down, X.

UNLOCK ALL LOCATIONS
Press Down, Z, R, L, Z.

UNLOCK ALL OBJECTS
Press Down, Z, Up, Y, R.

UNLOCK ALL SKINS
Press L, Y, A, R, Left.

UNLOCK ALL SOCIAL OPTIONS
Press L, R, Down, Down, Y.

SONIC ADVENTURE DX DIRECTOR'S CUT

You must first unlock these "mini-games" with emblems.

Sonic Chaos
LEVEL SELECT
At the title screen, press Up, Up, Up, Up, Right, Left, Right, Left, Start.

INSTANT CHAOS EMERALDS
At the character select, press Up, Down, Up, Down, B, A, B, A, B, A.

SOUND TEST
At the title screen, press Down, Down, Up, Up, Left, Right, Left, Right, B, A.

Sonic Labyrinth
LEVEL SELECT
At the title screen, press Up, Up, Right, Right, Right, Down, Down, Down, Down, Down, Down, Left, Left, Left, Left, Left, Left.

Sonic Spinball
LEVEL SELECT
At the Sound Test option, play the sounds in the following order: 0, 2, 1, 5, 6, 6.

NO GRAVITY
At the Sound Test option, play the sounds in the following order: 0, 9, 0, 1, 6, 8.

FAST BACKGROUND MUSIC
At the Sound Test option, play the sounds in the following order: 0, 4, 2, 5, 5, 7.

ZOOMED IN
At the Sound Test option, play the sounds in the following order: 0, 2, 1, 1, 6, 6.

SONIC GEMS COLLECTION

Sonic CD

STAGE SELECT
At the Title screen, press Up, Down, Down, Left, Right, A.

HIGH SCORES
At the Title screen, press Right, Right, Up, Up, Down, A.

SOUND TEST
At the Title screen, press Down, Down, Down, Left, Right, A.

Sonic R

SAME CHARACTER SELECT
When selecting your character in Multiplayer, hold L and press A or X. This will enable you to choose the same character as the other player.

Sonic Spinball

Enter the following codes by accessing the Options screen and entering them using the SFX option. The screen will shake to confirm that the code is entered correctly.

SKIP BOSS
Choose Sound Effects from the Options screen and play the following tracks in order: 00, 02, 01, 05, 06, 06. During a boss battle, pause the game, hold A + B + Start and press Down.

ANTI-GRAVITY SONIC
Choose Sound Effects from the Options screen and play the following tracks in order: 00, 09, 00, 01, 06, 08. Pause the game and press A + B + Start.

FAST MUSIC
Choose Sound Effects from the Options screen and play the following tracks in order: 00, 04, 02, 05, 05, 07.

Tails Skypatrol
SOUND AND STAGE TEST
At the Title screen, hold Up + A and press Start.

Vectorman 2
LEVEL SELECT AND SOUND TEST
Pause the game and press Up, Right, B, A, B, Down, Left, B, Down.

NEW WEAPONS
Pause the game and press X, B, Left, Left, Down, B, Down.

EXTRA LIFE
Pause the game and press Right, Up, A, B, Down, Up, A, Down, Up, A.

REFILL LIFE METER
Pause the game and press A, B, A, B, Left, Up, Up.

MAP COORDINATES
Pause the game and press A, B, Left, Left.

Vectorman
CHEAT MENU
At the Options screen, press B, A, A, B, Down, B, A, A, B.

REFILL LIFE METER
Pause the game and press B, A, Right, B, X, B, Down, B, A, Right, B.

SLOW MOTION
Pause the game and press Down, Right, B, X, Up, Left, B.

TAXI MODE
Pause the game and press X, B, Left, Left, B, X, B, A.

ALL ITEMS AND
LEVEL SELECT
Enter the password ADE7 AA2A 51A6 6D12.

SONIC HEROES

METAL CHARACTERS IN 2-PLAYER
After selecting a level in 2-Player mode, hold A + Y.

SPIDER-MAN 2

TREYARCH PASSWORD
Start a New Game and enter **HCRAYERT** as your name. This code starts the game at 44% complete, 201,000 Hero Points, some upgrades and more.

SPONGEBOB SQUAREPANTS: BATTLE FOR BIKINI BOTTOM

The following codes must be entered quickly.

RESTORE HEALTH
Pause the game, hold L + R and press X, X, X, X, Y, X, Y, X, Y, Y, Y, Y.

EXPERT MODE
Pause the game, hold L + R and press X, X, X, Y, Y, X, X, X, Y, X, Y, Y, Y, X, Y, Y.

EARN 1,000 SHINY OBJECTS
Pause the game, hold L + R and press Y, X, X, Y, Y, X, X, Y.

EARN 10 GOLD SPATULAS
Pause the game, hold L + R and press X, Y, Y, X, X, Y, Y, X.

BUBBLE BOWL POWER-UP
Pause the game, hold L + R and press X, Y, X, Y, X, X, Y, Y. Press X to use the power-up.

CRUISE BUBBLE POWER-UP
Pause the game, hold L + R and press Y, X, Y, X, Y, Y, X, X. Press L to use the power-up.

INCREASE VALUE OF SHINY OBJECTS
Pause the game, hold L + R and press Y, X, Y, X, X, Y, X, X, X, Y, Y, Y, Y, X, X, Y.

MODIFIED CRUISE BUBBLE CONTROLS
Pause the game, hold L + R and press X, X, X, X, X, Y, Y, X, X, Y, X, Y, Y.

VILLAGERS GIVE SHINY OBJECTS WHEN HIT
Pause the game, hold L + R and press Y, Y, Y, Y, Y, X, Y, X, X, Y, X, Y.

VILLAGERS RESTORE HEALTH WHEN NEAR
Pause the game, hold L + R and press Y, Y, Y, Y, Y, X, Y, X, X, X, Y, Y.

NO PANTS
Pause the game, hold L + R and press X, X, X, X, X, Y, X, X, Y, X, Y, Y, X.

BIG PLANKTON
Pause the game, hold L + R and press Y, Y, Y, Y, X, Y, X, Y, X, X, X, X.

SMALL CHARACTERS
Pause the game, hold L + R and press Y, Y, Y, Y, Y, X, Y, X, Y, Y, Y, Y, Y.

SMALL VILLAGERS
Pause the game, hold L + R and press Y, Y, Y, Y, Y, X, Y, X, Y, X, Y, X.

SPONGEBOB BREAKS APART WHEN DEFEATED
Pause the game, hold L + R and press X, X, X, X, Y, Y, X, Y, X, X, X, Y.

INVERT LEFT/RIGHT CAMERA CONTROLS
Pause the game, hold L + R and press Y, Y, X, X, X, X, X, Y, Y.

INVERT UP/DOWN CAMERA CONTROLS
Pause the game, hold L + R and press Y, X, X, X, X, X, X, X, Y.

SPONGEBOB SQUAREPANTS: CREATURE FROM THE KRUSTY KRAB

30,000 EXTRA Z'S
Select Cheat Codes from the Extras menu and enter ROCFISH.

PUNK SPONGEBOB IN DIESEL DREAMING
Select Cheat Codes from the Extras menu and enter SPONGE. Select Activate Bonus Items to enable this bonus item.

HOT ROD SKIN IN DIESEL DREAMING

Select Cheat Codes from the Extras menu and enter HOTROD. Select Activate Bonus Items to enable this bonus item.

PATRICK TUX IN STARFISHMAN TO THE RESCUE

Select Cheat Codes from the Extras menu and enter PATRICK. Select Activate Bonus Items to enable this bonus item.

SPONGEBOB PLANKTON IN SUPER-SIZED PATTY

Select Cheat Codes from the Extras menu and enter PANTS. Select Activate Bonus Items to enable this bonus item.

PATRICK LASER COLOR IN ROCKET RODEO

Select Cheat Codes from the Extras menu and enter ROCKET. Select Activate Bonus Items to enable this bonus item.

PATRICK ROCKET SKIN COLOR IN ROCKET RODEO

Select Cheat Codes from the Extras menu and enter SPACE. Select Activate Bonus Items to enable this bonus item.

PLANKTON EYE LASER COLOR IN REVENGE OF THE GIANT PLANKTON MONSTER

Select Cheat Codes from the Extras menu and enter LASER. Select Activate Bonus Items to enable this bonus item.

HOVERCRAFT VEHICLE SKIN IN HYPNOTIC HIGHWAY - PLANKTON

Select Cheat Codes from the Extras menu and enter HOVER. Select Activate Bonus Items to enable this bonus item.

SPONGEBOB SQUAREPANTS: LIGHTS, CAMERA, PANTS!

SILVER STORY MODE
Select Rewards from the Bonuses menu, then choose Codes and enter **486739**.

ALL ACTION FIGURES
Select Rewards from the Bonuses menu, then choose Codes and enter **977548**.

HOOK, LINE & CHEDDAR GAME
Select Rewards from the Bonuses menu, then choose Codes and enter **893634**.

SSX ON TOUR

NEW THREADS
Select Cheats from the Extras menu and enter **FLYTHREADS**.

THE WORLD IS YOURS
Select Cheats from the Extras menu and enter **BACKSTAGEPASS**.

SHOW TIME (ALL MOVIES)
Select Cheats from the Extras menu and enter **THEBIGPICTURE**.

BLING BLING (INFINITE CASH)
Select Cheats from the Extras menu and enter **LOOTSNOOT**.

FULL BOOST, FULL TIME
Select Cheats from the Extras menu and enter **ZOOMJUICE**.

MONSTERS ARE LOOSE (MONSTER TRICKS)
Select Cheats from the Extras menu and enter **JACKALOPESTYLE**.

SNOWBALL FIGHT
Select Cheats from the Extras menu and enter **LETSPARTY**.

FEEL THE POWER (STAT BOOST)
Select Cheats from the Extras menu and enter **POWERPLAY**.

CHARACTERS ARE LOOSE
Select Cheats from the Extras menu and enter **ROADIEROUNDUP**.

UNLOCK CONRAD
Select Cheats from the Extras menu and enter **BIGPARTYTIME**.

UNLOCK MITCH KOOBSKI
Select Cheats from the Extras menu and enter **MOREFUNTHANONE**.

UNLOCK NIGEL
Select Cheats from the Extras menu and enter **THREEISACROWD**.

UNLOCK SKI PATROL
Select Cheats from the Extras menu and enter **FOURSOME**.

STAR WARS ROGUE SQUADRON III: REBEL STRIKE

Select Passcodes from the Options screen and enter the following. When there are two passcodes, enter the first one and Enter Code and then enter the second one and Enter Code.

UNLIMITED LIVES
Enter **IIOUAOYE**, then enter **WIMPIAM!**.

ACE MODE
Enter **YNMSFY?P**, then enter **YOUDAMAN**.

LEVEL SELECT (COOPERATIVE MODE)
Enter **SWGRCQPL**, then enter **UCHEATED**.

ALL SINGLE-PLAYER MISSIONS
Enter **HYWSC!WS**, then enter **NONGAMER**.

ALL SINGLE-PLAYER MISSIONS & BONUS MISSIONS
Enter **EEQQ?YPL**, then enter **CHE!ATER**.

BEGGAR'S CANYON RACE (COOPERATIVE MODE)
Enter **FRLL!CSF**, then enter **FARMBOY?**.

ASTEROID FIELD MISSION (COOPERATIVE MODE)
Enter **RWALPIGC**, then enter **NOWAYOUT**.

DEATH STAR
ESCAPE MISSION
(COOPERATIVE MODE)
Enter **YFCEDFRH**, then enter **DSAGAIN?**.

ENDURANCE MISSION (COOPERATIVE MODE)
Enter **WPX?FGC!**, then enter **EXCERSIZ**.

ALL SHIPS
(VERSUS MODE)
Enter **W!WSTPQB**, then enter **FREEPLAY**.

MILLENNIUM FALCON
Enter **QZCRPTG!**, then enter **HANSRIDE**.

NABOO STARFIGHTER
Enter **RTWCVBSH**, then enter **BFNAGAIN**.

SLAVE I
Enter **TGBCWLPN**, then enter **ZZBOUNTY**.

TIE BOMBER
Enter **JASDJWFA**, then enter **!DABOMB!**.

TIE HUNTER
Enter **FRRVBMJK**, then enter **LOOKOUT!**.

TIE FIGHTER (COOPERATIVE MODE)
Enter **MCKEMAKD**, then enter **ONESHOT!**.

TIE ADVANCE IN COOPERATIVE
Enter **VDX?WK!H**, then enter **ANOKSHIP**.

RUDY'S CAR
Enter **AXCBPRHK**, then enter **WHATTHE?**.

CREDITS
Enter **LOOKMOM!**. You can find this option in the Special Features menu.

STAR WARS ARCADE GAME
Enter **RTJPFC!G**, then enter **TIMEWARP**.

EMPIRE STRIKES BACK ARCADE GAME
Enter **!H!F?HXS**, then enter **KOOLSTUF**.

DOCUMENTARY
Enter **THEDUDES**.

ART GALLERY
Enter **!KOOLART**.

MUSIC HALL
Enter **HARKHARK**.

BLACK AND WHITE
Enter **NOCOLOR?**.

TAK: THE GREAT JUJU CHALLENGE

BONUS SOUND EFFECTS
In Juju's Potions, select Universal Card and enter the following numbers for Bugs, Crystals and Fruit: 20, 17, 5.

BONUS SOUND EFFECTS 2
In Juju's Potions, select Universal Card and enter the following numbers for Bugs, Crystals and Fruit: 50, 84, 92.

BONUS MUSIC TRACK 1
In Juju's Potions, select Universal Card and enter the following numbers for Bugs, Crystals and Fruit: 67, 8, 20.

BONUS MUSIC TRACK 2
In Juju's Potions, select Universal Card and enter the following numbers for Bugs, Crystals and Fruit: 6, 18, 3.

MAGIC PARTICLES
In Juju's Potions, select Universal Card and enter the following numbers for Bugs, Crystals and Fruit: 24, 40, 11.

MORE MAGIC PARTICLES
In Juju's Potions, select Universal Card and enter the following numbers for Bugs, Crystals and Fruit: 48, 57, 57.

VIEW JUJU CONCEPT ART
In Juju's Potions, select Universal Card and enter the following numbers for Bugs, Crystals and Fruit: Art 33, 22, 28.

VIEW VEHICLE ART
In Juju's Potions, select Universal Card and enter the following numbers for Bugs, Crystals and Fruit: 11, 55, 44.

VIEW WORLD ART
In Juju's Potions, select Universal Card and enter the following numbers for Bugs, Crystals and Fruit: 83, 49, 34.

TEENAGE MUTANT NINJA TURTLES 3: MUTANT NIGHTMARE

INVINCIBILITY
Select Passwords from the Options screen and enter **MDLDSSLR**.

HEALTH POWER-UPS BECOME SUSHI
Select Passwords from the Options screen and enter **SLLMRSLD**.

NO HEALTH POWER-UPS
Select Passwords from the Options screen and enter **DMLDMRLD**.

ONE-HIT DEFEATS TURTLE
Select Passwords from the Options screen and enter **LDMSLRDD**.

MAX OUGI
Select Passwords from the Options screen and enter **RRDMLSDL**.

UNLIMITED SHURIKEN
Select Passwords from the Options screen and enter **LMDRRMSR**.

NO SHURIKEN
Select Passwords from the Options screen and enter **LLMSRDMS**.

DONATELLO'S LEVEL 2 DINO ARMOR SCROLL
Select Passwords from the Options screen and enter **MSSRDLMR**.

DONATELLO'S LEVEL 3 DINO ARMOR SCROLL
Select Passwords from the Options screen and enter **DLRLDMSR**.

LEO'S LEVEL 2 DINO ARMOR SCROLL
Select Passwords from the Options screen and enter **RLDMRMSD**.

LEO'S LEVEL 3 DINO ARMOR SCROLL
Select Passwords from the Options screen and enter **MLMSRRDS**.

MICHELANGELO'S LEVEL 2 DINO ARMOR SCROLL
Select Passwords from the Options screen and enter **SRDMMLRS**.

MICHELANGELO'S LEVEL 3 DINO ARMOR SCROLL
Select Passwords from the Options screen and enter **LSMRRDSL**.

RAPHAEL'S LEVEL 2 DINO ARMOR SCROLL
Select Passwords from the Options screen and enter **DRMDLLRS**.

RAPHAEL'S LEVEL 3 DINO ARMOR SCROLL
Select Passwords from the Options screen and enter **SMRDRSLD**.

DOUBLE ENEMY ATTACK
Select Passwords from the Options screen and enter **MSRLSMML**.

DOUBLE ENEMY DEFENSE
Select Passwords from the Options screen and enter **SLRMLSSM**.

TIGER WOODS PGA TOUR 06

ALL GOLFERS
Select Password from the Options screen and enter **WOOGLIN**.

ALL CLUBS
Select Password from the Options screen and enter **CLUB11**.

LEVEL 2 NIKE ITEMS
Select Password from the Options screen and enter **JUSTDOIT**.

ALL COURSES
Select Password from the Options screen and enter **ITSINTHEHOLE**.

TIGER WOODS IN HAT AND TIE

Select Password from the Options screen and enter **GOLDENAGE**.

TIGER WOODS IN STRIPED PANTS

Select Password from the Options screen and enter **TECHNICOLOR**.

TIGER WOODS IN OLD GOLF OUTFIT

Select Password from the Options screen and enter **OLDSKOOL**.

TIGER WOODS IN A DIFFERENT OLD GOLF OUTFIT

Select Password from the Options screen and enter **THROWBACK**.

ARNOLD PALMER

Select Password from the Options screen and enter **ARNIESARMY**.

BEN HOGAN

Select Password from the Options screen and enter **THEHAWK**.

JACK NICKLAUS

Select Password from the Options screen and enter **GOLDENBEAR**.

OLD TOM MORRIS

Select Password from the Options screen and enter **FEATHERIE**.

TOMMY BLACK

Select Password from the Options screen and enter **IDONTHAVEAPROBLEM**.

WESLEY ROUNDER

Select Password from the Options screen and enter **POCKETPAIR**.

TONY HAWK'S AMERICAN WASTELAND

ALWAYS SPECIAL

Select Cheat Codes from the Options screen and enter **uronfire**. Pause the game and select Cheats from the Game Options to enable the cheat.

PERFECT RAIL

Select Cheat Codes from the Options screen and enter **grindxpert**. Pause the game and select Cheats from the Game Options to enable the cheat.

PERFECT SKITCH

Select Cheat Codes from the Options screen and enter **h!tchar!de**. Pause the game and select Cheats from the Game Options to enable the cheat.

PERFECT MANUAL

Select Cheat Codes from the Options and enter **2wheels!**. Pause the game and select Cheats from the Game Options to enable the cheat.

MOON GRAVITY

Select Cheat Codes from the Options screen and enter **2them00n**. Pause the game and select Cheats from the Game Options to enable the cheat.

MAT HOFFMAN

Select Cheat Codes from the Options screen and enter **the_condor**.

JASON ELLIS

Select Cheat Codes from the Options screen and enter **sirius-dj**.

TONY HAWK'S UNDERGROUND 2

ALWAYS SPECIAL
Select Cheat Codes from the Game Options and enter likepaulie. Select Cheats from the Game Options to toggle the code on and off.

PERFECT RAIL
Select Cheat Codes from the Game Options and enter straightedge. Select Cheats from the Game Options to toggle the code on and off.

TY THE TASMANIAN TIGER 3: NIGHT OF THE QUINKAN

100,000 OPALS
During a game, press Start, Start, Y, Start, Start, Y, X, A, X, A.

ALL CHASSIS
During a game, press Start, Start, Y, Start, Start, Y, X, B, X, B.

ULTIMATE SPIDER-MAN

ALL CHARACTERS
Pause the game and select Controller Setup from the Options. Press Right, Down, Right, Down, Left, Up, Left, Right.

ALL COVERS
Pause the game and select Controller Setup from the Options. Press Left, Left, Right, Left, Up, Left, Left, Down.

ALL CONCEPT ART
Pause the game and select Controller Setup from the Options. Press Down, Down, Down, Up, Down, Up, Left, Left.

ALL LANDMARKS
Pause the game and select Controller Setup from the Options. Press Up, Right, Down, Left, Down, Up, Right, Left.

X-MEN LEGENDS II: RISE OF APOCALYPSE

ALL CHARACTERS
At the Team Management screen, press Right, Left, Left, Right, Up, Up, Up, Start.

ALL SKINS
At the Team Management screen, press Down, Up, Left, Right, Up, Up, Start.

ALL SKILLS
At the Team Management screen, press Left, Right, Left, Right, Down, Up, Start.

LEVEL 99
At the Team Management screen, press Up, Down, Up, Down, Left, Up, Left, Right, Start.

GOD MODE
Pause the game and press Down, Up, Down, Up, Right, Down, Right, Left, Start.

MOVE FASTER
Pause the game and press Up, Up, Up, Down, Up, Down, Start.

UNLIMITED XTREME TOKENS
Pause the game and press Left, Down, Right, Down, Up, Down, Up, Start.

TOUCH OF DEATH
During a game, press Left, Left, Right, Left, Right, Up, Start.

100,000 TECH-BITS
At Forge or Beast's store, press Up, Up, Up, Down, Right, Right, Start.

ALL DANGER ROOM COURSES
At the Danger Room Course menu, press Right, Right, Left, Left, Up, Down, Down, Start.

ALL COMICS
Select Review from the Main menu and press Right, Left, Left, Right, Up, Up, Right, Start.

ALL CUTSCENES
Select Review from the Main menu and press Left, Right, Right, Left, Down, Down, Left, Start.

ALL CONCEPTS
Select Review from the Main menu and press Left, Right, Left, Right, Up, Up, Down, Start.

ALL SCREENS
Select Review from the Main menu and press Right, Left, Right, Left, Up, Up, Down, Start.

X-MEN: THE OFFICIAL GAME

DANGER ROOM ICEMAN
At the Cerebro Files menu, press Right, Right, Left, Left, Down, Up, Down, Up, Start.

DANGER ROOM NIGHTCRAWLER
At the Cerebro Files menu, press Up, Up, Down, Down, Left, Right, Left, Right, Start.

DANGER ROOM WOLVERINE
At the Cerebro Files menu, press Down, Down, Up, Up, Right, Left, Right, Left, Start.

YU-GI-OH: FALSEBOUND KINGDOM

GOLD COINS
On an empty piece of land and during a mission, press Up, Up, Down, Down, Left, Right, Left, Right, B, A.

ZAPPER

INFINITE LIVES
Pause the game, hold L and press Up, Up, Up, Left, Left, Right, Left, Right.

INFINITE SHIELDS
Pause the game, hold L and press Up, Down, Up, Left, Right, Down, Up.

ZOIDS: BATTLE LEGENDS

ENERGY LIGER
Select Config and play the following voices: 004, 044, 019, 066, 034.

LIGER ZERO PHOENIX
Select Config and play the following voices: 021, 001, 018, 006, 023.

MEGASAURER IN VS MODE
Select Config and play the following voices: 000, 007, 077, 041, 054.

GAME BOY® ADVANCE

EVERYONE

ACE COMBAT ADVANCE

ACTION MAN: ROBOT ATAK

ALIENATORS: EVOLUTION CONTINUES

ANIMANIACS:
LIGHTS, CAMERA, ACTION!

BARBIE IN THE 12 DANCING PRINCESSES

BACKYARD BASEBALL 2006

BANJO PILOT

BATTLE B-DAMAN: FIRE SPIRITS!

BIONICLE: TALES OF THE TOHUNGA

BUTT UGLY MARTIANS:
B.K.M. BATTLES

CAR BATTLER JOE

CARS

CARTOON NETWORK SPEEDWAY

CLASSIC NES SERIES: PAC-MAN

CURIOUS GEORGE

DANNY PHANTOM:
THE ULTIMATE ENEMY

DISNEY'S EXTREME SKATE ADVENTURE

DISNEY'S HOME ON THE RANGE

DK: KING OF SWING

DONKEY KONG COUNTRY 2:
DIDDY KONG'S QUEST

DORA THE EXPLORER: SUPER SPIES

FINAL FANTASY I & II:
DAWN OF SOULS

HARLEM GLOBETROTTERS:
WORLD TOUR

HOT WHEELS VELOCITY X

JUSTICE LEAGUE HEROES: THE FLASH

KIEN

LEGO KNIGHT'S KINGDOM

LEGO STAR WARS

MEGA MAN BATTLE NETWORK 5:
TEAM PROTOMAN

MEGA MAN BATTLE NETWORK 5: TEAM
COLONEL

PIRATES OF THE CARIBBEAN:
DEAD MAN'S CHEST

ROCK 'EM SOCK 'EM ROBOTS

RUGRATS: I GOTTA GO PARTY

SECRET AGENT BARBIE:
ROYAL JEWELS MISSION

SHAMAN KING: LEGACY OF THE SPIRITS,
SOARING HAWK

SHAMAN KING: LEGACY OF THE SPIRITS,
SPRINTING WOLF

SHINING SOUL

SHINING SOUL II

SPIDER-MAN 2

SUPER COLLAPSE 2

THAT'S SO RAVEN 2:
SUPERNATURAL STYLE

TOM AND JERRY: THE MAGIC RING

TONY HAWK'S UNDERGROUND

TONY HAWK'S UNDERGROUND 2

TOP GUN: COMBAT ZONES

TRON 2.0: KILLER APP

THE URBZ: SIMS IN THE CITY

WINNIE THE POOH'S RUMBLY
TUMBLY ADVENTURE

WORLD CHAMPIONSHIP POKER

YOSHI TOPSY-TURVY

YU-GI-OH! 7 TRIALS TO GLORY: WORLD
CHAMPIONSHIP TOURNAMENT 2005

ZOIDS: LEGACY

E 10+

DRAGON BALL GT: TRANSFORMATION

POWER RANGERS: SPACE PATROL DELTA

TEEN

BLACKTHORNE

BLADES OF THUNDER

BUFFY THE VAMPIRE SLAYER:
WRATH OF THE DARKHUL KING

CASTLEVANIA: ARIA OF SORROW

RIVER CITY RANSOM EX

ROAD RASH: JAILBREAK

STREET FIGHTER ALPHA 3

URBAN YETI

Game Boy® Advance Table of Contents

ACE COMBAT ADVANCE

COMPLETE GAME WITH ALL PLANES AND LEVELS OPEN
Select Enter Code and enter QF9B9F59.

ACTION MAN: ROBOT ATAK

ADVENTURE LEVEL 2
Select Password from the main menu and enter REDWOLF.

ADVENTURE LEVEL 3
Select Password from the main menu and enter FLYNT.

ADVENTURE LEVEL 4
Select Password from the main menu and enter MOTHER.

ADVENTURE LEVEL 5
Select Password from the main menu and enter MOTOX.

ADVENTURE LEVEL 6
Select Password from the main menu and enter TEMPLE.

ADVENTURE LEVEL 7
Select Password from the main menu and enter ACTION.

ADVENTURE LEVEL 8
Select Password from the main menu and enter BEACH.

ADVENTURE LEVEL 9
Select Password from the main menu and enter JURA.

ADVENTURE LEVEL 10
Select Password from the main menu and enter AIR.

ADVENTURE LEVEL 11
Select Password from the main menu and enter SURF.

ADVENTURE LEVEL 12
Select Password from the main menu and enter SEWERS.

ADVENTURE LEVEL 13
Select Password from the main menu and enter TUNNEL.

ADVENTURE LEVEL 14
Select Password from the main menu and enter LABO.

ADVENTURE LEVEL 15
Select Password from the main menu and enter KONGO.

ADVENTURE LEVEL 16
Select Password from the main menu and enter BASIC.

ADVENTURE LEVEL 17
Select Password from the main menu and enter ROCKET.

ADVANCED MODE
Select Password from the main menu and enter JUNGLE.

ADVANCED LEVEL 2
Select Password from the main menu and enter AZTEC.

ADVANCED LEVEL 3
Select Password from the main menu and enter SPIDER.

ADVANCED LEVEL 4
Select Password from the main menu and enter DIRT.

ADVANCED LEVEL 5
Select Password from the main menu and enter CROCO.

ADVANCED LEVEL 6
Select Password from the main menu and enter QUEEN.

ADVANCED LEVEL 7
Select Password from the main menu and enter BOW.

ADVANCED LEVEL 8
Select Password from the main menu and enter LAVA.

ADVANCED LEVEL 9
Select Password from the main menu and enter ROCKS.

ADVANCED LEVEL 10
Select Password from the main menu and enter VOLCANO.

ADVANCED LEVEL 11
Select Password from the main menu and enter TRAPS.

ADVANCED LEVEL 12
Select Password from the main menu and enter DINO.

ADVANCED LEVEL 13
Select Password from the main menu and enter SHORE.

ADVANCED LEVEL 14
Select Password from the main menu and enter RAPTOR.

ADVANCED LEVEL 15
Select Password from the main menu and enter BATS.

ADVANCED LEVEL 16
Select Password from the main menu and enter TREX.

ADVANCED LEVEL 17
Select Password from the main menu and enter BIRD.

ADVANCED LEVEL 18
Select Password from the main menu and enter ATTACK.

ADVANCED LEVEL 19
Select Password from the main menu and enter SHELL.

ADVANCED LEVEL 20
Select Password from the main menu and enter PATROL.

ADVANCED LEVEL 21
Select Password from the main menu and enter WIND.

ADVANCED LEVEL 22
Select Password from the main menu and enter RATS.

ADVANCED LEVEL 23
Select Password from the main menu and enter SECRET.

ADVANCED LEVEL 24
Select Password from the main menu and enter WATER.

ADVANCED LEVEL 25
Select Password from the main menu and enter VAPOR.

ADVANCED LEVEL 26
Select Password from the main menu and enter MORAN.

ADVANCED LEVEL 27
Select Password from the main menu and enter LIANA.

ADVANCED LEVEL 28
Select Password from the main menu and enter BACK.

ADVANCED LEVEL 29
Select Password from the main menu and enter CLOCK.

ADVANCED LEVEL 30
Select Password from the main menu and enter UNITY.

ADVANCED LEVEL 31
Select Password from the main menu and enter FINAL.

ADVANCED LEVEL 32
Select Password from the main menu and enter DOCTORX.

TIME ATTACK MODE
Select Password from the main menu and enter HURRY.

TIME ATTACK 2
Select Password from the main menu and enter RUINS.

TIME ATTACK 3
Select Password from the main menu and enter VENOM.

TIME ATTACK 4
Select Password from the main menu and enter STORM.

TIME ATTACK 5
Select Password from the main menu and enter BAYOU.

TIME ATTACK 6
Select Password from the main menu and enter EGGS.

TIME ATTACK 7
Select Password from the main menu and enter ARROW.

TIME ATTACK 8
Select Password from the main menu and enter RACE.

TIME ATTACK 9
Select Password from the main menu and enter SLOPE.

TIME ATTACK 10
Select Password from the main menu and enter HASTE.

TIME ATTACK 11
Select Password from the main menu and enter PITFALL.

TIME ATTACK 12
Select Password from the main menu and enter DESCENT.

TIME ATTACK 13
Select Password from the main menu and enter RUN.

TIME ATTACK 14
Select Password from the main menu and enter CLAWS.

TIME ATTACK 15
Select Password from the main menu and enter STONES.

TIME ATTACK 16
Select Password from the main menu and enter WAOW.

TIME ATTACK 17
Select Password from the main menu and enter AERO.

TIME ATTACK 18
Select Password from the main menu and enter BREEZE.

TIME ATTACK 19
Select Password from the main menu and enter RUSH.

TIME ATTACK 20
Select Password from the main menu and enter CLOUDS.

TIME ATTACK 21
Select Password from the main menu and enter GUST.

TIME ATTACK 22
Select Password from the main menu and enter STINK.

TIME ATTACK 23
Select Password from the main menu and enter BASE.

TIME ATTACK 24
Select Password from the main menu and enter DANGER.

TIME ATTACK 25
Select Password from the main menu and enter STEAM.

TIME ATTACK 26
Select Password from the main menu and enter RESCUE.

TIME ATTACK 27
Select Password from the main menu and enter MONKEY.

TIME ATTACK 28
Select Password from the main menu and enter CHAMBER.

TIME ATTACK 29
Select Password from the main menu and enter BANANA.

TIME ATTACK 30
Select Password from the main menu and enter FORCE.

TIME ATTACK 31
Select Password from the main menu and enter TELE.

TIME ATTACK 32
Select Password from the main menu and enter BOSS.

GAME COMPLETE
Select Password from the main menu and enter MAXIM.

ALIENATORS: EVOLUTION CONTINUES

LEVEL 2
Enter MDKMZKCC as a password.

LEVEL 3
Enter BHSZSKTC as a password.

LEVEL 4
Enter ZKTSHKMC as a password.

LEVEL 5
Enter JLPFDKHB as a password.

LEVEL 6
Enter HMDBRKCB as a password.

LEVEL 7
Enter GLDKLKZB as a password.

LEVEL 8
Enter GLPKLKRB as a password.

LEVEL 9
Enter GLDJBKKF as a password.

LEVEL 10
Enter GLPJBKFF as a password.

LEVEL 11
Enter GLPKBKRF as a password.

LEVEL 12
Enter GLPKBKRF as a password.

LEVEL 13
Enter GLDJLKHD as a password.

UNLIMITED AMMO
Enter RBJPXCKC as a password.

ANIMANIACS: LIGHTS, CAMERA, ACTION!

SKIP LEVEL
Pause the game and press L, L, R, R, Down, Down.

DISABLE TIME
Pause the game and press L, R, Left, Left, Up, Up.

KINGSIZE PICKUPS
Pause the game and press Right, Right, Right, Left, Left, Left, R, L.

PASSWORDS

LEVEL	PASSWORD
1	Wakko, Wakko, Wakko, Wakko, Wakko
2	Dot, Yakko, Brain, Wakko, Pinky
3	Yakko, Dot, Wakko, Wakko, Brain
4	Pinky, Yakko, Yakko, Dot, Brain
5	Pinky, Pinky, Yakko, Wakko, Wakko
6	Brain, Dot, Brain, Pinky, Yakko
7	Brain, Pinky, Wakko, Pinky, Brain
8	Brain Pinky, Pinky, Wakko, Wakko

LEVEL	PASSWORD
9	Dot, Dot, Yakko, Pinky, Wakko
10	Brain, Dot, Brain, Yakko, Wakko
11	Wakko, Yakko, Pinky, Dot, Dot
12	Pinky, Pinky, Brain, Dot, Wakko
13	Yakko, Wakko, Pinky, Wakko, Brain
14	Pinky, Wakko, Brain, Wakko, Yakko
15	Dot, Pinky, Wakko, Wakko, Yakko

BACKYARD BASEBALL 2006

SAMMY SOSA
In a season, enter BABYBEAR as a coach's name.

DONTRELLE WILLIS
In a season, enter BIGFISH as a coach's name.

BANJO PILOT

GRUNTY
Defeat Grunty in the Broomstick battle race. Then, you can purchase Grunty from Cheato.

HUMBA WUMBA
Defeat Humba Wumba in the Jiggu battle race. Then, you can purchase Humba Wumba from Cheato.

JOLLY
Defeat Jolly in the Pumpkin battle race. Then, you can purchase Jolly from Cheato.

KLUNGO
Defeat Klungo in the Skull battle race. Then, you can purchase Klungo from Cheato.

BARBIE IN THE 12 DANCING PRINCESSES

EASY PASSWORDS

LEVEL	PASSWORD
2-a	Cat, Cat, Slippers, Prince
2-b	Cat, Old Lady, Bird, Monkey
3-a	Old Lady, Slippers, Slippers, Slippers
3-b	Blonde Girl, Blonde Girl, Monkey, Blonde Girl
4-a	Old Lady, Brunette Girl, Cat, Brunette Girl
4-b	Monkey, Prince, Blonde Girl, Bird
5-a	Old Lady, Bird, Slippers, Monkey
5-b	Brunette Girl, Bird, Blonde Girl, Old Lady
6-a	Prince, Monkey, Blonde, Old Lady
6-b	Brunette Girl, Cat, Old Lady, Slippers
7-a	Blonde Girl, Brunette Girl, Prince, Old Lady
7-b	Monkey, Cat, Blonde Girl, Old Lady
8	Blonde Girl, Blonde Girl, Prince, Brunette Girl

BATTLE B-DAMAN: FIRE SPIRITS!

2,000 B-DABUCKS
Enter HEY TOMMI! at the parts shop with a Bronze Pass.

3,000 B-DABUCKS
Enter B-DAFIRING at the parts shop with a Bronze Pass.

CHEESY MOUSE B-DAMAN
Enter HARD TEETH at the parts shop with a Bronze Pass.

SABER BARREL AND SHIELD STAND
Enter SHOOT IT!! at the parts shop with a Bronze Pass.

BERSERK OGRE B-DAMAN SET
Enter MONGREL FANG! at the parts shop with a Silver Pass.

BLOOD SHARK B-DAMAN SET
Enter A BLOODY BODY at the parts shop with a Silver Pass.

GAOTIGER B-DAMAN SET
Enter GLEAMING FANG at the parts shop with a Silver Pass.

KOKURYU-OH B-DAMAN SET
Enter SHADOWY ARMOR at the parts shop with a Silver Pass.

OAK RAVEN
Enter GUST OF WIND! at the parts shop with a Silver Pass.

OHRYU-OH B-DAMAN SET
Enter GOLDEN ARMOR! at the parts shop with a Silver Pass.

SABER MAGAZINE
Enter TONS OF BALLS at the parts shop with a Silver Pass.

VENOM STING B-DAMAN SET
Enter VENOMOUS TAIL at the parts shop with a Silver Pass.

YOKUSAIMARU B-DAMAN SET
Enter YOKUSAIMARU! at the parts shop with a Silver Pass.

ASSAULT BEAST AND STORM CHIMERA

Enter FEROCIOUS WOLF! at the parts shop with a Gold Pass.

BLITZ EAGLE

Enter THE SWIFT WINGS at the parts shop with a Gold Pass.

CHROME HARRIER

Enter STRONG RED GALE at the parts shop with a Gold Pass.

CRIMSON SABER

Enter THE RAZING FIRE at the parts shop with a Gold Pass.

LABYRINTH

Enter REVIVAL OF EVIL at the parts shop with a Gold Pass.

MEGA DIABROS

Enter DEVILISH FIGURE at the parts shop with a Gold Pass.

REVOLVER HEAVEN

Enter LET'S B-DAFIRE! at the parts shop with a Gold Pass.

STREAM PEGASUS

Enter GIFT FROM ATLUS at the parts shop with a Gold Pass.

BIONICLE: TALES OF THE TOHUNGA

EVERYTHING BUT THE MINI-GAMES

Enter B9RBRN as a name.

GALI MINI-GAME

Enter 9MA268 as a name.

KOPAKA MINI-GAME

Enter V33673 as a name.

LEWA MINI-GAME

Enter 3LT154 as a name.

ONUA MINI-GAME

Enter 8MR472 as a name.

POHATU MINI-GAME

Enter 5MG834 as a name.

TAHU MINI-GAME

Enter 4CR487 as a name.

BLACKTHORNE

INFINITE HEALTH

At the title screen, press Left, Right, Down, Up, B, B, Down.

INVISIBLE

At the title screen, press B, Down, Right, Down, Up, Up, Left, B, Up.

FALLING WON'T KILL YOU

At the title screen, press B, B, Up, Left, Down, Right, Right, Up.

BLADES OF THUNDER

LEVEL 1 ON EASY

Enter the password 4265.

LEVEL 2 ON EASY

Enter the password 7332.

LEVEL 3 ON EASY

Enter the password 6578.

LEVEL 4 ON EASY

Enter the password 7213.

LEVEL 5 ON EASY

Enter the password 8234.

LEVEL 6 ON EASY

Enter the password 9322

LEVEL 7 ON EASY

Enter the password 1279.

LEVEL 8 ON EASY

Enter the password 5682.

LEVEL 9 ON EASY

Enter the password 3211.

LEVEL 1 ON MEDIUM

Enter the password 6932.

LEVEL 2 ON MEDIUM

Enter the password 3682.

LEVEL 3 ON MEDIUM

Enter the password 5892.

LEVEL 4 ON MEDIUM

Enter the password 4468.

LEVEL 5 ON MEDIUM

Enter the password 1127.

LEVEL 6 ON MEDIUM
Enter the password 9902.

LEVEL 7 ON MEDIUM
Enter the password 2332.

LEVEL 8 ON MEDIUM
Enter the password 8658.

LEVEL 9 ON MEDIUM
Enter the password 7745.

LEVEL 1 ON HARD
Enter the password 1979.

LEVEL 2 ON HARD
Enter the password 2034.

LEVEL 3 ON HARD
Enter the password 7809.

LEVEL 4 ON HARD
Enter the password 6776.

LEVEL 5 ON HARD
Enter the password 9054.

LEVEL 6 ON HARD
Enter the password 4311.

LEVEL 7 ON HARD
Enter the password 8282.

LEVEL 8 ON HARD
Enter the password 2468.

LEVEL 9 ON HARD
Enter the password 1410.

BUFFY THE VAMPIRE SLAYER: WRATH OF THE DARKHUL KING

9 OF EVERYTHING
At the title screen, press Up, Down, Up, Down, B, A.

INFINITE LIVES
At the title screen, press L, L, L, R, R, R, Right, Right.

INVINCIBLE
At the title screen, press B, B, A, A, L, R, Down, Up.

BUTT UGLY MARTIANS: B.K.M. BATTLES

UNLIMITED LIVES
Enter KMIORMAO as a password.

MAX DEFENSE, FIREPOWER AND RESTORATION PICKUPS
Enter ALWMAA15 as a password.

2 DEFENSE UPGRADES
Enter JT2DU 4MP as a password.

2 EXTRA LIVES
Enter 2ELFM PLS as a password.

2 WEAPON UPGRADES
Enter GMACO EWU as a password.

4 DEFENSE UPGRADES
Enter DUATO U4M as a password.

4 EXTRA LIVES
Enter IAGAW 4EL as a password.

4 WEAPON UPGRADES
Enter IAGAW 4WU as a password.

START AT MECHTROPOLIS
Select Resume Game and enter IWTSOWN2.

START AT AQUATICA
Select Resume Game and enter TMTWN3PD.

START AT ARBOREA
Select Resume Game and enter IIALTSMO4.

START AT SILICON CITY
Select Resume Game and enter IOTJOWN5.

START AT MAGMA
Select Resume Game and enter FILGSOW6.

START AT KOO FOO SHIP
Select Resume Game and enter IWTSOWN7.

CAR BATTLER JOE

BIG BANG
At the main menu, select Battle League. When the game asks "Use which machine," choose password and enter HAMA!333.

BLUE GALPE EV
At the main menu, select Battle League. When the game asks "Use which machine," choose password and enter SHISYO!!.

CASEY'S WHLS
At the main menu, select Battle League. When the game asks "Use which machine," choose password and enter !KOKICHI.

CAVALIER
At the main menu, select Battle League. When the game asks "Use which machine," choose password and enter CUREWAND.

COPA ZONE23
At the main menu, select Battle League. When the game asks "Use which machine," choose password and enter CDMACAPA.

EMP FORCE X
At the main menu, select Battle League. When the game asks "Use which machine," choose password and enter EMPIRE!!.

ISSUE X
At the main menu, select Battle League. When the game asks "Use which machine," choose password and enter 8998981!.

JOE JIM ZERO
At the main menu, select Battle League. When the game asks "Use which machine," choose password and enter Todoroki.

LONG VALLEYZ
At the main menu, select Battle League. When the game asks "Use which machine," choose password and enter NAGOYADB.

MATSU K MK4
At the main menu, select Battle League. When the game asks "Use which machine," choose password and enter MR!HURRY.

MAX-K
At the main menu, select Battle League. When the game asks "Use which machine," choose password and enter GANKOMAX.

MEGA M
At the main menu, select Battle League. When the game asks "Use which machine," choose password and enter M!M!M!M!.

MILLENNIUM90
At the main menu, select Battle League. When the game asks "Use which machine," choose password and enter 90!60!92.

MRIN'S DREAM
At the main menu, select Battle League. When the game asks "Use which machine," choose password and enter MARRON!!.

MSSL DOLLY
At the main menu, select Battle League. When the game asks "Use which machine," choose password and enter KINNIKU!.

PISTON GH
At the main menu, select Battle League. When the game asks "Use which machine," choose password and enter GO!HOME!.

SOLID WIND
At the main menu, select Battle League. When the game asks "Use which machine," choose password and enter RED!GUNS.

TAKAH'S LSR
At the main menu, select Battle League. When the game asks "Use which machine," choose password and enter TK000056.

WNN SPECIAL
At the main menu, select Battle League. When the game asks "Use which machine," choose password and enter BOM!BOM!.

CARS

ALL LEVELS AND 90 BOLTS
At the title screen, press Up, Up, Down, Down, Left, Right, Left, Right, B, A.

ALL CARS
At the title screen, press Right, Down, Right, B.

ALL CAR COLORS
At the title screen, press Up, Up, Left, Right, Right, Left, Down, Down.

RADIATOR CAP SECRET CIRCUIT
At the title screen, press Left, Left, Right, Right, B, B, A.

ALL SCREENSHOTS AT THE DRIVE-IN
At the title screen, press Left, Down, Right, A.

CARTOON NETWORK SPEEDWAY

UNLOCK EVERYTHING
Enter 96981951 as a password.

ALL FIVE CHAMPIONSHIPS COMPLETE
Enter 34711154 as a password.

START AT FARM FROLICS
Enter 12761357 as a password.

START AT DOWN ON THE FARM
Enter 25731079 as a password.

START AT MURIEL
Enter 25731079 as a password.

START AT EDOPOLIS
Enter 38611791 as a password.

START AT JOHNNY 2X4
Enter 52681314 as a password.

START AT SCARY SPEEDWAY
Enter 68851752 as a password.

START AT DESERT DRIVE
Enter 81821475 as a password.

START AT LITTLE SUZY
Enter 81821475 as a password.

START AT HOT ROD JOHNNY
Enter 84891097 as a password.

START AT SWANKY
Enter 98761719 as a password.

START AT ALPINE ANTICS
Enter 98761719 as a password.

ACME AXEL AWARD TROPHY
Enter 50000050 as a password.

CARTOON SPEEDWAY TROPHY
Enter 10000010 as a password.

FENDER BENDER FRENZY TROPHY
Enter 32000010 as a password.

CASTLEVANIA: ARIA OF SORROW

NO ITEMS
Start a new game with the name NOUSE to use no items in the game.

NO SOULS
Start a new game with the name NOSOUL to use no soulds in the game.

CLASSIC NES SERIES: PAC-MAN

PAC-ATTACK PUZZLE MODE

STAGE	PASSWORD
1	STR
2	HNM
3	KST
4	TRT
5	MYX
6	KHL
7	RTS
8	SKB
9	HNT

STAGE	PASSWORD
10	SRY
11	YSK
12	RCF
13	HSM
14	PWW
15	MTN
16	TKY
17	RGH

CURIOUS GEORGE

PASSWORDS

LEVEL	PASSWORD
2	TNTDBHNQ
3	TNTDBHBQ
6	PSTDHHSS
8	TNSDBHAG

DANNY PHANTOM: THE ULTIMATE ENEMY

BOSS RUSH MODE
Select Password from the Options and enter Rush.

EASY AND HARD DIFFICULTY
Select Password from the Options and enter Vlad.

DASH'S HAUNTED LOCKER MINI GAME
Select Password from the Options and enter Dash.

HINDIN' GHOST SEEK
MINI GAME
Select Password from the Options and enter Seek.

LEVITATION MINI GAME
Select Password from the Options and enter Jazz.

SAM'S X-RAY ECTO DETECTOR MINI GAME
Select Password from the Options and enter Ecto.

DISNEY'S EXTREME SKATE ADVENTURE

PETER PAN
At the main menu, press L, R, L, R, L, L, Start.

DISNEY'S HOME ON THE RANGE

LEVEL 1
Enter DVHB as a password.

LEVEL 2
Enter VCFK as a password.

LEVEL 3
Enter BQMF as a password.

LEVEL 4
Enter HFKM as a password.

LEVEL 5
Enter DMCV as a password.

LEVEL 6
Enter BBKD as a password.

LEVEL 7
Enter KNLC as a password.

LEVEL 8
Enter BDJR as a password.

LEVEL 9
Enter BDRN as a password.

LEVEL 10
Enter PSBH as a password.

LEVEL 11
Enter QRNN as a password.

LEVEL 12
Enter MMKN as a password.

LEVEL 13
Enter PSFH as a password.

LEVEL 14
Enter DBVJ as a password.

DK: KING OF SWING

ATTACK BATTLE 3
At the title screen, press Up + L + A + B to bring up a password screen. Enter 65942922.

CLIMBING RACE 5
At the title screen, press Up + L + A + B to bring up a password screen. Enter 55860327.

OBSTACLE RACE 4
At the title screen, press Up + L + A + B to bring up a password screen. Enter 35805225.

UNLOCK TIME ATTACK
Complete the game as DK.

UNLOCK DIDDY MODE
Collect 24 medals as DK.

UNLOCK BUBBLES
Complete Diddy Mode with 24 Medals.

UNLOCK KREMLING
Collect 6 gold medals in Jungle Jam.

UNLOCK KING K. ROOL
Collect 12 gold medals in Jungle Jam.

DONKEY KONG COUNTRY 2: DIDDY KONG'S QUEST

ALL LEVELS
Select Cheats from the Options and enter freedom.

START WITH 15 LIVES
Select Cheats from the Options and enter helpme.

START WITH 55 LIVES
Select Cheats from the Options and enter weakling.

START WITH 10 BANANA COINS
Select Cheats from the Options and enter richman.

START WITH 50 BANANA COINS
Select Cheats from the Options and enter wellrich.

NO DK OR HALF WAY BARRELS
Select Cheats from the Options and enter rockard.

MUSIC PLAYER
Select Cheats from the Options and enter onetime.

CREDITS
Select Cheats from the Options and enter kredits.

DORA THE EXPLORER: SUPER SPIES

RAINFOREST 2 PASSWORD
Select Continue and enter Arrow up, Plus sign, Triangle, Star, Plus sign, Triangle, Frown.

DRAGON BALL GT: TRANSFORMATION

REFILL ENERGY
During a game, press Down, Up, Right. Right, Right, Left, Right, Left, B.

REFILL HEALTH
During a game, press Down, Up, Left, Left, Up, Right, Down, B.

PICCOLO
At the main menu, press Left, Right, Left Right, Up, Up, Down, B.

SUPER BABY VEGETA
At the main menu, press Left, Right, Left Right, Down, Down, Up, B.

SUPER SAIYAN 4 GOKU
At the main menu, press Left, Right, Left Right, Down, Down, Down, B.

SUPER SAIYAN KID GOKU
At the main menu, press Left, Right, Left Right, Up, Up, Up, B.

SUPER SAIYAN VEGETA
At the main menu, press Left, Right, Left Right, Up, Down, Down, B.

FINAL FANTASY I & II: DAWN OF SOULS

FF I TILE GAME
During a game of Final Fantasy I and after you get the ship, hold A and press B about 55 times.

FF II CONCENTRATION GAME
Once you obtain the Snowcraft, hold B and press A about 20 times.

HARLEM GLOBETROTTERS: WORLD TOUR

PASSWORDS

TEAMS BEATEN	PASSWORD
2	XCTXJK
3	XNSXHD
4	XYRXGT
5	X7QXFL
6	XHQXXG
7	XSPXWD
8	XZNXVS
10	X4LX9L
11	XDLXRH
12	XPKXQJ
13	XZJXPM
14	X8HXNQ
15	XTGX3H

HOT WHEELS VELOCITY X

PASSWORDS

LEVEL	PASSWORD
02	143-24-813
03	141-38-985
04	249-48-723
05	294-16-277
06	457-51-438
07	112-86-545
08	447-65-112
09	368-54-466
10	718-59-438
11	363-95-545
12	373-65-848
13	171-49-211
14	373-59-216
15	373-62-927
16	718-42-276
17	358-59-355
18	478-68-254
19	573-77-683

LEVEL	PASSWORD
20	188-58-352
21	766-46-341
22	187-98-394
23	188-12-234
24	786-84-747
25	466-59-979
26	477-58-369
27	447-62-191
28	614-81-432
29	641-18-239
30	399-68-584
31	662-84-635
32	476-63-843
33	616-67-341
34	384-97-475
35	363-13-298
36	521-71-135
37	543-17-658
38	782-57-387

JUSTICE LEAGUE HEROES: THE FLASH

ALL HEROES
At the title screen, hold B and press Up, Down, Left, Right, Right, Left, Down, Up, Select.

ALL POWERS
At the title screen, hold B and press Down, Down, Down, Down, Left, Right, Up, Down, Select.

LIVES
At the title screen, hold B and press Up, Up, Up, Down, Down, Up, Down, Select.

BIG FLASH
At the title screen, hold B and press Left, Up, Right, Down, Left, Up, Right, Down, Select.

SMALL FLASH
At the title screen, hold B and press Down, Down, Down, Left, Up, Up, Up, Right, Select.

BIG BAD GUYS
At the title screen, hold B and press Up, Up, Down, Down, Left, Right, Left, Right, Select.

SMALL BAD GUYS
At the title screen, hold B and press Down, Down, Up, Up, Right, Left, Right, Left, Select.

KIEN

QUEST II
Enter KA10LVQ1M as a password.

QUEST III
Enter KB18LVQ2L as a password.

QUEST IV
Enter KC30LVQ3G as a password.

QUEST V
Enter KD70LVQ4S as a password.

LEGO KNIGHT'S KINGDOM

STORY 100% COMPLETE
Enter YZZVZYZ as a password.

LEGO STAR WARS

SHEEP MODE
Pause the game and press L, R, L, Down, Up, R, R, Right, Left, Down, Right, Right, Select

YODA SAYS
Pause the game and press Down, L, R, Select.

WATCH CUTSCENES
Pause the game and press Down, Up, R, L, R, R, R, Down, Down, Up, Down, Down, Select.

REPAIR BOT
Pause the game and press Down, Down, Down, Down, L, Right, Down, Right, L.

TEMPORARY SPEED BOOST
Pause the game and press Right, Right, Down, Up, Right, L.

PLAY AS BATTLE DROID
On the start screen, Start, Start, Left, Down, Down, Down, Down, Right.

PLAY AS A DROIDEKA
Pause the game and press Start, Start, Down, Right, Left, Down, Right, Left.

PLAY AS A REPAIR DROID
Pause the game and press Start, Start, Up, Up, Up, Down, Down, Down.

PLAY AS BLUE GUNGAN
Pause the game and press Start, Start, Down, Left, Right, Down, Left, Right.

PLAY AS C-3PO
Pause the game and press Start, Start, Left, Down, Right, Up, Right, Right.

PLAY AS DROID ON HOVERSLED
Pause the game and press Start, Start, Down, Up, Down, Up, Down, Up.

PLAY AS GENERAL GRIEVOUS
Pause the game and press Start, Start, Down, Down, Down, Down, Down, Down.

PLAY AS WINGED GUY
Pause the game and press Start, Start, Right, Down, Right, Down, Left, Up.

PLAY AS R2-D2
Pause the game and press Start, Start, Up, Up, Up, Up, Up, Up.

PLAY AS R4-P17
Pause the game and press Start, Start, Up, Down, Up, Down, Up, Down.

POWERFUL BLASTERS
Pause the game and press Down, Down, Left, Right, Down, L.

A FEW LEGO PIECES
Pause the game and press L, L, L, Right, Left, R, R, R.

BLACK SABER
Pause the game and press L, L, R, Start.

BLUE SABER
Pause the game and press R, R, R, Start.

GREEN SABER
Pause the game and press R, L, R, Start.

PURPLE SABER
Pause the game and press L, R, L, Start.

RED SABER
Pause the game and press L, R, R, Start.

YELLOW SABER
Pause the game and press R, R, L, Start.

MEGA MAN BATTLE NETWORK 5: TEAM PROTOMAN & MEGA MAN BATTLE NETWORK 5: TEAM COLONEL

To compress the following Navi Customizer Programs, you must highlight that program and enter the appropriate code.

COMPRESS AIRSHOES
Highlight AirShoes, hold Right and press B, L, B, A, B, L, B, B, A, A.

COMPRESS ATTACKMAX
Highlight AttackMAX, hold Right and press L, L, L, R, R, B, A, R, B, L.

COMPRESS BATTERYMODE
Highlight BatteryMode, hold Right and press A, A, B, R, A, B, R, L, L, R.

COMPRESS BEATSUPPORT
Highlight BeatSupport, hold Right and press A, B, B, R, A, A, B, R, B, R.

COMPRESS BODYPACK
Highlight BodyPack, hold Right and press B, A, R, A, B, R, L, R, R, A.

COMPRESS BUGSTOPPER
Highlight bugstopper, hold Right and press B, A, B, L, A, B, R, L, R, B.

COMPRESS BUSTERPACK
Highlight BusterPack, hold Right and press L, L, R, A, R, L, B, L, A, R.

COMPRESS CHARGEMAX
Highlight ChargeMAX, hold Right and press A, L, A, A, R, B, R, B, A, R.

COMPRESS COLLECT
Highlight Collect, hold Right and press B, R, A, L, A, R, B, A, A, B.

COMPRESS CUSTOM +1
Highlight , hold Right and press A, A, R, L, B, A, B, A, L, B.

COMPRESS CUSTOM2
Highlight Custom, hold Right and press B, A, R, L, L, R, A, L, B, R.

COMPRESS DANDYISM
Highlight Dandyism, hold Right and press R, R, B, B, R, B, R, B, A, A.

COMPRESS FIRST BARRIER
Highlight Barrier, hold Right and press R, L, A, B, B, A, R, A, L, R.

COMPRESS FLOATSHOES
Highlight FloatShoes, hold Right and press A, L, L, B, R, L, A, A, A, L.

COMPRESS GIGAFOLDER1
Highlight GigaFolder, hold Right and press R, R, L, B, L, L, A, R, B, L.

COMPRESS GIGAVIRUS
Highlight GigaVirus, hold Right and press B, B, R, A, L, B, L, A, R, R.

COMPRESS HUMOURSENSE
Highlight HumourSense, hold Right and press A, B, L, A, R, A, B, L, R, L.

COMPRESS I'M FISH
Highlight I'm Fish, hold Right and press B, A, A, B, A, L, R, A, R, A, A.

COMPRESS THE JUNGLELAND
Highlight JungleLand, hold Right and press L, R, L, A, B, L, B, B, L, A.

COMPRESS KAWARIMIMAGIC
Highlight KawarimiMagic, hold Right and press R, B, B, A, R, B, R, A, R, B.

COMPRESS MEGAFOLDER 1
Highlight , hold Right and press B, B, A, B, B, R, R, L, A, R.

COMPRESS MEGAVIRUS
Highlight MegaVirus, hold Right and press A, A, B, L, A, R, B, L, A, A.

COMPRESS MILLIONARE
Highlight Millionare, hold Right and press R, L, R, A, R, R, L, L, L, R.

COMPRESS THE OIL BODY
Highlight Oil Body, hold Right and press L, B, R, A, R, L, A, B, L, B.

COMPRESS RAPIDMAX
Highlight RapidMAX, hold Right and press R, A, R, L, L, R, R, A, B, A.

COMPRESS THE REFLECT PROGRAM
Highlight program, hold Right and press L, L, R, B, L, L, A, A, L, B.

COMPRESS RUSHSUPPORT
Highlight RushSupport, hold Right and press R, B, L, R, B, R, L, L, R, L.

COMPRESS SAITOBATCH
Highlight SaitoBatch, hold Right and press A, L, R, A, B, L, R, A, L, R.

COMPRESS SELFRECOVERY
Highlight SelfRecovery, hold Right and press R, L, R, L, R, B, B, R, A, B.

COMPRESS SHIELD
Highlight Shield, hold Right and press A, B, A, R, A, L, R, B, B, A.

COMPRESS SHINOBIDASH
Highlight ShinobiDash, hold Right and press R, L, L, A, L, L, B, A, B, B.

COMPRESS SUPERARMOUR
Highlight SuperArmour, hold Right and press R, A, B, R, A, L, L, R, B, A.

COMPRESS TANGOSUPPORT
Highlight TangoSupport, hold Right and press L, B, L, A, B, L, A, B, A, L.

COMPRESS UNDERSHIRT
Highlight UnderShirt, hold Right and press A, R, B, B, R, L, R, A, L, A.

ANTI ELEC * NUMBERMAN CODE
Once the Numberman Machine is in Higsby's shop, use it and enter 35607360.

ANTI FIRE * NUMBERMAN CODE
Once the Numberman Machine is in Higsby's shop, use it and enter 73877466.

ANTI NAVI V NUMBERMAN CODE
Once the Numberman Machine is in Higsby's shop, use it and enter 05068930.

ANTI SWORD R NUMBERMAN CODE
Once the Numberman Machine is in Higsby's shop, use it and enter 10386794.

ANTI WATER * NUMBERMAN CODE
Once the Numberman Machine is in Higsby's shop, use it and enter 25465278.

ANTI WOOD * NUMBERMAN CODE
Once the Numberman Machine is in Higsby's shop, use it and enter 10133670.

ATTACK MAX (YELLOW NCP) NUMBERMAN CODE
Once the Numberman Machine is in Higsby's shop, use it and enter 63231870.

BEATSUPPORT NCP NUMBERMAN CODE
Once the Numberman Machine is in Higsby's shop, use it and enter 79877132.

BODY PACK NUMBERMAN CODE

Once the Numberman Machine is in Higsby's shop, use it and enter 30112002.

BUSTERPACK NCP NUMBERMAN CODE

Once the Numberman Machine is in Higsby's shop, use it and enter 80246758.

CHARGE MAX (WHITE NCP) NUMBERMAN CODE

Once the Numberman Machine is in Higsby's shop, use it and enter 87412146.

CUSTOM 2 NUMBERMAN CODE

Once the Numberman Machine is in Higsby's shop, use it and enter 15595587.

CUSTOM BOLT 3 G NUMBERMAN CODE

Once the Numberman Machine is in Higsby's shop, use it and enter 07765623.

DARK INVIS * NUMBERMAN CODE

Once the Numberman Machine is in Higsby's shop, use it and enter 68799876.

DJANGOSP D NUMBERMAN CODE

Once the Numberman Machine is in Higsby's shop, use it and enter 91098051.

FULL ENERGY NUMBERMAN CODE

Once the Numberman Machine is in Higsby's shop, use it and enter 12118790.

FULL ENERGY NUMBERMAN CODE

Once the Numberman Machine is in Higsby's shop, use it and enter 90914896.

GUN DEL SOL 3 O NUMBERMAN CODE

Once the Numberman Machine is in Higsby's shop, use it and enter 35321321.

HP +200 (PINK NCP) NUMBERMAN CODE

Once the Numberman Machine is in Higsby's shop, use it and enter 90630807.

HP+300 (WHITE NCP) NUMBERMAN CODE

Once the Numberman Machine is in Higsby's shop, use it and enter 13926561.

HP+400 (PINK NCP) NUMBERMAN CODE

Once the Numberman Machine is in Higsby's shop, use it and enter 03419893.

HP+400 NCP NUMBERMAN CODE

Once the Numberman Machine is in Higsby's shop, use it and enter 45654128.

HP+50 NCP NUMBERMAN CODE

Once the Numberman Machine is in Higsby's shop, use it and enter 31084443.

HP+500 (WHITE NCP) NUMBERMAN CODE

Once the Numberman Machine is in Higsby's shop, use it and enter 72846472.

LOCK ENEMY NUMBERMAN CODE

Once the Numberman Machine is in Higsby's shop, use it and enter 29789661.

RAPID MAX (PINK NCP) NUMBERMAN CODE

Once the Numberman Machine is in Higsby's shop, use it and enter 36695497.

RECOVERY-300 Y NUMBERMAN CODE

Once the Numberman Machine is in Higsby's shop, use it and enter 18746897.

RUSHSUPPORT NCP NUMBERMAN CODE

Once the Numberman Machine is in Higsby's shop, use it and enter 09609807.

SHINOBI DASH NUMBERMAN CODE

Once the Numberman Machine is in Higsby's shop, use it and enter 64892292.

SOULTIME +1 (YELLOW NCP) NUMBERMAN CODE

Once the Numberman Machine is in Higsby's shop, use it and enter 28256341.

SPIN BLUE NUMBERMAN CODE

Once the Numberman Machine is in Higsby's shop, use it and enter 12541883.

SPIN GREEN NUMBERMAN CODE

Once the Numberman Machine is in Higsby's shop, use it and enter 78987728.

SPIN RED NUMBERMAN CODE

Once the Numberman Machine is in Higsby's shop, use it and enter 30356451.

STATIC S NUMBERMAN CODE

Once the Numberman Machine is in Higsby's shop, use it and enter 48958798.

TANGOSUPPORT NCP NUMBERMAN CODE

Once the Numberman Machine is in Higsby's shop, use it and enter 54288793.

UNLOCKER NUMBERMAN CODE

Once the Numberman Machine is in Higsby's shop, use it and enter 64664560.

UNLOCKER NUMBERMAN CODE

Once the Numberman Machine is in Higsby's shop, use it and enter 28706568.

UNLOCKER NUMBERMAN CODE

Once the Numberman Machine is in Higsby's shop, use it and enter 73978713.

UNTRAP NUMBERMAN CODE

Once the Numberman Machine is in Higsby's shop, use it and enter 00798216.

PIRATES OF THE CARIBBEAN: DEAD MAN'S CHEST

1,000 GOLD

Pause the game, press Select and then press A, L, Select, R, Right, Right.

INVINCIBILITY

Pause the game, press Select and then press R, L, Up, Up, Left, Right.

RESTORE HEALTH

Pause the game, press Select and then press Select, R, A, L, Left, Right.

ALL SHIP UPGRADES

Pause the game, press Select and then press Right, Left, Left, Down, Up, Select.

BEST JACK UPGRADES

Pause the game, press Select and then press Right, L, Down, A, Left, Select.

RESTORE GROG/FOOD

Pause the game, press Select and then press A, Select, Left, Down, Right, Up.

UNLOCK RUMORS

Pause the game, press Select and then press A, L, Select, A, Right, Up.

MAGIC WIND

Pause the game, press Select and then press Up, R, Down, Left, Left, Right.

POWER RANGERS: SPACE PATROL DELTA

EPISODE 1 ON EASY
Enter ZZB as a password.

EPISODE 2A ON EASY
Enter ZVC as a password.

EPISODE 2B ON EASY
Enter QZB as a password.

EPISODE 3A ON EASY
Enter QVC as a password.

0G EPISODE 3B ON EASY
Enter ! as a password.

XH EPISODE 4A ON EASY
Enter ! as a password.

EPISODE 4B ON EASY
Enter ROG as a password.

EPISODE 5A ON EASY
Enter Z2B as a password.

EPISODE 5B ON EASY
Enter V6C as a password.

EPISODE 6A ON EASY
Enter L6C as a password.

4G EPISODE 6B ON EASY
Enter ! as a password.

EPISODE 7A ON EASY
Enter R4G as a password.

EPISODE 7B ON EASY
Enter M8H as a password.

EPISODE 8A ON EASY
Enter OBF as a password.

EPISODE 8B ON EASY
Enter SGD as a password.

FINAL BATTLE ON EASY
Enter SBF as a password.

RIVER CITY RANSOM EX

Select the status menu and change your name to the following:

MAX STATS
DAMAX

$999999.99
PLAYA

CUSTOM CHAR
XTRA0

CUSTOM SELF
XTRA1

CUSTOM MOVE
XTRA2

CLEAR SAVE
ERAZE

TECHNIQUES 1
FUZZY. This group includes Mach Punch, Dragon Kick, Acro Circus, Grand Slam, Javelin Man, Slick Trick, Nitro Port, Twin Kick, Deadly Shot, Top Spin, Helicopter, Torpedo.

TECHNIQUES 2
WUZZY. This group includes Slap Happy, Pulper, Headbutt, Kickstand, Big Bang, Wheel Throw, Glide Chop, Head Bomb, Chain Chump, Jet Kick, Shuriken, Flip Throw

TECHNIQUES 3
WAZZA. This group includes Boomerang, Charge It, Bat Fang, Flying Kick, Speed Drop, Bomb Blow, Killer Kick, Bike Kick, Slam Punk, Dragon Knee, God Fist, Hyperguard.

TECHNIQUES 4
BEAR*. This group includes PhoenixWing, Inlines, Springlines, Rocketeers, Air Merc's Narcishoes, Magic Pants, Pandora Box, Skaterz, Custom Fit.

ROAD RASH: JAILBREAK

ALL CHARACTERS AT LEVEL 4 AND ALL RACES
Press Select at the Player select and enter ALAKAZAMM.

ALL RACES
Press Select at the Player select and enter KEEPOUT.

ALL RACES IN COP PATROL
Press Select at the Player select and enter FELONY.

SURVIVAL
Press Select at the Player select and enter MENACE.

ACE LEVEL 2
Press Select at the Player select and enter SWING.

ACE LEVEL 3
Press Select at the Player select and enter FLUSH.

ACE LEVEL 4
Press Select at the Player select and enter BRUISE.

FAT HOAGIE
Press Select at the Player select and enter EDGY.

FAT HOAGIE LEVEL 2
Press Select at the Player select and enter SLAP.

FAT HOAGIE LEVEL 3
Press Select at the Player select and enter FURIOUS.

FAT HOAGIE LEVEL 4
Press Select at the Player select and enter HEADACHE.

HURL LEVEL 1
Press Select at the Player select and enter HOWDY.

HURL LEVEL 2
Press Select at the Player select and enter PULSE.

HURL LEVEL 3
Press Select at the Player select and enter STRIDER.

HURL LEVEL 4
Press Select at the Player select and enter BEATNIK.

LULU LEVEL 2
Press Select at the Player select and enter BLOW.

LULU LEVEL 3
Press Select at the Player select and enter SCOURGE.

LULU LEVEL 4
Press Select at the Player select and enter QUICKEN.

TINY LEVEL 2
Press Select at the Player select and enter AXLE.

TINY LEVEL 3
Press Select at the Player select and enter WHEEL.

TINY LEVEL 4
Press Select at the Player select and enter PROPER.

ROCK 'EM SOCK 'EM ROBOTS

TITLE FIGHT PASSWORDS

Select Passwords from the Select Game Mode screen and enter the following:

TITLE FIGHT	PASSWORD	TITLE FIGHT	PASSWORD
Black Bruiser	LSTL2B	Pink Pummeller	6QT1KK
Blue Bomber	B5T32J	Purple Pyro	O2TX2T
Brown Bully	J[]T7KH	Silver Stretcher	GZTV2K
Green Grappler	NMTZKQ	Yellow Yahoo	W8T52Q
Orange Oppressor	2XT9KN	End	3CTNKS

RUGRATS: I GOTTA GO PARTY

GO TO LEVEL 2
Enter CBKBBB as a password.

GO TO LEVEL 3
Enter RBHBNB as a password.

GO TO LEVEL 4
Enter SNFBBC as a password.

GO TO LEVEL 5
Enter TNHHBG as a password.

GO TO LEVEL 6
Enter VNFTNG as a password.

GO TO LEVEL 7
Enter XNHTFC as a password.

GO TO LEVEL 8
Enter ZNFTRJ as a password.

SECRET AGENT BARBIE: ROYAL JEWELS MISSION

ALL SECRETS
Enter TTTTTS as a password.

ENGLAND – THE ROYAL TOWER
Enter BBBBCG as a password.

ENGLAND – STREET CHASE
Enter DBBFCM as a password.

CHINA – CITY STREETS
Enter FBBFFQ as a password.

CHINA – SECRET HIDEOUT
Enter GBBPFH as a password.

CHINA – GOLDEN CITY
Enter HBBPKN as a password.

CHINA – THE PALACE
Enter JCBPKQ as a password.

ITALY – OPERA HOUSE
Enter KCBTKC as a password.

ITALY - CANAL CHASE
Enter LCGTKJ as a password.

ITALY – FASHION DISTRICT
Enter MCHTKL as a password.

ITALY – SCUBA SEARCH
Enter NCHTTC as a password.

MEXICO - SUNNY CITY
Enter PCRTTN as a password.

SHAMAN KING: LEGACY OF THE SPIRITS, SOARING HAWK

SPIRIT OF FIRE
At the title screen, press Right, Right, L, Left + R, Down, R, Right, B.

SHAMAN KING: LEGACY OF THE SPIRITS, SPRINTING WOLF

SPIRIT OF FIRE
At the title screen, press Right, Right, L, Left + R, Down, R, Right, B.

SHINING SOUL

2 EXTRA HERBS
Enter your name as Shining.

2 VALUING SCROLLS
Enter your name as Force.

HEALING DROP
Enter your name as Soul.

MONKEY DOLL
Enter your name as AiAi.

PAINTER'S SOUL
Enter your name as Salamander.

JUDO UNIFORM FOR DRAGONUTE
Select the Dragonute and enter your name as Segata.

LEAF BRIEFS FOR ARCHER
Select the Archer and enter your name as NomuNomu.

SHINING SOUL II

DREAM HAT
Enter Nindri as your name.

GENOME RING
Enter Genomes as your name.

ATLUS RING
Enter Vjum as your name.

POWER GLOVES
Enter VJxSS as your name.

STR +5
Enter Ninky as your name.

DEX +5
Enter Yoshi as your name.

VIT +5
Enter Taicho as your name.

INT +5, RTH +30
Enter Dengeki as your name.

RDK +30
Enter Montaka as your name.

RFR +30
Enter Iyoku as your name.

RIC +30
Enter Mizupin as your name.

RPO +30
Enter Hachi as your name.

SPIDER-MAN 2

INVINCIBILITY
At the title screen, press Up, Down, Right, A.

LEVEL SELECT
After completing the game, start a new game with the name FLUWDEAR.

STREET FIGHTER ALPHA 3

ALL FIGHTERS
At the title screen, press Left, Right, Down, Right, L, L, A, L, L, B, R, A, Up.

ALL MODES
At the title screen, press A, Up, A, L, R, Right, L, Right, A, Down, Right.
Now press L, Right, A, R, Up,L, Right, B, A, Up, Right, Down, Right.

PLAY AS SUPER BISON
At the character select, hold Start and select Bison.

PLAY AS SHIN AKUMA
At the character select, hold Start and select Akuma.

ALTERNATE COSTUMES
At the character select, press L or R.

FINAL BATTLE
At the speed select, hold A + B.

SUPER COLLAPSE 2

PUZZLE MODE PASSWORDS

PUZZLE	PASSWORD	PUZZLE	PASSWORD	PUZZLE	PASSWORD
2	G6CLG	6	RQCJD	10	GDXSV
3	69MR3	7	DL4NX	11	FVH4M
4	F6DHM	8	TCLV5	12	7TD4K
5	2XNSX	9	G5DYR	13	F6GS4

THAT'S SO RAVEN 2: SUPERNATURAL STYLE

COSTUME MODE
At the title screen, press Left, Right, Up, Down, B, B, B, Up, Down.

UNLIMITED ENERGY MODE
At the title screen, press B, B, L, R, Up, Down, Up, Left, Right.

TOM AND JERRY: THE MAGIC RING

LEVEL 1-1 AS JERRY
Enter 1236 as a password.

LEVEL 1-1 AS TOM
Enter 5488 as a password.

LEVEL 1-2 AS JERRY
Enter 6878 as a password.

LEVEL 1-2 AS TOM
Enter 4121 as a password.

LEVEL 1-3 AS JERRY
Enter 5121 as a password.

LEVEL 1-3 AS TOM
Enter 1353 as a password.

LEVEL 1-4 AS JERRY
Enter 2753 as a password.

LEVEL 1-4 AS TOM
Enter 8246 as a password.

LEVEL 1-5 AS JERRY
Enter 7616 as a password.

LEVEL 1-5 AS TOM
Enter 3868 as a password.

LEVEL 2 AS JERRY
Enter 7531 as a password.

LEVEL 2 AS TOM
Enter 3783 as a password.

LEVEL 3 AS JERRY
Enter 8358 as a password.

LEVEL 3 AS TOM
Enter 5423 as a password.

LEVEL 4-1 AS JERRY
Enter 1176 as a password.

LEVEL 4-1 AS TOM
Enter 5348 as a password.

LEVEL 4-2 AS JERRY
Enter 6718 as a password.

LEVEL 4-2 AS TOM
Enter 4281 as a password.

LEVEL 4-3 AS JERRY
Enter 5261 as a password.

LEVEL 4-3 AS TOM
Enter 1413 as a password.

LEVEL 5 AS JERRY
Enter 8251 as a password.

LEVEL 5 AS TOM
Enter 5126 as a password.

LEVEL 6 AS JERRY
Enter 2761 as a password.

LEVEL 6 AS TOM
Enter 8238 as a password.

LEVEL 7-1 AS JERRY
Enter 2856 as a password.

LEVEL 7-1 AS TOM
Enter 8143 as a password.

LEVEL 7-2 AS JERRY
Enter 5228 as a password.

LEVEL 7-2 AS TOM
Enter 1456 as a password.

TONY HAWK'S UNDERGROUND

SKIP TUTORIAL
At the Main Menu, hold R and press Left, Down, Start, Start, Right, Up, Up, L, Down.

TONY HAWK'S UNDERGROUND 2

TENNIS SHOOTER MINIGAME
Once you unlock Bam's character on the map, talk to him. Knock down the rollerbladers, then go back. He'll give you the Tennis Shooter minigame. Once you've completed three levels, save your game to access Tennis Shooter at any time from the main menu.

TOP GUN: COMBAT ZONES

LEVEL 2 - PACIFIC OCEAN ON EASY

Enter 9799 as a password.

LEVEL 3 - NORTHERN SIBERIA ON EASY

Enter 8457 as a password.

LEVEL 4 - BERING STRAIT ON EASY

Enter 6767 as a password.

LEVEL 5 - NORTH SEA ON EASY

Enter 6891 as a password.

LEVEL 6 - EASTERN EUROPE ON EASY

Enter 2468 as a password.

LEVEL 7 - ARABIAN PENINSULA ON EASY

Enter 4479 as a password.

LEVEL 8 - SOUTHEAST ASIA ON EASY

Enter 3232 as a password.

LEVEL 9 - MONGOLIAN DESERT ON EASY

Enter 1295 as a password.

LEVEL 10 - ARCTIC CIRCLE ON EASY

Enter 7783 as a password.

LEVEL 11 - SOUTH AMERICA ON EASY

Enter 8226 as a password.

LEVEL 12 - GULF OF MEXICO ON EASY

Enter 7453 as a password.

LEVEL 2 - PACIFIC OCEAN ON NORMAL

Enter 7294 as a password.

LEVEL 3 - NORTHERN SIBERIA ON NORMAL

Enter 4947 as a password.

LEVEL 4 - BERING STRAIT ON NORMAL

Enter 1599 as a password.

LEVEL 5 - NORTH SEA ON NORMAL

Enter 9145 as a password.

LEVEL 6 - EASTERN EUROPE ON NORMAL

Enter 8813 as a password.

LEVEL 7 - ARABIAN PENINSULA ON NORMAL

Enter 9915 as a password.

LEVEL 8 - SOUTHEAST ASIA ON NORMAL

Enter 8212 as a password.

LEVEL 9 - MONGOLIAN DESERT ON NORMAL

Enter 9215 as a password.

LEVEL 10 - ARCTIC CIRCLE ON NORMAL

Enter 4518 as a password.

LEVEL 11 - SOUTH AMERICA ON NORMAL

Enter 2121 as a password.

LEVEL 12 - GULF OF MEXICO ON NORMAL

Enter 4211 as a password.

LEVEL 2 - PACIFIC OCEAN ON HARD

Enter 3468 as a password.

LEVEL 3 - NORTHERN SIBERIA ON HARD

Enter 2345 as a password.

LEVEL 4 - BERING STRAIT ON HARD

Enter 8791 as a password.

LEVEL 5 - NORTH SEA ON HARD

Enter 6642 as a password.

LEVEL 6 - EASTERN EUROPE ON HARD

Enter 2918 as a password.

LEVEL 7 - ARABIAN PENINSULA ON HARD

Enter 5748 as a password.

LEVEL 8 - SOUTHEAST ASIA ON HARD

Enter 5367 as a password.

LEVEL 9 - MONGOLIAN DESERT ON HARD

Enter 3783 as a password.

LEVEL 10 - ARCTIC CIRCLE ON HARD

Enter 9818 as a password.

LEVEL 11 - SOUTH AMERICA ON HARD

Enter 9319 as a password.

LEVEL 12 - GULF OF MEXICO ON HARD

Enter 6161 as a password.

TRON 2.0: KILLER APP

ALL MINIGAMES
At the title screen, press Left, Left, Left, Left, Up, Right, Down, Down, Select.

URBAN YETI

UNLOCK EVERYTHING
Enter TONYGOLD as a password.

DISCUS TOURNAMENT
Enter PINGPONG as a password.

LAZY SEWER O' FUN
Enter YETIRAFT as a password.

SOUP KITCHEN MANAGER
Enter HAMSTEAK as a password.

YETI CHICKEN RANCHER
Enter PROVIDER as a password.

START AT LEVEL 1
Enter BUZZWORD as a password.

START AT LEVEL 2
Enter FOREWORD as a password.

START AT LEVEL 3
Enter COOKBOOK as a password.

START AT LEVEL 4
Enter FEEDBAGS as a password.

START AT LEVEL 5
Enter HAMSTEAK as a password.

START AT LEVEL 6
Enter DAYBREAK as a password.

START AT LEVEL 7
Enter SUNLIGHT as a password.

START AT LEVEL 8
Enter NITETIME as a password.

START AT LEVEL 9
Enter EASTSIDE as a password.

START AT LEVEL 10
Enter BEATDOWN as a password.

START AT LEVEL 11
Enter VENGEFUL as a password.

START AT LEVEL 12
Enter FRISBEES as a password.

START AT LEVEL 13
Enter ICESKATE as a password.

START AT LEVEL 14
Enter PINGPONG as a password.

START AT LEVEL 15
Enter DOWNTOWN as a password.

START AT LEVEL 16
Enter CITYMAPS as a password.

START AT LEVEL 17
Enter DUMPSTER as a password.

START AT LEVEL 18
Enter WATERWAY as a password.

START AT LEVEL 19
Enter TIRETUBE as a password.

START AT LEVEL 20
Enter YETIRAFT as a password.

START AT LEVEL 21
Enter SUBURBIA as a password.

START AT LEVEL 22
Enter HOUSETOP as a password.

START AT LEVEL 23
Enter CITIZENS as a password.

START AT LEVEL 24
Enter CHICKENS as a password.

START AT LEVEL 25
Enter SONGBIRD as a password.

START AT LEVEL 26
Enter PROVIDER as a password.

STRANGE COLORS AND SOUND
Enter BSWSBSWS as a password

THE URBZ: SIMS IN THE CITY

CLUB XIZZLE
Once you gain access to Club Xizzle, enter with the password "bucket."

WINNIE THE POOH'S RUMBLY TUMBLY ADVENTURE

GAME COMPLETED
Enter 3013736 as a password.

EEYORE'S FIRST AREA
Enter 9744991 as a password.

EEYORE'S SECOND AREA
Enter 9301241 as a password.

EEYORE'S THIRD AREA
Enter 3220311 as a password.

EEYORE'S AREA COMPLETE
Enter 3412121 as a password.

PIGLET'S FIRST AREA
Enter 5735172 as a password.

PIGLET'S SECOND AREA
Enter 7045732 as a password.

PIGLET'S THIRD AREA
Enter 1156612 as a password.

PIGLET'S AREA COMPLETE
Enter 1348422 as a password.

POOH'S FIRST AREA
Enter 1937986 as a password.

POOH'S SECOND AREA
Enter 1388596 as a password.

POOH'S THIRD AREA
Enter 5399476 as a password.

ROO'S FIRST AREA
Enter 3412773 as a password.

ROO'S SECOND AREA
Enter 9999053 as a password.

ROO'S THIRD AREA
Enter 5505553 as a password.

ROO'S AREA COMPLETE
Enter 3011033 as a password.

TIGGER'S FIRST AREA
Enter 7847570 as a password.

TIGGER'S SECOND AREA
Enter 5560830 as a password.

TIGGER'S THIRD AREA
Enter 3834540 as a password.

TIGGER'S FOURTH AREA
Enter 9172120 as a password.

TIGGER'S AREA COMPLETE
Enter 1749510 as a password.

WORLD CHAMPIONSHIP POKER

10 MILLION DOLLAR
Enter the following as a password: 7 Hearts, King Spades, 2 Hearts, Queen Clubs, 9 Hearts, Jack Hearts.

YOSHI TOPSY-TURVY

CHALLENGE MODE AND CHALLENGE 1
Defeat Bowser for the 2nd time in story mode.

CHALLENGES 2, 3, 4
Complete the Egg Gallery in story mode.

FINAL CHALLENGE
Earn all Golds in story mode.

YU-GI-OH! 7 TRIALS TO GLORY: WORLD CHAMPIONSHIP TOURNAMENT 2005

PURPLE TITLE SCREEN
Completing the game changes the title screen from blue to purple. To switch it back, press Up, Up, Down, Down, Left, Right, Left, Right, B, A at the title screen.

CREDITS
Defeat the game. Then, press Up, Up, Down, Down, Left, Right, Left, Right, B, A.

CARD PASSWORDS
At the password machine, press R and enter the following.

CARD	PASSWORD	CARD	PASSWORD
30,000-Year White Turtle	11714098	Alligator's Sword	64428736
7 Colored Fish	23771716	Alligator's Sword Dragon	03366982
7 Completed	86198326	Alpha The Magnet Warrior	99785935
A Hero Emerges	21597117	Amazon Archer	91869203
Acid Trap Hole	41356845	Amazon of the Seas	17968114
Air Eater	08353769	Amphibian Beast	67371383

CARD	PASSWORD	CARD	PASSWORD
Amphibious Bugroth	40173854	Dark Illusion Ritual	41426869
Ancient Brain	42431843	Dark-Eyes Illusionist	38247752
Ancient Elf	93221206	Darkfire Soldier #1	05388481
Ancient Lizard Warrior	43230671	Darkfire Soldier #2	78861134
Anti Raigeki	42364257	Des Koala	69579761
Aqua Chorus	95132338	Destroyer Golem	73481154
Aqua Dragon	86164529	Dissolverock	40826495
Archfiend Soldier	49881766	Dragonic Attack	32437102
Arma Knight	36151751	Dunames Dark Witch	12493482
Armaill	53153481	Durnames Dark Witch	12493482
Armed Ninja	09076207	Eatgaboon	42578427
Armored Lizard	15480588	Exile of the Wicked	26725158
Armored Rat	16246527	Exodia the Forbidden One	33396948
Armored Starfish	17535588	Fiend Reflection #2	02863439
Armored Zombie	20277860	Final Destiny	18591904
Axe of Despair	40619825	Firegrass	53293545
Axe Raider	48305365	Flame Champion	42599677
Baby Dragon	88819587	Flash Assailant	96890582
Banisher of the Light	61528025	Flower Wolf	95952802
Baron of the Fiend Sword	86325596	Flying Kamakiri #1	84834865
Barrel Dragon	81480460	Flying Kamakiri #2	03134241
Barrel Dragon	81480460	Gaia the Fierce Knight	06368038
Barrel Lily	67841515	Gamma The Magnet Warrior	11549357
Barrel Rock	10476868	Garnecia Elefantis	49888191
Beaver Warrior	32452818	Gemini Elf	69140098
Beta The Magnet Warrior	39256679	Giant Flea	41762634
Bite Shoes	50122883	Giant Rat	97017120
Black Luster Soldier - Envoy of the Beginning	72989439	Gift of the Mystical Elf	98299011
Black Pendant	65169794	Graverobber's Retribution	33737664
Bladefly	28470714	Great White	13429800
Blast Sphere	26302522	Harpie Lady	76812113
Blast Sphere	26302522	Headless Knight	05434080
Blue Eyes Toon Dragon	53183600	Humanoid Worm Drake	05600127
Blue Eyes White Dragon	89631139	Hyosube	02118022
Boneheimer	98456117	Hyozanryu	62397231
Book of SecretArts	91595718	Illusion Wall	13945283
Bottom Dweller	81386177	Iron Blacksmith Kotetsu	73431236
Catapult Turtle	95727991	Jellyfish	14851496
Celtic Guardian	91152256	Jinzo	77585513
Ceremonial Bell	20228463	Jinzo	77585513
Change of Heart	04031928	Jowgen the Spiritualist	41855169
Chaos Emperor Dragon - EotE	82301904	Karate Man	23289281
Crass Clown	93889755	Kojikocy	01184620
Curse of the Masked Beast	94377247	Kuriboh	40640057
Cyber Falcon	30655537	La Jinn	97590747
Cyber Harpie	80316585	Lady of Faith	17358176
Cyber Jar	34124316	Lady Panther	38480590
Cyber Shield	63224564	Last Day of Witch	90330453
Cyber Soldier of Darkworld	75559356	Lava Battleguard	20394040
Cyber-Stein	69015963	Left Arm of the Forbidden One	07902349
Cyber-Tech Alligator	48766543	Left Leg of the Forbidden One	44519536
D.D. Warrior Lady	07572887	Little Chimera	68658728
Dark Artist	72520073	Luminous Spark	81777047
		Mad Dog of Darkness	79182538

CARD	PASSWORD	CARD	PASSWORD
Mad Sword Beast	79870141	Silver Fang	90357090
Magic Swordsman Neo	50930991	Sinister Serpent	08131171
Magical Scientist	34206604	Skull Mark Ladybug	64306248
Magician of Faith	31560081	Skull Servant	32274490
Malevolent Nuzzler	99597615	Slate Warrior	78636495
Man Eating Treasure Chest	13723605	Slot Machine	03797883
Manga Ryu Ran	38369349	Soul of Purity and Light	77527210
Marauding Captain	02460565	Soul Release	05758500
Mask of Darkness	28933734	Spear Dragon	31553716
Mechanicalchaser	07359741	Spike Bot	87511987
Melchid the Four-Face Beast	86569121	Spirit of Flames	13522325
Metal Guardian	68339286	St. Joan	21175632
Millennium Shield	32012841	Sword of Deep-Seated	98495314
Milus Radiant	07489323	Swords of Revealing Light	72302403
Monster Reborn	83764718	Tainted Wisdom	28725004
Mother Grizzly	57839750	Talwar Demon	11761845
Mystic Plasma Zone	18161786	The 13th Grave	00032864
Mystic Tomato	83011277	The All-Seeing White Tiger	32269855
Offerings to the Doomed	19230407	The Bistro Butcher	71107816
Ooguchi	58861941	The Earl of Demise	66989694
Overdrive	02311603	The Gross Ghost of Fled Dreams	68049471
Pendulum Machine	24433920	The Portrait's Secret	32541773
Pinch Hopper	26185991	The Shallow Grave	43434803
Pot of Greed	55144522	The Unhappy Maiden	51275027
Red-Eyes Black Dragon	74677422	Thousand Eyes Idol	27125110
Red-Eyes Black Metal Dragon	64335804	Thousand Eyes Relinquised	63519819
Reflect Bounder	02851070	Time Seal	85316708
Relinquished	64631466	Tornado Bird	71283180
Relinquished	64631466	Total Defense Shogun	75372290
Restructer Revolution	99518961	Tribe Infecting Virus	33184167
Right Arm of the Forbidden One	70903634	Turtle Tiger	37313348
Right Leg of the Forbidden One	08124921	Two-Headed King Rex	94119974
Robbin' Zombie	83258273	UFO Turtle	60806437
Rogue Doll	91939608	Ultimate Offering	80604091
Ryu Ran	02964201	Ushi Oni	48649353
Ryu-Kishin Powered	24611934	Vorse Raider	14898066
Shining Abyss	87303357	Water Omotics	02483611
Shining Angel	95956346	Wingweaver	31447217
Shining Friendship	82085619	Yata-Garusa	03078576

ZOIDS: LEGACY

CYCLOPES TYPE ONE/TWO, DIABLO TIGER DATA AND ZOID CORES TO BUILD THEM

Complete the game. Then, at the title screen, press L, L, R, R, Up, Down, Up, Down, Left, Left, R, R, Right, Right, Left, Up, Start.

GILVADER, KING GOJULA ZI DATA AND ZOID CORES TO BUILD THEM

Complete the game. Then, at the title screen, press R, R, L, L, Down, Up, Down, Up, Right, Right, L, L, Left, Left, Right, Down, Start.

NINTENDO DS™

Everyone

ADVANCE WARS: DUAL STRIKE

ANIMANIACS: LIGHTS, CAMERA, ACTION!

ASPHALT URBAN GT

ATV: QUAD FRENZY

BIG MUTHA TRUCKERS

BRAIN AGE: TRAIN YOUR BRAIN IN MINUTES A DAY

BUBBLE BOBBLE REVOLUTION

BUST-A-MOVE DS

CARS

THE CHRONICLES OF NARNIA: THE LION, THE WITCH AND THE WARDROBE

DRAGON QUEST HEROES: ROCKET SLIME

FEEL THE MAGIC: XY/XX

KIRBY: CANVAS CURSE

LEGO STAR WARS II: THE ORIGINAL TRILOGY

MADDEN NFL 2005

METROID PRIME PINBALL

NEW SUPER MARIO BROS.

NINTENDOGS

PAC-PIX

PING PALS

PUYO POP FEVER

RIDGE RACER DS

THE SIMS 2

SPIDER-MAN 2

STAR WARS EPISODE III: REVENGE OF THE SITH

TEENAGE MUTANT NINJA TURTLES 3: MUTANT NIGHTMARE

TIGER WOODS PGA TOUR

TOM CLANCY'S SPLINTER CELL CHAOS THEORY

TONY HAWK'S DOWNHILL JAM

TRAUMA CENTER: UNDER THE KNIFE

THE URBZ: SIMS IN THE CITY

YU-GI-OH! NIGHTMARE TROUBADOUR

ZOO KEEPER

Teen

ALEX RIDER: STORMBREAKER

CASTLEVANIA: DAWN OF SORROW

PIRATES OF THE CARIBBEAN: DEAD MAN'S CHEST

THE RUB RABBITS!

Nintendo DS™ Table of Contents

ADVANCE WARS: DUAL STRIKE

ADVANCE WARS MAP

Select Map from the Design Room menu and immediately press and hold L + R. You will get a map that spells out Advance Wars.

By having old versions of advance wars inserted in your DS at the same time as the Battle Maps Shop!Unlockable How to Unlock Select Battle Maps

ADVANCE WARPAPER

Insert Advance Wars in the GBA slot of your Nintendo DS. Start Advance Wars: Dual Strike. Select Battle maps and purchase Advance Warpaper. Select Display from the Design Room and choose Classic 1.

HACHI'S LAND

Insert Advance Wars in the GBA slot of your Nintendo DS. Start Advance Wars: Dual Strike. Select Battle Maps and purchase Hachi's Land for 1.

NELL'S LAND

Insert Advance Wars in the GBA slot of your Nintendo DS. Start Advance Wars: Dual Strike. Select Battle Maps and purchase Nell's Land for 1.

ADVANCE WARPAPER 2

Insert Advance Wars 2: Black Hole Rising in the GBA slot of your Nintendo DS. Start Advance Wars: Dual Strike. Select Battle maps and purchase Advance Warpaper 2. Select Display from the Design Room and choose Classic 2.

LASH'S LAND

Insert Advance Wars 2: Black Hole Rising in the GBA slot of your Nintendo DS. Start Advance Wars: Dual Strike. Select Battle Maps and purchase Lash's Land for 1.

STRUM'S LAND

Insert Advance Wars 2: Black Hole Rising in the GBA slot of your Nintendo DS. Start Advance Wars: Dual Strike. Select Battle Maps and purchase Strum's Land for 1.

ALEX RIDER: STORMBREAKER

10,000 SPY POINTS

Select Password from the main menu and enter 5204025.

EVERYTHING HALF PRICE AT SHOP

Select Password from the main menu and enter 4298359.

BLACK BELT AVAILABLE FOR PURCHASE

Select Password from the main menu and enter JESSICA PARKER.

DISK 6 AVAILABLE AFTER COMPLETING GAME

Select Password from the main menu and enter 6943059.

FUGU AVAILABLE FOR PURCHASE

Select Password from the main menu and enter RENATO CELANI.

M16 BADGE AVAILABLE FOR PURCHASE

Select Password from the main menu and enter VICTORIA PARR.

SUNGLASSES AVAILABLE FOR PURCHASE

Select Password from the main menu and enter SARYL HIRSCH.

HARD LEVEL

Select Password from the main menu and enter 9785711.

GALLERY

Select Password from the main menu and enter 9603717.

OUTFIT CHANGE

Select Password from the main menu and enter 6894098.

ANIMANIACS: LIGHTS, CAMERA, ACTION!

SKIP LEVEL
Pause the game and press L, L, R, R, Down, Down.

DISABLE TIME
Pause the game and press L, R, Left, Left, Up, Up.

KINGSIZE PICKUPS
Pause the game and press Right, Right, Right, Left, Left, Left, R, L.

PASSWORDS

LEVEL	PASSWORD	LEVEL	PASSWORD
1	Wakko, Wakko, Wakko, Wakko, Wakko	9	Dot, Dot, Yakko, Pinky, Wakko
2	Dot, Yakko, Brain, Wakko, Pinky	10	Brain, Dot, Brain, Yakko, Wakko
3	Yakko, Dot, Wakko, Wakko, Brain	11	Akko, Yakko, Pinky, Dot, Dot
4	Pinky, Yakko, Yakko, Dot, Brain	12	Pinky, Pinky, Brain, Dot, Wakko
5	Pinky, Pinky, Yakko, Wakko, Wakko	13	Yakko, Wakko, Pinky, Wakko, Brain
6	Brain, Dot, Brain, Pinky, Yakko	14	Pinky, Wakko, Brain, Wakko, Yakko
7	Brain, Pinky, Wakko, Pinky, Brain	15	Dot, Pinky, Wakko, Wakko, Yakko
8	Brain Pinky, Pinky, Wakko, Wakko		

ASPHALT URBAN GT

MONEY FOR NOTHING
Buy the Chevrolet 2005 Corvette C6 for $45,000. Then, go to your garage and sell it for $45,500.

ATV: QUAD FRENZY

FLY MODE
At the title screen, press A + Y + X.

BIG MUTHA TRUCKERS

EVIL BOB TRUCK
At the title screen, press X, L, R, R, A, B, Y, Y, R.

BRAIN AGE: TRAIN YOUR BRAIN IN MINUTES A DAY

BRAIN AGE CHECK SELECTION MENU
At the Daily Training Menu, hold Select while choosing Brain Age Check.

TOP 3 LISTS
At the Daily Training Menu, hold Select while choosing Graph.

BUBBLE BOBBLE REVOLUTION

BONUS LEVELS IN CLASSIC MODE
At the Classic mode title screen, press L, R, L, R, L, R, Right, Select. Touch the door at Level 20.

POWER UP! MODE IN CLASSIC VERSION
At the Classic mode title screen, press Select, R, L, Left, Right, R, Select, Right.

SUPER BUBBLE BOBBLE IN CLASSIC VERSION
You must first defeat the boss with two players. At the Classic mode title screen, press Left, R, Left, Select, Left, L, Left, Select.

BUST-A-MOVE DS

DARK WORLD
First you must complete the game. At the title screen, press A Left Right A.

SOUND TEST
At the main menu, press Select, A, B, Left, Right, A, Select, Right.

CARS

SECRET MUSIC TRACK FOR RAMONES STYLE
At the title screen, press Up, Down, Up, Down, A, B, X, Y.

EVERYTHING EXCEPT HIDDEN MUSIC
At the title screen press Up, Up, Down, Down, Left, Right, Left, Right, B, A, B.

CASTLEVANIA: DAWN OF SORROW

POTION
Complete Boss Rush Mode.

RPG
Complete Boss Rush Mode in less than 5 minutes.

DEATH'S ROBE
Complete Boss Rush Mode in less than 6 minutes.

TERROR BEAR
Complete Boss Rush Mode in less than 7 minutes.

NUNCHAKUS
Complete Boss Rush Mode in less than 8 minutes.

THE CHRONICLES OF NARNIA: THE LION, THE WITCH AND THE WARDROBE

RESTORE HEALTH
At the main menu, press Left, Right, Up, Down, A (x4).

INVINCIBILITY
At the main menu, press A, Y, X, B, Up, Up, Down, Down.

ARMOR
At the main menu, press A, X, Y, B, Up, Up, Up, Down.

EXTRA MONEY
At the main menu, press Up, X, Up, X, Down, B, Down, B.

ALL BLESSINGS.
At the main menu, press Left, Up, A, B, Right, Down, X, Y.

MAXIMUM ATTRIBUTES
At the main menu, press Left, B, Up, Y, Down, X, Right, A.

MAX SKILLS
At the main menu, press A, Left, Right, B, Down, Up, X, X.

STRONGER ATTACKS
At the main menu, press A, Up, B, Down, X, X, Y, Y.

DRAGON QUEST HEROES: ROCKET SLIME

KNIGHTRO TANK IN MULTIPLAYER
While in the church, press Y, L, L, Y, R, R, Y, Up, Down, Select.

THE NEMESIS TANK IN MULTIPLAYER
While in the church, press Y, R, R, up, L, L, Y, Down, Down, Down, Y, Select.

FEEL THE MAGIC: XY/XX

RECORD YOUR VOICE ON THE TITLE SCREEN

While at the title screen, hold Down + Y to record whatever you want into the microphone. It will now play back whatever you recorded at random intervals while the title music plays. However, if you wish to play it back immediately, press Down + X. Down-Left + X will play it back slowly, while Down-Right + X will speed it up.

HARD MODE

Defeat the game on Normal difficulty.

HELL MODE

Defeat the game on Hard difficulty.

KIRBY: CANVAS CURSE

JUMP GAME

Defeat the game with all five characters. Select the game file to get Jump Game next to options on the main menu.

LEGO STAR WARS II: THE ORIGINAL TRILOGY

10 STUDS
At the Mos Eisley cantina, enter 4PR28U.

OBI WAN GHOST
At the Mos Eisley cantina, enter BEN917.

MADDEN NFL 2005

THREE DOWNS FOR OPPONENT

Touch the spot in the middle of the main menu and enter SHORTTIME.

FIVE DOWNS

Touch the spot in the middle of the main menu and enter LONGTIME.

HARDER HITS

Touch the spot in the middle of the main menu and enter SMASHMOUTH.

MORE FUMBLES

Touch the spot in the middle of the main menu and enter SUPERSLICK.

MORE INTERCEPTIONS

Touch the spot in the middle of the main menu and enter BADPASS.

MORE SACKS

Touch the spot in the middle of the main menu and enter SAD SACK.

METROID PRIME PINBALL

PHAZON MINES

Complete Omega Pirate in Multi Mission Mode.

PHENDRANA DRIFTS

Complete Thardus in Multi Mission Mode.

NEW SUPER MARIO BROS.

PLAY AS LUIGI IN SINGLE PLAYER

At the Select a File screen, hold L + R while selecting a saved game.

SECRET CHALLENGE MODE

On the map, pause the game and press L, R, L, R, X, X, Y, Y.

NINTENDOGS

FEED DOG LIGHT BULB

When the light bulb appears above your dog, grab it and drag it to his/her mouth.

PAC-PIX

BUTTERFLY HIDDEN GESTURE
Select Sketchbook from the Gallery. Draw a figure eight. The drawing should fly upwards.

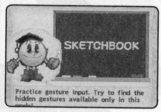

Practice gesture input. Try to find the hidden gestures available only in this

CHERRIES HIDDEN GESTURE
Select Sketchbook from the Gallery. Draw a pair of cherries starting with one of the circles.

POGO STICK HIDDEN GESTURE
Select Sketchbook from the Gallery. Draw a P and it will bounce off the screen.

RAIN CLOUD HIDDEN GESTURE
Select Sketchbook from the Gallery. Draw a cloud and it will turn blue and rain will fall from the drawing.

SNAKE HIDDEN GESTURE
Select Sketchbook from the Gallery. Draw an a squiggly line. It will turn green and slither away.

TREBLE CLEF HIDDEN GESTURE
Select Sketchbook from the Gallery. Draw a treble clef.

SHOOT ARROWS AT PAC-MAN
After you have earned the Arrow gesture in Chapter 4, select Sketchbook from the Gallery. Draw an arrow facing Pac-man.

Practice gesture input. Try to find the hidden gestures available only in this

PING PALS

50 COINS
Select Credits and let them run to the end.

HOLIDAY ITEMS
Set the date on your Nintendo DS to the following dates to get access to special Holiday Items:

DATE	ITEM	COST
February 14	Valentine (Boy)	300 Coins
February 14	Valentine (Girl)	200 Coins
February 21	Vessel Top	700 Coins
March 17	Snowflake	250 Coins
October 31	Bat Treats	400 Coins
October 31	Jack Hat	4000 Coins

DATE	ITEM	COST
October 31	Succubus	321 Coins
December 25	Elf Skirt	300 Coins
December 25	Jolly Suit	300 Coins
December 25	Merry Cap	10 Coins
Birthday	Birthday (Boy)	5 Coins
Birthday	Birthday (Girl)	5 Coins

SHANTAE BACKGROUND
Touch the Ping Pals logo exactly at midnight.

PIRATES OF THE CARIBBEAN: DEAD MAN'S CHEST

10 GOLD
During a game, press Right, X, X, Right, Left.

INVINCIBILITY
During a game, press Up, Down, Left, Right (x5), Left, Right, Up, Down, Left, Right, Up (x5), Left.

UNLIMITED POWER
During a game, press Up, Up, Down, Down, Left, Right, Left, Right, L, R.

RESTORE HEALTH
During a game, press Y, Y, Select, Left, Right, Left, Right, Left.

RESTORE SAVVY
During a game, press X, X, Select, Up, Down, Up, Down, Up.

GHOST FORM MODE
During a game, press Y, X, Y, X, Y, X.

SEASICKNESS MODE
During a game, press X, X, Y, X, X, Y.

SILLY WEAPONS
During a game, press Y, Y, X, Y (x3).

AXE
During a game, press Left, L, L, Down, Down, Left, Up, Up, Down, Down.

BLUNDERBUSS
During a game, press Down, L, L, Down (x3).

CHICKEN
During a game, press Right, L, L, Up, Down, Down.

EXECUTIONER AXE
During a game, press Right, L, L, Up, Down, Up, Right, Right, Left(x2).

PIG
During a game, press Right, R, R, Down, Up, Up.

PISTOL
During a game, press Down, L, L, Down, Down, Right.

RIFLE
During a game, press Left, L, L, Up (x3).

FAST MUSIC
During a game, press Y, Select, Y (x4).

SLOW MUSIC
During a game, press Y, Select, X (x4).

DISABLE CHEATS
During a game, press X (x6).

PUYO POP FEVER

ALL CHARACTERS AND CUTSCENES
Select Gallery from the Options. Highlight cutscene viewer, hold X and press Up, Down, Left, Right.

RIDGE RACER DS

00-AGENT CAR
Finish more than ten races in multi-player.

CADDY CAR
Finish more than ten races in multi-player.

GALAGA '88 CAR
Finish more than ten races in multi-player.

MARIO RACING CAR
Finish more than ten races in multi-player.

POOKA CAR
Finish more than ten races in multi-player.

RED SHIRT RAGE CAR
Finish more than ten races in multi-player.

SHY GUY CAR
Finish more than ten races in multi-player.

GALAGA PAC JAM SONG
Unlock the Pooka car.

MUSHROOM KINGDOM II SONG
Unlock the DK Team Racing car.

THE RUB RABBITS!

BOXING GLOVES
Start the game with Sonic Battle in the GBA slot of your Nintendo DS.

FIST GLOVES
Start the game with Chu Chu Rocket in the GBA slot of your Nintendo DS.

HAND PUPPETS
Start the game with Sonic Advance 3 in the GBA slot of your Nintendo DS.

PINK GLOVES
Start the game with Sonic Advance 1 or 2 in the GBA slot of your Nintendo DS.

WHITE GLOVES
Start the game with Puyo Pop in the GBA slot of your Nintendo DS.

THE SIMS 2

MONGOO MONKEY FOR THE CASINO
Start the game with Sims 2 in the GBA slot of your Nintendo DS.

SPIDER-MAN 2

ALL SPECIAL MOVES
Load the game with Spider-Man: Mysterio's Menace for Game Boy Advance in the Nintendo DS.

STAR WARS EPISODE III: REVENGE OF THE SITH

MASTER DIFFICULTY
Defeat the game.

ANAKIN'S STARFIGHTER
Beat the Anakin bot in multiplayer.

DARTH VADER'S TIE FIGHTER
Defeat Darth Vader bot in multiplayer.

GENERAL GREVIOUS'S STARFIGHTER
Defeat General Grevious bot in multiplayer.

MILLENIUM FALCON
Defeat the Solo bot in multiplayer.

SLAVE I
Defeat Fett bot in multiplayer.

X-WING
Defeat Luke bot in multiplayer.

TEENAGE MUTANT NINJA TURTLES 3: MUTANT NIGHTMARE

CRYSTALS ARE EASTER EGGS
Select Input Password from the options and enter SRDSLLMS.

CRYSTALS ARE JACK-O-LANTERNS
Select Input Password from the options and enter DRSSMRLD.

CRYSTALS ARE SANTAS
Select Input Password from the options and enter LLDMSRMD.

LIFE ICONS ARE PIZZA
Select Input Password from the options and enter DDRMLRDS.

COWABUNGA
At the title screen, press U, U, D, D, L, R, L, R, B, A.

TIGER WOODS PGA TOUR 2005

EMERALD DRAGON
Earn $1,000,000.

GREEK ISLES
Earn $1,500,000.

PARADISE COVER
Earn $2,000,000.

EA SPORTS FAVORITES
Earn $5,000,000

MEAN8TEEN
Earn $10,000,000.

FANTASY SPECIALS
Earn $15,000,000.

LEGEND COMPILATION 1
Defeat Hogan in Legend Tour.

LEGEND COMPILATION 2
Defeat Gary Player in Legend Tour.

LEGEND COMPILATION 3
Defeat Ballesteros in Legend Tour.

LEGEND COMPILATION 4
Defeat Palmer in Legend Tour.

LEGEND COMPILATION 5
Defeat Nicklaus in Legend Tour.

THE HUSTLER'S DREAM 18
Defeat The Hustler in Legend Tour.

TIGER'S DREAM 18
Defeat Tiger Woods in Legend Tour.

TOM CLANCY'S SPLINTER CELL CHAOS THEORY

UNLIMITED AMMO/ GADGETS
Defeat the game.

CHARACTER SKINS
Defeat the game.

TONY HAWK'S DOWNHILL JAM

ALWAYS SNOWSKATE
Select Buy Stuff from the Skateshop. Choose Enter Code and enter SNOWSK8T.

MIRRORED MAPS
Select Buy Stuff from the Skateshop. Choose Enter Code and enter MIRRORBALL.

ABOMINABLE SNOWMAN OUTFIT
Select Buy Stuff from the Skateshop. Choose Enter Code and enter BIGSNOWMAN.

ZOMBIE SKATER OUTFIT
Select Buy Stuff from the Skateshop. Choose Enter Code and enter ZOMBIEALIVE.

TRAUMA CENTER: UNDER THE KNIFE

X1: KYRIAKI MISSION
Defeat the game. Find the X Missions under Challenge Mode.

X2: DEFTERA MISSION
Defeat X1 : Kyriaki Mission. Find the X Missions under Challenge Mode.

X3: TRITI MISSION
Defeat X2 : Deftera Mission. Find the X Missions under Challenge Mode.

X4: TETARTI MISSION
Defeat X3 : Triti Mission. Find the X Missions under Challenge Mode.

X5: PEMPTI MISSION
Defeat X4 : Tetarti Mission. Find the X Missions under Challenge Mode.

X6: PARAKEVI MISSION
Defeat X5 : Pempti Mission. Find the X Missions under Challenge Mode.

X7: SAVATO MISSION
Defeat X6 : Parakevi Mission. Find the X Missions under Challenge Mode.

THE URBZ: SIMS IN THE CITY

CLUB XIZZLE
Once you gain access to Club Xizzle, enter with the password "bucket."

YU-GI-OH! NIGHTMARE TROUBADOUR

CREDITS
Unlock the Password Machine by defeating the Expert Cup. Enter the Duel Shop and select the Slot maching. Enter 00000375.

SOUND TEST
Unlock the Password Machine by defeating the Expert Cup. Enter the Duel Shop and select the Slot maching. Enter 57300000.

ZOO KEEPER

GEKIMUZU DIFFICULTY
Earn a high score in all 4 modes.
Here are the high scores needed for each mode:

Zoo keeper	200000
Tokotan 100	800000
Quest mode	10000
Time attack	600000

PLAYSTATION® 2

EVERYONE

ALIEN HOMINID
AND 1 STREETBALL
APE ESCAPE 3
ATV OFFROAD FURY 3
AVATAR: THE LAST AIRBENDER
BRATZ: FOREVER DIAMONDZ
BRATZ: ROCK ANGELZ
BUTT UGLY MARTIANS: ZOOM OR DOOM
CARS
CHICKEN LITTLE
DROME RACERS
DUEL MASTERS
EA SPORTS ARENA FOOTBALL
FIFA STREET 2
FROGGER: ANCIENT SHADOW
GRAFFITI KINGDOM
GRAN TURISMO 4
HOT SHOTS GOLF FORE!
ICE AGE 2: THE MELTDOWN
THE INCREDIBLES:
    RISE OF THE UNDERMINER
IN THE GROOVE
KARAOKE REVOLUTION VOLUME 2
KARAOKE REVOLUTION VOLUME 3
KATAMARI DAMACY
LEGO STAR WARS: THE VIDEO GAME
LEGO STAR WARS II:
    THE ORIGINAL TRILOGY
MADDEN NFL 06
MADDEN NFL 07
MAJOR LEAGUE BASEBALL 2K6
MASTERS OF THE UNIVERSE HE-MAN:
    DEFENDER OF GRAYSKULL
MEGA MAN X COLLECTION
MEGA MAN X8

MIDWAY ARCADE TREASURES 3
MLB 06: THE SHOW
MLB SLUGFEST 2006
MVP 06 NCAA BASEBALL
MX VS. ATV UNLEASHED
NASCAR 06: TOTAL TEAM CONTROL
NASCAR 07
NBA '06: FEATURING THE LIFE VOL. 1
NBA 2K6
NBA 2K7
NBA BALLERS
NBA BALLERS PHENOM
NBA LIVE 06
NBA LIVE 07
NCAA FOOTBALL 06
NCAA FOOTBALL 07
NCAA MARCH MADNESS 06
NEED FOR SPEED CARBON
NFL STREET 2
NHL 2K6
OUTRUN 2006: COAST 2 COAST
OVER THE HEDGE
PAC-MAN WORLD 3
R-TYPE FINAL
RAMPAGE: TOTAL DESTRUCTION
ROBOTS
SATURDAY NIGHT SPEEDWAY
SCALER
SD GUNDAM FORCE: SHOWDOWN!
SHARK TALE
SHREK 2
SHREK SUPERSLAM
SLY 3: HONOR AMONG THIEVES
SONIC MEGA COLLECTION PLUS
SPONGEBOB SQUAREPANTS:
    BATTLE FOR BIKINI BOTTOM

SPONGEBOB SQUAREPANTS:
LIGHTS, CAMERA, PANTS!

SPONGEBOB SQUAREPANTS:
THE MOVIE

SSX ON TOUR

SUZUKI TT SUPERBIKES

TAK: THE GREAT JUJU CHALLENGE

TEENAGE MUTANT NINJA TURTLES 2:
BATTLE NEXUS

TEENAGE MUTANT NINJA TURTLES 3:
MUTANT NIGHTMARE

TIGER WOODS PGA TOUR 06

TIGER WOODS PGA TOUR 07

TIM BURTON'S THE NIGHTMARE BEFORE
CHRISTMAS: OOGIE'S REVENGE

TOM AND JERRY IN WAR
OF THE WHISKERS

TY THE TASMANIAN TIGER 3:
NIGHT OF THE QUINKAN

YU-GI-OH! THE DUELIST OF THE ROSES

ZAPPER

TEEN

TEEN
T
CONTENT RATED BY
ESRB

AEON FLUX

ALIAS

AMERICAN CHOPPER

APE ESCAPE: PUMPED & PRIMED

CABELA'S DANGEROUS HUNTS 2

CAPCOM CLASSICS COLLECTION

CHAMPIONS OF NORRATH: REALMS OF
EVERQUEST

THE CHRONICLES OF NARNIA: THE LION,
THE WITCH AND THE WARDROBE

THE DA VINCI CODE

DESTROY ALL HUMANS!

DESTROY ALL HUMANS! 2

DOG'S LIFE

DRAGON BALL Z: SAGAS

EPHEMERAL FANTASIA

FANTASTIC 4

FLATOUT

FLATOUT 2

GODZILLA: SAVE THE EARTH

GRADIUS V

GRAFFITI KINGDOM

GRAN TURISMO 4

GROWLANSER GENERATIONS

GUITAR HERO

.HACK//G.U. VOL. 1//REBIRTH

HEROES OF THE PACIFIC

JAK X: COMBAT RACING

JUICED

JUSTICE LEAGUE HEROES

L.A. RUSH

MARVEL NEMESIS: RISE OF THE
IMPERFECTS

MARVEL ULTIMATE ALLIANCE

MLB SLUGFEST: LOADED

MOTOCROSS MANIA 3

NEED FOR SPEED MOST WANTED

ONE PIECE: GRAND BATTLE

PETER JACKSON'S KING KONG:
THE OFFICIAL GAME OF THE MOVIE

PSYCHONAUTS

PUMP IT UP: EXCEED

RATCHET AND CLANK: UP YOUR ARSENAL

ROGUE TROOPER

SAMURAI JACK: THE SHADOW OF AKU

SECRET WEAPONS OVER NORMANDY

SHAMAN KING: POWER OF SPIRIT

THE SIMS 2: PETS

SPIDER-MAN 2

SPY HUNTER: NOWHERE TO RUN

SPY VS SPY

STAR WARS: BATTLEFRONT

STAR WARS: BATTLEFRONT II

STREET RACING SYNDICATE

TAITO LEGENDS

TONY HAWK'S AMERICAN WASTELAND

TONY HAWK'S PROJECT 8

TONY HAWK'S UNDERGROUND 2
TRANSFORMERS
URBAN REIGN
ULTIMATE SPIDER-MAN

VICTORIOUS BOXERS 2: FIGHTING SPIRIT
X-MEN LEGENDS II: RISE OF APOCALYPSE
X-MEN: THE OFFICIAL GAME
YS: THE ARK OF NAPISHTIM

PlayStation® 2 Table of Contents

AEON FLUX

BOMBER JACKET OUTFIT

Select Enter Cheat from the Extras menu and enter
**JULIET ALPHA CHARLIE KILO ECHO
TANGO**. Find the outfit under Outfits in the Extras
menu.

FAME OUTFIT

Select Enter Cheat from the Extras menu and enter **GOLF ROMEO ALPHA YANKEE**. Find the outfit under Outfits in the Extras menu.

ALTERNATE OUTFITS

Select Enter Cheat from the Extras menu and enter **CHARLIE LIMA OSCAR TANGO HOTEL ECHO SIERRA**. Find the outfits under Outfits in the Extras menu. These outfits include the following: Freya, Monican Freya, Hostess Judy, Una, and Fashion Una.

MRS. GOODCHILD OUTFIT

Select Enter Cheat from the Extras menu and enter **WHISKEY HOTEL INDIA TANGO ECHO**. Find the outfit under Outfits in the Extras menu.

REVELATION OUTFIT

Select Enter Cheat from the Extras menu and enter **ALPHA ROMEO MIKE SIERRA**. Find the outfit under Outfits in the Extras menu.

SEEDS OUTFIT

Select Enter Cheat from the Extras menu and enter **MIKE OSCAR VICTOR INDIA ECHO**. Find the outfit under Outfits in the Extras menu.

WAR OUTFIT

Select Enter Cheat from the Extras menu and enter **BRAVO LIMA UNIFORM ROMEO**. Find the outfit under Outfits in the Extras menu.

ALL REPLAY EPISODES

Select Enter Cheat from the Extras menu and enter **BRAVO ALPHA YANKEE OSCAR UNIFORM**. Select Replay Episode from the Extras menu.

ALL SLIDESHOWS

Select Enter Cheat from the Extras menu and enter **PAPA INDIA XRAY ECHO SIERRA**. Select Slideshows from the Extras menu.

ACTION MOVIE CHEAT

Select Enter Cheat from the Extras menu and enter **BRAVO ALPHA GOLF MIKE ALPHA NOVEMBER** or **UNIFORM KILO GOLF ALPHA MIKE ECHO ROMEO**. Pause the game and select Cheats to access the code.

GOD MODE CHEAT

Select Enter Cheat from the Extras menu and enter **TANGO ROMEO INDIA ROMEO OSCAR XRAY**. Pause the game and select Cheats to access the code.

FREE FATALITIES CHEAT

Select Enter Cheat from the Extras menu and enter **CHARLIE UNIFORM TANGO INDIA OSCAR NOVEMBER ECHO**. Pause the game and select Cheats to access the code.

ONE-STRIKE KILLS CHEAT

Select Enter Cheat from the Extras menu and enter **BRAVO UNIFORM CHARLIE KILO FOXTROT SIERRA TANGO**. Pause the game and select Cheats to access the code.

RESTORE HEALTH CHEAT

Select Enter Cheat from the Extras menu and enter **HOTEL ECHO ALPHA LIMA MIKE ECHO**. Pause the game and select Cheats to access the code.

UNLIMITED AMMO CHEAT

Select Enter Cheat from the Extras menu and enter **FOXTROT UNIFORM GOLF**. Pause the game and select Cheats to access the code.

UNLIMITED HEALTH CHEAT

Select Enter Cheat from the Extras menu and enter **CHARLIE LIMA OSCAR NOVEMBER ECHO**. Pause the game and select Cheats to access the code.

UNLIMITED POWER STRIKES CHEAT

Select Enter Cheat from the Extras menu and enter **LIMA CHARLIE VICTOR GOLF**. Pause the game and select Cheats to access the code.

ALIAS

LEVEL SELECT

Complete the game, then press **L1** + **R1** at the new game screen.

ALIEN HOMINID

ALL LEVELS, MINI-GAMES, & HATS
Select Player 1 Setup or Player 2 Setup and change the name to **ROYGBIV**.

HATS FOR 2-PLAYER GAME
Go to the Options and rename your alien one of the following:

Abe	behemoth	dandy	grrl	superfly
april	cletus	Goodman	princess	

AMERICAN CHOPPER

UNLOCK EVERYTHING
During a game, press **R1, R2, L2, L1, R2, L3, R3**.

AND 1 STREETBALL

GLOBAL UNLOCK
Select Cheat Codes from the Options menu and enter △, △, ✕, ✕, ●, ○, ●, ○. This unlocks all Bonus Stuff

ALL BREAKDOWNS
Select Cheat Codes from the Options menu and enter ✕, ✕, ○, ●, ●, △, △.

WARDROBE UNLOCK
Select Cheat Codes from the Options menu and enter ✕, △, ○, ✕, ●, △, ○.

ALL BLACKTOPS
Select Cheat Codes from the Options menu and enter ○, ✕, ✕, ●, △, △, ○, ✕.

CHATTERBOX UNLOCK
Select Cheat Codes from the Options menu and enter △, ●, ○, △, ✕, ●, △.

SIDE GAMES
Select Cheat Codes from the Options menu and enter ○, ●, △, ✕, ✕, ○, ●.

DJ GREEN LANTERN
Select Cheat Codes from the Options menu and enter ○, ○, △, ✕, ●, ✕, △, ○.

PLAY AS FLASH
Select Cheat Codes from the Options menu and enter △, ✕, ✕, ○, ✕, △, ●.

PLAY AS SHANE
Select Cheat Codes from the Options menu and enter ●, ✕, △, ✕, △, ○, △, ✕.

PLAY AS SKIP TO MY LOU
Select Cheat Codes from the Options menu and enter ○, ✕, ○, ●, △, ✕, ○, ●.

HAMILTONS
Select Cheat Codes from the Options menu and enter ○, △, ●, ●, △, ○, ✕, ●. This gives you $1,000,000.

ALWAYS ON FIRE
Select Cheat Codes from the Options menu and enter ●, △, ✕, △, ●, ✕, ●, ●.

IBALL MOVES
Select Cheat Codes from the Options menu and enter ✕, △, ○, ✕, ●, ✕, ●.

LIKE WATER
Select Cheat Codes from the Options menu and enter ●, ✕, ○, ●, ✕, ○, △, △.

THE OG WAY
Select Cheat Codes from the Options menu and enter △, ○, ●, ●, △, ○, ✕, ●.

SHOT TIMING TEXT
Select Cheat Codes from the Options menu and enter △, ●, ○, ○, ●, △, ●, △.

APE ESCAPE 3

SECRET PASSWORDS
At the Title screen, press **L1 + R1 + L2 + R2**. Now you can enter the following codes.

DARK MASTER ON THE LOOSE!
Enter **blackout** at the Secret Password screen.

MOVIE 28 AND 2 CINEMA FILES
Enter **2 snakes** at the Secret Password screen.

SHIMMY ON THE LOOSE!
Enter **2nd man** at the Secret Password screen.

MONKEY AS SPIKE
Enter **krops** at the Secret Password screen.

BLUE PIPOTRON
Enter **coolblue** at the Secret Password screen.

RED PIPOTRON
Enter **redmon** at the Secret Password screen.

YELLOW PIPOTRON
Enter **yellowy** at the Secret Password screen.

SAL-1000 MONKEY
Enter **grobyc** at the Secret Password screen.

SAL-3000 MONKEY
Enter **SAL3000** at the Secret Password screen.

APE ESCAPE: PUMPED & PRIMED

ALL GADGETS
Complete Story Mode. At the mode select, hold **R1** + **L1** + **R2** + **L2** to access the password screen. Enter **Go Wild!**.

DISABLE ALL GADGETS CHEAT
Complete Story Mode. At the mode select, hold **R1** + **L1** + **R2** + **L2** to access the password screen. Enter **Limited!**.

NORMAL DIFFICULTY
Complete Story Mode. At the mode select, hold **R1** + **L1** + **R2** + **L2** to access the password screen. Enter **NORMAL!**.

HARD DIFFICULTY
Complete Story Mode. At the mode select, hold **R1** + **L1** + **R2** + **L2** to access the password screen. Enter **HARD!**.

ATV OFFROAD FURY 3

UNLOCK EVERYTHING, EXCEPT THE FURY BIKE
Select Player Profile from the options. Then, select Enter Cheat and enter **!SLACKER!** This will not give the Fury.

ALL ATVS IN TRAINING
Select Player Profile from the options. Then, select Enter Cheat and enter **NOSKILLS**.

ALL RIDER GEAR
Select Player Profile from the options. Then, select Enter Cheat and enter **FITS**.

$1500
Select Player Profile from the options. Then, select Enter Cheat and enter **+foodstamps+**.

MUSIC VIDEOS
Select Player Profile from the options. Then, select Enter Cheat and enter **ROCKNROLL**.

AVATAR: THE LAST AIRBENDER

ALL TREASURE MAPS
Select Code Entry from Extras and enter 37437.

1 HIT DISHONOR
Select Code Entry from Extras and enter 54641.

DOUBLE DAMAGE
Select Code Entry from Extras and enter 34743.

UNLIMITED COPPER
Select Code Entry from Extras and enter 23637.

UNLIMITED CHI
Select Code Entry from Extras and enter 24463.

UNLIMITED HEALTH
Select Code Entry from Extras and enter 94677.

NEVERENDING STEALTH
Select Code Entry from Extras and enter 53467.

CHARACTER CONCEPT ART GALLERY
Select Code Entry from Extras and enter 97831.

BRATZ: FOREVER DIAMONDZ

1000 BLINGZ
While in the Bratz Office, use the Cheat computer to enter SIZZLN.

2000 BLINGZ
While in the Bratz Office, use the Cheat computer to enter FLAUNT.

PET TREATS
While in the Bratz Office, use the Cheat computer to enter TREATZ.

GIFT SET A
While in the Bratz Office, use the Cheat computer to enter STYLIN.

GIFT SET B
While in the Bratz Office, use the Cheat computer to enter SKATIN.

GIFT SET C
While in the Bratz Office, use the Cheat computer to enter JEWELZ.

GIFT SET E
While in the Bratz Office, use the Cheat computer to enter DIMNDZ.

BRATZ: ROCK ANGELZ

CAMERON CHANGED
While in the Bratz Office, use the Cheat computer to enter STYLIN.

CHLOE CHANGED
While in the Bratz Office, use the Cheat computer to enter SPARKLE, FASHION, STRUT or FLAIR.

DYLAN CHANGED
While in the Bratz Office, use the Cheat computer to enter MEYGEN.

JADE CHANGED
While in the Bratz Office, use the Cheat computer to enter FUNKALISH, SLAMMIN or HOT.

LONDON BOY CHANGED
While in the Bratz Office, use the Cheat computer to enter BLINGZ.

PARIS BOY CHANGED
While in the Bratz Office, use the Cheat computer to enter ROCKIN.

SASHA CHANGED
While in the Bratz Office, use the Cheat computer to enter FUNKY, SCORCHIN, PRETTY or MODEL

YASMIN CHANGED
While in the Bratz Office, use the Cheat computer to enter COOL, CRAZY or SASSY.

RECEIVE 1000 BLINGZ
While in the Bratz Office, use the Cheat computer to enter YASMIN.

RECEIVE 2000 BLINGZ
While in the Bratz Office, use the Cheat computer to enter PHOEBE.

RECEIVE 2100 BLINGZ
While in the Bratz Office, use the Cheat computer to enter DANCIN.

RECEIVE 3000 BLINGZ
While in the Bratz Office, use the Cheat computer to enter WAYFAB.

RECEIVE 6000 BLINGZ
While in the Bratz Office, use the Cheat computer to enter HOTTIE.

UNLOCKED RINGTONE 12
While in the Bratz Office, use the Cheat computer to enter BLAZIN.

UNLOCKED RINGTONE 15
While in the Bratz Office, use the Cheat computer to enter FIANNA.

UNLOCKED RINGTONE 16
While in the Bratz Office, use the Cheat computer to enter ANGELZ.

BUTT UGLY MARTIANS: ZOOM OR DOOM

ALL RACERS
During a game, hold **L1 + R1** and press △, ○, ✕, ○.

CABELA'S DANGEROUS HUNTS 2

DOUBLE HEALTH
Select Codes and enter Eye, Bolt, Skull, Hand, Boot.

HEALTH REGENERATES FASTER
Select Codes and enter Skull, Eye, Boot, Bolt, Hand.

DOUBLE DAMAGE
Select Codes and enter Hand, Boot, Skull, Eye, Bolt.

INFINITE AMMO
Select Codes and enter Bolt, Hand, Eye, Boot, Skull.

CAPCOM CLASSICS COLLECTION

ALL LOCKS OPENED
At the Title screen, press **L1**, **R1**, Up on Right Analog Stick, Down on Right Analog Stick, **L1**, **R1**, Up on Left Analog Stick, Down on Left Analog Stick, **L1**, **R1**, Up, Down.

CARS

UNLOCK EVERYTHING
Select Cheat Codes from the Options and enter IF900HP.

ALL CHARACTERS
Select Cheat Codes from the Options and enter YAYCARS.

ALL CHARACTER SKINS
Select Cheat Codes from the Options and enter R4MONE.

ALL MINI-GAMES AND COURSES
Select Cheat Codes from the Options and enter MATTL66.

MATER'S COUNTDOWN CLEAN-UP MINI-GAME AND MATER'S SPEEDY CIRCUIT
Select Cheat Codes from the Options and enter TRGTEXC.

FAST START
Select Cheat Codes from the Options and enter IMSPEED.

INFINITE BOOST
Select Cheat Codes from the Options and enter VROOOOM.

ART
Select Cheat Codes from the Options and enter CONC3PT.

VIDEOS
Select Cheat Codes from the Options and enter WATCHIT.

CHAMPIONS OF NORRATH: REALMS OF EVERQUEST

LEVEL 20 CHARACTER
During a game, press and hold **L1** + **R2** + ● + **R3**. This makes your character level 20 with 75,000 coins and 999 skill points. This does *not* increase your character's main attributes.

CHICKEN LITTLE

INVINCIBILITY
Select Cheat Codes from the Extras menu and enter Baseball, Baseball, Baseball, Shirt.

BIG FEET
Select Cheat Codes from the Extras menu and enter Hat, Glove, Glove, Hat.

BIG HAIR
Select Cheat Codes from the Extras menu and enter Baseball, Bat, Bat, Baseball.

BIG HEAD
Select Cheat Codes from the Extras menu and enter Hat, Helmet, Helmet, Hat.

PAPER PANTS
Select Cheat Codes from the Extras menu and enter Bat, Bat, Hat, Hat.

SUNGLASSES
Select Cheat Codes from the Extras menu and enter Glove, Glove, Helmet, Helmet.

UNDERWEAR
Select Cheat Codes from the Extras menu and enter Hat, Hat, Shirt, Shirt.

THE CHRONICLES OF NARNIA: THE LION, THE WITCH AND THE WARDROBE

ENABLE CHEATS
At the Title screen, press ✖ and hold **L1** + **R1**, then press Down, Down, Right, Up. The text should turn green when entered correctly. Now you can enter the following codes.

LEVEL SELECT
At the wardrobe, hold **L1** and press Up, Up, Right, Right, Up, Right, Down.

ALL BONUS LEVELS
At the Bonus Drawer, hold **L1** and press Down, Down, Right, Right, Down, Right, Up.

LEVEL SKIP
During gameplay, hold **L1** and press Down, Left, Down, Left, Down, Right, Down, Right, Up.

INVINCIBILITY
During gameplay, hold **L1** and press Down, Up, Down, Right, Right.

RESTORE HEALTH
During gameplay, hold **L1** and press Down, Left, Left, Right.

10,000 COINS
During gameplay, hold **L1** and press Down, Left, Right, Down, Down.

ALL ABILITIES
During gameplay, hold **L1** and press Down, Left, Right, Left, Up.

FILL COMBO METER
During gameplay, hold **L1** and press Up, Up, Right, Up.

THE DA VINCI CODE

GOD MODE
Select Codes from the Options and enter VITRUVIAN MAN.

EXTRA HEALTH
Select Codes from the Options and enter SACRED FEMININE.

MISSION SELECT
Select Codes from the Options and enter CLOS LUCE 1519.

ONE HIT FIST KILL
Select Codes from the Options and enter PHILLIPS EXETER.

ONE HIT WEAPON KILL
Select Codes from the Options and enter ROYAL HOLLOWAY.

ALL VISUAL DATABASE
Select Codes from the Options and enter APOCRYPHA.

ALL VISUAL DATABASE AND CONCEPT ART
Select Codes from the Options and enter ET IN ARCADIA EGO.

DESTROY ALL HUMANS!

AMMO-A-PLENTY
Pause the game, hold **L2** and press Left, ●, **R2**, Right, **R1**, ●. This gives you unlimited ammo.

BULLETPROOF CRYPTO
Pause the game, hold **L2** and press ●, ●, Left, Left, ●, ●. This makes you invincible.

DEEP THINKER
Pause the game, hold **L2** and press **R1**, **R2**, ●, Right, **R2**, ●. This gives you unlimited Concentration.

AWARE LIKE A FOX
Pause the game, hold **L2** and press Right, ●, **R2**, **R1**, Right, **R2**. This maxes out the alert meter.

NOBODY LOVES YOU
Pause the game, hold **L2** and press **R2**, Right, **R2**, **R1**, ●, Right. This resets the alert meter.

FOUND KEY TO ORTHOPOX'S LAB
On the Mothership, hold **L2** and press ●, ●, Left, Left, ●, ●. This gives you access to the Upgrades at Pox's Lab.

MMMM BRAINS!
On the Mothership, hold **L2** and press **R1**, **R1**, **R2**, **R2**, Left, Right, Left, Right, **R2**, **R1**. This gives you extra DNA.

DESTROY ALL HUMANS! 2

SALAD DAYS WITH POX & CRYPTO
Pause the game and select Archives. Hold **L3** and press ⊗, ⊕, ⊖, ⊖, ⊕, ⊕, ⊖, ⊗, ⊗.

DOG'S LIFE

CHEAT MENU
During a game, press ⊕ (Bark), ⊕ (Bark), ⊕ (Bark), hold ⊕ (Growl), hold ⊕ (Growl), hold ⊕ (Growl), Left, Right, Down (Fart).

DRAGON BALL Z: SAGAS

PENDULUM ROOMS
Select Options from the Main menu and press Up, Down, Up, Down, Left, Right, Left, Right, Select, Start, Select, Start, ⊕, ⊕, ⊕, ⊕, ⊗, ⊗, Start. When entered correctly, the message "Pendulum Rooms Unlocked" will appear on-screen. This unlocks the Pendulum mode, all Extras, all Sagas, and all Upgrades.

INVINCIBILITY
Pause the game, select Controller and press Down, ⊗, Select, Start, Right, ⊕, Left, ⊕, Up, ⊖.

ALL UPGRADES
Pause the game, select Controller and press Up, Left, Down, Right, Select, Start, ⊕, ⊗, ⊕, ⊖.

DROME RACERS

INSTANT WIN
At the Main menu, press Left, Right, Left, Right, Up, Down, Up, Down, ⊕, ⊖, ⊕. Press **L3** during a race to win.

ALL TRACKS
At the Main menu, press Left, Right, Left, Right, Up, Down, Up, Down, ⊖, ⊖, ⊗.

PURPLE RAIN
At the Main menu, press Left, Right, Left, Right, Up, Down, Up, Down, Up, Down, ⊕ (x3).

WIREFRAME MODE
At the Main menu, press Left, Right, Left, Right, Up, Down, Up, Down, ⊕, ⊕, ⊗.

DUEL MASTERS

ALL LOCATIONS
At the map screen, hold **R3** and press ⊕ (x3).

4 OF EVERY CARD AND UNLOCK CHUCK IN ARCADE MODE
At the deck building screen, hold **R3** and press **L1, L1, L1**.

PLAYER 1 LOSES SHIELD
During a duel, hold **R3** and press ⊖, ⊕, ⊗. Release **R3**.

PLAYER 2 LOSES SHIELD
During a duel, hold **R3** and press ⊖, ⊕, ⊗. Release **R3**.

PLAYER 1 GAINS SHIELD
During a duel, hold **R3** and press ⊗, ⊕, ⊖. Release **R3**.

PLAYER 2 GAINS SHIELD
During a duel, hold **R3** and press ⊗, ⊕, ⊖. Release **R3**.

PLAYER 1 WINS
During a duel, hold **R3** and press **L1, R1, L1**.

PLAYER 2 WINS
During a duel, hold **R3** and press **R1, L1, R1**.

TURN OFF DECK OUTS
During a duel, hold **R3** and press ⊕ (x3).

EA SPORTS ARENA FOOTBALL

BIG BALL
At the line of scrimmage, press **L1** + ⬤, Up, Up.

SMALL BALL
At the line of scrimmage, press **L1** + ⬤, Down, Down.

NORMAL SIZE BALL
At the line of scrimmage, press **L1** + ⬤, Up, Down.

MAX STATS IN QUICK PLAY
Load a profile with the name **IronMen**. This will maximize all players' stats in Quick Play.

EPHEMERAL FANTASIA

ALL NOTES IN MIDDLE BAR
Select Pattimo from Items. Press **L2** (x3), **L1**, **L1**, Right (x3), ⬤ before selecting your song.

NOTES MOVE FASTER AND FURTHER APART
Select Pattimo from Items. Press **L2**, **L1**, Right, ⬤, ⬤ before selecting your song.

NOTES MOVE EVEN FASTER AND FURTHER APART
Select Pattimo from Items. Press **L2**, **L1**, Right, ⬤, ⬤, **L2**, **L1**, Right, ⬤, ⬤ before selecting your song.

NOTES DISAPPEAR BEFORE HITTING TOP BAR
Select Pattimo from Items. Press **L2**, Right, **L1**, Right, **L2**, **L1** before selecting your song.

NOTES IN DIFFERENT PLACES
Select Pattimo from Items. Press Right, **L1**, **L1**, **L2**, **L1**, ⬤ before selecting your song.

FANTASTIC 4

BARGE ARENA AND STAN LEE INTERVIEW #1
At the Main menu, press ⬤, ⬤, ⬤, Down, Down, ⬤, Up.

INFINITE COSMIC POWER
At the Main menu, press Up, ⬤, ⬤, ⬤, Left, Right, ⬤.

BONUS LEVEL
At the Main menu, press Right, Right, ⬤, ⬤, Left, Up, Down.

FIFA STREET 2

ALL VENUES
At the Main menu, hold **L1** + ⬤ and press Left, Up, Up, Right, Down, Down, Right, Down.

FLATOUT

ALL CARS, CLASSES AND RACES
Create a new profile with the name **GIVEALL**.

$40,000
Create a new profile with the name **GIVECASH**.

EJECT YOURSELF FROM CAR
Create a new profile with the name **RAGDOLL**. Use the Gear Up button to throw yourself from the car without hitting anything.

FLATOUT 2

ALL CARS AND 1,000,000 CREDITS
Select Enter Code from the Extras and enter GIEVEPIX.

1,000,000 CREDITS
Select Enter Code from the Extras and enter GIVECASH.

PIMPSTER CAR
Select Enter Code from the Extras and enter RUTTO.

FLATMOBILE CAR
Select Enter Code from the Extras and enter WOTKINS.

MOB CAR
Select Enter Code from the Extras and enter BIGTRUCK.

SCHOOL BUS
Select Enter Code from the Extras and enter GIEVCARPLZ.

ROCKET CAR
Select Enter Code from the Extras and enter KALJAKOPPA.

TRUCK
Select Enter Code from the Extras and enter ELPUEBLO.

FROGGER: ANCIENT SHADOW

LEVEL SELECT

For the following codes, choose Secret Code and enter the appropriate code to unlock the levels.

LEVEL	ENTER
Level 4-1	Berry, Lily, Lumpy, Lily.
Level 4-2	Finnius, Frogger, Frogger, Wani.
Level 5-1	Lily, Lily, Wani, Wani.
Level 5-2	Frogger, Berry, Finnius, Frogger.
Level 6-1	Lily, Wani, Lily, Wani.

LEVEL	ENTER
Level 6-2	Frogger, Lily, Lily, Lily.
Level 6-3	Frogger, Frogger, Frogger, Berry.
Level 7-1	Lily, Lily, Wani, Lumpy.
Level 7-2	Lily, Frogger, Frogger, Lumpy.

UNLOCK LETTERS

To unlock the various letter, choose Secret Code and enter the following codes.

LETTER	ENTER
Hyacinth Letter	Lumpy, Frogger, Frogger, Berry
Cosmos Letter	Berry, Lumpy, Frogger, Lumpy
Rose Letter	Wani, Lily, Wani, Frogger
Pansy Letter	Lumpy, Berry, Lumpy, Finnius

UNLOCK WIGS

To unlock the various wigs, choose Secret Code and enter the following codes.

WIG	ENTER
Lobster Wig	Finnius, Wani, Lumpy, Frogger.
Bird Nest Wig	Lily, Lily, Lily, Lily.
Sail Boat Wig	Lumpy, Lumpy, Lumpy, Lumpy.
Skull Wig	Frogger, Lumpy, Lily, Frogger.

DEVELOPER PICTURE 1

Select Secret Code and enter Wani, Frogger, Wani, Frogger.

DEVELOPER PICTURE 2

Select Secret Code and enter Berry, Berry, Berry, Wani.

UNLOCK ARTWORK

To unlock the various artwork pieces, choose Secret Code and enter the following codes.

ART NAME	ENTER
Programmer Art 1	Wani, Wani, Wani, Wani.
Programmer Art 2	Lumpy, Frogger, Berry, Lily.
Programmer Art 3	Wani, Frogger, Lily, Finnius.
Additional Art 1	Frogger, Frogger, Frogger, Frogger.
Additional Art 2	Finnius, Finnius, Finnius, Finnius.
Additional Art 3	Berry, Berry, Berry, Berry.

GODZILLA: SAVE THE EARTH

CHEAT MENU

At the Main menu, press and hold **L2**, ●, **R2** in order, then let go of ●, **R2**, **L2** in order. Now you can enter the following cheats.

ALL CITIES

Enter 659996.

ALL MONSTERS

Enter 525955.

UNLOCK CHALLENGES

Enter 975013.

HEALTH REGENERATES
Enter 536117.

ENERGY DOES NOT REGENERATE
Enter 122574.

INDESTRUCTIBLE BUILDINGS
Enter 812304.

100,000 POINTS
Enter 532459.

150,000 POINTS
Enter 667596.

200,000 POINTS
Enter 750330.

PLAYER 1: 4X DAMAGE
Enter 259565.

PLAYER 1: INFINITE ENERGY
Enter 819342.

PLAYER 1: INVISIBLE
Enter 531470.

PLAYER 1: INVULNERABLE
Enter 338592.

PLAYER 2: 4X DAMAGE
Enter 927281.

PLAYER 2: INFINITE ENERGY
Enter 324511.

PLAYER 2: INVISIBLE
Enter 118699.

PLAYER 2: INVULNERABLE
Enter 259333.

PLAYER 3: 4X DAMAGE
Enter 500494.

PLAYER 3: INFINITE ENERGY
Enter 651417.

PLAYER 3: INVISIBLE
Enter 507215.

PLAYER 3: INVULNERABLE
Enter 953598.

PLAYER 4: 4X DAMAGE
Enter 988551.

PLAYER 4: INFINITE ENERGY
Enter 456719.

PLAYER 4: INVISIBLE
Enter 198690.

PLAYER 4: INVULNERABLE
Enter 485542.

GALLERY
Enter 294206.

GODZILLA FINAL WARS
Enter 409014.

GRADIUS V

You can use one of these each level completed.

DOUBLE SHOT POWER
After the first boss, pause the game and press Up, Up, Down, Down, Left, Right, Left, Right, **L2**, **R2**.

LASER POWER
After the first boss, pause the game and press Up, Up, Down, Down, Left, Right, Left, Right, **L1**, **R1**.

GRAFFITI KINGDOM

PLAY AS FAKE PASTEL IN VS BOSSES
After completing the game, select VS Mode. Then hold **L2 + R1** while selecting VS Bosses.

PLAY AS FAKE PIXEL IN VS BOSSES
After completing the game, select VS Mode. Then hold **L1 + L2** while selecting VS Bosses.

PLAY AS PASTEL IN VS BOSSES
After completing the game, select VS Mode. Then hold **L1 + R1** while selecting VS Bosses.

PLAY AS PIXEL IN VS BOSSES
After completing the game, select VS Mode. Then hold **L1 + R2** while selecting VS Bosses.

FAKE PASTEL VS PASTEL IN 2-PLAYER TOURNAMENT
After completing the game, select VS Mode. Then hold **L1 + L2 + R1** while selecting 2 Player Tournament.

FAKE PASTEL VS PIXEL IN 2-PLAYER TOURNAMENT
After completing the game, select VS Mode. Then hold **L2 + R1** while selecting 2 Player Tournament.

FAKE PIXEL VS FAKE PASTEL IN 2-PLAYER TOURNAMENT
After completing the game, select VS Mode. Then hold **L2 + R2** while selecting 2 Player Tournament.

FAKE PIXEL VS PIXEL IN 2-PLAYER TOURNAMENT

After completing the game, select VS Mode. Then hold L1 + L2 while selecting 2 Player Tournament.

PASTEL VS FAKE PASTEL IN 2-PLAYER TOURNAMENT

After completing the game, select VS Mode. Then hold L1 + R1 while selecting 2 Player Tournament.

PASTEL VS FAKE PIXEL IN 2-PLAYER TOURNAMENT

After completing the game, select VS Mode. Then hold R1 + R2 while selecting 2 Player Tournament.

PIXEL VS FAKE PIXEL IN 2-PLAYER TOURNAMENT

After completing the game, select VS Mode. Then hold L1 + R2 while selecting 2 Player Tournament.

GRAN TURISMO 4

EXTRA TRACKS FOR ARCADE MODE

Play through the indicated amount of days to unlock the corresponding track in Arcade Mode.

DAYS	UNLOCK	DAYS	UNLOCK
15	Deep Forest Raceway	197	Tahiti Maze
29	Opera Paris	211	Twin Ring Motegi Road Course
43	Fuji Speedway 80s	225	George V Paris
57	Special Stage Route 5	239	Cathedral Rocks Trail I
71	Suzuka Circuit	253	Costa di Amalfi
85	Twin Ring Motegi Road Course East Short	267	Circuit de la Sarthe 1
99	Grand Valley Speedway	281	Autumn Ring
113	Hong Kong	309	Chamonix
127	Suzuka Circuit West Course	309	Infineon Raceway Stock Car Course
141	Fuji Speedway 2005 GT	323	Fuji Speedway 2005 F
155	Ice Arena	337	Tsukuba Circuit Wet
169	Apricot Hill Raceway	351	Circuit de la Sarthe 2 (not chicaned)
183	Cote d Azur		

GROWLANSER GENERATIONS

ALL ARMOR, GEMS AND MAX MONEY

At the world map, press Up, Right, L2, L2, Down, R2, R2 Up, Down, R2, L2, Right, Left, ●, ●, ●.

GUITAR HERO

UNLOCK ALL CHEATS

At the Main menu, press Yellow, Orange, Blue, Blue, Orange, Yellow, Yellow.

GUITAR HERO GUITAR CHEAT

At the Main menu, press Blue, Orange, Yellow, Blue, Blue.

CROWD METER CHEAT

At the Main menu, press Yellow, Blue, Orange, Orange, Blue, Blue, Yellow, Orange.

MONKEY HEAD CROWD CHEAT

At the Main menu, press Blue, Orange, Yellow, Yellow, Yellow, Blue, Orange.

SKULL HEAD CROWD CHEAT

At the Main menu, press Orange, Yellow, Blue, Blue, Orange, Yellow, Blue, Blue.

AIR GUITAR CHEAT

At the Main menu, press Orange, Orange, Blue, Yellow, Orange.

NO VENUE CHEAT

At the Main menu, press Blue, Yellow, Orange, Blue, Yellow, Orange.

.HACK//G.U. VOL. 1//REBIRTH

VOL.2 PREVIEW

On the desktop, hold R1 + R2 and press ●, ▲, ●, ▲. Release R1 and R2. Hold L1 + L2 and press Right, Up, Right, Up. Release L1 and L2 and press R3 + L3.

HEROES OF THE PACIFIC

The following cheats will disable game saving.

CHEAT MENU
At the Main menu, press **L1, R2, L2, R3, R1, L3**.

PLANES AND MISSIONS
At the Main menu, press Up on Right Analog Stick, Down on Right Analog Stick, Left, **R2, L1**, Right on Right Analog Stick.

UPGRADE PLANES
At the Main menu, press **L1**, Left on Right Analog Stick, **R2**, Right on Right Analog Stick, Right, Down.

JAPANESE
At the Main menu, press ●, **R2, L1, L2**, Left, Up.

HOT SHOTS GOLF FORE!

Select Password from the Options menu and enter the following codes to enable these cheats:

ALL CHARACTERS AVAILABLE IN VS MODE
Enter **REZTWS**.

PRICE REDUCTION SALE IN SHOP
Enter **MKJEFQ**.

ALOHA BEACH RESORT COURSE IN SHOP
Enter **XSREHD**.

BAGPIPE CLASSIC COURSE IN SHOP
Enter **CRCNHZ**.

BLUE LAGOON C.C. COURSE IN SHOP
Enter **WVRJQS**.

DAY DREAM G.C. IN SHOP
Enter **OQUTNA**.

MINI-GOLF 2 G.C. IN SHOP
Enter **RVMIRU**.

SILKROAD CLASSIC COURSE IN SHOP
Enter **ZKOGJM**.

UNITED FOREST G.C. IN SHOP
Enter **UIWHLZ**.

WESTERN VALLEY COUNTRY CLUB COURSE AVAILABLE IN SHOP
Enter **LIBTFL**.

WILD GREEN C.C. COURSE IN SHOP
Enter **YZLOXE**.

CAPSULE 01 IN SHOP
Enter **WXAFSJ**.

CAPSULE 2 IN SHOP
Enter **OEINLK**.

CAPSULE 3 IN SHOP
Enter **WFKVTG**.

CAPSULE 4 IN SHOP
Enter **FCAVDO**.

CAPSULE 5 IN SHOP
Enter **YYPOKK**.

CAPSULE 6 IN SHOP
Enter **GDQDOF**.

CAPSULE 7 IN SHOP
Enter **HHXKPV**.

CAPSULE 8 IN SHOP
Enter **UOKXPS**.

CAPSULE 9 IN SHOP
Enter **LMIRYD**.

CAPSULE 10 IN SHOP
Enter **MJLJEQ**.

CAPSULE 11 IN SHOP
Enter **MHNCQI**

LOWER TOURNEY STAGE
Enter **XKWGFZ**.

CADDIE CLANK AVAILABLE IN SHOP
Enter **XCQGWJ**.

CADDIE DAXTER AVAILABLE IN SHOP
Enter **WSIKIN**.

CADDIE KAYLA AVAILABLE IN SHOP
Enter MZIMEL.

CADDIE KAZ AVAILABLE IN SHOP
Enter LNNZJV.

CADDIE MOCHI AVAILABLE IN SHOP
Enter MYPWPA.

CADDIE SIMON AVAILABLE IN SHOP
Enter WRHZNB.

CADDIE SOPHIE AVAILABLE IN SHOP
Enter UTWIVQ.

BEGINNER'S BALL AVAILABLE IN SHOP
Enter YFQJJI.

BIR AIR BALL AVAILABLE IN SHOP
Enter CRCGKR.

INFINITY BALL AVAILABLE IN SHOP
Enter DJXBRG.

PIN HOLE BALL AVAILABLE IN SHOP
Enter VZLSGP.

SIDESPIN BALL AVAILABLE IN SHOP
Enter JAYQRK.

TURBO SPIN BALL AVAILABLE IN SHOP
Enter XNETOK.

100T HAMMER CLUB (B-CLASS) AVAILABLE IN SHOP
Enter NFSNHR.

UPGRADE 100T HAMMER CLUB (A-CLASS) AVAILABLE IN SHOP
Enter BVLHSI.

UPGRADE 100T HAMMER CLUB (S-CLASS) AVAILABLE IN SHOP
Enter MCSRUK.

BIG AIR CLUB (B-CLASS) AVAILABLE IN SHOP
Enter DLJMFZ.

UPGRADE BIG AIR CLUB (A-CLASS) AVAILABLE IN SHOP
Enter TOSXUJ.

UPGRADE BIG AIR CLUB (S-CLASS) AVAILABLE IN SHOP
Enter JIDTQI.

INFINITY CLUB AVAILABLE IN SHOP
Enter RZTQGV.

UPGRADE INFINITY CLUB (A-CLASS) AVAILABLE IN SHOP
Enter WTGFOR.

UPGRADE INFINITY CLUB (S-CLASS) AVAILABLE IN SHOP
Enter EIPCUL.

PIN HOLE CLUB (B-CLASS) AVAILABLE IN SHOP
Enter DGHFRP.

UPGRADE PIN HOLE CLUB (A-CLASS) AVAILABLE IN SHOP
Enter TTIMHT.

UPGRADE PIN HOLE CLUB (S-CLASS) AVAILABLE IN SHOP
Enter RBXVEL.

UPGRADE TURBO SPIN CLUB (A-CLASS) AVAILABLE IN SHOP
Enter NIWKWP.

UPGRADE TURBO SPIN CLUB (S-CLASS) AVAILABLE IN SHOP
Enter DTIZAB.

EXTRA POSE CAM AVAILABLE IN SHOP
Enter UEROOK.

EXTRA SWING CAM AVAILABLE IN SHOP
Enter RJIFQS.

EXTRA VIDEO AVAILABLE IN SHOP
Enter DPYHIU.

HECKLETS AVAILABLE IN SHOP
Enter DIXWFE.

HSG CD/VOICE AVAILABLE IN SHOP
Enter UITUGF.

HSG CD/MUSIC AVAILABLE IN SHOP
Enter PAJXLI.

HSG RULES AVAILABLE IN SHOP
Enter FKDHDS.

LANDING GRID AVAILABLE IN SHOP
Enter **MQTIMV**.

REPLAY CAM A AVAILABLE IN SHOP
Enter **PVJEMF**.

REPLAY CAM B AVAILABLE IN SHOP
Enter **EKENCR**.

REPLAY CAM C AVAILABLE IN SHOP
Enter **ZUHHAC**.

MENU CHARACTER BRAD AVAILABLE IN SHOP
Enter **ZKJSIO**.

MENU CHARACTER PHOEBE AVAILABLE IN SHOP
Enter **LWVLCB**.

MENU CHARACTER RENEE AVAILABLE IN SHOP
Enter **AVIQXS**.

WALLPAPER SET 2 AVAILABLE IN SHOP
Enter **RODDHQ**.

MIKE'S COSTUME AVAILABLE IN SHOP
Enter **YKCFEZ**.

LIN'S COSTUME AVAILABLE IN SHOP
Enter **BBLSKQ**.

MEL'S COSTUME AVAILABLE IN SHOP
Enter **ARFLCR**.

PHOEBE'S COSTUME AVAILABLE IN SHOP
Enter **GJBCHY**.

ICE AGE 2: THE MELTDOWN

INFINITE PEBBLES
Pause the game and press Down, Down, Left, Up, Up, Right, Up, Down.

INFINITE ENERGY
Pause the game and press Down, Left, Right, Down, Down, Right, Left, Down.

INFINITE HEALTH
Pause the game and press Up, Right, Down, Up, Left, Down, Right, Left.

THE INCREDIBLES: RISE OF THE UNDERMINER

Pause the game, select Secrets, and enter the following.

EGOPROBLEM
Mr. Incredible and Frozone have big huge funny heads!

MRIPROF
Mr. Incredible gains 1000 Experience Points.

FROZPROF
Frozone 1000 gains Experience Points.

MRIBOOM
Mr. Incredible gains a Super-Move.

FROZBOOM
Frozone gains a Super-Move.

ROLLCALL
Shows the game credits.

THISISTOOEASY
Cuts damage done to enemies in half, doubles damage done to the Supers, no health recovery, and Experience Points are halved!

THISISTOOHARD
Doubles damage done to enemies, halves damage done to the Supers, doubles amount of health recovery and Experience Points!

SHOWME
Unlocks every item in the Gallery!

MAXIMILLION
Doubles Experience Point rewards!

IN THE GROOVE

ALL SONGS
At the Main menu, press Up, Right, Up, Right, Left, Down, Left, Down, Up, Right, Down, Left, Up, Left, Down, Right.

JAK X: COMBAT RACING

DAXTER
Play for 5 hours to unlock Daxter in the Secrets Shop for 50,000 Orbs.

KIERA
Defeat the game.

KLEVER
Defeat Beachfront Drive Circuit Race

RAZER
Defeat Northern Tour Circuit Race

SIG
Defeat Spargus City Death Race

UR-86
Defeat Kras City Qualifier

JAK
Make sure you have a Jak and Daxter save file on your memory card. Select Scan for Secret Characters from the Secrets Shop.

JAK II
Make sure you have a Jak II save file on your memory card. Select Scan for Secret Characters from the Secrets Shop.

JAK 3
Make sure you have a Jak 3 save file on your memory card. Select Scan for Secret Characters from the Secrets Shop.

RATCHET
Make sure you have a Ratchet: Deadlocked save file on your memory card. Select Scan for Secret Characters from the Secrets Shop.

HERO MODE
Complete the game with 100%. You can now purchase it for 50,000 Orbs at the Secret Shop.

DAXTERMOBILE, KAEDEN, OSMO, TARYN AND XIMON
With Daxter in your PSP, connect it to the PS2. Scan for Secrets in the Secrets Shop.

JUICED

ARCADE/CUSTOM MODE UNLOCKED
Select Cheats from the Extras menu and enter PINT.

JUSTICE LEAGUE HEROES

UNLOCK EVERYTHING
Pause the game, hold L1 + R1 + L2 + R2 and press Down, Left, Up, Right.

UNLIMITED ENERGY
Pause the game, hold L1 + R1 + L2 + R2 and press Down, Down, Right, Right, Up, Up, Left, Left.

KARAOKE REVOLUTION VOLUME 2

Cheats
At the Title screen, enter the following:

ALL SONGS
Press ●, ▲, Down, Left, Up, Right, L2, R2, Start.

ALL CHARACTERS
Press Up, ●, Right, ●, ●, Left, ●, Up, L3, R3.

ALL COSTUMES
Press Up, ●, Left, ●, ●, Down, ●, Right, R3, L3.

ALL VENUES
Press ●, ▲, Right, Up, Left, Down, R2, L2, Start.

GAME INFORMER T-SHIRT FOR ANGELA
Press Down, L3(2), R3(2), ●, Right, ●, L3, R3.

GAMEPRO T-SHIRT
Press Down, R3, Up, R3, L3, Down, L3, Up, Down, ●.

GAME STAR T-SHIRT
Press Up, R3, Right, R3(2), Left, R3, Down, ●, ●.

HARMONIX T-SHIRT FOR ISHANI
Press L3, ●, Up, ●, ●, L3, Down, Down, R3.

KONAMI T-SHIRT FOR DWAYNE
Press Right, R3, Right, R3, ●, Right, ●, ●, Down, Left.

PSM T-SHIRT FOR DEVRON
Press Left, Right, Left, L3, R3, Down, Up, Up, ●, ●.

More Cheats

Select Cheat Collection from Extras and enter the following or enter during a game:

BANANA MICROPHONE
Press L1, L1, R2, R2, Right, Down, ●, Left, Up, ●.

DWAYNE DOLLMICROPHONE
Press ●, R2, ●, L1, R1, L2, ●, Up, ●, ●.

TOOTHBRUSH MICROPHONE
Press R1, L1, R2, L2, Right, Left, Down, Up, ●, ●.

BIG HEAD CHARACTER
Press Down (x3), Up, R1, L2, R2, L1, ●, ●.

SMALL HEAD CHARACTER
Press Right, Right, Up, Up, L2, L2, R2, R1, L1.

BIG EYE CHARACTER
Press ●(x4), ●, Down, Down, R2, L2, R1.

GLASS CHARACTER
Press ●, ●, ●, R2, R2, L2, Down, Right, Right, Up.

OIL SLICK CHARACTER
Press L2, R2, L2, R2, ●, Down, ●, Up, Left, Right.

MERCURY CHARACTER
Press ●, L1, R2, Up, Up, Left, Left, ●, ●, R1.

WRAITH CHARACTER
Press R2, Left, R1, Right, Up, Up, ●, ●, Down, L2.

Even More Cheats

Select Cheat Collection from Extras and enter the following:

TOUGH CROWD
Press Right, Up, ● (x3), R2, R1, R1, L2, Down.

PIRATE CROWD
Press ●, ●, Left, Left, R2, L1, R2, R1, ●, L2.

ROBOT CROWD
Press ●, ●, Right, Right, R2, R1, R1, R2, ●, R2.

ZOMBIE CROWD
Press Left, L1, L2, ●, ●, L2, L2, L1, Left, Left.

KARAOKE REVOLUTION VOLUME 3

BANANA MICROPHONE
Score gold at each venue in Showtime mode. At the Extras menu, press Down, Up, Left, Right, ●, ●, ●, ● at Cheat Collection 1.

BIG EYED CHARACTER
Score gold at each venue in Showtime mode. At the Extras menu, press ●, ●, ●, ●, Down, Left, Left, Down at Cheat Collection 1.

DWAYNE DOLLMICROPHONE
Score gold at each venue in Showtime mode. At the Extras menu, press ●, ●, R3, ●, Up, Down, Right, Left at Cheat Collection 1.

TOOTHBRUSH MICROPHONE
Score gold at each venue in Showtime mode. At the Extras menu, press L2, L2, ●, ●, Down, Up, Left, L3 at Cheat Collection 1.

BIG HEAD CHARACTER
Score gold at each venue in Showtime mode. At the Extras menu, press ●, ●, ●, ●, Up, Right, Down, Left at Cheat Collection 2.

FISH MICROPHONE
Score gold at each venue in Showtime mode. At the Extras menu, press ●, Down, Up, Left, ●, ●, L2, L1 at Cheat Collection 2.

MERCURY CHARACTER
Score gold at each venue in Showtime mode. At the Extras menu, press Down, Down, Right, Left, Right, Left, ●, ● at Cheat Collection 2.

WRAITH CHARACTER
Score gold at each venue in Showtime mode. At the Extras menu, press L2, L2, Right, Right, ●, ●, R1, R1 at Cheat Collection 2.

GLASS CHARACTER
Score gold at each venue in Showtime mode. At the Extras menu, press Down, L2, R1, R2, L1, ●, ●, ● at Cheat Collection 3.

ICE CREAM MICROPHONE
Score gold at each venue in Showtime mode. At the Extras menu, press ●, ●, ●, ●, R2, L2, R1, L1 at Cheat Collection 3.

OIL SLICK CHARACTER
Score gold at each venue in Showtime mode. At the Extras menu, press L3, L3, R2, R1, L2, L2, L1, Down, Up at Cheat Collection 3.

SMALL HEAD CHARACTER
Score gold at each venue in Showtime mode. At the Extras menu, press ●, R2, L2, R1, L1, Down, Down, Up at Cheat Collection 3.

ALIEN CROWD
Score gold at each venue in Showtime mode. At the Extras menu, press Up, Up, Down, ●, ●, L2, R2, ● at Cheat Collection 4.

PIRATE CROWD
Score gold at each venue in Showtime mode. At the Extras menu, press Down, L2, L2, R2, R2, ●, ●, ● at Cheat Collection 4.

ROBOT CROWD
Score gold at each venue in Showtime mode. At the Extras menu, press L3, Down, Down, R1, ●, ●, ●, ● at Cheat Collection 4.

TOUGH AUDIO CROWD
Score gold at each venue in Showtime mode. At the Extras menu, press ●, L1, L2, R1, R2, Right, Right, Down at Cheat Collection 4.

ZOMBIE CROWD
Score gold at each venue in Showtime mode. At the Extras menu, press ●, ●, ●, ●, Up, Right, Right, Up at Cheat Collection 4.

KATAMARI DAMACY

COMETS

Finish a "Make a Star" level under a certain time to earn a comet. Use the following table to find the times you must beat to earn a comet.

LEVEL	FINISH WITHIN	LEVEL	FINISH WITHIN
Make a Star 1	1 minute	Make a Star 6	8 minutes
Make a Star 2	3 minutes	Make a Star 7	8 minutes
Make a Star 3	4 minutes	Make a Star 8	12 minutes
Make a Star 4	6 minutes	Make a Star 9	15 minutes
Make a Star 5	8 minutes	Make the Moon	20 minutes

L.A. RUSH

$5,000
During a game, press Up, Down, Left, Right, ●, Left, R2, Up.

UNLIMITED N20
During a game, press Up, Down, Left, Right, ●, Up, Down, ●, Up.

ALL CARS IN GARAGE PIMPED
During a game, press Up, Down, Left, Right, ●, ●, R2, R1, Up, Down, Left, Right.

DISABLE POLICE
During a game, press Up, Down, Left, Right, R2, ●, Right, R1, Left.

FAST TRAFFIC
During a game, press Up, Down, Left, Right, ●, Right, ●, Left.

NO CATCH UP
Use C-VHARD as a profile name.

LEGO STAR WARS: THE VIDEO GAME

Extras
Pause the game and select Extras to toggle these cheats on and off.

INVINCIBILITY
At Dexter's Diner, select Enter Code and enter 4PR28U.

BIG BLASTERS
At Dexter's Diner, select Enter Code and enter IG72X4.

CLASSIC BLASTERS
At Dexter's Diner, select Enter Code and enter L449HD.

SILLY BLASTERS
At Dexter's Diner, select Enter Code and enter NR37W1.

BRUSHES
At Dexter's Diner, select Enter Code and enter SHRUB1.

TEA CUPS
At Dexter's Diner, select Enter Code and enter PUCEAT.

MINIKIT DETECTOR
At Dexter's Diner, select Enter Code and enter LD116B.

MOUSTACHES
At Dexter's Diner, select Enter Code and enter RP924W.

PURPLE
At Depxter's Diner, select Enter Code and enter YD77GC.

SILHOUETTES
At Dexter's Diner, select Enter Code and enter MS999Q.

Characters
These codes make each character available for purchase from Dexter's Diner.

BATTLE DROID
At Dexter's Diner, select Enter Code and enter 987UYR.

BATTLE DROID (COMMANDER)
At Dexter's Diner, select Enter Code and enter EN11K5.

BATTLE DROID (GEONOSIS)
At Dexter's Diner, select Enter Code and enter LK42U6.

BATTLE DROID (SECURITY)
At Dexter's Diner, select Enter Code and enter KF999A.

BOBA FETT
At Dexter's Diner, select Enter Code and enter LA811Y.

CLONE
At Dexter's Diner, select Enter Code and enter F8B4L6.

CLONE (EPISODE III)
At Dexter's Diner, select Enter Code and enter **ER33JN**.

CLONE (EPISODE III, PILOT)
At Dexter's Diner, select Enter Code and enter **BHU72T**.

CLONE (EPISODE III, SWAMP)
At Dexter's Diner, select Enter Code and enter **N3T6P8**.

CLONE (EPISODE III, WALKER)
At Dexter's Diner, select Enter Code and enter **RS6E25**.

COUNT DOOKU
At Dexter's Diner, select Enter Code and enter **14PGMN**.

DARTH MAUL
At Dexter's Diner, select Enter Code and enter **H35TUX**.

DARTH SIDIOUS
At Dexter's Diner, select Enter Code and enter **A32CAM**.

DISGUISED CLONE
At Dexter's Diner, select Enter Code and enter **VR832U**.

DROIDEKA
At Dexter's Diner, select Enter Code and enter **DH382U**.

GENERAL GRIEVOUS
At Dexter's Diner, select Enter Code and enter **SF321Y**.

GEONOSIAN
At Dexter's Diner, select Enter Code and enter **19D7NB**.

GRIEVOUS' BODYGUARD
At Dexter's Diner, select Enter Code and enter **ZTY392**.

GONK DROID
At Dexter's Diner, select Enter Code and enter **U63B2A**.

JANGO FETT
At Dexter's Diner, select Enter Code and enter **PL47NH**.

KI-ADI MUNDI
At Dexter's Diner, select Enter Code and enter **DP55MV**.

KIT FISTO
At Dexter's Diner, select Enter Code and enter **CBR954**.

LUMINARA
At Dexter's Diner, select Enter Code and enter **A725X4**.

MACE WINDU (EPISODE III)
At Dexter's Diner, select Enter Code and enter **MS952L**.

PADMÉ
At Dexter's Diner, select Enter Code and enter **92UJ7D**.

PK DROID
At Dexter's Diner, select Enter Code and enter **R840JU**.

PRINCESS LEIA
At Dexter's Diner, select Enter Code and enter **BEQ82H**.

REBEL TROOPER
At Dexter's Diner, select Enter Code and enter **L54YUK**.

ROYAL GUARD
At Dexter's Diner, select Enter Code and enter **PP43JX**.

SHAAK TI
At Dexter's Diner, select Enter Code and enter **EUW862**.

SUPER BATTLE DROID
At Dexter's Diner, select Enter Code and enter **XZNR21**.

LEGO STAR WARS II: THE ORIGINAL TRILOGY

BEACH TROOPER
At Mos Eisley Canteena, select Enter Code and enter UCK868. You still need to select Characters and purchase this character for 20,000 studs.

BEN KENOBI (GHOST)
At Mos Eisley Canteena, select Enter Code and enter BEN917. You still need to select Characters and purchase this character for 1,100,000 studs.

BESPIN GUARD
At Mos Eisley Canteena, select Enter Code and enter VHY832. You still need to select Characters and purchase this character for 15,000 studs.

BIB FORTUNA
At Mos Eisley Canteena, select Enter Code and enter WTY721. You still need to select Characters and purchase this character for 16,000 studs.

BOBA FETT
At Mos Eisley Canteena, select Enter Code and enter HLP221. You still need to select Characters and purchase this character for 175,000 studs.

DEATH STAR TROOPER
At Mos Eisley Canteena, select Enter Code and enter BNC332. You still need to select Characters and purchase this character for 19,000 studs.

EWOK

At Mos Eisley Canteena, select Enter Code and enter TTT289. You still need to select Characters and purchase this character for 34,000 studs.

GAMORREAN GUARD

At Mos Eisley Canteena, select Enter Code and enter YZF999. You still need to select Characters and purchase this character for 40,000 studs.

GONK DROID

At Mos Eisley Canteena, select Enter Code and enter NFX582. You still need to select Characters and purchase this character for 1,550 studs.

GRAND MOFF TARKIN

At Mos Eisley Canteena, select Enter Code and enter SMG219. You still need to select Characters and purchase this character for 38,000 studs.

GREEDO

At Mos Eisley Canteena, select Enter Code and enter NAH118. You still need to select Characters and purchase this character for 60,000 studs.

HAN SOLO (HOOD)

At Mos Eisley Canteena, select Enter Code and enter YWM840. You still need to select Characters and purchase this character for 20,000 studs.

IG-88

At Mos Eisley Canteena, select Enter Code and enter NXL973. You still need to select Characters and purchase this character for 30,000 studs.

IMPERIAL GUARD

At Mos Eisley Canteena, select Enter Code and enter MMM111. You still need to select Characters and purchase this character for 45,000 studs.

IMPERIAL OFFICER

At Mos Eisley Canteena, select Enter Code and enter BBV889. You still need to select Characters and purchase this character for 28,000 studs.

IMPERIAL SHUTTLE PILOT

At Mos Eisley Canteena, select Enter Code and enter VAP664. You still need to select Characters and purchase this character for 29,000 studs.

IMPERIAL SPY

At Mos Eisley Canteena, select Enter Code and enter CVT125. You still need to select Characters and purchase this character for 13,500 studs.

JAWA

At Mos Eisley Canteena, select Enter Code and enter JAW499. You still need to select Characters and purchase this character for 24,000 studs.

LOBOT

At Mos Eisley Canteena, select Enter Code and enter UUB319. You still need to select Characters and purchase this character for 11,000 studs.

PALACE GUARD

At Mos Eisley Canteena, select Enter Code and enter SGE549. You still need to select Characters and purchase this character for 14,000 studs.

REBEL PILOT

At Mos Eisley Canteena, select Enter Code and enter CYG336. You still need to select Characters and purchase this character for 15,000 studs.

REBEL TROOPER (HOTH)

At Mos Eisley Canteena, select Enter Code and enter EKU849. You still need to select Characters and purchase this character for 16,000 studs.

SANDTROOPER

At Mos Eisley Canteena, select Enter Code and enter YDV451. You still need to select Characters and purchase this character for 14,000 studs.

SKIFF GUARD

At Mos Eisley Canteena, select Enter Code and enter GBU888. You still need to select Characters and purchase this character for 12,000 studs.

SNOWTROOPER

At Mos Eisley Canteena, select Enter Code and enter NYU989. You still need to select Characters and purchase this character for 16,000 studs.

STROMTROOPER

At Mos Eisley Canteena, select Enter Code and enter PTR345. You still need to select Characters and purchase this character for 10,000 studs.

THE EMPEROR

At Mos Eisley Canteena, select Enter Code and enter HHY382. You still need to select Characters and purchase this character for 275,000 studs.

TIE FIGHTER

At Mos Eisley Canteena, select Enter Code and enter HDY739. You still need to select Characters and purchase this character for 60,000 studs.

TIE FIGHTER PILOT

At Mos Eisley Canteena, select Enter Code and enter NNZ316. You still need to select Characters and purchase this character for 21,000 studs.

TIE INTERCEPTOR

At Mos Eisley Canteena, select Enter Code and enter QYA828. You still need to select Characters and purchase this character for 40,000 studs.

TUSKEN RAIDER

At Mos Eisley Canteena, select Enter Code and enter PEJ821. You still need to select Characters and purchase this character for 23,000 studs.

UGNAUGHT

At Mos Eisley Canteena, select Enter Code and enter UGN694. You still need to select Characters and purchase this character for 36,000 studs.

MADDEN NFL 06

Select Madden Cards from My Madden. Then select
Madden Codes and enter the following:

PASSWORD	CARD
6W5J6Z	#1 Rex Grossman Gold
6X7W2O	#2 Thomas Jones Gold
6Y5Z6H	#3 Brian Urlacher Gold
6Z9X5Y	#4 Olin Kreutz Gold
7A7Z2G	#5 Tommie Harris Gold
7C6U4H	#6 Carson Palmer Gold
7D1B2H	#7 Chad Johnson Gold
7D1X8K	#8 Rudi Johnson Gold
7D5W8J	#9 Brian Simmons Gold
7D8S6J	#10 J.P. Losman Gold
7E3G7Y	#11 Willis McGahee Gold
7F5B2Y	#12 Eric Moulds Gold
7H3B2Y	#13 Takeo Spikes Gold
7H9E8L	#14 Lawyer Milloy Gold
7J3Y7F	#15 Jake Plummer Gold
7J8F4J	#16 Ashley Lelie Gold
7K5C8V	#17 Al Wilson Gold
7L8C2W	#18 Champ Bailey Gold
1A2D9F	#19 John Lynch Gold
7O1J3F	#20 D.J. Williams Gold
7P5G3N	#21 Lee Suggs Gold
7Q2E45	#22 Kellen Winslow Jr. Gold
7Q6F4G	#23 Simeon Rice Gold
7Q6X4L	#24 Derrick Brooks Gold
7R7V2E	#25 Ronde Barber Gold
7S4C4D	#26 Anthony McFarland Gold
7T1G2Y	#27 Michael Clayton Gold
7T3V5K	#28 Anquan Boldin Gold
7T6B5N	#29 Larry Fitzgerald Gold
7U4M9B	#30 Bertrand Berry Gold
7U6B3L	#31 LaDainian Tomlinson Gold
8Q2J2R	#55 Donovan McNabb Bronze
8Q2J2X	#55 Donovan McNabb Gold

8V9Y3X	#62 Michael Vick Gold
8X2Y9G	#64 Alge Crumpler Gold
2W4P9T	#188 First and Fifteen Bronze
2W4P9G	#188 First and Fifteen Silver
2Y7L88	#189 First and Five Bronze
2Z2F4H	#190 Unforced Errors Bronze

PASSWORD	CARD
2Z2F4G	#190 Unforced Errors Silver
3D3Q3P	#191 Extra Credit Bronze

3D8X6Z	#191 Extra Credit Gold
3D8X6T	#192 Tight Fit Bronze
3E9R4V	#193 5th Down Bronze

3E9R4I	#193 5th Down Silver
3F9G4J	#194 3rd Down Bronze
3F9G4O	#194 3rd Down Silver
3H3U7T	#194 3rd Down Gold
3H3U7F	#195 Human Plow Bronze

| 3H8M5U | #196 Super Dive Bronze |
| 3J3S9Y | #197 Da Boot Bronze |

PASSWORD	CARD		PASSWORD	CARD
3J3S9E	#197 Da Boot Silver		4F9D2H	#221 Super Bowl XLI Gold
3T4E3Y	#208 Pocket Protectors Gold		4I1V6T	#222 Super Bowl XLII Gold
3X1V2H	#210 QB on Target Gold		4F3D7E	#223 Super Bowl XLIII Gold
4D1V2Y	#217 Ouch Gold		4I1V6K	#224 Aloha Stadium Gold
4F9D2B	#220 Super Bowl XL Gold			

MADDEN NFL 07

#199 GOLD LAME DUCK CHEAT CARD
In My Madden, select Madden Codes from Madden Cards. Enter 5LAWOO.

#200 GOLD MISTAKE FREE CHEAT CARD
In My Madden, select Madden Codes from Madden Cards. Enter XL7SP1.

#210 GOLD QB ON TARGET CHEAT CARD
In My Madden, select Madden Codes from Madden Cards. Enter WROA0R.

MAJOR LEAGUE BASEBALL 2K6

UNLOCK EVERYTHING
Select Enter Cheat Code from the My 2K6 menu and enter **Derek Jeter**.

TOPPS 2K STARS
Select Enter Cheat Code from the My 2K6 menu and enter **Dream Team**.

SUPER WALL CLIMB
Select Enter Cheat Code from the My 2K6 menu and enter **Last Chance**. Enable the cheats by selecting My Cheats or selecting Cheat Codes from the Options screen in-game.

SUPER PITCHES
Select Enter Cheat Code from the My 2K6 menu and enter **Unhittable**. Enable the cheats by selecting My Cheats or selecting Cheat Codes from the Options screen in-game.

ROCKET ARMS
Select Enter Cheat Code from the My 2K6 menu and enter **Gotcha**. Enable the cheats by selecting My Cheats or selecting Cheat Codes from the Options screen in-game.

BOUNCY BALL
Select Enter Cheat Code from the My 2K6 menu and enter **Crazy Hops**. Enable the cheats by selecting My Cheats or selecting Cheat Codes from the Options screen in-game.

MARVEL NEMESIS: RISE OF THE IMPERFECTS

UNLOCKS ALL FANTASTIC FOUR COMICS
Select Cheats from the Options and enter SAVAGELAND.

UNLOCKS ALL TOMORROW PEOPLE COMICS
Select Cheats from the Options and enter NZONE.

MARVEL ULTIMATE ALLIANCE

UNLOCK ALL SKINS
At the Team Menu, press Up, Down, Left, Right, Left, Right, Start.

UNLOCKS ALL HERO POWERS
At the Team Menu, press Left, Right, Up, Down, Up, Down, Start.

ALL HEROES TO LEVEL 99
At the Team Menu, press Up, Left, Up, Left, Down, Right, Down, Right, Start.

UNLOCK ALL HEROES
At the Team Menu, press Up, Up, Down, Down, Left, Left, Left, Start.

UNLOCK DAREDEVIL

At the Team Menu, press Left, Left, Right, Right, Up, Down, Up, Down, Start.

UNLOCK SILVER SURFER

At the Team Menu, press Down, Left, Left, Up, Right, Up, Down, Left, Start.

GOD MODE

During gameplay, press Up, Down, Up, Down, Up, Left, Down, Right, Start.

TOUCH OF DEATH

During gameplay, press Left, Right, Down, Down, Right, Left, Start.

SUPER SPEED

During gameplay, press Up, Left, Up, Right, Down, Right, Start.

FILL MOMENTUM

During gameplay, press Left, Right, Right, Left, Up, Down, Down, Up, Start.

UNLOCK ALL COMICS

At the Review menu, press Left, Right, Right, Left, Up, Up, Right, Start.

UNLOCK ALL CONCEPT ART

At the Review menu, press Down, Down, Down, Right, Right, Left, Down, Start.

UNLOCK ALL MOVIES

At the Review menu, press Up, Left, Left, Up, Right, Right, Up, Start.

UNLOCK ALL LOAD SCREENS

At the Review menu, press Up, Down, Right, Left, Up, Up Down, Start.

UNLOCK ALL COURSES

At the Comic Missions menu, press Up, Right, Left, Down, Up, Right, Left, Down, Start.

MASTERS OF THE UNIVERSE HE-MAN: DEFENDER OF GRAYSKULL

INVULNERABILITY

Select cheats from the Options menu and enter Right, ●, Up, Left, ✖.

UNLIMITED GRAYSKULL POWER

Select cheats from the Options menu and enter Down, Right, ✖, ●, Down.

DOUBLE DAMAGE

Select cheats from the Options menu and enter ●, Right, ✖, Up, ✖.

ALL LEVELS

Select cheats from the Options menu and enter ✖, Left, Up, ●, Down.

MEGA MAN X COLLECTION

Mega Man X4

BLACK ZERO

At the Character Select screen, highlight Zero, hold **R1** and press Right (x6). Then release **R1**, hold ● and press Start. Continue holding ● until the game starts.

ULTIMATE ARMOR FOR MEGA MAN X

At the Character Select screen, highlight Mega Man X, press ●, ●, Left (x6), hold **L1 + R2** and press Start. Continue holding **L1 + R2** until the game starts. Complete the level, then find the Leg power-up in the Jungle.

Mega Man X5

BLACK ZERO

At the Character Select screen, highlight Zero and press Down, Down, Up (x9).

ULTIMATE ARMOR FOR MEGA MAN X

At the Character Select screen, highlight Mega Man X and press Up, Up, Down (x9).

Mega Man X6

BLACK ZERO

At the Main menu, highlight Game Start and press **L1, L1, L1, R2.**

ULTIMATE ARMOR FOR MEGA MAN X

At the Main menu, highlight Game Start and press Left, Left, Left, Right.

MEGA MAN X8

PLAY AS ALIA
At the Title screen, press Down, **R1**, Up, **L1**, ●, ✕, ▲, ●.

PLAY AS LAYER
At the Title screen, press ●, ▲, Right, ✕, **R1**.

BATTLE CUTMAN
At the Title screen, press Left, ●, Up, ▲, Down, ✕, Right, ●, **L1**, **R1**, **L2**, **R2**.

SIGMA BLADE
At the Title screen, press **L3, L3, R3, L3, L3, R3, L3, L3, R3, L3, L3, R3**.

BLACK ZERO
At the Title screen, press **L1, L1, R1, R1, L1, L1, L1, L1**.

PALLETE
At the Title screen, press **R1**, ✕, Left, ●, ●.

ULTIMATE ARMOR X
At the Title screen, press Left, Left, Left, Right, Right, Right, Left, Left, Left, Left, Right, Right, Right, Right.

WHITE AXL
At the Title screen, press **L2, L2, L2, R2, R2, R2, L2, L2, R2**.

MIDWAY ARCADE TREASURES 3

HYDRO THUNDER

ALL TRACKS AND BOATS
Get a high score and enter ?PB as your initials.

Offroad Thunder

CLIFFHANGER TRACK
Select Rally and press Right at the Choose Track screen press Right to bring up the Secret Code option. Press Right, Up, Left, to unlock the Cliffhanger track.

CHIEFTAIN & GENERAL VEHICLES
Select Rally and press Right at the Choose Machine screen press Right to bring up the Secret Code option. Press Left (x3) to unlock Chieftain. Press Left (x3) again to unlock General.

DUST DEVIL & SILVER STREAK VEHICLES
Select Rally and press Right at the Choose Machine screen press Right to bring up the Secret Code option. Press Left, Up, Right to unlock Dust Devil. Press Left, Up, Right again to unlock Silver Streak.

HYENA & BAD OMEN VEHICLES
Select Rally and press Right at the Choose Machine screen press Right to bring up the Secret Code option. Press Right (x3) to unlock Hyena. Press Right (x3) again to unlock Bad Omen.

WILDCAT & THRASHER VEHICLES
Select Rally and press Right at the Choose Machine screen press Right to bring up the Secret Code option. Press Up (x3) to unlock Wildcat. Press Up (x3) again to unlock Thrasher.

SAN FRANCISCO: RUSH 2049

ACTIVATE CHEAT MENU
At the Main menu, highlight Options and press **L1** + **R1** + ● + ●. Now you can enter the following cheats.

ALL CARS

At the Cheat Menu, highlight All Cars and press ✕, ✕, ●, ●, L1, L1. Hold R1 and press ●. Release R1, hold L1 and press ✕.

ALL TRACKS

At the Cheat Menu, highlight All Tracks, hold ✕ + ● and press R1. Release ✕ and ●. Hold ● + ● and press L1. Release ● and ●. Press ✕, ✕, ●, ●, hold L1 + R1 and press ●.

ALL PARTS

At the Cheat Menu, highlight All Parts, hold ● and press ●, ✕, L1, R1. Release ●, hold ● and press ✕. Release ● and press ●, ●.

RESURRECT IN PLACE

At the Cheat Menu, highlight Resurrect in Place and press R1, R1, L1, L1, ✕, ●, ●.

FRAME SCALE

At the Cheat Menu, highlight Frame Scale hold L1 and press ✕, ✕, ●. Release L1, hold R1 and press ✕, ✕, ●.

TIRE SCALING

At the Cheat Menu, highlight Tire Scaling press and press ●, ●, ✕, ●, ●, ✕. Hold R1 and press ✕.

FOG COLOR

At the Cheat Menu, highlight Fog Color hold L1 and press ●, release L1, hold ✕ and press ●, release ✕, hold ● and press ●, release ●, hold R1 and press ●.

CAR COLLISIONS

At the Cheat Menu, highlight Car Collisions hold L1 + R1 and press ●, ●, ✕. Release L1 and R1 and press ●, ●, ✕.

CONE MINES

At the Cheat Menu, highlight Cone Mines hold ● and press R1, L1. Release ● and press ●. Hold ✕ and press ●. Release ✕ and press ●.

CAR MINES

At the Cheat Menu, highlight Car Mines, hold L1 + R1 + ● and press ✕, ●. Release L1, R1 and ●. Press ✕, ●.

TRACK ORIENTATION

At the Cheat Menu, highlight Track Orientation hold L1 + R1 and press ●. Release L1 and R1 and press ✕, ●, ●. Hold L1 + R1 and press ●.

AUTO ABORT

At the Cheat Menu, highlight Auto Abort and press ✕, L1, ●, R1, ●. Hold L1 + R1 and press ✕, ●.

SUPER SPEED

At the Cheat Menu, highlight Super Speed hold ● + R1 and press L1. Release ● and R1. Hold ✕ and press ●. Release ✕ and press ✕, ✕, ✕.

INVINCIBLE

At the Cheat Menu, highlight Invincible hold L1 + ● and press ●, ✕. Release L1 + ●. Hold R1 and press ✕, ●, ●.

INVISIBLE CAR

At the Cheat Menu, highlight Invisible Car hold L1 and press ●. Release L1. Hold R1 and press ●. Release R1 and press ✕. Hold L1 + R1 and press ●. Release L1 and R1 and press ●, ●, ●.

INVISIBLE TRACK

At the Cheat Menu, highlight Invisible Track press R1, L1, ●, ●, ✕, ✕, ●, ●. Hold L1 + R1 and press ✕.

BRAKES

At the Cheat Menu, highlight Brakes press ●, ●, ●. Hold L1 + ● + ✕ and press R1.

SUPER TIRES

At the Cheat Menu, highlight Super Tires hold R1 and press ●, ●, ●. Release R1. Hold L1 and press ✕, ✕, ●.

MASS

At the Cheat Menu, highlight Mass hold ✕ and press ●, ●, ●. Release ✕ and press L1, R1.

SUICIDE MODE

At the Cheat Menu, highlight Suicide Mode hold ● and press R1, L1, R1, L1. Release ●. Hold ● and press R1, L1, R1, L1.

BATTLE PAINT SHOP

At the Cheat Menu, highlight Battle Paint Shop hold ✕ and press L1, R1, L1, R1. Release ✕ and press ●, ●, ●.

DEMOLITION BATTLE

At the Cheat Menu, highlight Demolition Battle hold L1 + ✕ and press ●, ●. Release L1 and ✕. Hold R1 + ✕ and press ●, ●.

RANDOM WEAPONS

At the Cheat Menu, highlight Random Weapons hold L1 + ✕ and press ●, ●. Release L1 and ✕. Hold R1 + ✕ and press ●, ●.

MLB '06: THE SHOW

ALL TEAMS
At the Main menu, press Left, Right, Right, Down, Down, Left, Up, Up.

ALL PLAYERS
At the Main menu, press Left, Up, Left, Right, Down, Right, Left, Up.

ALL UNIFORMS
At the Main menu, press Up, Down, Right, Left, Down, Right, Down, Up.

ALL STADIUMS
At the Main menu, press Down, Up, Left, Right, Up, Right, Up, Down.

BIG BALL
Pause the game and press Up, Right, Down, Left, Right, Down, Left, Up.

MAX PITCH
Pause the game and press Right, Right, Up, Up, Down, Down, Left, Left Break.

MAX PITCH SPEED
Pause the game and press Up, Up, Left, Right, Left, Right, Up, Up.

RUN FASTER
Pause the game and press Left, Left, Left, Up, Right, Right, Right, Down.

RUN SLOWER
Pause the game and press Right, Right, Right, Up, Left, Left, Left, Down.

MLB SLUGFEST 2006

ATLANTIS
Hit a Homer in AT&T Park.

COLISEUM
Hit a Homer in Fenway.

EMPIRE
Hit a Homer in Yankee Stadium.

FORBIDDEN CITY
Hit Homer in PetCo Park.

MONUMENT STADIUM
Hit homer in Citizens Bank Park.

ROCKET PARK
Hit a Homer in Minute Maid Park.

TEAM BOBBLE HEAD
Hit 10 homers in one game.

TEAM CASEY
Hit a Triple in Wrigley Field.

TEAM DOLPHINS
Hit a homer in Atlantis.

TEAM EAGLES
Walk 3 times in one game.

TEAM EVIL CLOWNS
Hit a homer in Empire Park with the Yankees.

TEAM GLADIATOR
Hit homer in The Coliseum.

TEAM HORSE
Steal 5 bases in one game.

TEAM LIONS
Hit a homer with the Tigers in Comerica Park.

TEAM MARTIANS
Hit a Triple in Rocket Park.

TEAM MINTAUR
Hit a homer in The Forbidden City.

TEAM PINTO
Hit an inside-the-park homer in Busch Stadium.

TEAM RODEO CLOWN
Perform a double play.

MLB SLUGFEST: LOADED

CHEATS
At the Match-Up screen, press ●, ▲, and ● to enter the following codes, then press the appropriate direction. For example, for 16" Softball press ●(x2), ▲(x4), ●(x2), then press Down.

CODE	ENTER	CODE	ENTER
Bone Bat	0-0-1 Up	Unlimited Turbo	4-4-4 Down
Blade Bat	0-0-2 Up	Extra Time After Plays	1-2-3 Left
Ice Bat	0-0-3 Up	Little League Mode	1-0-1 Down
Log Bat	0-0-4 Up	16" Softball	2-4-2 Down
Spike Bat	0-0-5 Up	Rubber Bball	2-4-2 Up
Whiffle Bat	0-0-4 Right	Tiny Head	2-0-0 Left
Max Batting	3-0-0 Left	Big Head	2-0-0 Right
Max Power	0-3-0 Left	Alien Team	2-3-1 Down
Max Speed	0-0-3 Left	Bobblehead Team	1-3-3 Down

CODE	ENTER	CODE	ENTER
Casey team	2-3-3 Down	Rivera Team	2-2-2 Up
Dolphin Team	1-0-2 Down	Rodeo Clown Team	1-3-2 Down
Dwarf Team	1-0-3 Down	Scorpion team	1-1-2 Down
Eagle Team	2-1-2 Right	Terry Fitzgerald team	3-3-3 Right
Evil Clown Team	2-1-1 Down	Todd McFarlane team	2-2-2 Right
Gladiator Team	1-1-3 Down	Atlantis stadium	3-2-1 Left
Horse Team	2-1-1 Right	Coliseum stadium	3-3-3 Up
Lion Team	2-2-0 Right	Empire Park stadium	3-2-1 Right
Minotaur Team	1-1-0 Down	Forbidden City stadium	3-3-3 Left
Napalitano Team	2-3-2 Down	Midway Park stadium	3-2-1 Down
Olshan Team	2-2-2 Down	Monument stadium	3-3-3 Down
Pinto Team	2-1-0 Right	Rocket Park stadium	3-2-1 Up

MOTOCROSS MANIA 3

ALL TRACKS

At the Main menu, press Up, Left, Down, Right, Up, Left, Down, Left, Left, ●.

ALL RIDERS & BIKES

At the Main menu, press Up, Left, Down, Right, Up, Left, Down, Up, ●.

ALL BIKE UPGRADES

At the Main menu, press Up, Left, Down, Right, Up, Down, Down, Left, Down, ●.

ALL WEAPONS & ARMOR

At the Main menu, press Up, Left, Down, Right, Up, Left, Down, Left, Down, ●.

FREESTYLE

At the Main menu, press Up, Left, Down, Right, Up, Left, Down, Left, Left, ●. Go into another menu and back out to access Freestyle.

MVP 06 NCAA BASEBALL

ALL CHALLENGE ITEMS

In Dynasty Mode, create a player with the name **Dee Jay Randall**.

LEVEL 1 CHALLENGE ITEMS

In Dynasty Mode, create a player with the name **Peter Trenouth**.

ALL LEVEL 2 CHALLENGE ITEMS

In Dynasty Mode, create a player with the name **Trey Smith**.

ALL LEVEL 3 CHALLENGE ITEMS

In Dynasty Mode, create a player with the name **Chris Chung**.

ALL LEVEL 4 CHALLENGE ITEMS

In Dynasty Mode, create a player with the name **Federico Rahal**.

BIG BAT

In Dynasty Mode, create a player with the name **Chris Deas**.

SHORT PLAYER WITH BIG BAT
In Dynasty Mode, create a player with the name **Alan Blouin**.

THICK BAT
In Dynasty Mode, create a player with the name **Melissa Shim**.

LARGE PLAYER WITH THIN BAT
In Dynasty Mode, create a player with the name **Neale Genereux**.

SHORT PLAYER WITH THIN BAT
In Dynasty Mode, create a player with the name **Julia Kwan**.

SUPER HITTER
In Dynasty Mode, create a player with the name **Tim Regel**.

MX VS. ATV UNLEASHED

UNLOCK EVERYTHING
Select Cheat Codes from the Options and enter **TOOLAZY**.

1,000,000 POINTS
Select Cheat Codes from the Options and enter **BROKEASAJOKE**. After entering the code, press Done multiple times for more points.

ALL PRO RIDERS
Select Cheat Codes from the Options and enter **WANNABE**.

ALL GEAR
Select Cheat Codes from the Options and enter **WARDROBE**.

50CC BIKE CLASS
Select Cheat Codes from the Options and enter **MINIMOTO**.

ALL MACHINES
Select Cheat Codes from the Options and enter **LEADFOOT**.

ALL FREESTYLE TRACKS
Select Cheat Codes from the Options and enter **HUCKIT**.

NASCAR 06: TOTAL TEAM CONTROL

UNLOCK EVERYTHING
In Fight to the Top mode, select Edit Driver. Enter **Gimme Gimme** as the first and last names.

$10,000,000
In Fight to the Top mode, select Edit Driver. Enter **Walmart Money** as the first and last names.

MAX FAN LEVEL
In Fight to the Top mode, select Edit Driver. Enter **Super Star** as the first and last names.

MAX PRESTIGE
In Fight to the Top mode, select Edit Driver. Enter **MeMyself AndI** as the first and last names.

MAX TEAM PRESTIGE
In Fight to the Top mode, select Edit Driver. Enter **All ForOne** as the first and last names.

WALMART TRACKS AND CARS
In Fight to the Top mode, select Edit Driver. Enter **Walmart Exclusive** as the first and last names.

OLD SPICE TRACKS AND CARS
In Fight to the Top mode, select Edit Driver. Enter **KeepCool SmellGreat** as the first and last names.

DALE EARNHARDT SR.
In Fight to the Top mode, select Edit Driver. Enter **The Intimidator** as the first and last names.

NASCAR 07

$10,000,000
In Fight to the Top mode, enter your name as **GiveMe More**.

10,000,000 FANS
In Fight to the Top mode, enter your name as **AllBow ToMe**.

PRESTIGE LEVEL 10 WITH 2,000,000 POINTS
In Fight to the Top mode, enter your name as **Outta MyWay**.

100% TEAM PRESTIGE
In Fight to the Top mode, enter your name as **MoMoney BlingBling**.

ALL CHASE PLATES
In Fight to the Top mode, enter your name as **ItsAll ForMe**.

OLD SPICE TRACKS AND CARS.
In Fight to the Top mode, enter your name as **KeepCool SmellGreat**.

WALMART TRACK AND CARS
In Fight to the Top mode, enter your name as **Walmart EveryDay**.

NBA '06: FEATURING THE LIFE VOL. 1

CAVALIERS ALT JERSEY
Select NBA.com from the Trophy Room and enter
J8E5RAMI7E.

NUGGETS ALT JERSEY
Select NBA.com from the Trophy Room and enter
4J52U2N64E.

PISTONS ALT JERSEY
Select NBA.com from the Trophy Room and enter
7C43H21A8D.

CELTICS ALT JERSEY
Select NBA.com from the Trophy Room and enter
C83A22G93E.

PACERS AWAY JERSEY
Select NBA.com from the Trophy Room and enter
D2A7LL2A3S.

PACERS HOME JERSEY
Select NBA.com from the Trophy Room and enter
3E98M2I6LY.

CHICAGO BULLS CLASSIC JERSEY
Select NBA.com from the Trophy Room and enter
S60T9E2V9E.

LOS ANGELES CLIPPERS CLASSIC JERSEY
Select NBA.com from the Trophy Room and enter
3W6E2ST1ON.

MEMPHIS GRIZZLIES CLASSIC JERSEY
Select NBA.com from the Trophy Room and enter
N76I33A4L2.

NEW JERSEY NETS CLASSIC JERSEY
Select NBA.com from the Trophy Room and enter
T73R387HF2.

NEW YORK KNICKS CLASSIC JERSEY
Select NBA.com from the Trophy Room and enter
S25LFG33Z4.

ORLANDO MAGIC CLASSIC JERSEY
Select NBA.com from the Trophy Room and enter
IX55LD1A9P.

PHOENIX SUNS CLASSIC JERSEY
Select NBA.com from the Trophy Room and enter
L76HJY52K6.

SEATTLE SUPERSONICS CLASSIC JERSEY
Select NBA.com from the Trophy Room and enter
S27T3E9V1E.

WASHINGTON WIZARDS CLASSIC JERSEY
Select NBA.com from the Trophy Room and enter
J44X9YLL3F.

NBA 2K6

CELEBRITY STREET OPTION
Select Codes from the Features menu and enter
ballers.

2KSPORTS TEAM
Select Codes from the Features menu and enter
2ksports.

2K6 TEAM
Select Codes from the Features menu and enter
nba2k6.

VC TEAM
Select Codes from the Features menu and enter
vcteam.

NIKE SHOX MTX SHOES
Select Codes from the Features menu and enter
crazylift.

NIKE ZOOM 20-5-5 SHOES
Select Codes from the Features menu and enter
lebronsummerkicks.

NIKE ZOOM KOBE 1 SHOES
Select Codes from the Features menu and enter **kobe**.

NIKE ZOOM LEBRON III ALL-STAR COLORWAY SHOES
Select Codes from the Features menu and enter **lb allstar**.

NIKE ZOOM LEBRON III BLACK/CRIMSON SHOES
Select Codes from the Features menu and enter **lb crimsonblack**.

NIKE ZOOM LEBRON III SPECIAL BIRTHDAY EDITION SHOES
Select Codes from the Features menu and enter **lb bday**.

NIKE ZOOM LEBRON III WHITE/GOLD SHOES
Select Codes from the Features menu and enter **lb whitegold**.

NIKE UP TEMPO PRO SHOES
Select Codes from the Features menu and enter
anklebreakers.

ALTERNATE UNIFORMS   ENTER

For the following codes, choose Codes from the Features menu and enter the appropriate code.

UNIFORM	ENTER	UNIFORM	ENTER
2006 All-Star	fanfavorites.	Knicks Retro	ny retro.
St. Patrick's Day	gogreen.	Magic Retro	orl retro.
Bulls Retro	chi retro.	Nets Retro	nj retro.
Cavaliers Alternate	cle 2nd.	Nuggets Alternate	den 2nd.
Celtics Alternate	bos 2nd.	2005-06 Pacers Uniform	31andonly.
Clippers Retro	lac retro.	Pistons Alternate	det 2nd.
Grizzlies Retro	mem retro.	Rockets Retro	hou retro.
Heat Retro	mia retro.	Sonics Retro	sea retro.
Hornets Retro	no retro.	Suns Retro	phx retro.
Kings Alternate	sac 2nd.	Wizards Retro	was retro.

+10 BONUS FOR DEFENSIVE AWARENESS

Find the PowerBar vending machine in The Crib. Choose Enter Code and enter **lockdown**.

+10 BONUS FOR OFFENSIVE AWARENESS

Find the PowerBar vending machine in The Crib. Choose Enter Code and enter **getaclue**.

MAX DURABILITY

Find the PowerBar vending machine in The Crib. Choose Enter Code and enter **noinjury**.

UNLIMITED STAMINA

Find the PowerBar vending machine in The Crib. Choose Enter Code and enter **nrgmax**.

POWERBAR TATTOO

Find the PowerBar vending machine in The Crib. Choose Enter Code and enter **pbink**. You can now use it in the game's Create Player feature.

ALL ITEMS IN THE CRIB

Find the PowerBar vending machine in The Crib. Choose Enter Code and enter **criball**.

NBA 2K7

MAX DURABILITY

Select Codes from the Features menu and enter ironman.

UNLIMITED STAMINA

Select Codes from the Features menu and enter norest.

+10 DEFFENSIVE AWARENESS

Select Codes from the Features menu and enter getstops.

+10 OFFENSIVE AWARENESS

Select Codes from the Features menu and enter inthezone.

TOPPS 2K SPORTS ALL-STARS

Select Codes from the Features menu and enter topps2ksports.

ABA BALL

Select Codes from the Features menu and enter payrespect.

NBA BALLERS

VERSUS SCREEN CHEATS

You can enter the following codes at the Versus screen. The ● button corresponds to the first number in the code, the ● is the second number, and the ● button corresponds to the last number. Press the D-pad in any direction to enter the code.

EFFECT	CODE	EFFECT	CODE
Big Head	1 3 4	Super Push	3 1 5
Baby Ballers	4 2 3	Super Block Ability	1 2 4
Kid Ballers	4 3 3	Great Handles	3 3 2
Young Ballers1	4 4 3	Unlimited Juice	7 6 3
Paper Ballers	3 5 4	Super Steals	2 1 5
Alternate Gear	1 2 3	Perfect Free Throws	3 2 7
Show Shot Percentage	0 1 2	Speedy Players	2 1 3
Expanded Move Set	5 1 2	Better Free Throws	3 1 7

EFFECT	CODE
Fire Ability	7 2 2
Hotspot Ability	6 2 7
Back-In Ability	1 2 2
2x Juice Replenish	4 3 1
Stunt Ability	3 7 4
Pass 2 Friend Ability	5 3 6
Alley-Oop Ability	7 2 5
Put Back Ability	3 1 3
Legal Goal Tending	7 5 6
R2R Mode	0 0 8
Play As Coach	5 6 7

EFFECT	CODE
Play As Agent	5 5 7
Play As Secretary	5 4 7
Play As BiznezMan-A	5 3 7
Play As BiznezMan-B	5 2 7
Play As Afro Man	5 1 7
Super Back-Ins	2 3 5
Half House	3 6 7
Random Moves	3 0 0
Pygmy	4 2 5
Tournament Mode	0 1 1

PHRASE-OLOGY CODES/ALTERNATE GEAR

Select Phrase-ology from the Inside Stuff option and enter the following codes to unlock the Alternate Gear for the corresponding player.

PLAYER	PHRASE
Allan Houston	KNICKER BOCKER PLEASE
Allen Iverson	KILLER CROSSOVER
Alonzo Mourning	ZO
Amare Stoudemire	RISING SUN
Antoine Walker	BALL HAWK
Baron Davis	STYLIN' & PROFILIN'
Ben Wallace	RADIO CONTROLLED CARS
Bill Russell	CELTICS DYNASTY
Bill Walton	TOWERS OF POWER
Carmelo Anthony	NEW TO THE GAME
Chris Webber	24 SECONDS
Clyde Drexler	CLYDE THE GLIDE
Darko Milicic	NBA FASTBREAK
Darryl Dawkins	RIM WRECKER
Dejuan Wagner	NBA HANGTIME
Dikembe Mutombo	IN THE PAINT
Dominique Wilkins	DUNK FEST
Eddie Jones	BALLER UPRISING
Elton Brand	REBOUND
Emanuel Ginobili	MANU
Gary Payton	GLOVE IS IN LA
George Gervin	THE ICE MAN COMETH
Grant Hill	GONE GOLD WITH IT
Isiah Thomas	TRUE BALLER
Jalen Rose	BRING IT
Jason Kidd	PASS THE ROCK
Jason Terry	BALL ABOVE ALL
Jason Williams	GIVE AND GO
Jerry Stackhouse	STOP DROP AND ROLL
John Stockton	COURT VISION
Julius Irving	ONE ON ONE
Karl Malone	SPECIAL DELIVERY
Kenyon Martin	TO THE HOLE
Kevin Garnett	BOSS HOSS
Kevin McHale	HOLLA BACK
Kobe Bryant	JAPANESE STEAK

PLAYER	PHRASE
Larry Bird	HOOSIER
Latrell Sprewell	SPREE
Lebron James	KING JAMES
Magic Johnson	LAKER LEGENDS
Michael Finley	STUDENT OF THE GAME
Mike Bibby	DREAMS & SCHEMES
Moses Malone	LOST FREESTYLE FILES
Nate "Tiny" Archibald	NATE THE SKATE
Nene Hilario	RAGS TO RICHES
Oscar Robertson	AINT NO THING
Pau Gasol	POW POW POW
Paul Pierce	CELTICS SUPREME
Pete Maravich	PISTOL PETE
Rashard Lewis	FAST FORWARD
Rasheed Wallace	BRING DOWN THE HOUSE
Ray Allen	ALL STAR
Reggie Miller	FROM DOWNTOWN
Richard Hamilton	RIP
Robert Parish	THE CHIEF
Scottie Pippen	PLAYMAKER
Shaquille O'Neal	DIESEL RULES THE PAINT
Shawn Marion	MAKE YOUR MARK
Stephon Marbury	PLATINUM PLAYA
Steve Francis	ANKLE BREAKER
Steve Francis	RISING STAR
Steve Nash	HAIR CANADA
Tim Duncan	MAKE IT TAKE IT
Tony Parker	RUN AND SHOOT
Tracy McGrady	LIVING LIKE A BALLER
Vince Carter	CHECK MY CRIB
Wally Szczerbiak	WORLD
Walt Frazier	PENETRATE AND PERPETRATE
Wes Unseld	OLD SCHOOL
Willis Reed	HALL OF FAME
Wilt Chamberlain	WILT THE STILT
Yao Ming	CENTER OF ATTENTION

CRIBS

Select Phrase-ology from the Inside Stuff option and enter the following to unlock player cribs.

CRIB	PHRASE
Allen Iverson's Recording Studio	THE ANSWER
Karl Malone's Devonshire Estate	ICE HOUSE
Kobe Bryant's Italian Estate	EURO CRIB
Scottie Pippen's Yacht	NICE YACHT
Yao Ming's Childhood Grade School	PREP SCHOOL

OTHER PHRASE-OLOGY CODES

Select Phrase-ology from the Inside Stuff option and enter the following to unlock that bonus.

BONUS	PHRASE
All Players, Alternate Gear, and Cinemas	NBA BALLERS TRUE PLAYA
Special Movie #1	JUICE HOUSE
Special Movie #2	NBA SHOWTIME
Special Movie #3	NBA BALLERS RULES
Special Movie #4	HATCHET MAN
Special Movie #5	SLAM IT
Special Shoe #2	COLD STREAK
Special Shoe #3	LOST YA SHOES

NBA BALLERS: PHENOM

VERSUS SCREEN CHEATS

You can enter the following codes at the Vs screen. The ● button corresponds to the first number in the code, the ● is the second number, and the ● button corresponds to the last number. Press the D-pad in any direction to enter the code.

EFFECT	CODE	EFFECT	CODE
Tournament Mode	0 1 1	Unlimited Juice	7 6 3
Big Head	1 3 4	House Meter Half-Full at Start	3 6 7
Baby Ballers	4 2 3	Super Block Ability	1-2-4
Kid Ballers	4 3 3	Show Shot Percentage	0 1 2
2D Ballers	3 5 4	Alternate Gear	1 2 3
Speedy Players	2 1 3		

NBA LIVE 06

EASTERN ALL-STARS 2005-06 AWAY JERSEYS

Select NBA Codes from My NBA Live and enter XCVB5387EQ.

EASTERN ALL-STARS 2005-06 HOME JERSEY

Select NBA Codes from My NBA Live and enter 234SDFGHMO.

WESTERN ALL-STARS 2005-06 AWAY JERSEY

Select NBA Codes from My NBA Live and enter 39N56B679J.

WESTERN ALL-STARS 2005-06 HOME JERSEY

Select NBA Codes from My NBA Live and enter 2J9UWABNP1.

BOSTON CELTICS 2005-06 ALTERNATE JERSEY

Select NBA Codes from My NBA Live and enter 193KSHU88J.

CLEVELAND CAVALIERS 2005-06 ALTERNATE JERSEY

Select NBA Codes from My NBA Live and enter 9922NVDKVT.

DENVER NUGGETS 2005-06 ALTERNATE JERSEYS

Select NBA Codes from My NBA Live and enter XWETJK72FC.

DETROIT PISTONS 2005-06 ALTERNATE JERSEY

Select NBA Codes from My NBA Live and enter JANTWIKBS6.

INDIANA PACERS 2005-06 ALTERNATE AWAY JERSEY

Select NBA Codes from My NBA Live and enter **PSDF90PPJN**.

INDIANA PACERS 2005-06 ALTERNATE HOME JERSEY

Select NBA Codes from My NBA Live and enter **SDF786WSHW**.

SACRAMENTO KINGS 2005-06 ALTERNATE JERSEY

Select NBA Codes from My NBA Live and enter **654NNBFDWA**.

A3 GARNETT 3

Select NBA Codes from My NBA Live and enter **DRI239CZ49**.

JORDAN MELO V.5 WHITE & BLUE

Select NBA Codes from My NBA Live and enter **5223WERPII**.

JORDAN MELO V.5 WHITE & YELLOW

Select NBA Codes from My NBA Live and enter **ZXDR7362Q1**.

JORDAN XIV BLACK & RED

Select NBA Codes from My NBA Live and enter **144FVNHM35**.

JORDAN XIV WHITE & GREEN

Select NBA Codes from My NBA Live and enter **67YFH9839F**.

JORDAN XIV WHITE & RED

Select NBA Codes from My NBA Live and enter **743HFDRAU8**.

S. CARTER III LE

Select NBA Codes from My NBA Live and enter **JZ3SCARTVY**.

T-MAC 5 BLACK

Select NBA Codes from My NBA Live and enter **258SHQW95B**.

T-MAC 5 WHITE

Select NBA Codes from My NBA Live and enter **HGS83KP234P**.

ANSWER DMX 10

Select NBA Codes from My NBA Live and enter **RBKAIUSAB7**.

ANSWER IX AND THE RBK ANSWER IX VIDEO

Select NBA Codes from My NBA Live and enter **AI9BUBBA7T**.

THE QUESTION AND THE MESSAGE FROM ALLEN IVERSON VIDEO

Select NBA Codes from My NBA Live and enter **HOYAS3AI6L**.

NBA LIVE 07

ADIDAS ARTILLERY II BLACK AND THE RBK ANSWER 9 VIDEO

Select NBA Codes from My NBA Live and enter **99B6356HAN**.

ADIDAS ARTILLERY II

Select NBA Codes and enter NTGNFUE87H.

ADIDAS BTB LOW AND THE MESSAGE FROM ALLEN IVERSON VIDEO

Select NBA Codes and enter 7FB3KS9JQ0.

ADIDAS C-BILLUPS

Select NBA Codes and enter BV6877HB9N.

ADIDAS C-BILLUPS BLACK

Select NBA Codes and enter 85NVLDMWS5.

ADIDAS CAMPUS LT

Select NBA Codes and enter CLT2983NC8.

ADIDAS CRAZY 8

Select NBA Codes and enter CC98KKL814.

ADIDAS EQUIPMENT BBALL

Select NBA Codes and enter 220IUJKMDR.

ADIDAS GARNETT BOUNCE

Select NBA Codes and enter HYIOUHCAAN.

ADIDAS GARNETT BOUNCE BLACK

Select NBA Codes and enter KDZ2MQL17W.

ADIDAS GIL-ZERO

Select NBA Codes and enter 23DN1PPOG4.

ADIDAS GIL-ZERO BLACK

Select NBA Codes and enter QQQ3JCUYQ7.

ADIDAS GIL-ZERO MID

Select NBA Codes and enter 1GSJC8JWRL.

ADIDAS GIL-ZERO MID BLACK

Select NBA Codes and enter 369V6RVU3G.

ADIDAS STEALTH

Select NBA Codes and enter FE454DFJCC.

ADIDAS T-MAC 6

Select NBA Codes and enter MCJK843NNC.

ADIDAS T-MAC 6 WHITE

Select NBA Codes and enter 84GF7EJG8V.

CHARLOTTE BOBCATS 2006-07 ALTERNATE JERSEY

Select NBA Codes and enter WEDX671H7S.

NCAA FOOTBALL 06

IMPACT PLAYERS IN THE ZONE IN PRACTICE

Create a Profile with the name **ZoneOut**.

PENNANT	CODE
Sic Em	#16 Baylor
Oskee Wow	#63 Illinois
Fight	#160 Texas Tech
Thanks	#200 First and Fifteen
For	#201 Blink
Registering	#202 Boing
With EA	#204 Butter Fingers
Tiburon	#205 Crossed The Line
EA Sports	#206 Cuffed
Touchdown	#207 Extra Credit
In The Zone	#208 Helium
Turnover	#209 Hurricane
Impact	#210 Instant Freplay
Heisman	#211 Jumbalaya
Game Time	#212 Molasses
Break Free	#213 Nike Free
Hand Picked	#214 Nike Magnigrip
No Sweat	#215 Nike Pro
Light Speed	#216 Nike Speed TD
Elite 11	#219 QB Dud
NCAA	#222 Stiffed
Football	#224 Take Your Time
06	#225 Thread & Needle
Offense	#226 Tough As Nails
Defense	#227 Trip
Blitz	#228 What a Hit!
Sideline	#229 Kicker Hex
Fumble	#273 2004 All-Americans
Roll Tide	#274 All-Alabama
Woopigsooie	#276 All-Arkansas
War Eagle	#277 All-Auburn
Death Valley	#278 All-Clemson
Glory	#279 All-Colorado
Great To Be	#280 All-Florida
Uprising	#281 All-FSU
Hunker Down	#282 All-Georgia
On Iowa	#283 All-Iowa
Victory	#284 All-Kansas State

PENNANT CODES

Select Pennant Collection from My NCAA. Press Select and enter the following codes:

PENNANT	CODE
Geaux Tigers	#285 All-LSU
Raising Cane	#286 All-Miami
Go Blue	#287 All-Michigan
Hail State	#288 All-Mississippi State
Go Big Red	#289 All-Nebraska
Rah Rah	#290 All-North Carolina
Golden Domer	#291 All-Notre Dame
Killer Nuts	#292 All-Ohio State
Boomer	#293 All-Oklahoma
Go Pokes	#294 All-Oklahoma State
Quack Attack	#295 All-Oregoen
We Are	#296 All-Penn State
Lets Go Pitt	#297 All-Pittsburgh
Boiler Up	#298 All-Purdue
Orange Crush	#299 All-Syracuse
Big Orange	#300 All-Tennessee
Hook Em	#301 All-Texas
Gig Em	#302 All-Texas A&M
Mighty	#303 All-UCLA
Fight On	#304 All-USC
Wahoos	#305 All-Virginia
Tech Triumph	#306 All-Virginia Tech
Bow Down	#307 All-Washington
U Rah Rah	#308 All-Wisconsin
Bear Down	#311 Ark Mascot
Red And Gold	#333 ISU Mascot
Rock Chalk	#335 KU Mascot
Go Green	#346 Michigan State Mascot
Rah Rah Rah	#341 Minn Mascot
Hotty Totty	#342 Miss Mascot
Mizzou Rah	#344 Mizzou Mascot
Go Pack	#349 NCSU Mascot
Go Cats	#352 NU Mascot
On On UK	#371 UK Mascot
Go Deacs Go	#382 Wake Mascot
All Hail	#385 WSU Mascot
Hail WV	#386 WVU Mascot

NCAA FOOTBALL 07

#16 BAYLOR
Select Pennant Collection from My NCAA. Press Select and enter Sic Em.

#16 NIKE SPEED TD
Select Pennant Collection from My NCAA. Press Select and enter Light Speed.

#63 ILLINOIS
Select Pennant Collection from My NCAA. Press Select and enter Oskee Wow.

#160 TEXAS TECH
Select Pennant Collection from My NCAA. Press Select and enter Fight.

#200 FIRST AND FIFTEEN
Select Pennant Collection from My NCAA. Press Select and enter Thanks.

#201 BLINK
Select Pennant Collection from My NCAA. Press Select and enter For.

#202 BOING
Select Pennant Collection from My NCAA. Press Select and enter Registering.

#204 BUTTER FINGERS
Select Pennant Collection from My NCAA. Press Select and enter With EA.

#205 CROSSED THE LINE
Select Pennant Collection from My NCAA. Press Select and enter Tiburon.

#206 CUFFED
Select Pennant Collection from My NCAA. Press Select and enter EA Sports.

#207 EXTRA CREDIT
Select Pennant Collection from My NCAA. Press Select and enter Touchdown.

#208 HELIUM
Select Pennant Collection from My NCAA. Press Select and enter In The Zone.

#209 HURRICANE
Select Pennant Collection from My NCAA. Press Select and enter Turnover.

#210 INSTANT FREPLAY
Select Pennant Collection from My NCAA. Press Select and enter Impact.

#211 JUMBALAYA
Select Pennant Collection from My NCAA. Press Select and enter Heisman.

#212 MOLASSES
Select Pennant Collection from My NCAA. Press Select and enter Game Time.

#213 NIKE FREE
Select Pennant Collection from My NCAA. Press Select and enter Break Free.

#214 NIKE MAGNIGRIP
Select Pennant Collection from My NCAA. Press Select and enter Hand Picked.

#215 NIKE PRO
Select Pennant Collection from My NCAA. Press Select and enter No Sweat.

#219 QB DUD
Select Pennant Collection from My NCAA. Press Select and enter Elite 11.

#221 STEEL TOE
Select Pennant Collection from My NCAA. Press Select and enter Gridiron.

#222 STIFFED
Select Pennant Collection from My NCAA. Press Select and enter NCAA.

#223 SUPER DIVE
Select Pennant Collection from My NCAA. Press Select and enter Upset.

#224 TAKE YOUR TIME
Select Pennant Collection from My NCAA. Press Select and enter Football.

#225 THREAD & NEEDLE
Select Pennant Collection from My NCAA. Press Select and enter 06.

#226 TOUGH AS NAILS
Select Pennant Collection from My NCAA. Press Select and enter Offense.

#227 TRIP
Select Pennant Collection from My NCAA. Press Select and enter Defense.

#228 WHAT A HIT
Select Pennant Collection from My NCAA. Press Select and enter Blitz.

#229 KICKER HEX
Select Pennant Collection from My NCAA. Press Select and enter Sideline.

#273 2004 ALL-AMERICANS
Select Pennant Collection from My NCAA. Press Select and enter Fumble.

#274 ALL-ALABAMA
Select Pennant Collection from My NCAA. Press Select and enter Roll Tide.

#276 ALL-ARKANSAS
Select Pennant Collection from My NCAA. Press Select and enter Woopigsooie.

#277 ALL-AUBURN
Select Pennant Collection from My NCAA. Press Select and enter War Eagle.

#278 ALL-CLEMSON
Select Pennant Collection from My NCAA. Press Select and enter Death Valley.

#279 ALL-COLORADO
Select Pennant Collection from My NCAA. Press Select and enter Glory.

#280 ALL-FLORIDA
Select Pennant Collection from My NCAA. Press Select and enter Great To Be.

#281 ALL-FSU
Select Pennant Collection from My NCAA. Press Select and enter Uprising.

#282 ALL-GEORGIA
Select Pennant Collection from My NCAA. Press Select and enter Hunker Down.

#283 ALL-IOWA
Select Pennant Collection from My NCAA. Press Select and enter On Iowa.

#284 ALL-KANSAS STATE
Select Pennant Collection from My NCAA. Press Select and enter Victory.

#285 ALL-LSU
Select Pennant Collection from My NCAA. Press Select and enter Geaux Tigers.

#286 ALL-MIAMI
Select Pennant Collection from My NCAA. Press Select and enter Raising Cane.

#287 ALL-MICHIGAN
Select Pennant Collection from My NCAA. Press Select and enter Go Blue.

#288 ALL-MISSISSIPPI STATE
Select Pennant Collection from My NCAA. Press Select and enter Hail State.

#289 ALL-NEBRASKA
Select Pennant Collection from My NCAA. Press Select and enter Go Big Red.

#290 ALL-NORTH CAROLINA
Select Pennant Collection from My NCAA. Press Select and enter Rah Rah.

#291 ALL-NOTRE DAME
Select Pennant Collection from My NCAA. Press Select and enter Golden Domer.

#292 ALL-OHIO STATE
Select Pennant Collection from My NCAA. Press Select and enter Killer Nuts.

#293 ALL-OKLAHOMA
Select Pennant Collection from My NCAA. Press Select and enter Boomer.

#294 ALL-OKLAHOMA STATE
Select Pennant Collection from My NCAA. Press Select and enter Go Pokes.

#295 ALL-OREGON
Select Pennant Collection from My NCAA. Press Select and enter Quack Attack.

#296 ALL-PENN STATE
Select Pennant Collection from My NCAA. Press Select and enter We Are.

#297 ALL-PITTSBURGH
Select Pennant Collection from My NCAA. Press Select and enter Lets Go Pitt.

#298 ALL-PURDUE
Select Pennant Collection from My NCAA. Press Select and enter Boiler Up.

#299 ALL-SYRACUSE
Select Pennant Collection from My NCAA. Press Select and enter Orange Crush.

#300 ALL-TENNESSEE
Select Pennant Collection from My NCAA. Press Select and enter Big Orange.

#301 ALL-TEXAS
Select Pennant Collection from My NCAA. Press Select and enter Hook Em.

#302 ALL-TEXAS A&M
Select Pennant Collection from My NCAA. Press Select and enter Gig Em.

#303 ALL-UCLA
Select Pennant Collection from My NCAA. Press Select and enter MIGHTY.

#304 ALL-USC
Select Pennant Collection from My NCAA. Press Select and enter Fight On.

#305 ALL-VIRGINIA
Select Pennant Collection from My NCAA. Press Select and enter Wahoos.

#306 ALL-VIRGINIA TECH
Select Pennant Collection from My NCAA. Press Select and enter Tech Triumph.

#307 ALL-WASHINGTON
Select Pennant Collection from My NCAA. Press Select and enter Bow Down.

#308 ALL-WISCONSIN
Select Pennant Collection from My NCAA. Press Select and enter U Rah Rah.

#311 ARK MASCOT
Select Pennant Collection from My NCAA. Press Select and enter Bear Down.

#329 GT MASCOT
Select Pennant Collection from My NCAA. Press Select and enter RamblinWreck.

#333 ISU MASCOT
Select Pennant Collection from My NCAA. Press Select and enter Red And Gold.

#335 KU MASCOT
Select Pennant Collection from My NCAA. Press Select and enter Rock Chalk.

#341 MINN MASCOT
Select Pennant Collection from My NCAA. Press Select and enter Rah Rah Rah.

#344 MIZZOU MASCOT
Select Pennant Collection from My NCAA. Press Select and enter Mizzou Rah.

#346 MSU MASCOT
Select Pennant Collection from My NCAA. Press Select and enter Go Green.

#349 NCSU MASCOT
Select Pennant Collection from My NCAA. Press Select and enter Go Pack.

#352 NU MASCOT
Select Pennant Collection from My NCAA. Press Select and enter Go Cats.

#360 S CAR MASCOT
Select Pennant Collection from My NCAA. Press Select and enter Go Carolina.

#371 UK MASCOT
Select Pennant Collection from My NCAA. Press Select and enter On On UK.

#382 WAKE FOREST
Select Pennant Collection from My NCAA. Press Select and enter Go Deacs Go.

#385 WSU MASCOT
Select Pennant Collection from My NCAA. Press Select and enter All Hail.

#386 WVU MASCOT
Select Pennant Collection from My NCAA. Press Select and enter Hail WV.

NCAA MARCH MADNESS 06

ALL TEAMS
Select My NCAA, then Cheat Codes from the lounge. Enter **PSDF9078VT**.

AIR JORDAN III SHOES
Select My NCAA, then Cheat Codes from the lounge. Enter **39N56BXC4S**.

FIRST AIR JORDANS
Select My NCAA, then Cheat Codes from the lounge. Enter **2J9UWAS44L**.

NEED FOR SPEED CARBON

CASTROL CASH
At the main menu, press Down, Up, Left, Down, Right, Up, ●, ▲. This gives you 10,000 extra cash.

INFINITE CREW CHARGE
At the main menu, press Down, Up, Up, Right, Left, Left, Right, ●.

INFINITE NITROUS
At the main menu, press Left, Up, Left, Down, Left, Down, Right, ●.

INFINITE SPEEDBREAKER
At the main menu, press Down, Right, Right, Left, Right, Up, Down, ●.

NEED FOR SPEED CARBON LOGO VINYLS
At the main menu, press Right, Up, Down, Up, Down, Left, Right, ●.

NEED FOR SPEED CARBON SPECIAL LOGO VINYLS
At the main menu, press Up, Up, Down, Down, Down, Down, Up, ●.

NEED FOR SPEED MOST WANTED

BURGER KING CHALLENGE
At the Title screen, press Up, Down, Up, Down, Left, Right, Left, Right.

CASTROL SYNTEC VERSION OF THE FORD GT
At the Title screen, press Left, Right, Left, Right, Up, Down, Up, Down.

MARKER IN BACKROOM OF THE ONE-STOP SHOP
At the Title screen, press Up, Up, Down, Down, Left, Right, Up, Down.

NFL STREET 2

FUMBLE MODE
Enter **GreasedPig** as a code.

MAX CATCH
Enter **MagnetHands** as a code.

NO CHAINS MODE
Enter **NoChains** as a code.

NO FUMBLE MODE
Enter **GlueHands** as a code.

UNLIMITED TURBO
Enter **NozBoost** as a code.

EA FIELD
Enter **EAField** as a code.

AFC EAST ALL STARS
Enter **EAASFSCT** as a code.

AFC NORTH ALL STARS
Enter **NAOFRCTH** as a code.

AFC SOUTH ALL STARS
Enter **SAOFUCTH** as a code.

AFC WEST ALL STARS
Enter **WAEFSCT** as a code.

NFC EAST ALL STARS
Enter **NNOFRCTH** as a code.

NFC NORTH ALL STARS
Enter **NNAS66784** as a code.

NFC SOUTH ALL STARS
Enter **SNOFUCTH** as a code.

NFC WEST ALL STARS
Enter **ENASFSCT** as a code.

TEAM REEBOK
Enter **Reebok** as a code.

TEAM XZIBIT
Enter **TeamXzibit** as a code.

NHL 2K6

UNLOCK EVERYTHING
Select Manage Profiles from the Options screen. Create a New Profile with the name **Turco813**.

ONE PIECE: GRAND BATTLE

CHOPPER'S 3RD COSTUME
At the title screen, hold **L1** or **L2** and press Left, Right
❌, ⬤, ❌, 🔺.

LUFFY'S 3RD COSTUME
At the title screen, hold **L1** or **L2** and press Up, Up, ❌,
⬤, ❌, ❌.

ROBIN'S 3RD COSTUME
At the title screen, hold **L1** or **L2** and press Down, Right,
❌, ⬤, ❌, ❌.

SANJI'S 3RD COSTUME
At the title screen, hold **L1** or **L2** and press Up, Down,
❌, ⬤, ❌, ⬤.

🔵 NAMI'S 3RD COSTUME
At the title screen, hold **L1** or **L2** and press Left, Left,
❌, ⬤, ❌.

USOPP'S 3RD COSTUME
At the title screen, hold **L1** or **L2** and press Right, Right,
❌, ⬤, ❌, 🔺.

ZORO'S 3RD COSTUME
At the title screen, hold **L1** or **L2** and press Down, Down,
❌, ⬤, ❌, 🔺.

OUTRUN 2006: COAST 2 COAST

100% COMPLETE/UNLOCK EVERYTHING
Edit your license and change the name to
ENTIRETY. Select Done, then back out of all menus.

1000000 OUTRUN MILES
Edit your license and change the name to
MILESANDMILES. Select Done, then back out of all menus.

OVER THE HEDGE

COMPLETE LEVELS
Pause the game, hold **L1 + R1** and press 🔺, ⬤, 🔺,
⬤, ⬤, ⬤.

ALL MINIGAMES
Pause the game, hold **L1 + R1** and press 🔺, ⬤, 🔺,
🔺, ⬤, ⬤.

ALL MOVES
Pause the game, hold **L1** + **R1** and press ▲, ●, ▲, ■, ■, ●.

EXTRA DAMAGE
Pause the game, hold **L1** + **R1** and press ▲, ●, ▲, ●, ▲, ■.

MORE HP FROM FOOD
Pause the game, hold **L1** + **R1** and press ▲, ●, ▲, ●, ■, ▲.

ALWAYS POWER PROJECTILE
Pause the game, hold **L1** + **R1** and press ▲, ●, ▲, ●, ■, ●.

BONUS COMIC 14
Pause the game, hold **L1** + **R1** and press ▲, ●, ■, ■, ●, ▲.

BONUS COMIC 15
Pause the game, hold **L1** + **R1** and press ▲, ▲, ■, ●, ■, ●.

PAC-MAN WORLD 3

ALL LEVELS AND MAZE GAMES
At the main menu, press Left, Right, Left, Right, ●, Up.

SUPER PUNCH
During gameplay, press ✕, L1, R1, ●, ●, R2.

PETER JACKSON'S KING KONG: THE OFFICIAL GAME OF THE MOVIE

At the Main menu, hold **L1** + **R1** and press Down, ●, Up, ■, Down, Down, Up, Up. Release **L1** + **R1** to get the Cheat option on the menu. The Cheat option will also be available from the pause menu.

GOD MODE
Select Cheat and enter **8wonder**.

ALL CHAPTERS
Select Cheat and enter **KKst0ry**.

INFINITE SPEARS
Select Cheat and enter **lance 1nf**.

ONE-HIT KILLS
Select Cheat and enter **GrosBras**.

AMMO 999
Select Cheat and enter **KK 999 mun**.

MACHINE GUN
Select Cheat and enter **KKcapone**.

REVOLVER
Select Cheat and enter **KKtigun**.

SNIPER RIFLE
Select Cheat and enter **KKsn1per**.

EXTRAS
Select Cheat and enter **KKmuseum**.

PSYCHONAUTS

INVINCIBILITY
Hold **L1** and **R1** and press ◉, **R2**, ◉, ◉, ◉, **L2**.

ALL POWERS
Hold **L1** and **R1** and press ◉, ◉, ◉, **R2**, **L3**, ◉.

9999 LIVES
Hold **L1** and **R1** and press **L3**, **R2**, **R2**, ◉, ⊗, **R3**.

9999 AMMO
Hold **L1** and **R1** and press **R3**, ⊗, **L3**, **L3**, ◉, ◉.

GLOBAL ITEMS
Hold **L1** and **R1** and press **R3**, ◉, **R2**, **R2**, **L3**, ◉.

ALL POWERS UPGRADED
Hold **L1** and **R1** and press **L3**, **R3**, **L3**, **R2**, ◉, **R2**.

10K ARROWHEADS
Hold **L1** and **R1** and press ⊗, **R3**, **R3**, **R2**, ◉, ◉.

CHANGE TEXT
Hold **L1** and **R1** and press **R2**, X, **L3**, **R2**, **R2**, ◉.

PUMP IT UP: EXCEED

ARROWS DISAPPEAR
At the song select, press Up/Left, Up/Right, Down/Left, Down/Right, Center.

ARROW SPEED CHANGES THROUGHOUT SONG
At the song select, press Up/Left, Up/Right, Up/Left, Up/Right, Up/Left, Up/Right, Up/Left, Up/Right, Center.

DOUBLE SPEED
At the song select, press Up/Left Up/Right Up/Left Up/Right center 2X speed. Enter this code again to get 3x speed. A third time for 4x speed. A fourth time to get 8x speed.

DEACTIVATES THESE MODIFIERS
At the song select, press Down/Left, Down/Right, Down/Left, Down/Right, Down/Left, Down/Right.

R-TYPE FINAL

INVINCIBILITY
Pause the game, press and hold **L2**, then press Right, Right, Left, Right, Left, Left, Right, Left, **L1**, Up, Up, Down, Down, Up, Down, Up, Down, **L1**. Re-enter the code to disable it.

99.9% CHARGE DOSE
Pause the game, press and hold **L2**, then press **R2**, **R2**, Left, Right, Up, Down, Right, Left, Up, Down, ◉.

FULL BLUE POWER, MISSILES, AND BITS
Pause the game, press and hold **L2**, then press **R2**, **R2**, Left, Right, Up, Down, Right, Left, Up, Down, ◉.

FULL RED POWER, MISSILES, AND BITS
Pause the game, press and hold **L2**, then press **R2**, **R2**, Left, Right, Up, Down, Right, Left, Up, Down, ◉.

FULL YELLOW POWER, MISSILES, AND BITS
Pause the game, press and hold **L2**, then press **R2**, **R2**, Left, Right, Up, Down, Right, Left, Up, Down, ⊗.

LADY LOVE SHIP (#3)
At the R Museum, enter **5270 0725** as a password.

STRIDER SHIP (#24)
At the R Museum, enter **2078 0278** as a password.

MR. HELI SHIP (#59)
At the R Museum, enter **1026 2001** as a password.

CURTAIN CALL SHIP (#100)
At the R Museum, enter **1009 9201** as a password.

RAMPAGE: TOTAL DESTRUCTION

ALL MONSTERS
At the Main menu, press **R2** + **L2** to access the Cheat menu and enter **141421**.

INVULNERABLE TO ATTACKS
At the Main menu, press **R2** + **L2** to access the Cheat menu and enter **986960**.

ALL SPECIAL ABILITIES
At the Main menu, press **R2** + **L2** to access the Cheat menu and enter **011235**.

ALL LEVELS
At the Main menu, press **R2** + **L2** to access the Cheat menu and enter **271828**.

CPU VS CPU DEMO

At the Main menu, press **R2** + **L2** to access the cheat menu and enter **082864**.

FAST CPU VS CPU DEMO

At the Main menu, press **R2** + **L2** to access the Cheat menu and enter **874098**.

ONE-HIT DESTROYS BUILDINGS

At the Main menu, press **R2** + **L2** to access the Cheat menu and enter **071767**.

OPENING MOVIE

At the Main menu, press **R2** + **L2** to access the Cheat menu and enter **667300**.

ENDING MOVIE

At the Main menu, press **R2** + **L2** to access the Cheat menu and enter **667301**.

CREDITS

At the Main menu, press **R2** + **L2** to access the Cheat menu and enter **667302**.

VERSION INFORMATION

At the Main menu, press **R2** + **L2** to access the Cheat menu and enter **314159**.

CLEAR CHEATS

At the Main menu, press **R2** + **L2** to access the Cheat menu and enter **000000**.

RATCHET AND CLANK: UP YOUR ARSENAL

DUEL BLADE LASER SWORD

Pause the game and press ●, ●, ●, ●, Up, Down, Left, Left.

QWARK'S ALTERNATE COSTUME

Start a game of Qwark Vid-Comic and press Up, Up, Down, Down, Left, Right, ●, ●, ●.

PIRATE VS NINJA MINI GAME

At the Qwark Comics Issue select, press ● to bring up a password screen. Enter **_MEGHAN_** as a password.

4-PLAYER BOMB MINIGAME

At the Qwark Comics Issue select, press ● to bring up a password screen. Enter **YING_TZU** as a password. Press Start, Select to return to Starship Phoenix.

SLY 2: BAND OF THIEVES DEMO

At the Title screen, hold **L1** + **L2** + **R1** + **R2**.

ROBOTS

BIG HEAD
Pause the game and press Up, Down, Down, Up, Right, Right, Left, Right.

UNLIMITED HEALTH
Pause the game and press Up, Right, Down, Up, Left, Down, Right, Left.

UNLIMITED SCRAP
Pause the game and press Down, Down, Left, Up, Up, Right, Up, Down.

ROGUE TROOPER

INFINITE HEALTH
At the Extra menu, press Left, Right, Up, Down, **L3**, ●.

INFINITE SUPPLIES
At the Extra menu, press Select, **R1**, **L1**, Select, **R3**, **L1**.

LOW GRAVITY RAGDOLL
At the Extra menu, press ●, ●, ●, ●, Up, Down.

EXTREME RAGDOLL
At the Extra menu, press Up, Up, Up, **R2**, **R2**, Up.

HIPPY BLOOD
At the Extra menu, press **L2**, Right, ●, Down, **R1**, Select.

SAMURAI JACK: THE SHADOW OF AKU

MAXIMUM HEALTH
During a game, hold Left on the Left Analog Stick + Right on the Right Analog Stick, and press ✖, ●, ▲, ●.

MAXIMUM ZEN
During a game, hold Left on the Left Analog Stick + Right on the Right Analog Stick, and press ●, ✖, ●, ▲.

CRYSTAL SWORD
During a game, press Left on the Left Analog Stick Down + Up on the Right Analog Stick, then press ✖, ●, ●, ▲.

FIRE SWORD
During a game, press Down on the Left Analog Stick + Up on the Right Analog Stick, then press ●, ✖, ●, ▲.

LIGHTNING SWORD
During a game, press Down on the Left Analog Stick + Up on the Right Analog Stick, then press ●, ✖, ▲, ●.

SATURDAY NIGHT SPEEDWAY

UNLOCK EVERYTHING
Start a new career, and enter mudeater as your name.

SCALER

FULL HEALTH
Pause the game, select audio from the options and press **R1**, **L1**, **R1**, **L1**, ●, ●, ●, ●, **R1**, ●.

200,000 KLOKKIES
Pause the game, select audio from the options and press **L1**, **L1**, **R1**, **R1**, ●, ●, ●.

INFINITE ELECTRIC BOMBS
Pause the game, select audio from the options and press **R1**, **R1**, **L1**, **L1**, ●, ●, ●.

SD GUNDAM FORCE: SHOWDOWN!

BAKUNETSUMARU
At Kao Lyn's Laboratory, enter ▲, ●, ✕, ▲, ●, ✕, ▲, ●, ✕, ▲, ●, ●.

CAPTAIN GUNDAM
At Kao Lyn's Laboratory, enter ●, ■, ▲, ✕, ✕, ▲, ■, ●, ▲, ●, ■, ✕.

ZERO THE WINGED KNIGHT
At Kao Lyn's Laboratory, enter ▲, ▲, ●, ●, ✕, ■, ✕, ■, ●, ✕, ▲, ■.

SECRET WEAPONS OVER NORMANDY

ALL PLANES, ENVIRONMENTS, AND MISSIONS
At the Main menu, press ■(x3), ●(x3), ▲, ■, then enter **R2, R2, L2, L2**.

ALL ENVIRONMENTS IN INSTANT ACTION
At the Main menu, press Up, Down, Left, Right, **L1, R1, L1, R1**.

INVINCIBILITY
At the Main menu, press Up, Down, Left, Right, Left, Left, Right, Right, **L1, L1, R1, R1, L2, R2**.

UNLIMITED AMMUNITION
At the Main menu, press Up, Right, Down, Left, Up, Right, Down, Left, **L1, R1**.

BIG HEADS
At the Main menu, press Right, Up, Left, Down, Right, Up, Left, Down, Right, **L1, R1, L1, R1**.

SHAMAN KING: POWER OF SPIRIT

VERSUS MODE
Complete all 20 episodes in story mode.

MASKED MERIL IN VERSUS MODE
Press select on Meril.

MATILDA IN VERSUS MODE
Press select on Kanna.

MARION FAUNA IN VERSUS MODE
Press select on Matilda.

ZEKE ASAKURA IN VERSUS MODE
Press select on Yoh Asakura.

SHARK TALE

REPLACE PEARLS WITH FISH KING COINS
During a level with Pearls, press Select, then hold **L1** and press ●, ✕, ●(x3), ✕, ●, ●. Release **L1** to enable the cheat.

ATTACK
During a game, press Select, then hold **L1** and press ●(x4), ✕, ●x4). Release **L1** to enable the cheat.

CLAMS AND FAME
During a game, press Select, then hold **L1** and press ●, ●, ✕, ●, ✕, ●, ✕, ●, ●. Release **L1** to enable the cheat.

SHREK 2

BONUS GAMES

Pause the game and select Scrapbook. Press Left, Up, ✖, ◉, Left, Up, ✖, ◉, Left, Up, ✖, ◉, ◉, ◉, ◉, ◉, ◉. Exit the level and select Bonus to access the games.

CHAPTER SELECT

Pause the game and select Scrapbook. Press Left, Up, ✖, ◉, Left, Up, ✖, ◉, Left, Up, ✖, ◉, Up, Up, Up, Up, Up. Exit the level and select Chapter Select to change chapters.

FULL HEALTH

Pause the game and select Scrapbook. Press Left, Up, ✖, ◉, Left, Up, ✖, ◉, Left, Up, ✖, ◉, Up, Right, Down, Left, Up.

1,000 COINS

Pause the game and select Scrapbook. Press Left, Up, ✖, ◉, Left, Up, ✖, ◉, Left, Up, ✖, ◉ (x6).

SHREK SUPERSLAM

ALL CHARACTERS AND LEVELS

At the Title screen, press **L1**, **R1**, ◉, ◉.

ALL CHALLENGES

At the Title screen, press ▲, ▲, ▲, ◉, ◉, ◉, ▲, ◉, ◉, ◉, ◉, ◉, Up, Down, Left, Right, **L1**, **R1**.

ALL STORY MODE CHAPTERS

At the Title screen, press ▲, ◉, **R1**, ◉.

ALL MEDALS & TROPHIES

At the Title screen, press **R1**, **L1**, ▲, ◉.

SUPER SPEED MODIFIER

At the Title screen, press **L1**, **L1**, **R1**, **R1**, **L1**, **R1**, **L1**, **R1**, ◉, ◉, ▲, ▲.

PIZZA ONE

At the Title screen, press Up, Up, ▲, ▲, Right, Right, ◉, ◉, Down, Down, **L1**, **R1**, Left, Left, ◉, ◉, **L1**, **R1**.

PIZZA TWO

At the Title screen, press ◉, ◉, ◉, ◉, Right, Right, Left, Left, **L1**, **L1**.

PIZZA THREE

At the Title screen, press Down, Down, Right, ◉, Up, ▲, Left, ◉, **L1**, **L1**.

SLAMMAGEDDON

At the Title screen, press Up, Up, Down, Down, Left, Right, Left, Right, ▲, ◉, ◉, **L1**, **R1**.

THE SIMS 2: PETS

CHEAT GNOME

At the EA logo screen, press **L1**, **L1**, **R1**, ✖, ✖, Up.

GIVE SIM PET POINTS

After activating the Cheat Gnome, press ▲, ◉, ✖, ◉, **L1**, **R1**.

CAT AND DOG CODES

Select New Key from Game Options and enter the following codes for the corresponding cat or dog.

PET	CODE	PET	CODE
Bandit Mask Cats	EEGJ2YRQZZAIZ9QHA64	Blue Camouflage Dogs	EEGJ2YRZZZ1RQ9QHA64
Bandit Mask Dogs	EEGJ2YRQZQARQ9QHA64	Blue Cats	EEGJ2YRQZZAIQ9QHA64
Black Dot Cats	EEGJ2YRQZQ1IQ9QHA64	Blue Dogs	EEGJ2YRQQQ1IZ9QHA64
Black Dot Dogs	EEGJ2YRQZZ1IQ9QHA64	Blue Star Cats	EEGJ2YRQQZ1IZ9QHA64
Black Smiley Cats	EEGJ2YRQQZ1RQ9QHA64	Blue Star Dogs	EEGJ2YRQZQ1IQ9QHA64
Black Smiley Dogs	EEGJ2YRQQQARQ9QHA64	Deep Red Cats	EEGJ2YRQQQAIQ9QHA64
Blue Bones Cats	EEGJ2YRQZZARQ9QHA64	Deep Red Dogs	EEGJ2YRQZQ1RQ9QHA64
Blue Bones Dogs	EEGJ2YRZZZ1IZ9QHA64	Goofy Cats	EEGJ2YRQZQ1IZ9QHA64
Blue Camouflage Cats	EEGJ2YRZZQ1IQ9QHA64	Goofy Dogs	EEGJ2YRZZZARQ9QHA64

PET	CODE	PET	CODE
Green Cats	EEGJ2YRZQQAIZ9QHA64	Panda Cats	EEGJ2YRQZQAIZ9QHA6
Green Dogs	EEGJ2YRQZQAIQ9QHA64	Pink Cats	EEGJ2YRQZZ1IZ9QHA64
Green Flower Cats	EEGJ2YRZQZAIQ9QHA64	Pink Dogs	EEGJ2YRZQZ1RQ9QHA64
Green Flower Dogs	EEGJ2YRQZZ1RQ9QHA64	Pink Vertical Strip Cats	EEGJ2YRQQQARQ9QHA6
Light Green Cats	EEGJ2YRZZQ1RQ9QHA64	Pink Vertical Strip Dogs	EEGJ2YRZZZAIQ9QHA64
Light Green Dogs	EEGJ2YRZQQ1RQ9QHA64	Purple Cats	EEGJ2YRQQZARQ9QHA64
Navy Hearts Cats	EEGJ2YRQZQ1IQ9QHA64	Purple Dogs	EEGJ2YRQQZAIZ9QHA64
Navy Hearts Dogs	EEGJ2YRQQZ1IQ9QHA64	Star Cats	EEGJ2YRQZQARQ9QHA6
Neon Green Cats	EEGJ2YRZZQAIQ9QHA64	Star Dogs	EEGJ2YRQZQZAIZ9QHA64
Neon Green Dogs	EEGJ2YRZQQAIQ9QHA64	White Paws Cats	EEGJ2YRQQQ1RQ9QHA64
Neon Yellow Cats	EEGJ2YRZZQAR09QHA64	White Paws Dogs	EEGJ2YRZQQ1IZ9QHA64
Neon Yellow Dogs	EEGJ2YRQQQAIZ9QHA64	White Zebra Stripe Cats	EEGJ2YRZZQ1IZ9QHA6
Orange Diagonal Cats	EEGJ2YRQQZAIQ9QHA64	White Zebra Stripe Dogs	EEGJ2YRZZZ1IQ9QHA64
Orange Diagonal Dogs	EEGJ2YRQZQZ1IZ9QHA64	Zebra Stripes Dogs	EEGJ2YRZZQAIZ9QHA64

SLY 3: HONOR AMONG THIEVES

TOONAMI PLANE

While flying the regular plane, pause the game and press **R1**, **R1**, Right, Down, Down, Right.

SONIC MEGA COLLECTION PLUS

Comix Zone

INVINCIBILITY

Select the jukebox from the options and play the following tracks in order: 3, 12, 17, 2, 2, 10, 2, 7, 7, 11.

STAGE SELECT

Select the jukebox from the options and play the following tracks in order: 14, 15, 18, 5, 13, 1, 3, 18, 15, 6.

Dr. Robotnik's Mean Bean Machine

EASY PASSWORDS

Continue a game with the following passwords:

LEVEL	PASSWORD	LEVEL	PASSWORD
2	Red Bean, Red Bean, Red Bean, Has Bean	8	Yellow Bean, Green Bean, Purple Bean, Has Bean
3	Clear Bean, Purple Bean, Clear Bean, Green Bean	9	Yellow Bean, Purple Bean, Has Bean, Blue Bean
4	Red Bean, Clear Bean, Has Bean, Yellow Bean	10	Red Bean, Yellow Bean, Clear Bean, Has Bean
5	Clear Bean, Blue Bean, Blue Bean, Purple Bean	11	Green Bean, Purple Bean, Blue Bean, Clear Bean
6	Clear Bean, Red Bean, Clear Bean, Purple Bean	12	Red Bean, Has Bean, Has Bean, Yellow Bean
7	Purple Bean, Yellow Bean, Red Bean, Blue bean	13	Yellow Bean, Has Bean, Blue Bean, Blue Bean

NORMAL PASSWORDS

LEVEL	PASSWORD	LEVEL	PASSWORD
2	Has Bean, Clear Bean, Yellow Bean, Yellow Bean	8	Green Bean, Has Bean, Clear Bean, Yellow Bean
3	Blue Bean, Clear Bean, Red Bean, Yellow Bean	9	Blue Bean, Purple Bean, Has Bean, Has Bean
4	Yellow Bean, Blue Bean, Clear Bean, Purple Bean	10	Has Bean, Red Bean, Yellow Bean, Clear Bean
5	Has Bean, Green Bean, Blue Bean, Yellow Bean	11	Clear Bean, Red Bean, Red Bean, Blue Bean
6	Green Bean, Purple Bean, Purple Bean, Yellow Bean	12	Green Bean, Green Bean, Clear Bean, Yellow Bean
7	Purple Bean, Blue Bean, Green Bean, Has Bean	13	Purple Bean, Yellow Bean, Has Bean, Clear Bean

HARD PASSWORDS

LEVEL	PASSWORD	LEVEL	PASSWORD
2	Green Bean, Clear Bean, Yellow Bean, Yellow Bean	8	Clear Bean, Yellow Bean, Has Bean, Yellow Bean
3	Yellow Bean, Clear Bean, Purple Bean, Clear Bean	9	Purple Bean, Blue Bean, Blue Bean, Green Bean
4	Blue Bean, Green Bean, Clear Bean, Blue Bean	10	Clear Bean, Green Bean, Red Bean, Yellow Bean
5	Red Bean, Purple Bean, Green Bean, Green Bean	11	Blue Bean, Yellow Bean, Yellow Bean, Has Bean
6	Yellow Bean, Yellow Bean, Clear Bean, Green Bean	12	Green Bean, Clear Bean, Clear Bean, Blue bean
7	Purple Bean, Clear Bean, Blue Bean, Blue Bean	13	Has Bean, Clear Bean, Purple Bean, Has Bean

HARDEST PASSWORDS

LEVEL	PASSWORD	LEVEL	PASSWORD
2	Blue Bean, Blue Bean, Green Bean, Yellow Bean	8	Clear Bean, Purple Bean, Has Bean, Yellow Bean
3	Green Bean, Yellow Bean, Green Bean, Clear Bean	9	Purple Bean, Green Bean, Has Bean, Clear Bean
4	Purple Bean, Purple Bean, Red Bean, Has Bean	10	Green Bean, Blue Bean, Yellow Bean, Has Bean
5	Green Bean, Red Bean, Purple Bean, Blue Bean	11	Green Bean, Purple Bean, Has Bean, Red Bean
6	Blue Bean, Purple Bean, Green Bean, Yellow Bean	12	Red Bean, Green Bean, Has Bean, Blue Bean
7	Blue Bean, Purple Bean, Green Bean, Has Bean	13	Red Bean, Red Bean, Clear Bean, Yellow Bean

RISTAR

LEVEL SELECT
Enter **ILOVEU** as a password.

FIGHT ONLY BOSSES
Enter **MUSEUM** as a password.

TIME ATTACK
Enter **DOFEEL** as a password.

TONE DEAF SOUNDS
Enter **MAGURO** as a password.

TRUE SIGHT
Enter **MIEMIE** as a password.

SUPER HARD
Enter **SUPER** as a password.

VERY HARD
Enter **SUPERB** as a password.

CANCEL CODES
Enter **XXXXXX** as a password.

Sonic the Hedgehog

LEVEL SELECT
At the title screen press Up, Down, Right, Left. Hold ● and press Start.

Sonic the Hedgehog 2

LEVEL SELECT
Select Sound Test from the Options. Play the following in this order: 19, 65, 09, 17. Exit the Options and immediately hold ● and press Start.

Sonic the Hedgehog 3

LEVEL SELECT
While the game is loading, press Up, Up, Down, Down, Up, Up, Up, Up. Scroll down past Competition.

Sonic Spinball

ROUND SELECT
At the Options, press ●, Down, ✖, Down, ●, Down, ●, ✖, Up, ●, ●, Up, ✖, ●, Up.
Then, at the title screen, hold ● and press Start for Round 2. Hold ✖ and press Start for Round 3. Hold ● and press Start for Round 4.

SPIDER-MAN 2

TREYARCH PASSWORD
Start a New Game and enter **HCRAYERT** as your name. You will start at 44% complete, 201,000 Hero Points, some upgrades, and more.

SPONGEBOB SQUAREPANTS: BATTLE FOR BIKINI BOTTOM

You must quickly enter the following codes.

RESTORE HEALTH
Pause the game, hold **L1** + **L2** + **R1** + **R2** and press
●, ●, ●, ●, ●, ●, ●, ●, ●, ●, ●, ●, ●.

EXPERT MODE
Pause the game, hold **L1** + **L2** + **R1** + **R2** and press
●, ●, ●, ●, ●, ●, ●, ●, ●, ●, ●, ●, ●, ●, ●, ●, ●.

EARN 1,000 SHINY OBJECTS
Pause the game, hold **L1** + **L2** + **R1** + **R2** and press
●,●,●,●,●,●,●,●.

EARN 10 GOLD SPATULAS
Pause the game, hold **L1** + **L2** + **R1** + **R2** and press
●,●,●,●,●,●,●,●.

BUBBLE BOWL POWER-UP
Pause the game, hold **L1** + **L2** + **R1** + **R2** and press
●,●,●,●,●,●,●,●. Press ● to use the
power-up.

CRUISE BUBBLE POWER-UP
Pause the game, hold **L1** + **L2** + **R1** + **R2** and press
●,●,●,●,●,●,●,●. Press **L1** to use the
power-up.

INCREASE VALUE OF SHINY OBJECTS
Pause the game, hold **L1** + **L2** + **R1** + **R2** and press
●,●,●,●,●,●,●,●,●,●,●,●,●,
●,●,●.

MODIFIED CRUISE BUBBLE CONTROLS
Pause the game, hold **L1** + **L2** + **R1** + **R2** and press
●,●,●,●,●,●,●,●,●,●.

VILLAGERS GIVE SHINY OBJECTS WHEN HIT
Pause the game, hold **L1** + **L2** + **R1** + **R2** and press
●,●,●,●,●,●,●,●,●,●,●.

VILLAGERS RESTORE HEALTH WHEN NEAR
Pause the game, hold **L1** + **L2** + **R1** + **R2** and press
●,●,●,●,●,●,●,●,●,●,●,●.

NO PANTS
Pause the game, hold **L1** + **L2** + **R1** + **R2** and press
●,●,●,●,●,●,●,●,●,●,●.

BIG PLANKTON
Pause the game, hold **L1** + **L2** + **R1** + **R2** and press
●,●,●,●,●,●,●,●,●,●,●,●.

SMALL CHARACTERS
Pause the game, hold **L1** + **L2** + **R1** + **R2** and press
●,●,●,●,●,●,●,●,●,●,●,●.

SMALL VILLAGERS
Pause the game, hold **L1** + **L2** + **R1** + **R2** and press
●,●,●,●,●,●,●,●,●,●,●.

SPONGEBOB BREAKS APART WHEN DEFEATED
Pause the game, hold **L1** + **L2** + **R1** + **R2** and press
●,●,●,●,●,●,●,●,●,●,●.

SPONGEBOB SQUAREPANTS: LIGHTS, CAMERA, PANTS!

SILVER STORY MODE
Select Rewards from the Bonuses menu. Then select
Codes and enter **486739**.

ALL ACTION FIGURES
Select Rewards from the Bonuses menu. Then select
Codes and enter **977548**.

HOOK, LINE & CHEDDAR GAME
Select Rewards from the Bonuses menu. Then select
Codes and enter **893634**.

SPONGEBOB SQUAREPANTS: THE MOVIE

SIX HEALTH SLOTS
Pause the game, hold **R1** + **L1** + **R2** + **L2** and press
●,●,●,●,●,●,●,●,●.

ALL MOVES
Pause the game, hold **R1** + **L1** + **R2** + **L2** and press
●,●,●,●,●,●,●,●.

ALL MOVES TO MACHO
Pause the game, hold **R1** + **L1** + **R2** + **L2** and press
●,●,●,●,●,●,●,●.

DOUBLE MANLINESS POINTS
Pause the game, hold **R1** + **L1** + **R2** + **L2** and press
●,●,●,●,●,●,●,●.

ALL UNKNOWN TASKS
Pause the game, hold **R1** + **L1** + **R2** + **L2** and press
●,●,●,●,●,●,●.

SPONGEBOB CAVEMAN
Pause the game, hold **R1** + **L1** + **R2** + **L2** and press
●,●,●,●,●,●,●,●.

SPONGEBOB RIPPED SHORTS
Pause the game, hold **R1** + **L1** + **R2** + **L2** and press
●,●,●,●,●,●.

PATRICK CAVEMAN
Pause the game, hold **R1** + **L1** + **R2** + **L2** and press
●,●,●,●,●,●,●.

PATRICK GOOFY GOOBER
Pause the game, hold **R1** + **L1** + **R2** + **L2** and press
●,●,●,●,●,●.

SPY HUNTER: NOWHERE TO RUN

SPY HUNTER ARCADE

This is a version of the old *Spy Hunter* arcade game, using the new 3D models, weapons, and enemies found in *Nowhere to Run*. As in the original game, you'll transform from a car to a boat and back again. You don't need to earn a certain ranking to unlock it; all you must do is activate the machine when you come across it in the safe house on Level 7 (Cleaning Up).

SPY VS SPY

ALL CLASSIC MAPS
Enter RETROSPY at the password screen.

ALL STORY MODE LEVELS
Enter ANTONIO at the password screen.

ALL LEVELS FOR SINGLE-PLAYER MODERN MODE
Enter PROHIAS at the password screen.

ALL MULTIPLAYER MAPS
Enter MADMAG at the password screen.

ALL OUTFITS
Enter DISGUISE at the password screen.

ALL WEAPONS
Enter WRKBENCH at the password screen.

INVULNERABILITY
Enter ARMOR at the password screen.

SUPER DAMAGE
Enter BIGGUNZ at the password screen.

PERMANENT FAIRY IN MODERN MODE
Enter FAIRY at the password screen.

NO DROPPED ITEMS WHEN KILLED
Enter NODROP at the password screen.

INVISIBLE HUD
Enter BLINK at the password screen.

ALL MOVIES
Enter SPYFLIX at the password screen.

CONCEPT ART
Enter SPYPICS at the password screen.

SSX ON TOUR

NEW THREADS
Select Cheats from the Extras menu and enter FLYTHREADS.

THE WORLD IS YOURS
Select Cheats from the Extras menu and enter BACKSTAGEPASS.

SHOW TIME (ALL MOVIES)
Select Cheats from the Extras menu and enter THEBIGPICTURE.

BLING BLING (INFINITE CASH)
Select Cheats from the Extras menu and enter LOOTSNOOT.

FULL BOOST, FULL TIME
Select Cheats from the Extras menu and enter ZOOMJUICE.

MONSTERS ARE LOOSE (MONSTER TRICKS)
Select Cheats from the Extras menu and enter JACKALOPESTYLE.

SNOWBALL FIGHT
Select Cheats from the Extras menu and enter LETSPARTY.

FEEL THE POWER (STAT BOOST)
Select Cheats from the Extras menu and enter POWERPLAY.

CHARACTERS ARE LOOSE
Select Cheats from the Extras menu and enter ROADIEROUNDUp.

UNLOCK CONRAD
Select Cheats from the Extras menu and enter BIGPARTYTIME.

UNLOCK MITCH KOOBSKI
Select Cheats from the Extras menu and enter MOREFUNTHANONE.

UNLOCK NIGEL
Select Cheats from the Extras menu and enter THREEISACROWD.

UNLOCK SKI PATROL
Select Cheats from the Extras menu and enter FOURSOME.

STAR WARS: BATTLEFRONT

ALL MISSIONS
Select Historical Campaign, then press ●, ●, ●, ● at the Mission Select.

SMALL PEOPLE
Create a profile named **Jub Jub**.

STAR WARS: BATTLEFRONT II

INFINITE AMMO
Pause the game, hold **L2 + R2** and press Up, Down, Left, Down, Down, Left, Down, Down, Left, Down, Down, Down, Left, Right.

INVINCIBILITY
Pause the game, hold **L2 + R2** and press Up, Up, Up, Left, Down, Down, Down, Left, Up, Up, Up, Left, Right.

NO HUD
Pause the game, hold **L2 + R2** and press Up, Up, Up, Left, Up, Up, Down, Left, Down, Up, Up, Left, Right. Re-enter the code to enable HUD again.

ALTERNATE SOLDIERS
Pause the game, hold **L2 + R2** and press Down, Down, Down, Up, Up, Left, Down, Down, Down, Down, Left, Up, Up, Up, Left.

ALTERNATE SOUNDS
Pause the game, hold **L2 + R2** and press Up, Up, Up, Left, Up, Down, Up, Up, Left, Down, Down, Down, Left, Up, Down, Down, Left, Right.

FUNNY MESSAGES WHEN REBELS DEFEATED
Pause the game, hold **L2 + R2** and press Up, Down, Left, Down, Left, Right.

STREET RACING SYNDICATE

At the Main menu, press Up, Down, Left, Right. This will bring up the code entry screen. Enter the following codes to enable these cheats:

MAZDA RX-8
Enter **RENESIS**.

TOYOTA SUPRA 3.0L RZ
Enter **SICKJZA**.

MITSUBISHI ECLIPSE GS-T
Enter **IGOTGST**.

TOYOTA CELICA GT-S
Enter **MYTCGTS**.

SUBARU IMPREZA S202 STI
Enter **SICKGDB**.

POLICE CAR
Enter **GOTPOPO**.

PAC MAN VINYL
Enter **GORETRO**.

FREE CAR REPAIR
Enter **FIXITUP**. Your first car repair is free.

GET WARNING FOR FIRST 3 BUSTS
Enter **LETMEGO**. The first three times you are pulled over, you get a warning.

SUZUKI TT SUPERBIKES

CHEAT SCREEN
At the Main menu, press R1, R2, L1, L2, R1, R2, L1, L2. Now you can enter the following:

ALL EVENTS
Enter **BORN FREE**.

RED BULL MAD SUNDAY EVENTS
Enter **SUNDAYSUNDAY**.

ALL HELMETS
Enter **SKID LIDS**.

ALL LEATHERS
Enter **COLORED HIDE**.

ALL BIKES
Enter **ROCKETS**.

ALL WHEELS
Enter **TIRE CITY**.

ALL COLLECTION BOOK
Enter **COUCH POTATO**.

TAITO LEGENDS

EXTRA GAMES
At the title screen, press L1, R1, R2, L2, Select, Start.

TAK: THE GREAT JUJU CHALLENGE

BONUS SOUND EFFECTS
In Juju's Potions, select Universal Card and enter 20, 17, 5 for Bugs, Crystals and Fruits respectively.

BONUS SOUND EFFECTS 2
In Juju's Potions, select Universal Card and enter 50, 84, 92 for Bugs, Crystals and Fruits respectively.

BONUS MUSIC TRACK 1
In Juju's Potions, select Universal Card and enter 67, 8, 20 for Bugs, Crystals and Fruits respectively.

BONUS MUSIC TRACK 2
In Juju's Potions, select Universal Card and enter 6, 18, 3 for Bugs, Crystals and Fruits respectively.

MAGIC PARTICLES
In Juju's Potions, select Universal Card and enter 24, 40, 11 for Bugs, Crystals and Fruits respectively.

MORE MAGIC PARTICLES
In Juju's Potions, select Universal Card and enter 48, 57, 57 for Bugs, Crystals and Fruits respectively.

VIEW JUJU CONCEPT ART
In Juju's Potions, select Universal Card and enter Art 33, 22, 28 for Bugs, Crystals and Fruits respectively.

VIEW VEHICLE ART
In Juju's Potions, select Universal Card and enter 11, 55, 44 for Bugs, Crystals and Fruits respectively.

VIEW WORLD ART
In Juju's Potions, select Universal Card and enter 83, 49, 34 for Bugs, Crystals and Fruits respectively.

TEENAGE MUTANT NINJA TURTLES 2: BATTLE NEXUS

Select Password from the Options menu and enter the following. Hold **L1** while selecting a turtle to get his New Nexus Turtle outfit.

EFFECT	PASSWORD	EFFECT	PASSWORD
Challenge Code Abyss	SDSDRLD	Cheat Code Self Recovery	DRMSRLR
Challenge Code Endurance	MRMDRMD	Cheat Code Squeaking	MLDSRDM
Challenge Code Fatal Blow	LRSRDRD	Cheat Code Super Defense Power	LDRMRLM
Challenge Code Lose Shuriken	RLMRDSL	Cheat Code Super Offense Power	SDLSRLL
Challenge Code Nightmare	SLSDRDL	Cheat Code Toddling	SSSMRDD
Challenge Code Poison	DRSLLSR	New Nexus Turtle outfit for Donatello	DSLRDRM
Challenge Code Super-Tough	RDSRMRL	New Nexus Turtle outfit for Leonardo	LMRMDRD
Cheat Code All-You-Can-Throw Shuriken	RSRLRSM	New Nexus Turtle outfit for Michelangelo	MLMRDRM
Cheat Code Health	DSRDRMR	New Nexus Turtle outfit for Raphael	RMSRMDR
Cheat Code Mighty Turtle	LSDRRDR	Playmates added to Bonus Materials	SRMLDDR
Cheat Code Pizza Paradise	MRLMRMR		

TEENAGE MUTANT NINJA TURTLES 3: MUTANT NIGHTMARE

INVINCIBILITY
Select Passwords from the Options screen and enter MDLDSSLR.

HEALTH POWER-UPS BECOME SUSHI
Select Passwords from the Options screen and enter SLLMRSLD.

NO HEALTH POWER-UPS
Select Passwords from the Options screen and enter DMLDMRLD.

ONE-HIT DEFEATS TURTLE
Select Passwords from the Options screen and enter LDMSLRDD.

MAX OUGI
Select Passwords from the Options screen and enter RRDMLSDL.

UNLIMITED SHURIKEN
Select Passwords from the Options screen and enter LMDRRMSR.

NO SHURIKEN
Select Passwords from the Options screen and enter LLMSRDMS.

DOUBLE ENEMY ATTACK
Select Passwords from the Options screen and enter MSRLSMML.

DOUBLE ENEMY DEFENSE
Select Passwords from the Options screen and enter SLRMLSSM.

TIGER WOODS PGA TOUR 06

ALL GOLFERS
Select from the Options and enter **WOOGLIN**.

ALL CLUBS
Select Password from the Options and enter **CLUB11**.

LEVEL 2 NIKE ITEMS
Select Password from the Options and enter **JUSTDOIT**.

ALL COURSES
Select Password from the Options and enter **ITSINTHEHOLE**.

TIGER WOODS IN HAT AND TIE
Select Password from the Options and enter **GOLDENAGE**.

TIGER WOODS IN STRIPED PANTS
Select Password from the Options and enter **TECHNICOLOR**.

TIGER WOODS IN OLD GOLF OUTFIT
Select Password from the Options and enter **OLDSKOOL**.

TIGER WOODS IN A DIFFERENT OLD GOLF OUTFIT
Select Password from the Options and enter **THROWBACK**.

ARNOLD PALMER
Select Password from the Options and enter **ARNIESARMY**.

BEN HOGAN
Select Password from the Options and enter **THEHAWK**.

JACK NICKLAUS
Select Password from the Options and enter **GOLDENBEAR**.

OLD TOM MORRIS
Select Password from the Options and enter **FEATHERIE**.

TOMMY BLACK
Select Password from the Options and enter **IDONTHAVEAPROBLEM**.

WESLEY ROUNDER
Select Password from the Options and enter **POCKETPAIR**.

TIGER WOODS PGA TOUR 07

NIKE ITEMS
Select the Password option and enter JUSTDOIT.

TIM BURTON'S THE NIGHTMARE BEFORE CHRISTMAS: OOGIE'S REVENGE

PUMPKIN JACK AND SANTA JACK COSTUMES
During gameplay, press Down, Up, Right, Left, **L3**, **R3**.

TOM AND JERRY IN WAR OF THE WHISKERS

INFINITE LIFE
During a game, press ✕, ○, ✕, △, △, □, ○, △.

INFINITE AMMUNITION
During a game, press ○, □, ○, △, ✕, □, ✕, ✕.

ALL ARENAS
During a game, press △, ○, △, △, ✕, □, ○, □.

COSTUMES
During a game, press ○, ○, ✕, □, ○, △, ✕, ○.

TONY HAWK'S AMERICAN WASTELAND

ALWAYS SPECIAL
Select Cheat Codes from the Options screen and enter **uronfire**. Pause the game and select Cheats from the Game Options to enable the cheat.

PERFECT RAIL
Select Cheat Codes from the Options screen and enter **grindxpert**. Pause the game and select Cheats from the Game Options to enable the cheat.

PERFECT SKITCH

Select Cheat Codes from the Options screen and enter **h!tchar!de**. Pause the game and select Cheats from the Game Options to enable the cheat.

PERFECT MANUAL

Select Cheat Codes from the Options screen and enter **2wheels!**. Pause the game and select Cheats from the Game Options to enable the cheat.

MOON GRAVITY

Select Cheat Codes from the Options screen and enter **2them00n**. Pause the game and select Cheats from the Game Options to enable the cheat.

MAT HOFFMAN

Select Cheat Codes from the Options screen and enter **the_condor**.

JASON ELLIS

Select Cheat Codes from the Options screen and enter **sirius-dj**.

TONY HAWK'S PROJECT 8

SPONSOR ITEMS

As you progress through Career mode and move up the rankings, you gain sponsors and each comes with its own Create-a-skater item.

RANK REQUIRED	CAS ITEM UNLOCKED	RANK REQUIRED	CAS ITEM UNLOCKED
Rank 040	Adio Kenny V2 Shoes	Rank 120	Almost Watch What You Say Deck
Rank 050	Quiksilver_Hoody_3	Rank 140	DVS Adage Shoe
Rank 060	Birdhouse Tony Hawk Deck	Rank 150	Element Illuminate Deck
Rank 080	Vans No Skool Gothic Shoes	Rank 160	Etnies Sheckler White Lavender Shoes
Rank 100	Volcom Scallero Jacket	Complete Skateshop Goal	Stereo Soundwave Deck
Rank 110	eS Square One Shoes		

SKATERS

All of the skaters, except for Tony Hawk, must be unlocked by completing challenges in the Career Mode. They are useable in Free Skate and 2 Player modes.

SKATER	HOW THEY ARE UNLOCKED	SKATER	HOW THEY ARE UNLOCKED
Tony Hawk	Always Unlocked	Zombie	Complete Pro Challenge
Lyn-z Adams Hawkins	Complete Pro Challenge	Christian Hosoi	Animal Chin Challenge
Bob Burquist	Complete Pro Challenge	Jason Lee	Complete Final Tony Hawk Goal
Dustin Dollin	Complete Pro Challenge	Photographer	Unlock Shops
Nyjah Huston	Complete Pro Challenge	Security Guard	Unlock School
Bam Margera	Complete Pro Challenge	Bum	Unlock Car Factory
Rodney Mullen	Complete Pro Challenge	Beaver Mascot	Unlock High School
Paul Rodriguez	Complete Pro Challenge	Real Estate Agent	Unlock Downtown
Ryan Sheckler	Complete Pro Challenge	Filmer	Unlock High School
Daewon Song	Complete Pro Challenge	Skate Jam Kid	Rank #4
Mike Vallely	Complete Pro Challenge	Dad	Rank #1
Stevie Willams	Complete Pro Challenge	Colonel	All Gaps
Travis Barker	Complete Pro Challenge	Nerd	Complete School Spirit Goal
Kevin Staab	Complete Pro Challenge		

CHEAT CODES

Select Cheat Codes from the Options and enter the following codes. In game you can access some codes from the Options menu.

CHEAT CODE	RESULTS	CHEAT CODE	RESULTS
plus44	Unlocks Travis Barker	themedia	Unlocks Photog Girl & Filmer
hohohosoi	Unlocks Christian Hosoi	militarymen	Unlocks Colonel & Security Guard
notmono	Unlocks Jason Lee	jammypack	Unlocks Always Special
mixitup	Unlocks Kevin Staab	balancegalore	Unlocks Perfect Rail
strangefellows	Unlocks Dad & Skater Jam Kid	frontandback	Unlocks Perect Manual

CHEAT CODE	RESULTS	CHEAT CODE	RESULTS
shellshock	Unlocks Unlimited Focus	enterandwin	Unlocks Bum
shescaresme	Unlocks Big Realtor	wearelosers	Unlocks Nerd
birdhouse	Unlocks Inkblot deck	manineedadate	Unlocks Mascot
allthebest	Full Stats	suckstobedead	Unlocks Zombie
needaride	All Decks unlocked and free, except for inkblot deck and gamestop deck	sellsellsell	Unlocks Skinny real estate agent
		newshound	Unlocks Anchor man
yougotitall	All specials unlocked and in player's special list and set as owned in skate shop	badverybad	Unlocks Twin

TONY HAWK'S UNDERGROUND 2

Select Cheat Codes from the Game Options and enter the following. For the cheats, pause the game and select Cheats to turn them on.

ALL LEVELS
Enter **d3struct**.

ALL SKATERS EXCEPT FOR SECRET SKATERS
Enter **costars!**.

THPS1 TONY HAWK AND ALL THUG2 MOVIES
Enter **boxoffice**.

NATAS KAUPAS
Enter **oldskool**.

NIGEL BEAVERHAUSEN
Enter **sellout**.

PHIL MARGERA
Enter **aprilsman**.

INFINITE RAIL CHEAT
Enter **straightedge**.

ALWAYS SPECIAL
Enter **likepaulie**.

SECRETS

Tony Hawk's Underground 2 has a wealth of unlockable skaters, videos, and levels for those who complete the various modes of play. Newcomers to the series will be happy to learn that some of the unlockables are earned through completion of Story Mode on the Easy and Normal difficulty settings, as well as the Sick setting. Similarly, veterans and completionists can take joy in knowing that completing both modes on the Sick setting also unlocks more skaters and that finding all of the gaps on all 15 levels unlocks the various cheat codes.

REWARDS TABLE

GOAL ACHIEVED	LEVEL UNLOCKED	SKATERS UNLOCKED	MOVIES UNLOCKED
Complete Story Mode on "Easy"	Pro Skater	Shrek, Phil Margera, Peds Group A	World Destruction Tour
Complete Story Mode on "Normal"	Pro Skater	The Hand, Paulie, Peds Group B	World Destruction Tour
Complete Story Mode on "Sick"	Pro Skater	Call of Duty Soldier, Nigel, Peds Group C	World Destruction Tour
Complete Story Mode with 100%	N/A	Peds Group F	Pro Bails 2
Complete Classic Mode on "Normal"	The Triangle	Steve-O, THPS1 Tony, Peds Group D	Pro Bails 1
Complete Classic Mode on "Sick"	The Triangle	Jesse James, Natas Kaupas, Peds Group E	Pro Bails 1
Complete Classic Mode with 100%	N/A	Peds Group G	Neversoft Skates
Get all gaps on all 15 levels	N/A	Peds Group H	Cheat Codes
Complete Boston in Story Mode	N/A	Ben Franklin	N/A
Complete Barcelona in Story Mode	N/A	Bull Fighter	N/A
Complete Berlin in Story Mode	N/A	Graffiti Tagger	N/A
Complete Australia in Story Mode	N/A	Shrimp Vendor	N/A
Complete New Orleans in Story Mode	N/A	Jester	N/A
Complete Skatopia in Story Mode	N/A	Ryan Sheckler	N/A

TRANSFORMERS

ALL EXTRAS
Select Extras and press ●, ●, ●, ●, ●, ●, L1, L2.

INVINCIBILITY
Pause the game and press R1, ●, R1, R2, L1, L1, L2.

STEALTH ENEMIES
Pause the game and press Left, Right, Left, R1, R2, R1, Right, Right.

ONE-HIT KILLS
Pause the game and press ●, ●, ●, ●, L1, L1, L2, L1.

At the Autobot Headquarters menu, enter the following:

BIG HEAD CHEAT MODE
Press ●(x3), ●, L1(x3), L2.

TURBO CHEAT MODE
Press L1, R2, R2, ●(x4), L1.

UNLIMITED STEALTH
Press Up, Up, Down, Down, L1, L2, L1, L2.

UNLIMITED POWERLINK
Press Up, Down, Up, Down, ●, ●, ●, ●.

DISABLE MINI-CON OVERLOAD
Press R1, R1, L2, R1, R1, L2, ●, ●.

Enter the following at the difficulty select screen:

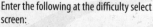

ALASKA LEVEL COMPLETE
Press R1, ●, R1, ●, Left, Left, Right, Left

DEEP AMAZON LEVEL COMPLETE
Press Left, Right, Left, Left, Right, R1, R2, ●.

EARTH LEVEL COMPLETE
Press R2, R1, L1, L2, ●, ●, ●, ●.

MID ATLANTIC LEVEL COMPLETE
Press ●, ●, ●, ●, Right, Left, Left, Right.

STARSHIP LEVEL COMPLETE
Press Left, Left, Right, ●, ●, Right, Right, Left.

AMAZON BOSS FIGHT
Press Left, Left, Right, L1, R2, Left, Left, Right.

AMAZON LEVEL COMPLETE
Press L1, L1, L2, ●, ●, ●, R1, R2.

ANARCTICA BOSS FIGHT
Press L1, Left, L2, Right, ●, ●, ●, ●.

ANARCTICA LEVEL COMPLETE
Press R1, R1, R2, L2, L1, L1, R1, R1.

MID ATLANTIC BOSS FIGHT
Press L2, Left, Right, Right, Left, L2, L2, L2.

STARSHIP BOSS FIGHT
Press Right, Right, ●, R1, R2, ● Left, Left.

TY THE TASMANIAN TIGER 3: NIGHT OF THE QUINKAN

100,000 OPALS
During a game, press Start, Start, ●, Start, Start, ●, ●, ✕, ●, ✕.

ALL 'RANG CHASSIS
During a game, press Start, Start, ●, Start, Start, ●, ●, ●, ●, ●.

ULTIMATE SPIDER-MAN

ALL CHARACTERS
Pause the game and select Controller Setup from the Options. Press Right, Down, Right, Down, Left, Up, Left, Right.

ALL COVERS
Pause the game and select Controller Setup from the Options. Press Left, Left, Right, Left, Up, Left, Left, Down.

ALL CONCEPT ART
Pause the game and select Controller Setup from the Options. Press Down, Down, Down, Up, Down, Up, Left, Left.

ALL LANDMARKS
Pause the game and select Controller Setup from the Options. Press Up, Right, Down, Left, Down, Up, Right, Left.

URBAN REIGN

ALL CHARACTERS
At the Title screen, press R1, R2, ✖, Left, Right, ⬤ (x4), L1, ⬤, ▲, ⬤

ALL WEAPONS
At the Title screen, press L1, R1, ✖, X, ▲, R1, R1, ▲, ⬤, ✖, R1.

BONUS WEAPON IN MULTI-PLAYER MODE
At the title screen, press L2, L2, ✖, ✖, ▲, R1, R1, ⬤, R1.

CHALLENGE MODE
At the title screen, press L2, R2, ▲, Right, Left, Up, Up, Left, R2, R2, R2, ⬤.

FREE MODE
At the title screen, press L1, R1, Left, Left, Left, Left, Left, Left, L2, Up, ▲, ⬤, Right.

TWO PLAYERS IN STORY MODE
At the title screen, press L1, R2, ⬤, ⬤, ▲, L2, R1, ⬤, ▲, ⬤.

VICTORIOUS BOXERS 2: FIGHTING SPRIRT

EXTRA CHARACTERS IN EXHIBITION
Select Password from the Options and enter NEL SAZ UMA.

BROCCOMAN IN EXHIBITION MODE
Select Password from the Options and enter BRC MAN EXH.

LUNSAKU PAUDY, JUNICHI HOTTA AND HIROSHI YAMANAKA
Select Password from the Options and enter ALL *ST ARS.

KAMOGAWA, NEKOTA AND HAMA IN EXHIBITION MODE
Select Password from the Options and enter MRS AND MAN.

DATE VS. RAMIREZ MATCH IN STORY MODE
Select Password from the Options and enter DAT EVS RMZ.

TAKAMURA VS. YAJIMA MATCH IN STORY MODE
Select Password from the Options and enter ASA CT3 CLR.

EXTRA STAGES
Select Password from the Options and enter DAM ATA MAQ.

X-MEN LEGENDS II: RISE OF APOCALYPSE

ALL CHARACTERS
At the Team Management screen, press Right, Left, Left, Right, Up, Up, Up, Start.

ALL SKINS
At the Team Management screen, press Down, Up, Left, Right, Up, Up, Start

ALL SKILLS
At the Team Management screen, press Left, Right, Left, Right, Down, Up, Start.

LEVEL 99
At the Team Management screen, press Up, Down, Up, Down, Left, Up, Left, Right, Start.

GOD MODE
Pause the game and press Down, Up, Down, Up, Right, Down, Right, Left, Start.

MOVE FASTER
Pause the game and press Up, Up, Up, Down, Up, Down, Start.

UNLIMITED XTREME TOKENS
Pause the game and press Left, Down, Right, Down, Up, Up, Down, Up, Start.

TOUCH OF DEATH
During a game, press Left, Left, Right, Left, Right, Up, Start.

100,000 TECH-BITS
At Forge or Beast's store, press Up, Up, Up, Down, Right, Right, Start.

ALL DANGER ROOM COURSES
At the Danger Room Course menu, press Right, Right, Left, Left, Up, Down, Up, Down, Start.

ALL COMICS
Select Review from the Main menu and press Right, Left, Left, Right, Up, Up, Right, Start.

ALL CINEMATICS
Select Review from the Main menu and press Left, Right, Right, Left, Down, Down, Left, Start.

ALL CONCEPTS
Select Review from the Main menu and press Left, Right, Left, Right, Up, Up, Down, Start.

ALL SCREENS
Select Review from the Main menu and press Right, Left, Right, Left, Up, Up, Down, Start.

X-MEN: THE OFFICIAL GAME

DANGER ROOM ICEMAN
At the Cerebro Files menu, press Right, Right, Left, Left, Down, Up, Down, Up, Start.

DANGER ROOM NIGHTCRAWLER
At the Cerebro Files menu, press Up, Up, Down, Down, Left, Right, Left, Right, Start.

DANGER ROOM WOLVERINE
At the Cerebro Files menu, press Down, Down, Up, Up, Right, Left, Right, Left, Start.

YS: THE ARK OF NAPISHTIM

HOW TO ENTER CHEAT CODES
1. Select **New Game**.
2. Select **Cheat** to enter the Cheat Room.
3. To activate Cheat Mode, strike the colored crystals in this sequence: Red, Blue, Yellow, Red, Blue, Yellow. The sequence appears at the top left as you strike each crystal.
4. Perform a Downward Thrust strike on the center pedestal to complete the code and activate Cheat Mode.
5. You can now use the same method to enter one of the cheat codes listed below, then exit the Cheat Room.
6. The game selection buttons are now red. Games saved with the Cheat Mode enabled will appear in red.

CLEARFLAG

Hit the crystals in the following order: Red, Red, Red, Red, Blue, Blue, Blue, Blue, Yellow, Yellow, Yellow, Yellow, Blue, Blue, Yellow, Yellow, Red, Red. Turns on all special features normally available only after you've completed the game once—Nightmare Mode, Time Attack, and Red Spirit Monuments. **Note:** When enabled, Red Spirit Monuments appear after you reach Port Rimorge. They allow you to warp between the Rehdan Village and Port Rimorge monuments to save travel time.

OPENING MOVIE WITH ENGLISH VOICE/ENGLISH TEXT

Hit the crystals in the following order: Blue, Blue, Yellow, Red.

OPENING MOVIE WITH ENGLISH VOICE/JAPANESE TEXT

Hit the crystals in the following order: Blue, Blue, Blue, Yellow, Red.

OPENING MOVIE WITH JAPANESE VOICE/ENGLISH TEXT

Hit the crystals in the following order: Blue, Blue, Blue, Blue, Yellow, Red.

OPENING MOVIE WITH JAPANESE VOICE/NO TEXT

Hit the crystals in the following order: Blue, Yellow, Red.

ALTERNATE OPENING MOVIE

Hit the crystals in the following order: Red, Blue, Red.

BEACH MOVIE WITH ENGLISH VOICE/ENGLISH TEXT

Hit the crystals in the following order: Blue, Blue, Red, Yellow

BEACH MOVIE WITH ENGLISH VOICE/JAPANESE TEXT

Hit the crystals in the following order: Blue, Blue, Blue, Red, Yellow.

BEACH MOVIE WITH JAPANESE VOICE/ENGLISH TEXT

Hit the crystals in the following order: Blue, Red, Red, Yellow.

BEACH MOVIE WITH JAPANESE VOICE/JAPANESE TEXT

Hit the crystals in the following order: Blue, Red, Yellow.

ROMUN FLEET ENTRANCE ANIME MOVIE

Hit the crystals in the following order: Blue, Red, Yellow, Red, Red, Yellow, Blue, Blue, Blue.

ROMUN FLEET ENTRANCE CG MOVIE

Hit the crystals in the following order: Blue, Red, Yellow, Red, Red, Yellow, Blue.

ROMUN FLEET DESTROYED ANIME MOVIE

Hit the crystals in the following order: Blue, Red, Yellow, Red, Red, Yellow, Red, Red, Red.

ROMUN FLEET DESTROYED CG MOVIE

Hit the crystals in the following order: Blue, Red, Yellow, Red, Red, Yellow, Red.

NAPISHTIM DESTROYED MOVIE WITH ENGLISH VOICE/ENGLISH TEXT

Hit the crystals in the following order: Blue, Red, Yellow, Red, Red, Blue, Yellow, Yellow.

NAPISHTIM DESTROYED MOVIE WITH ENGLISH VOICE/JAPANESE TEXT

Hit the crystals in the following order: Blue, Red, Yellow, Red, Red, Blue, Yellow, Yellow, Yellow.

NAPISHTIM DESTROYED MOVIE WITH JAPANESE VOICE/ENGLISH TEXT

Hit the crystals in the following order: Blue, Red, Yellow, Red, Red, Blue, Yellow, Yellow, Yellow, Yellow.

NAPISHTIM DESTROYED MOVIE WITH JAPANESE VOICE/JAPANESE TEXT

Hit the crystals in the following order: Blue, Red, Yellow, Red, Red, Blue, Yellow.

OLHA IN BIKINI

Hit the crystals in the following order: Blue, Blue, Blue, Blue, Yellow, Yellow, Yellow, Red, Blue, Yellow, Yellow, Red, Red, Red.

OLHA DEMO AFTER CLEARING TIME ATTACK ON HARD (JAPANESE)

Hit the crystals in the following order: Red, Red, Red, Red, Red, Blue, Blue, Yellow, Red, Blue, Blue, Yellow, Yellow, Yellow.

GAME IN JAPANESE

Hit the crystals in the following order: Yellow, Yellow, Red, Blue.

LEVEL 10

Hit the crystals in the following order: Red, Blue, Blue, Red, Red, Blue.

LEVEL 20

Hit the crystals in the following order: Red, Blue, Blue, Red, Red, Blue, Blue.

LEVEL 30

Hit the crystals in the following order: Red, Red, Blue, Blue, Red, Red, Blue, Blue.

LEVEL 40

Hit the crystals in the following order: Red, Red, Blue, Red, Red, Blue, Blue, Yellow.

LEVEL 60

Hit the crystals in the following order: Red, Red, Blue, Blue, Yellow, Yellow, Red, Red, Blue, Blue, Yellow, Yellow.

HALF PRICE ITEMS

Hit the crystals in the following order: Yellow, Yellow, Blue, Blue, Red, Red, Red, Yellow, Yellow, Yellow, Red, Red, Blue, Blue.

20 ITEM TOOL MAX INCREASE

Hit the crystals in the following order: Yellow, Yellow, Red, Red, Blue, Blue, Yellow, R.

MAXED OUT BLIRANTE SWORD

Hit the crystals in the following order: Blue, Blue, Yellow, Yellow, Yellow, Red, Blue, Red, Red, Red, Yellow, Yellow.

MAXED OUT LIVART SWORD

Hit the crystals in the following order: Blue, Blue, Blue, Yellow, Yellow, Red, Blue, Red, Red, Yellow, Yellow, Yellow.

MAXED OUT ERICCIL SWORD

Hit the crystals in the following order: Blue, Yellow, Yellow, Red, Red, Red, Blue, Blue, Blue, Red, Red, Yellow.

MAXED OUT ALL 3 SWORDS

Hit the crystals in the following order: Blue, Yellow, Red, Blue, Blue, Blue, Red, Red, Red, Yellow, Yellow, Yellow, Blue, Yellow, Red.

ALTERNATE ENDING MOVIES

In the Rehdan Village (Festival at Night): Toksa and Nahrya look toward Adol as he walks by.

At the Entrance of the Village: Isha runs toward the back, then returns.

On the *Tres Mares*: The cat is on the front of the ship.

ENDING CHANGE CRITERIA

Direction Calman is facing: Faces Adol if he has gotten the Gold Locket.

Number of Pikkards: Found all four pikkards and returned them to Emilio.

YU-GI-OH! THE DUELIST OF THE ROSES

PASSWORDS

At the Build Deck screen, press **R3** and enter the following passwords:

NUMBER	CARD	PASSWORD
#001	Seiyaryu	2H4D85J7
#019	Meteor Dragon	86985631
#042	Fairy's Gift	NVE7A3EZ
#043	Magician of Faith	GME1S3UM
#057	Left Arm of the Forbidden One	A5CF6HSH
#058	Exodia the Forbidden One	37689434
#146	Swordstalker	AHOPSHEB
#149	Greenkappa	YBJMCD6Z
#152	Tactical Warrior	054TC727
#191	Swordsman from a Foreign Land	C781UVGR
#478	Aqua Dragon	JXCB6FU7
#655	Ancient Tree of Enlightenment	EKJHQ109
#502	Barrel Dragon	GTJXSBJ7
#567	Beastking of the Swamps	QXNTQPAX
#291	Birdface	N54T4TY5
#348	Dragon Seeker	81EZCH8B
#372	Mystical Capture Chains	N1NDJMQ3

NUMBER	CARD	PASSWORD
#458	Serpentine Princess	UMQ3WZUZ
#506	Blast Sphere	CZN5GD2X
#510	Robotic Knight	S5S7NKNH
#670	Fairy King Truesdale	YF07QVEZ
#674	Slate Warrior	73153736
#687	Mimicat	69YDQM85
#699	Dark Hole	UMJ10MQB
#702	Harpy's Feather Duster	8HJHQPNP
#732	Change of Heart	SBYDQM8B
#750	Earthshaker	Y34PN1SV
#758	Elf's Light	E5G3NRAD
#765	Horn of the Unicorn	S14FGKQ1
#794	Crush Card	SRA7L5YR
#806	Gravity Bind	0HNFG9WX
#814	Goblin Fan	92886423
#825	Royal Decree	8TETQHE1
#829	Mirror Wall	53297534

ZAPPER

INFINITE LIVES

Pause the game, hold **L1** and press Up, Up, Left, Left, Right, Left, Right.

INFINITE SHIELDS

Pause the game, hold **L1** and press Up, Down, Up, Left, Right, Down, Up.

PLAYSTATION® PORTABLE

Everyone

ATV OFFROAD FURY: BLAZIN' TRAILS

BURNOUT LEGENDS

CARS

CRASH TAG TEAM RACING

DAXTER

EXIT

FRANTIX

FROGGER HELMET CHAOS

GRADIUS COLLECTION

GRETZKY NHL

GRETZKY NHL '06

HOT SHOTS GOLF: OPEN TEE

LEGO STAR WARS II:
THE ORIGINAL TRILOGY

MAJOR LEAGUE BASEBALL 2K6

MVP BASEBALL

MX VS. ATV UNLEASHED:
ON THE EDGE

NASCAR

NBA BALLERS: REBOUND

NBA LIVE 06

NEOPETS PETPET ADVENTURE:
THE WAND OF WISHING

NFL STREET 2 UNLEASHED

OUTRUN 2006: COAST 2 COAST

PAC-MAN WORLD 3

PINBALL HALL OF FAME

TIGER WOODS PGA TOUR

VIRTUA TENNIS: WORLD TOUR

WRC: FIA WORLD RALLY CHAMPIONSHIP

Teen

DARKSTALKERS CHRONICLE:
THE CHAOS TOWER

DEATH JR.

DRAGON BALL Z: SHIN BUDOKAI

JUICED: ELIMINATOR

KINGDOM OF PARADISE

MARVEL NEMESIS:
RISE OF THE IMPERFECTS

MARVEL ULTIMATE ALLIANCE

PIRATES OF THE CARIBBEAN:
DEAD MAN'S CHEST

THE SIMS 2

SPIDER-MAN 2

TOMB RAIDER: LEGEND

TONY HAWK'S UNDERGROUND 2 REMIX

WORLD CHAMPIONSHIP POKER 2:
FEATURING HOWARD LEDERER

X-MEN LEGENDS II: RISE OF APOCALYPSE

Playstation® Portable Contents

PLAYSTATION® PORTABLE

ATV OFFROAD FURY: BLAZIN' TRAILS

UNLOCK EVERYTHING EXCEPT THE FURY BIKE
Select Player Profile from Options. Choose Enter Cheat and enter **All Access**.

1500 CREDITS
Select Player Profile from Options. Choose Enter Cheat and enter **$moneybags$**.

ALL RIDER GEAR
Select Player Profile from Options. Choose Enter Cheat and enter **Duds**.

TIRES
Select Player Profile from Options. Choose Enter Cheat and enter **Dubs**.

MUSIC VIDEOS
Select Player Profile from Options. Choose Enter Cheat and enter **Billboards**.

BURNOUT LEGENDS

COP RACER
Earn a Gold in all Pursuit events.

FIRE TRUCK
Earn a Gold on all Crash Events.

GANGSTER BOSS
Earn Gold in all Race events.

CARS

BONUS SPEEDWAY (REVERSED) IN CUSTOM RACE
At the main menu hold L and press ✕, ⬛, ●, ✕, ▲, ⬛.

CRASH TAG TEAM RACING

FASTER VEHICLES
At the Main menu, hold L + R and press ◉, ◉, ▲, ▲.

ONE-HIT KO
At the Main menu, hold L + R and press ✕, ◉, ◉, ✕.

DISABLE HUD
At the Main menu, hold L + R and press ✕, ■, ◉, ◉

CHICKEN HEADS
At the Main menu, hold L + R and press ✕, ◉, ◉, ■

JAPANESE CRASH
At the Main menu, hold L + R and press ■, ◉, ■, ◉.

DRIVE A BLOCK VEHICLE
At the Main menu, hold L + R and press ◉, ◉, ▲, ■.

DARKSTALKERS CHRONICLE: THE CHAOS TOWER

EX OPTIONS
At the Main menu, hold L and select Options.

MARIONETTE IN ARCADE MODE
At the character select, highlight ? and press START (x7), then press P or K.

OBORO BISHAMON IN ALL MODES
At the character select, highlight Bishamon, hold START, and press P or K.

SHADOW IN ARCADE MODE
At the character select, highlight ? and press START (x5), then press P or K.

DAXTER

THE MATRIX DREAM SEQUENCE
Collect 1 Precursor Orb.

BRAVEHEART DREAM SEQUENCE
Collect 100 Precursor Orbs.

THE LORD OF THE RINGS DREAM SEQUENCE
Collect 200 Precursor Orbs.

INDIANA JONES DREAM SEQUENCE
Collect 300 Precursor Orbs.

THE MATRIX DREAM SEQUENCE 2
Collect 400 Precursor Orbs.

THE LORD OF THE RINGS DREAM SEQUENCE 2
Collect 500 Precursor Orbs.

E3 2005 TRAILER
Collect 600 Precursor Orbs, then pause the game and select Extras from the Secrets menu.

CONCEPT ART
Collect 700 Precursor Orbs, then pause the game and select Extras from the Secrets menu.

INTRO ANIMATIC
Collect 800 Precursor Orbs, then pause the game and select Extras from the Secrets menu.

GAME IN CONSTRUCTION
Collect 900 Precursor Orbs, then pause the game and select Extras from the Secrets menu.

BEHIND THE SCENES
Collect 1000 Precursor Orbs, then pause the game and select Extras from the Secrets menu.

PANTS
Earn Gold on The Lord of the Rings Dream Sequence 2, then pause the game and select Cheats from the Secrets menu.

HAT
Earn Gold on the Indiana Jones Dream Sequence, then pause the game and select Cheats from the Secrets menu.

WEBSITE CLUE A

Earn Gold on The Matrix Dream Sequence 2, then pause the game and select Cheats from the Secrets menu.

WEBSITE CLUE B

Earn Gold on the Braveheart Dream Sequence, then pause the game and select Cheats from the Secrets menu.

WEBSITE CLUE C

Earn Gold on The Lord of the Rings Dream Sequence, then pause the game and select Cheats from the Secrets menu.

WEBSITE CLUE D

Earn Gold on The Matrix Dream Sequence 2, then pause the game and select Cheats from the Secrets menu.

DEATH JR.

CAN'T TOUCH THIS (INVINCIBILITY)

Pause the game, hold L + R and press Up, Up, Down, Down, Left, Left, Right, Right, ●, ▲.

INCREASED HEALTH

Pause the game, hold L + R and press Up, Up, Down, Down, ✖, ●, ▲, ●, ✖, ✖.

WEAPONS UPGRADED (GIVES ALL WEAPONS)

Pause the game, hold L + R and press Up, Up, Down, Down, Left, Right, Left, Right, ✖, ●.

AMMO REFILLED

Pause the game, hold L + R and press ▲, ▲, ✖, ✖, ●, ●, ●, ●, Down, Right.

UNLIMITED AMMO

Pause the game, hold L + R and press ▲, ▲, ✖, ✖, ●, ●, ●, ●, Right, Down.

MY HEAD FEELS FUNNY (BIG HEAD)

Pause the game, hold L + R and press ▲, ●, ✖, ●, ▲, Up, Right, Down, Left, Up. Re-enter the code for normal head.

GIANT BLADE (BIG SCYTHE)

Pause the game, hold L + R and press ▲, ●, ✖, ●, ▲, Up, Left, Down, Right, Up.

FREE SEEP

Pause the game, hold L + R and press Left, Left, Right, Right, Left, Right, Left, Right, ✖, ✖.

A LITTLE MORE HELP (ASSIST EXTENDER)

Pause the game, hold L + R and press Up, Up, Down, Down, ▲, ▲, ✖, ✖, ▲, ▲.

FREE WIDGET

Pause the game, hold L + R and press Right, Up, Down, Up, ▲, Up, Left, ●, ▲, Right.

ALL LEVELS AND FREE ALL CHARACTERS

Pause the game, hold L + R and press Up, Up, Up, Up, Down, Down, Down, Down, ✖, ✖. Enter a stage and exit back to the museum for code to take effect.

I'D BUY THAT FOR A DOLLAR (FILL PANDORA ASSIST METER)

Pause the game, hold L + R and press Up, Up, Down, Down, Up, Right, Down, Left, ✖, ✖.

THIS WAS JED'S IDEA (ATTACKS HAVE DIFFERENT NAMES)

Pause the game, hold L + R and press Up, Up, Down, Left, ▲, ▲, ●, ✖, ●, ●.

WEAPON NAMES = NORMAL (WEAPONS HAVE DIFFERENT NAMES)

Pause the game, hold L + R and press Down, Down, Up, Up, Left, Right, Left, Right, ●, ▲.

EYEDOOR SOLIDITY QUESTIONABLE (NO LONGER REQUIRE SOULS)

Pause the game, hold L + R and press Up, Left, Down, Right, Left, ▲, ●, ✖, ●, ●.

BUDDY DECALS (BULLET HOLES BECOME PICTURES)

Pause the game, hold L + R and press Up, Right, Down, Left, Up, ▲, ●, ✖, ●, ▲.

STAGE WARP

Pause the game, hold L + R and enter the following codes to warp to that stage.

STAGE	CODE
Advanced Training	Down, K, Down, K, Down, K, Down, K, Down, I
The Basement	Down, K, Down, K, Down, K, Down, K, Up, J
Basic Training	Up, J, Up, K, Down, K, Down, K, Down, K
Big Trouble in Little Downtown	Up, J, Down, K, Down, K, Down, K, Down, K
Bottom of the Bell Curve	Down, K, Down, K, Down, K, Down, K, Down, J
The Burger Tram	Down, K, Down, K, Down, K, Up, K, Down, K
Burn it Down	Down, K, Up, J, Down, K, Down, K, Down, K
The Corner Store	Down, K, Up, K, Down, K, Down, K, Down, K

STAGE	CODE
Final Battle	Down, K, Down, K, Down, K, Down, J, Up, K
Growth Spurt	Down, K, Down, K, Down, K, Down, K, Up, K
Happy Trails Insanitarium	Down, K, Down, J, Up, K, Down, K, Down, K
Higher Learning	Down, K, Down, K, Down, K, Down, J, Down, K
How a Cow Becomes a Steak	Down, K, Down, K, Down, J, Down, K, Down, K
Inner Madness	Down, K, Down, K, Up, J, Down, K, Down, K
Into the Box	Down, K, Down, K, Down, K, Up, J, Down, K
Moving on Up	Down, J, Up, K, Down, K, Down, K, Down, K
The Museum	Up, K, Down K, Down, K, Down, K, Down, K
My House	Down, K, Down, J, Down, K, Down, K, Down, K
Seep's Hood	Down, J, Down, K, Down, K, Down, K, Down, K
Shock Treatment	Down, K, Down, K, Down, J, Up, K, Down, K
Udder Madness	Down, K, Down, K, Up, K, Down, K, Down, K

DRAGON BALL Z: SHIN BUDOKAI

MINI-GAME
At the Main menu, press L and then press R to begin the mini-game.

EXIT

SITUATION 8
Complete Situation 1. Then at the Title screen, press L, R, Left, Right, ◉, ◉, ✕, ▲.

SITUATION 9
Complete Situation 1 and unlock Situation 8. Then at the Title screen, press ▲, Down, ◉, Left, ✕, Up, ◉, Right.

SITUATION 10
Complete Situation 1 and unlock Situations 8 and 9. Then at the Title screen, press Right, Down, Up, Left, ◉, ✕, R, L.

FRANTIX

INVINCIBILITY
At the Level Select screen, hold R + L to access the codes screen. Enter **INVINC1**.

DISABLE INVINCIBILITY
At the Level Select screen, hold R + L to access the codes screen. Enter **INVINC0**.

ALL LEVELS
At the Level Select screen, hold R + L to access the codes screen. Enter **LVLANY1**. The levels will still appear locked, but you can select them.

DISABLE ALL LEVELS
At the Level Select screen, hold R + L to access the codes screen. Enter **LVLANY0**.

FROGGER HELMET CHAOS

MOHAWK WIG
Enter Berry, Lily, Lumpy, Lily as a password.

AFRO WIG
Enter Finnius, Frogger, Frogger, Wani as a password.

SANTA HAT
Enter Lily, Lily, Wani, Wani as a password.

PIRATE HAT
Enter Frogger, Berry, Finnius, Frogger as a password.

BASEBALL CAP
Enter Frogger, Frogger, Frogger, Berry as a password.

CROC HAT
Enter Lily, Lily, Wani, Lumpy as a password.

BUNNY EARS
Enter Lily, Frogger, Frogger, Lumpy as a password.

CAMOUFLAGE COSTUME
Enter Lily, Wani, Lily, Wani as a password.

COWBOY COSTUME
Enter Frogger, Lily, Lily, Lily as a password.

SANTA COSTUME
Play the game for four hours.

PIRATE COSTUME
Play the game for six hours.

PUNK COSTUME
Pause the game and press Up, Up, Down, Down, Left, Right, Left, Right, ▲, ◉, Start.

GRADIUS COLLECTION

ALL WEAPONS & POWER-UPS ON EASY DIFFICULTY

Pause the game and press Up, Up, Down, Down, Left, Right, Left, Right, ✕, ◯.

GRETZKY NHL

ALL UNLOCKABLES AVAILABLE

At the Gretzky Challenge Unlockables screen, press START, and enter **SHOENLOC**.

ONE GRETZKY CHALLANGE POINT

At the Gretzky Challenge Unlockables screen, press START, and enter **CANADIAN DOLLAR**.

BIG BOARDS CHECKING OPTION

At the Gretzky Challenge Unlockables screen, press START, and enter **ALL ABOARD**. You can turn this option on by selecting Unlocked Options when starting a game.

NO SKATER FATIGUE OPTION

At the Gretzky Challenge Unlockables screen, press START, and enter **CAFFEINATED**. You can turn this option on by selecting Unlocked Options when starting a game.

PERFECT AIM MODE OPTION

At the Gretzky Challenge Unlockables screen, press START, and enter **THREAD THE NEEDLE**. You can turn this option on by selecting Unlocked Options when starting a game.

PERFECT SLAP SHOTS OPTION

At the Gretzky Challenge Unlockables screen, press START, and enter **SLAP THAT PUCK**. You can turn this option on by selecting Unlocked Options when starting a game.

ROBOENFORCER MODEL-44

At the Gretzky Challenge Unlockables screen, press START, and enter **ROBO CHECKS**.

WAYNE GRETZKY: 1979 EDMONTON OILERS

At the Gretzky Challenge Unlockables screen, press START, and enter **UNSTOPPABLE GREATNESS**.

WAYNE GRETZKY: 1987 TEAM CANADA

At the Gretzky Challenge Unlockables screen, press START, and enter **GLORY DAZE**.

WAYNE GRETZKY: 1994 LOS ANGELES KINGS

At the Gretzky Challenge Unlockables screen, press START, and enter **WEST COAST WAYNE**.

WAYNE GRETZKY: 1999 NEW YORK RANGERS

At the Gretzky Challenge Unlockables screen, press START, and enter **A LEGEND ON ICE**.

ALTERNATE ANAHEIM MIGHTY DUCKS UNIFORM

At the Gretzky Challenge Unlockables screen, press START, and enter **FLYING VEE**.

ALTERNATE ATLANTA THRASHERS UNIFORM

At the Gretzky Challenge Unlockables screen, press START, and enter **THRASHED TO THE MAX**.

ALTERNATE BOSTON BRUINS UNIFORM

At the Gretzky Challenge Unlockables screen, press START, and enter **NOMAR STILL RULES**.

ALTERNATE BUFFALO SABERS UNIFORM

At the Gretzky Challenge Unlockables screen, press START, and enter **IN THE SNOW BELT**.

ALTERNATE CALGARY FLAMES UNIFORM

At the Gretzky Challenge Unlockables screen, press START, and enter **THREE ALARM BLAZE**.

ALTERNATE CHICAGO BLACKHAWKS UNIFORM

At the Gretzky Challenge Unlockables screen, press START, and enter **WINDY CITY**.

ALTERNATE COLORADO AVALANCHE UNIFORM

At the Gretzky Challenge Unlockables screen, press START, and enter **SNOW DRIFTS**.

ALTERNATE COLUMBUS BLUE JACKETS UNIFORM

At the Gretzky Challenge Unlockables screen, press START, and enter **BLUE SHOES**.

ALTERNATE DALLAS STARS UNIFORM

At the Gretzky Challenge Unlockables screen, press START, and enter **HOCKEY IN TEXAS**.

ALTERNATE EDMONTON OILERS UNIFORM

At the Gretzky Challenge Unlockables screen, press START, and enter **PUMPIN OIL**.

ALTERNATE FLORIDA PANTHERS UNIFORM

At the Gretzky Challenge Unlockables screen, press START, and enter **SOUTH BEACH**.

ALTERNATE LOS ANGELES KINGS UNIFORM

At the Gretzky Challenge Unlockables screen, press START, and enter **IT IS GOOD TO BE THE KING**.

ALTERNATE MINNESOTA WILD UNIFORM

At the Gretzky Challenge Unlockables screen, press START, and enter **COLD AS HECK**.

ALTERNATE NASHVILLE PREDATORS UNIFORM

At the Gretzky Challenge Unlockables screen, press START, and enter **ALIEN VS NASHVILLE**.

ALTERNATE NEW YORK ISLANDERS UNIFORM

At the Gretzky Challenge Unlockables screen, press START, and enter **LAWNG ISLAND**.

ALTERNATE NEW YORK RANGERS UNIFORM

At the Gretzky Challenge Unlockables screen, press START, and enter **GREAT WHITE WAY**.

ALTERNATE OTTAWA SENATORS UNIFORM

At the Gretzky Challenge Unlockables screen, press START, and enter **MAJORITY RULE**.

ALTERNATE PHILADELPHIA FLYERS UNIFORM

At the Gretzky Challenge Unlockables screen, press START, and enter **FANATICAL**.

ALTERNATE SAN JOSE SHARKS UNIFORM

At the Gretzky Challenge Unlockables screen, press START, and enter **GET A BIGGER BOAT**.

ALTERNATE TORONTO MAPLE LEAFS UNIFORM

At the Gretzky Challenge Unlockables screen, press START, and enter **HEY TERRANCE**.

ALTERNATE VANCOUVER CANUCKS UNIFORM

At the Gretzky Challenge Unlockables screen, press START, and enter **WEST COAST EH**.

1910 MONTREAL CANADIENS UNIFORM

At the Gretzky Challenge Unlockables screen, press START, and enter **THE HABS**.

1924 MONTREAL CANADIENS UNIFORM

At the Gretzky Challenge Unlockables screen, press START, and enter **LE HABITANT**.

1927 DETROIT RED WINGS UNIFORM

At the Gretzky Challenge Unlockables screen, press START, and enter **BEEP BEEP**.

1928 BOSTON BRUINS UNIFORM

At the Gretzky Challenge Unlockables screen, press START, and enter **WICKED HAAAAAHD**.

1929 OTTAWA SENATORS UNIFORM

At the Gretzky Challenge Unlockables screen, press START, and enter **THE SENATOR**.

1930 TORONTO MAPLE LEAFS UNIFORM

At the Gretzky Challenge Unlockables screen, press START, and enter **NORTH OF THE BORDER**.

1967 LOS ANGELES KINGS AWAY UNIFORM

At the Gretzky Challenge Unlockables screen, press START, and enter **VOLLEY DOLLY**.

1967 PHILADELPHIA FLYERS AWAY UNIFORM

At the Gretzky Challenge Unlockables screen, press START, and enter **CHEESESTEAK**.

1967 PITTSBURGH PENGUINS AWAY UNIFORM

At the Gretzky Challenge Unlockables screen, press START, and enter **POPPIN TALK**.

1970 MINNESOTA NORTH STARS UNIFORM

At the Gretzky Challenge Unlockables screen, press START, and enter **TWIN STARS**.

1975 KANSAS CITY SCOUTS UNIFORM

At the Gretzky Challenge Unlockables screen, press START, and enter **YOU LITTLE DEVIL**.

1976 NEW YORK RANGERS AWAY UNIFORM

At the Gretzky Challenge Unlockables screen, press START, and enter **NEW YORK NEW YORK**.

1977 CALGARY FLAMES AWAY UNIFORM

At the Gretzky Challenge Unlockables screen, press START, and enter **FLAME ON**.

1977 COLORADO ROCKIES UNIFORM

At the Gretzky Challenge Unlockables screen, press START, and enter **DEVIL MADE ME DO IT**.

1977 VANCOUVER CANUCKS HOME UNIFORM

At the Gretzky Challenge Unlockables screen, press START, and enter **GREAT WHITE NORTH**.

1977 WASHINGTON CAPITALS AWAY UNIFORM

At the Gretzky Challenge Unlockables screen, press START, and enter **CONGRESSIONAL WISDOM**.

1978 NEW YORK ISLANDERS AWAY UNIFORM

At the Gretzky Challenge Unlockables screen, press START, and enter **ORDWAY MADE ME DO IT**.

1979 EDMONTON OILERS AWAY UNIFORM

At the Gretzky Challenge Unlockables screen, press START, and enter **A SCARY SIGHT TO THE HOME CROWD**.

1979 EDMONTON OILERS HOME UNIFORM

At the Gretzky Challenge Unlockables screen, press START, and enter **THREADS OF CHAMPS**.

1979 ST. LOUIS BLUES AWAY UNIFORM

At the Gretzky Challenge Unlockables screen, press START, and enter **A BLUE NOTE**.

1979 ST. LOUIS BLUES HOME UNIFORM

At the Gretzky Challenge Unlockables screen, press START, and enter **MARDI GRAS**.

1980 QUEBEC NORDIQUES UNIFORM

At the Gretzky Challenge Unlockables screen, press START, and enter **FRENCH FOR CANADIAN**.

1983 EDMONTON OILERS AWAY UNIFORM

At the Gretzky Challenge Unlockables screen, press START, and enter **ALL HAIL WAYNE**.

1988 PITTSBURGH PENGUINS AWAY UNIFORM

At the Gretzky Challenge Unlockables screen, press START, and enter **STEEL TOWN**.

1989 LOS ANGELES KINGS AWAY UNIFORM

At the Gretzky Challenge Unlockables screen, press START, and enter **KING GRETZKY**.

1989 LOS ANGELES KINGS HOME UNIFORM

At the Gretzky Challenge Unlockables screen, press START, and enter **KING WAYNE**.

1990 WINNIPEG JETS AWAY UNIFORM

At the Gretzky Challenge Unlockables screen, press START, and enter **PORTAGE AND MAIN**.

1990 WINNIPEG JETS HOME UNIFORM

At the Gretzky Challenge Unlockables screen, press START, and enter **MIDDLE OF CANADA**.

1993 SAN JOSE SHARKS AWAY UNIFORM

At the Gretzky Challenge Unlockables screen, press START, and enter **SHARK BAIT**.

1995 ST. LOUIS BLUES AWAY UNIFORM

At the Gretzky Challenge Unlockables screen, press START, and enter **VINTAGE BLUES**.

1999 NEW YORK RANGERS HOME UNIFORM

At the Gretzky Challenge Unlockables screen, press START, and enter **UPPER WEST SIDE**.

GRETZKY NHL '06

UNLOCK EVERYTHING

Select Gretzky Challenge from the Features menu. Choose Unlockables, press Start, and enter **CONHEOSL**.

1 GRETZKY POINT

Select Gretzky Challenge from the Features menu. Choose Unlockables, press Start, and enter **CULKY NETC**.

ALL ALTERNATE UNIFORMS

Select Gretzky Challenge from the Features menu. Choose Unlockables, press Start, and enter **NNIADOUAMFM**.

ALL VINTAGE UNIFORMS

Select Gretzky Challenge from the Features menu. Choose Unlockables, press Start, and enter **DLEONG ARE**.

ALL WAYNE GRETZKYS

Select Gretzky Challenge from the Features menu. Choose Unlockables, press Start, and enter **TEH ESATGRTE NOES**.

BIG BOARDS CHECKING

Select Gretzky Challenge from the Features menu. Choose Unlockables, press Start, and enter **LAL ABRAOD**.

NO SKATER FATIGUE

Select Gretzky Challenge from the Features menu. Choose Unlockables, press Start, and enter **EFDTAFEACIN**.

PERFECT AIM MODE

Select Gretzky Challenge from the Features menu. Choose Unlockables, press Start, and enter **TADHRE TEH EDNELE**.

PERFECT SLAP SHOTS

Select Gretzky Challenge from the Features menu. Choose Unlockables, press Start, and enter **SAPL TATH CUKP**.

BIGGER PLAYERS

Select Gretzky Challenge from the Features menu. Choose Unlockables, press Start, and enter **ARGLE NI RAGECH**.

SMALLER PLAYERS

Select Gretzky Challenge from the Features menu. Choose Unlockables, press Start, and enter **IGHTMY UOSEM**.

ROBOENFORCER MODEL-44

Select Gretzky Challenge from the Features menu. Choose Unlockables, press Start, and enter **OBOR SKHECC**.

STANLEY CUP CHAMPIONSHIP VIDEO

Select Gretzky Challenge from the Features menu. Choose Unlockables, press Start, and enter **VINIOS FO LYRGO**.

HOT SHOTS GOLF: OPEN TEE

UNLOCK EVERYTHING

Start a new game with the name **5TNEPO**.

EASY DIFFICULTY FOR CHALLENGE MODE

Lose two matches or tournaments in a row. This can be changed in the Options.

AUTUMN PAGODA COURSE

Reach Beginner level in Challenge Mode.

GOLDEN DESERT COURSE

Reach Senior level in Challenge Mode.

OLIVE COAST COURSE

Reach Mid-Rank level in Challenge Mode.

5TH LOYALTY HEART

Defeat the character with a Super Win to get the 5th Loyalty Heart.

MANUAL REPLAY MODE

Reach Senior level in Challenge Mode.

JUICED: ELIMINATOR

ALL CARS AND TRACKS IN ARCADE MODE

Select Cheats from the Extras menu and enter PIES.

KINGDOM OF PARADISE

MOUNTAIN WIZARD SWORD

Select Download and get connected. Enter rkjulvj as a password and download the item.

SEIMA ANKLET

Select Download and get connected. Enter ydkvcex as a password and download the item.

SEIMA BRACELET

Select Download and get connected. Enter jticgek as a password and download the item.

SEIMA EAR ORNAMENT

Select Download and get connected. Enter lfiynvg as a password and download the item.

SEIMA HAIR ORNAMENT

Select Download and get connected. Enter otkciet as a password and download the item.

SEIMA NECKLACE

Select Download and get connected. Enter aietmaw as a password and download the item.

SEIMA RING

Select Download and get connected. Enter xktmvut as a password and download the item.

BYAKKO FREE STYLE & BYAKKO 6TH DAN, MU KATA

Select Download and get connected. Enter ptiuquc as a password and download the item.

GENBU FREE STYLE & GENBU 6TH DAN, MU KATA

Select Download and get connected. Enter zoeuiss as a password and download the item.

KIRIN FREE STYLE & KIRIN 6TH DAN, MU KATA

Select Download and get connected. Enter qucmtkb as a password and download the item.

SEIRYU FREE STYLE & SEIRYU 6TH DAN, MU KATA

Select Download and get connected. Enter kakeiti as a password and download the item.

SUZAKU FREE STYLE & SUZAKU 6TH DAN, MU KATA

Select Download and get connected. Enter myuicei as a password and download the item.

LEGO STAR WARS II: THE ORIGINAL TRILOGY

BEACH TROOPER
At Mos Eisley Canteena, select Enter Code and enter UCK868. You still need to select Characters and purchase this character for 20,000 studs.

BEN KENOBI (GHOST)
At Mos Eisley Canteena, select Enter Code and enter BEN917. You still need to select Characters and purchase this character for 1,100,000 studs.

BESPIN GUARD
At Mos Eisley Canteena, select Enter Code and enter VHY832. You still need to select Characters and purchase this character for 15,000 studs.

BIB FORTUNA
At Mos Eisley Canteena, select Enter Code and enter WTY721. You still need to select Characters and purchase this character for 16,000 studs.

BOBA FETT
At Mos Eisley Canteena, select Enter Code and enter HLP221. You still need to select Characters and purchase this character for 175,000 studs.

DEATH STAR TROOPER
At Mos Eisley Canteena, select Enter Code and enter BNC332. You still need to select Characters and purchase this character for 19,000 studs.

EWOK
At Mos Eisley Canteena, select Enter Code and enter TTT289. You still need to select Characters and purchase this character for 34,000 studs.

GAMORREAN GUARD
At Mos Eisley Canteena, select Enter Code and enter YZF999. You still need to select Characters and purchase this character for 40,000 studs.

GONK DROID
At Mos Eisley Canteena, select Enter Code and enter NFX582. You still need to select Characters and purchase this character for 1,550 studs.

GRAND MOFF TARKIN
At Mos Eisley Canteena, select Enter Code and enter SMG219. You still need to select Characters and purchase this character for 38,000 studs.

GREEDO
At Mos Eisley Canteena, select Enter Code and enter NAH118. You still need to select Characters and purchase this character for 60,000 studs.

HAN SOLO (HOOD)
At Mos Eisley Canteena, select Enter Code and enter YWM840. You still need to select Characters and purchase this character for 20,000 studs.

IG-88
At Mos Eisley Canteena, select Enter Code and enter NXL973. You still need to select Characters and purchase this character for 30,000 studs.

IMPERIAL GUARD
At Mos Eisley Canteena, select Enter Code and enter MMM111. You still need to select Characters and purchase this character for 45,000 studs.

IMPERIAL OFFICER
At Mos Eisley Canteena, select Enter Code and enter BBV889. You still need to select Characters and purchase this character for 28,000 studs.

IMPERIAL SHUTTLE PILOT
At Mos Eisley Canteena, select Enter Code and enter VAP664. You still need to select Characters and purchase this character for 29,000 studs.

IMPERIAL SPY
At Mos Eisley Canteena, select Enter Code and enter CVT125. You still need to select Characters and purchase this character for 13,500 studs.

JAWA
At Mos Eisley Canteena, select Enter Code and enter JAW499. You still need to select Characters and purchase this character for 24,000 studs.

LOBOT
At Mos Eisley Canteena, select Enter Code and enter UUB319. You still need to select Characters and purchase this character for 11,000 studs.

PALACE GUARD
At Mos Eisley Canteena, select Enter Code and enter SGE549. You still need to select Characters and purchase this character for 14,000 studs.

REBEL PILOT
At Mos Eisley Canteena, select Enter Code and enter CYG336. You still need to select Characters and purchase this character for 15,000 studs.

REBEL TROOPER (HOTH)
At Mos Eisley Canteena, select Enter Code and enter EKU849. You still need to select Characters and purchase this character for 16,000 studs.

SANDTROOPER
At Mos Eisley Canteena, select Enter Code and enter YDV451. You still need to select Characters and purchase this character for 14,000 studs.

SKIFF GUARD
At Mos Eisley Canteena, select Enter Code and enter GBU888. You still need to select Characters and purchase this character for 12,000 studs.

SNOWTROOPER
At Mos Eisley Canteena, select Enter Code and enter NYU989. You still need to select Characters and purchase this character for 16,000 studs.

STROMTROOPER
At Mos Eisley Canteena, select Enter Code and enter PTR345. You still need to select Characters and purchase this character for 10,000 studs.

THE EMPEROR
At Mos Eisley Canteena, select Enter Code and enter HHY382. You still need to select Characters and purchase this character for 275,000 studs.

TIE FIGHTER
At Mos Eisley Canteena, select Enter Code and enter HDY739. You still need to select Characters and purchase this character for 60,000 studs.

TIE FIGHTER PILOT
At Mos Eisley Canteena, select Enter Code and enter NNZ316. You still need to select Characters and purchase this character for 21,000 studs.

TIE INTERCEPTOR
At Mos Eisley Canteena, select Enter Code and enter QYA828. You still need to select Characters and purchase this character for 40,000 studs.

TUSKEN RAIDER
At Mos Eisley Canteena, select Enter Code and enter PEJ821. You still need to select Characters and purchase this character for 23,000 studs.

UGNAUGHT
At Mos Eisley Canteena, select Enter Code and enter UGN694. You still need to select Characters and purchase this character for 36,000 studs.

MAJOR LEAGUE BASEBALL 2K6

UNLOCK EVERYTHING
Select Enter Cheat Code from the My 2K6 menu and enter **Derek Jeter**. This does not unlock Topps 2K Stars.

TOPPS 2K STARS
Select Enter Cheat Code from the My 2K6 menu and enter **Dream Team**.

SUPER WALL CLIMB
Select Enter Cheat Code from the My 2K6 menu and enter **Last Chance**. Enable the cheats by selecting My Cheats or selecting Cheat Codes from the Options screen in-game.

SUPER PITCHES
Select Enter Cheat Code from the My 2K6 menu and enter **Unhittable**. Enable the cheats by selecting My Cheats or selecting Cheat Codes from the Options screen in-game.

ROCKET ARMS
Select Enter Cheat Code from the My 2K6 menu and enter **Gotcha**. Enable the cheats by selecting My Cheats or selecting Cheat Codes from the Options screen in-game.

BOUNCY BALL
Select Enter Cheat Code from the My 2K6 menu and enter **Crazy Hops**. Enable the cheats by selecting My Cheats or selecting Cheat Codes from the Options screen in-game.

MARVEL NEMESIS: RISE OF THE IMPERFECTS

BRIGADE
Finish story mode with the Thing.

IRON MAN
Finish story mode with Johnny Ohm.

SPIDER-MAN
Finish story mode with Venom.

VENOM
Finish story mode with Iron Man.

MARVEL ULTIMATE ALLIANCE

UNLOCK ALL SKINS
At the Team Menu, press Up, Down, Left, Right, Left, Right, Start.

UNLOCKS ALL HERO POWERS
At the Team Menu, press Left, Right, Up, Down, Up, Down, Start.

ALL HEROES TO LEVEL 99
At the Team Menu, press Up, Left, Up, Left, Down, Right, Down, Right, Start.

UNLOCK ALL HEROES
At the Team Menu, press Up, Up, Down, Down, Left, Left, Left, Start.

UNLOCK DAREDEVIL
At the Team Menu, press Left, Left, Right, Right, Up, Down, Up, Down, Start.

UNLOCK SILVER SURFER
At the Team Menu, press Down, Left, Left, Up, Right, Up, Down, Left, Start.

GOD MODE
During gameplay, press Up, Down, Up, Down, Up, Left, Down, Right, Start.

TOUCH OF DEATH
During gameplay, press Left, Right, Down, Down, Right, Left, Start.

SUPER SPEED
During gameplay, press Up, Left, Up, Right, Down, Right, Start.

FILL MOMENTUM
During gameplay, press Left, Right, Right, Left, Up, Down, Down, Up, Start.

UNLOCK ALL COMICS
At the Review menu, press Left, Right, Right, Left, Up, Up, Right, Start.

UNLOCK ALL CONCEPT ART
At the Review menu, press Down, Down, Down, Right, Right, Left, Down, Start.

UNLOCK ALL CINEMATICS
At the Review menu, press Up, Left, Left, Up, Right, Right, Up, Start.

UNLOCK ALL LOAD SCREENS
At the Review menu, press Up, Down, Right, Left, Up, Up Down, Start.

UNLOCK ALL COURSES
At the Comic Missions menu, press Up, Right, Left, Down, Up, Right, Left, Down, Start.

MVP BASEBALL

ALL REWARDS
Select My MVP and create a player with the name **Dan Carter**.

MX VS. ATV UNLEASHED: ON THE EDGE

UNLOCK EVERYTHING
Select Cheat Codes from the Options screen and enter **TOOLAZY**.

1,000,000 POINTS
Select Cheat Codes from the Options screen and enter **BROKEASAJOKE**.

PRO PHYSICS
Select Cheat Codes from the Options screen and enter **IAMTOOGOOD**.

ALL GEAR
Select Cheat Codes from the Options screen and enter **WARDROBE**.

ALL BIKES
Select Cheat Codes from the Options screen and enter **BRAPP**.

50CC BIKE CLASS
Select Cheat Codes from the Options screen and enter **MINIMOTO**.

500CC BIKE CLASS
Select Cheat Codes from the Options screen and enter **BIGBORE**.

ALL ATVS
Select Cheat Codes from the Options screen and enter **COUCHES**.

ALL MACHINES
Select Cheat Codes from the Options screen and enter **LEADFOOT**.

ALL FREESTYLE TRACKS
Select Cheat Codes from the Options screen and enter **HUCKIT**.

ALL NATIONAL TRACKS
Select Cheat Codes from the Options screen and enter **GOOUTSIDE**.

ALL OPEN CLASS TRACKS
Select Cheat Codes from the Options screen and enter **NOTMOTO**.

ALL SUPERCROSS TRACKS
Select Cheat Codes from the Options screen and enter **GOINSIDE**.

ALL TRACKS
Select Cheat Codes from the Options screen and enter **PITPASS**.

NASCAR

ALL CHASE PLATES
Go to Fight to the top mode. Edit driver's first and last name. Code is case sensitive ItsAll ForMe

$10,000,000
In Fight to the Top mode, enter your driver's name as GiveMe More.

10,000,000 FANS
In Fight to the Top mode, enter your driver's name as AllBow ToMe.

ALL CHASE PLATES
In Fight to the Top mode, enter your driver's name as ItsAll ForMe.

OLD SPICE TRACKS AND CARS
In Fight to the Top mode, enter your driver's name as KeepCool SmellGreat.

NBA BALLERS: REBOUND

VERSUS SCREEN CHEATS

You can enter the following codes at the Vs screen. The ⬤ button corresponds to the first number in the code, the ▲ is the second number, and the ◉ button corresponds to the last number. Press the D-pad in any direction to enter the code. The name of the code will appear if entered correctly. Some of the codes will give you the wrong code name when entered.

EFFECT	CODE
Big Head	1 3 4
Pygmy	4 2 5
Alternate Gear	1 2 3
Show Shot Percentage	0 1 2
Expanded Move Set	5 1 2
Super Push	3 1 5
Super Block Ability	1 2 4
Great Handles	3 3 2
Unlimited Juice	7 6 3
Super Steals	2 1 5
Perfect Free Throws	3 2 7
Better Free Throws	3 1 7
Speedy Players	2 1 3
Alley-Oop Ability	7 2 5
Back-In Ability	1 2 2
Hotspot Ability	6 2 7

EFFECT	CODE
Pass 2 Friend Ability	5 3 6
Put Back Ability	3 1 3
Stunt Ability	3 7 4
2x Juice Replenish	4 3 1
Legal Goal Tending	7 5 6
Play As Afro Man	5 1 7
Play As Agent	5 5 7
Play As Business-A	5 3 7
Play As Business-B	5 2 7
Play As Coach	5 6 7
Play As Secretary	5 4 7
Super Back-Ins	2 3 5
Half House	3 6 7
Random Moves	3 0 0
Tournament Mode	0 1 1

PHRASE-OLOGY CODES

Select Phrase-ology from the Inside Stuff option and enter the following to unlock that bonus.

BONUS	PHRASE
All Players and Cinemas	NBA BALLERS TRUE PLAYA
Special Shoe #2	COLD STREAK

BONUS	PHRASE
Special Shoe #3	LOST YA SHOES

CRIBS

Select Phrase-ology from the Inside Stuff option and enter the following to unlock player cribs.

CRIB	PHRASE
Allen Iverson's Recording Studio	THE ANSWER
Karl Malone's Devonshire Estate	ICE HOUSE
Kobe Bryant's Italian Estate	EURO CRIB

CRIB	PHRASE
Ben Gordon's Yacht	NICE YACHT
Yao Ming's Childhood Grade School	PREP SCHOOL

NBA LIVE 06

1960'S ALL-STAR TEAM
Earn all golds in Tier 1 of Superstar Challenge.

1970'S ALL-STAR TEAM
Earn all golds in Tier 2 of Superstar Challenge.

1980'S ALL-STAR TEAM
Earn all golds in Tier 3 of Superstar Challenge.

1990'S ALL-STAR TEAM
Earn all golds in Tier 4 of Superstar Challenge.

ATLANTIC DIVISION VINTAGE JERSEYS
Earn silver in Tier 1 of Superstar Challenge.

NORTHWEST DIVISION VINTAGE JERSEYS
Earn silver in Tier 2 of Superstar Challenge.

NEOPETS PETPET ADVENTURE: THE WAND OF WISHING

START GAME WITH 5 CHOCOLATE TREATS
Enter **treat4u** as your Petpet's name. You can then rename name your character. The chocolate treats are shaped according to the character you chose.

NFL STREET 2 UNLEASHED

Select Cheats and Codes from the Options and enter the following codes.

AFC EAST ALL STARS
Enter **EAASFSCT** as a code.

AFC NORTH ALL STARS
Enter **NAOFRCTH** as a code.

AFC SOUTH ALL STARS
Enter **SAOFUCTH** as a code.

AFC WEST ALL STARS
Enter **WAEFSCT** as a code.

NFC EAST ALL STARS
Enter **NNOFRCTH** as a code.

NFC NORTH ALL-STARS
Enter **NNAS66784** as a code.

NFC SOUTH ALL STARS
Enter **SNOFUCTH** as a code.

NFC WEST ALL STARS
Enter **ENASFSCT** as a code.

REEBOK TEAM
Enter **Reebok** as a code.

TEAM XZIBIT
Enter **TeamXzibit** as a code.

EA FIELD
Enter **EAField** as a code.

GRIDIRON FIELD
Enter **GRIDIRONPRK** as a code.

HUGE PLAYERS
Enter **BIGSmash** as a code.

BIG BALL
Enter **BIGPig** as a code.

MAX CATCH IN QUICK GAME
Enter **MagnetHands** as a code.

MAX SPEED IN QUICK GAME
Enter **GottaBdshoes** as a code.

MAX TACKLING IN QUICK GAME
Enter **BlastTackle** as a code.

DIFFICULT TO JUMP
Enter **CementShoes** as a code.

10X GAMEBREAKER
Enter **XxGBCraZ** as a code.

1X GAMEBREAKER
Enter **IIxGBCraZ** as a code.

NO FUMBLE MODE IN QUICK GAME
Enter **GlueHands** as a code.

FUMBLE MODE IN QUICK GAME
Enter **GreasedPig** as a code.

UNLIMITED TURBO IN QUICK GAME
Enter **NozBoost** as a code.

NO FIRST DOWNS
Enter **NoChains** as a code.

OUTRUN 2006: COAST 2 COAST

100% COMPLETE/UNLOCK EVERYTHING
Edit your license and change the name to **ENTIRETY**. Select Done, then back out of all menus.

1000000 OUTRUN MILES
Edit your license and change the name to **MILESANDMILES**. Select Done, then back out of all menus.

PAC-MAN WORLD 3

ALL LEVELS AND MAZES
At the Main menu, press Left, Right, Left, Right, ●, Up.

PINBALL HALL OF FAME

CUSTOM BALLS OPTION
Enter **CKF** as a code.

TILT OPTION
Enter **BZZ** as a code.

PAYOUT MODE
Enter **WGR** as a code.

ACES HIGH IN FREEPLAY
Enter **UNO** as a code.

CENTRAL PARK IN FREEPLAY
Enter **NYC** as a code.

LOVE MACHINE IN FREEPLAY
Enter **HOT** as a code.

PLAYBOY TABLE IN FREEPLAY
Enter **HEF** as a code.

STRIKES 'N SPARES IN FREEPLAY
Enter **PBA** as a code.

TEE'D OFF IN FREEPLAY
Enter **PGA** as a code.

XOLTEN IN FREEPLAY
Enter **BIG** as a code.

PIRATES OF THE CARIBBEAN: DEAD MAN'S CHEST

GOD MODE
During a game, press ▲, ●, ●, ▲, ▲, ■, ✕, ✕.

FULL HEALTH
During a game, press ▲, ●, ▲, ●, ▲, ●, ●, ✕.

UNLIMITED POWER MOVES
During a game, press ▲, ▲, ▲, ■, ■, ✕, ●, ●.

ONE-SHOT KILL
During a game, press ▲, ●, ●, ▲, ▲, ■, ■, ●.

ALL TREASURE LEVELS
During a game, press ●, ●, ▲, ▲, ▲, ▲, ✕, ✕.

KRAKEN BATTLE
During a game, press ●, ●, ●, ▲, ▲, ▲, ■, ■.

THE SIMS 2

PERK CHEAT
At the Buy Perks screen, hold L + R + Square. Buy the Cheat Perk to get some money, skills and more.

SPIDER-MAN 2

LEVEL WARP
Select Specials from the Options. Choose Cheats and enter **WARPULON**.

ALL MOVES
Select Specials from the Options. Choose Cheats and enter **MYHERO**.

INFINITE HEALTH
Select Specials from the Options. Choose Cheats and enter **NERGETS**.

INFINITE WEBBING
Select Specials from the Options. Choose Cheats and enter **FILLMEUP**.

ENEMIES BIG HEADS AND FEET
Select Specials from the Options. Choose Cheats and enter **BAHLOONIE**.

SPIDER-MAN BIG HEAD AND FEET
Select Specials from the Options. Choose Cheats and enter **HEAVYHEAD**.

TINY SPIDER-MAN
Select Specials from the Options. Choose Cheats and enter **SPIDEYMAN**.

MOVIE VIEWER
Select Specials from the Options. Choose Cheats and enter **POPPYCORN**.

STORYBOARD VIEWER
Select Specials from the Options. Choose Cheats and enter **FRZFRAME**.

PRODUCTION ART
Select Specials from the Options. Choose Cheats and enter **SHUTT**.

TIGER WOODS PGA TOUR

EMERALD DRAGON
Earn $1,000,000.

GREEK ISLES
Earn $1,500,000.

PARADISE COVER
Earn $2,000,000.

EA SPORTS FAVORITES
Earn $5,000,000

MEAN8TEEN
Earn $10,000,000.

FANTASY SPECIALS
Earn $15,000,000.

THE HUSTLER'S DREAM 18
Defeat The Hustler in Legend Tour.

TIGER'S DREAM 18
Defeat Tiger Woods in Legend Tour.

TOMB RAIDER: LEGEND

You need to unlock the following cheats before they can be used.

BULLETPROOF
During a game, hold L and press ✕, R, ▲, R, ●, R

DRAW ENEMY HEALTH
During a game, hold L and press ●, ●, ✕, R, R, ▲

INFINITE ASSUALT RIFLE AMMO
During a game, hold L and press ✕, O, ✕, R, ●, ▲

INFINITE GRENADE LAUNCHER
During a game, hold L and press R, ▲, R, ●, R, ●

INFINITE SHOTGUN AMMO
During a game, hold L and press R, ●, ●, R, ●, ✕

INFINITE SMG AMMO
During a game, hold L and press {CR}, ▲, R, R, ✕, ●

ONE SHOT KILL
During a game, hold L and press ▲, ✕, ▲, ●, R, ●

TEXTURELESS MODE
hold L and press R, ✕, ●, ✕, ▲, R.

WIELD EXCALIBUR
During a game, hold L and press ▲, ✕, ●, R, ▲, R

TONY HAWK'S UNDERGROUND 2 REMIX

PERFECT RAIL BALANCE
Select Cheat Codes from the Game Options and enter tightrope.

THPS1 TONY HAWK
Select Cheat Codes from the Game Options and enter birdman.

VIRTUA TENNIS: WORLD TOUR

KING & QUEEN
At the Main menu, hold L and press Up, Down, Up, Down, ●, ▲, ●.

ALL RACQUETS AND CLOTHING
At the Main menu, hold L and press Right, Left, Right, Right, Up, Up, Up.

ALL STADIUMS
At the Main menu, hold L and press Up, Down, Left, Right, ●, ●, ●.

BEGIN WORLD TOUR WITH $1,000,000
At the Main menu, hold L and press Up, Down, Left, Down, ▲, ▲, ▲.

$2000 A WEEK IN WORLD TOUR
At the Main menu, hold L and press Up, Down, Right, Down, ▲, ●, ▲.

SEPIA MODE
At the Main menu, hold L and press Up, Down, Left, Right, Left, Left, Left.

WORLD CHAMPIONSHIP POKER 2: FEATURING HOWARD LEDERER

SKIP WEEK AND MONEY CHEATS
At the career world map, hold R1. Hold L1 and release R1. Hold Up and release L1. Hold L1 and release Up. Hold R1 and release L1. While still holding R1, press Up/Down to skip weeks and Right/Left for money.

WRC: FIA WORLD RALLY CHAMPIONSHIP

UNLOCK EVERYTHING
Create a new profile with the name **PADLOCK.**

EXTRA AVATARS
Create a new profile with the name **UGLYMUGS**.

GHOST CAR
Create a new profile with the name **SPOOKY**.

SUPERCHARGER
Create a new profile with the name **MAXPOWER**.

TIME TRIAL GHOST CARS
Create a new profile with the name **AITRIAL**.

BIRD CAMERA
Create a new profile with the name **dovecam**.

REVERSES CONTROLS
Create a new profile with the name **REVERSE**.

X-MEN LEGENDS II: RISE OF APOCALYPSE

ALL CHARACTERS
At the Team Management screen, press Right, Left, Left, Right, Up, Up, Up, Start.

LEVEL 99 CHARACTERS
At the Team Management screen, press Up, Down, Up, Down, Left, Up, Left, Right, Start.

ALL SKILLS
At the Team Management screen, press Left, Right, Left, Right, Down, Up, Start.

SUPER SPEED
Pause the game and press Up, Up, Up, Down, Up, Down, Start.

UNLIMITED XTREME POWER
Pause the game and press Left, Down, Right, Down, Up, Up, Down, Up Start.

100,000 TECHBITS
At Forge or Beast's equipment screen, press Up, Up, Up, Down, Right, Right, Start.

ALL CINEMATICS
A the Review Menu, press Left, Right, Right, Left, Down, Down, Left, Start.

ALL COMIC BOOKS
At the Review Menu, press Right, Left, Left, Right, Up, Up, Right, Start.

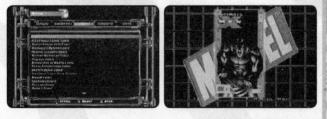

XBOX®

EVERYONE

AND 1 STREETBALL

AVATAR: THE LAST AIRBENDER

BRATZ: FOREVER DIAMONDZ

CARS

CHICKEN LITTLE

CRASH TAG TEAM RACING

DANCE DANCE REVOLUTION ULTRAMIX 2

DANCE DANCE REVOLUTION ULTRAMIX 3

EA SPORTS ARENA FOOTBALL

FORZA MOTORSPORT

FROGGER: ANCIENT SHADOW

ICE AGE 2: THE MELTDOWN

THE INCREDIBLES:
  RISE OF THE UNDERMINER

LEGO STAR WARS: THE VIDEO GAME

LEGO STAR WARS II: THE ORIGINAL
  TRILOGY

MADDEN NFL 06

MADDEN NFL 07

MAJOR LEAGUE BASEBALL 2K6

MIDNIGHT CLUB 3: DUB EDITION REMIX

MIDWAY ARCADE TREASURES 3

MLB SLUGFEST 2006

MVP 06 NCAA BASEBALL

MX vs. ATV UNLEASHED

NASCAR 06: TOTAL TEAM CONTROL

NASCAR 07

NBA 2K6

NBA 2K7

NBA BALLERS

NBA BALLERS: PHENOM

NBA LIVE 06

NBA LIVE 07

NCAA FOOTBALL 06

NCAA FOOTBALL 07

NCAA MARCH MADNESS 06

NEED FOR SPEED CARBON

NEED FOR SPEED MOST WANTED

NEED FOR SPEED UNDERGROUND 2

NFL HEAD COACH

NFL STREET 2

NHL 2K6

OUTRUN 2

OUTRUN 2006: COAST 2 COAST

OVER THE HEDGE

PAC-MAN WORLD 3

RALLISPORT CHALLENGE 2

ROBOTS

RUGBY LEAGUE 2

SCALER

SHREK 2

SONIC HEROES

SONIC MEGA COLLECTION PLUS

SPONGEBOB SQUAREPANTS:
  BATTLE FOR BIKINI BOTTOM

SPONGEBOB SQUAREPANTS:
  LIGHTS, CAMERA, PANTS!

SSX ON TOUR

TAK 2: THE STAFF OF DREAMS

TAK: THE GREAT JUJU CHALLENGE

TAZ WANTED

TEENAGE MUTANT NINJA TURTLES 3:
  MUTANT NIGHTMARE

TIGER WOODS PGA TOUR 06

TIGER WOODS PGA TOUR 07

TIM BURTON'S THE NIGHTMARE BEFORE
  CHRISTMAS: OOGIE'S REVENGE

TY THE TASMANIAN TIGER 2:
  BUSH RESCUE

TY THE TASMANIAN TIGER 3:
  NIGHT OF THE QUINKAN

WORLD RACING 2

YU-GI-OH! THE DAWN OF DESTINY

ZAPPER

EVERYONE

CONTENT RATED BY
ESRB

TEEN

AEON FLUX

ALIEN HOMINID

BLAZING ANGELS: SQUADRONS OF WWII

CABELA'S DANGEROUS HUNTS 2

CAPCOM CLASSICS COLLECTION

THE CHRONICLES OF NARNIA: THE LION, THE WITCH AND THE WARDROBE

COLD WAR

CRIMSON SKIES: HIGH ROAD TO REVENGE

THE DA VINCI CODE

DESTROY ALL HUMANS!

DESTROY ALL HUMANS! 2

DIGIMON RUMBLE ARENA 2

DRAGON BALL Z: SAGAS

FANTASTIC 4

FLATOUT 2

FUTURE TACTICS: THE UPRISING

GODZILLA: SAVE THE EARTH

GREG HASTINGS' TOURNAMENT PAINTBALL

GUN METAL

HEROES OF THE PACIFIC

THE INCREDIBLE HULK: ULTIMATE DESTRUCTION

JUICED

JUSTICE LEAGUE HEROES

L.A. RUSH

MAGIC: THE GATHERING— BATTLEGROUNDS

MARVEL NEMESIS: RISE OF THE IMPERFECTS

MARVEL ULTIMATE ALLIANCE

MLB SLUGFEST: LOADED

ODDWORLD: STRANGER'S WRATH

PANZER DRAGOON ORTA

PETER JACKSON'S KING KONG: THE OFFICIAL GAME OF THE MOVIE

PIRATES OF THE CARIBBEAN

POWERDROME

PSYCHONAUTS

ROGUE TROOPER

SECRET WEAPONS OVER NORMANDY

SHATTERED UNION

SID MEIER'S PIRATES!

THE SIMS 2

SPIDER-MAN 2

SPIKEOUT: BATTLE STREET

SPY HUNTER: NOWHERE TO RUN

SPY VS. SPY

STAR WARS: BATTLEFRONT II

STAR WARS EPISODE III: REVENGE OF THE SITH

STAR WARS KNIGHTS OF THE OLD REPUBLIC II: THE SITH LORDS

STOLEN

TOMB RAIDER: LEGEND

TONY HAWK'S AMERICAN WASTELAND

TONY HAWK'S PROJECT 8

ULTIMATE SPIDER-MAN

WARPATH

XGRA: EXTREME-G RACING ASSOCIATION

X-MEN LEGENDS II: RISE OF APOCALYPSE

X-MEN: THE OFFICIAL GAME

YAGER

YU-GI-OH! THE DAWN OF DESTINY

ZAPPER

XBOX®

Xbox® Table of Contents

AEON FLUX

BOMBER JACKET OUTFIT

Select Enter Cheat from the Extras menu and enter **JULIET ALPHA CHARLIE KILO ECHO TANGO**. Look for the outfit under Outfits in the Extras menu.

FAME OUTFIT

Select Enter Cheat from the Extras menu and enter **GOLF ROMEO ALPHA YANKEE**. Look for the outfit under Outfits in the Extras menu.

MULTIPLE OUTFITS

Select Enter Cheat from the Extras menu and enter **CHARLIE LIMA OSCAR TANGO HOTEL ECHO SIERRA**. Look for the outfits under Outfits in the Extras menu. The outfits include the following: Freya, Monican Freya, Hostess Judy, Una, and Fashion Una.

MRS. GOODCHILD OUTFIT

Select Enter Cheat from the Extras menu and enter **WHISKEY HOTEL INDIA TANGO ECHO**. Look for the outfit under Outfits in the Extras menu.

REVELATION OUTFIT

Select Enter Cheat from the Extras menu and enter **ALPHA ROMEO MIKE SIERRA**. Look for the outfit under Outfits in the Extras menu.

SEEDS OUTFIT

Select Enter Cheat from the Extras menu and enter **MIKE OSCAR VICTOR INDIA ECHO**. Look for the outfit under Outfits in the Extras menu.

WAR OUTFIT

Select Enter Cheat from the Extras menu and enter **BRAVO LIMA UNIFORM ROMEO**. Look for the outfit under Outfits in the Extras menu.

ALL REPLAY EPISODES

Select Enter Cheat from the Extras menu and enter **BRAVO ALPHA YANKEE OSCAR UNIFORM**. Then select Replay Episode from the Extras menu to view the episodes.

ALL SLIDESHOWS

Select Enter Cheat from the Extras menu and enter **PAPA INDIA XRAY ECHO SIERRA**. Then select Slideshows from the Extras menu to view the slideshows.

ACTION MOVIE CHEAT

Select Enter Cheat from the Extras menu and enter **BRAVO ALPHA GOLF MIKE ALPHA NOVEMBER**. Or, enter **UNIFORM KILO GOLF ALPHA MIKE ECHO ROMEO**. Pause the game and select Cheats to access the code.

GOD MODE

Select Enter Cheat from the Extras menu and enter **TANGO ROMEO INDIA ROMEO OSCAR XRAY**. Pause the game and select Cheats to access God Mode.

FREE FATALITIES CHEAT

Select Enter Cheat from the Extras menu and enter **CHARLIE UNIFORM TANGO INDIA OSCAR NOVEMBER ECHO**. Pause the game and select Cheats to access the code.

ONE-STRIKE KILLS

Select Enter Cheat from the Extras menu and enter **BRAVO UNIFORM CHARLIE KILO FOXTROT SIERRA TANGO**. Pause the game and select Cheats to access the code.

RESTORE HEALTH

Select Enter Cheat from the Extras menu and enter **HOTEL ECHO ALPHA LIMA MIKE ECHO**. Pause the game and select Cheats to access the code.

UNLIMITED AMMO

Select Enter Cheat from the Extras menu and enter **FOXTROT UNIFORM GOLF**. Pause the game and select Cheats to access the code.

UNLIMITED HEALTH

Select Enter Cheat from the Extras menu and enter **CHARLIE LIMA OSCAR NOVEMBER ECHO**. Pause the game and select Cheats to access the code.

UNLIMITED POWER STRIKES

Select Enter Cheat from the Extras menu and enter **LIMA CHARLIE VICTOR GOLF**. Pause the game and select Cheats to access the code.

ALIEN HOMINID

ALL LEVELS, MINI-GAMES, AND HATS

Select Player 1 Setup or Player 2 Setup and change the name to **ROYGBIV**.

HATS FOR 2-PLAYER GAME

Go to the Options menu and rename your alien one of the following:

HEAD 1	HEAD 2	HEAD 3	HEAD 1	HEAD 2	HEAD 3
ABE	Top Hat	#11	GOODMAN	Black Curly Hair	#7
APRIL	Blond Wig	#4	GRRL	Flowers	#10
BEHEMOTH	Red Cap	#24	PRINCESS	Tiara	#12
CLETUS	Hunting Hat	#3	SUPERFLY	Afro	#6
DANDY	Flower Petal Hat	#13	TOMFULP	Brown Messy Hair	#2

AND 1 STREETBALL

GLOBAL UNLOCK

Select Cheat Codes from the Options menu and enter B, B, A, A, X, Y, X, Y. This unlocks all Bonus Stuff

ALL CHARACTERS

Select Cheat Codes from the Options menu and enter B, X, X, Y, B, X, A, A.

ALL BREAKDOWNS

Select Cheat Codes from the Options menu and enter A, A, Y, X, X, B, Y, B.

CHATTERBOX UNLOCK

Select Cheat Codes from the Options menu and enter B, X, Y, X, B, A, X, B.

SIDE GAMES

Select Cheat Codes from the Options menu and enter Y, X, B, A, A, Y, Y, X.

DJ GREEN LANTERN

Select Cheat Codes from the Options menu and enter Y, Y, B, A, X, A, B, Y.

PLAY AS FLASH

Select Cheat Codes from the Options menu and enter B, A, A, Y, A, B, B, X.

PLAY AS SHANE

Select Cheat Codes from the Options menu and enter X, A, B, A, B, Y, B, A.

PLAY AS SKIP TO MY LOU

Select Cheat Codes from the Options menu and enter Y, A, Y, X, B, A, Y, X.

HAMILTONS

Select Cheat Codes from the Options menu and enter Y, B, X, X, B, Y, A, Y. This gives you $1,000,000.

ALWAYS ON FIRE

Select Cheat Codes from the Options menu and enter X, B, A, B, X, A, X, Y.

IBALL MOVES

Select Cheat Codes from the Options menu and enter A, B, B, A, X, Y, A, X.

LIKE WATER

Select Cheat Codes from the Options menu and enter X, A, Y, X, A, Y, B, B.

THE OG WAY

Select Cheat Codes from the Options menu and enter B, Y, X, X, Y, B, A, X.

SHOT TIMING TEXT

Select Cheat Codes from the Options menu and enter B, X, Y, Y, X, X, Y, B.

AVATAR: THE LAST AIRBENDER

ALL TREASURE MAPS
Select Code Entry from Extras and enter 37437.

1 HIT DISHONOR
Select Code Entry from Extras and enter 54641.

DOUBLE DAMAGE
Select Code Entry from Extras and enter 34743.

UNLIMITED COPPER
Select Code Entry from Extras and enter 23637.

UNLIMITED CHI
Select Code Entry from Extras and enter 24463.

UNLIMITED HEALTH
Select Code Entry from Extras and enter 94677.

NEVERENDING STEALTH
Select Code Entry from Extras and enter 53467.

CHARACTER CONCEPT ART GALLERY
Select Code Entry from Extras and enter 97831.

BLAZING ANGELS: SQUADRONS OF WWII

ALL MISSIONS, MEDALS, & PLANES
At the Main menu, hold Left Trigger + Right Trigger and press X, White, Black, Y, Y, Black, White, X.

GOD MODE
Pause the game, hold Left Trigger and press X, Y, Y, X. Release Left Trigger, hold Right Trigger and press Y, X, X, Y. Re-enter the code to disable it.

DAMAGE INCREASED
Pause the game, hold Left Trigger and press White, White, Black. Release Left Trigger, hold Right Trigger and press Black, Black, White. Re-enter the code to disable it.

BRATZ: FOREVER DIAMONDZ

1000 BLINGZ
While in the Bratz Office, use the Cheat computer to enter SIZZLN.

2000 BLINGZ
While in the Bratz Office, use the Cheat computer to enter FLAUNT.

PET TREATS
While in the Bratz Office, use the Cheat computer to enter TREATZ.

GIFT SET A
While in the Bratz Office, use the Cheat computer to enter STYLIN.

GIFT SET B
While in the Bratz Office, use the Cheat computer to enter SKATIN.

GIFT SET C
While in the Bratz Office, use the Cheat computer to enter JEWELZ.

GIFT SET E
While in the Bratz Office, use the Cheat computer to enter DIMNDZ.

CABELA'S DANGEROUS HUNTS 2

DOUBLE HEALTH
Select Codes and enter Eye, Bolt, Skull, Hand, Boot.

HEALTH REGENERATES FASTER
Select Codes and enter Skull, Eye, Boot, Bolt, Hand.

DOUBLE DAMAGE
Select Codes and enter Hand, Boot, Skull, Eye, Bolt.

INFINITE AMMO
Select Codes and enter Bolt, Hand, Eye, Boot, Skull.

CAPCOM CLASSICS COLLECTION

ALL LOCKS OPENED
At the Title screen, press Left Trigger, Right Trigger, Up on Right Thumbstick, Down on Right Thumbstick, Left Trigger, Right Trigger, Up on Left Thumbstick, Down on Left Thumbstick, Left Trigger, Right Trigger, Up, Down.

CARS

UNLOCK EVERYTHING
Select Cheat Codes from the Options and enter IF900HP.

ALL CHARACTERS
Select Cheat Codes from the Options and enter YAYCARS.

ALL CHARACTER SKINS
Select Cheat Codes from the Options and enter R4MONE.

ALL MINI-GAMES AND COURSES
Select Cheat Codes from the Options and enter MATTL66.

MATER'S COUNTDOWN CLEAN-UP MINI-GAME AND MATER'S SPEEDY CIRCUIT
Select Cheat Codes from the Options and enter TRGTEXC.

FAST START
Select Cheat Codes from the Options and enter IMSPEED.

INFINITE BOOST
Select Cheat Codes from the Options and enter VROOOOM.

ART
Select Cheat Codes from the Options and enter CONC3PT.

VIDEOS
Select Cheat Codes from the Options and enter WATCHIT.

CHICKEN LITTLE

INVINCIBILITY
Select Cheat Codes from the Extras menu and enter Baseball, Baseball, Baseball, Shirt.

BIG FEET
Select Cheat Codes from the Extras menu and enter Hat, Glove, Glove, Hat.

BIG HAIR
Select Cheat Codes from the Extras menu and enter Baseball, Bat, Bat, Baseball.

BIG HEAD
Select Cheat Codes from the Extras menu and enter Hat, Helmet, Helmet, Hat.

PAPER PANTS
Select Cheat Codes from the Extras menu and enter Bat, Bat, Hat, Hat.

SUNGLASSES
Select Cheat Codes from the Extras menu and enter Glove, Glove, Helmet, Helmet.

UNDERWEAR
Select Cheat Codes from the Extras menu and enter Hat, Hat, Shirt, Shirt.

THE CHRONICLES OF NARNIA: THE LION, THE WITCH AND THE WARDROBE

ENABLE CHEATS

At the Title screen, press A and hold Left Trigger + Right Trigger and press Down, Down, Right, Up. The text should turn green when entered correctly. When this occurs, you can enter the following codes.

LEVEL SELECT

At the wardrobe, hold Left Trigger and press Up, Up, Right, Right, Up, Right, Down.

ALL BONUS LEVELS

At the Bonus Drawer, hold Left Trigger and press Down, Down, Right, Right, Down, Right, Up.

LEVEL SKIP

During gameplay, hold Left Trigger and press Down, Left, Down, Left, Down, Right, Down, Right, Up.

INVINCIBILITY

During gameplay, hold Left Trigger and press Down, Up, Down, Right, Right.

RESTORE HEALTH

During gameplay, hold Left Trigger and press Down, Left, Left, Right.

10,000 COINS

During gameplay, hold Left Trigger and press Down, Left, Right, Down, Down.

ALL ABILITIES

During gameplay, hold Left Trigger and press Down, Left, Right, Left, Up.

FILL COMBO METER

During gameplay, hold Left Trigger and press Up, Up, Right, Up.

COLD WAR

INVULNERABILITY

Pause the game and press X, White, Y, Black, Left.

WIN CURRENT LEVEL

Pause the game and press X, White, Y, Black, X.

ALL ITEMS, GADGETS, & TECH POINTS

Pause the game and press X, White, Y, Black, Y.

CRASH TAG TEAM RACING

FASTER VEHICLES

At the Main menu, hold Left Trigger + Right Trigger and press B, B, Y, Y.

ONE-HIT KO

At the Main menu, hold Left Trigger + Right Trigger and press A, B, B, A.

DISABLE HUD

At the Main menu, hold Left Trigger + Right Trigger and press A, X, Y, B.

CHICKEN HEADS

At the Main menu, hold Left Trigger + Right Trigger and press A, B, B, X.

JAPANESE CRASH

At the Main menu, hold Left Trigger + Right Trigger and press X, B, X, B.

DRIVE A BLOCK VEHICLE

At the Main menu, hold Left Trigger + Right Trigger and press B, B, Y, X.

CRIMSON SKIES: HIGH ROAD TO REVENGE

GOD MODE

During a game, press Y, A, X, B, Black.

$5,000

During a game, press A, Y, A, Y, Black.

10 TOKENS

During a game, press X, B, X, B, Black.

ALL PLANES

During a game, press Y, X, B, Y, Black.

SUPER PRIMARY WEAPON

During a game, press B, X, A, B, Black.

ULTRA HARD DIFFICULTY

During a game, press X, B, A, X, Black.

DANCE DANCE REVOLUTION ULTRAMIX 2

ALL SONGS
With a controller in port four, select Credits from the Options screen. Then press Up, Up, Down, Down, Left, Right, Left, Right, B, A, Up, Up, Down, Down, Left, Right, Left, Right, A, B.

KONSENTO:03 AND MAID-ZUKIN CHARACTERS
With a controller in port four, select Dancers from the Options screen. Then press and hold X + Y for five seconds.

DANCE DANCE REVOLUTION ULTRAMIX 3

ALL SONGS
Select Credits from the Options screen and play the Credits mini-game, then press the opposite of what the game indicates. (For example, press Up when it says Down and so on. Or, if it says Left + Right, press Up + Down.) You'll hear applause when the code is entered correctly.

THE DA VINCI CODE

GOD MODE
Select Codes from the Options screen and enter **VITRUVIAN MAN**.

EXTRA HEALTH
Select Codes from the Options screen and enter **SACRED FEMININE**.

MISSION SELECT
Select Codes from the Options screen and enter **CLOS LUCE 1519**.

ONE-HIT FIST KILL
Select Codes from the Options screen and enter **PHILLIPS EXETER**.

ONE-HIT WEAPON KILL
Select Codes from the Options screen and enter **ROYAL HOLLOWAY**.

ALL VISUAL DATABASE
Select Codes from the Options screen and enter **APOCRYPHA**.

ALL VISUAL DATABASE AND CONCEPT ART
Select Codes from the Options screen and enter **ET IN ARCADIA EGO**.

DESTROY ALL HUMANS!

AMMO-A-PLENTY
Pause the game, hold Left Trigger and press Left, Y, White, Right, Black, X. This gives you unlimited ammo.

BULLETPROOF CRYPTO
Pause the game, hold Left Trigger and press X, Y, Left, Left, Y, X. This makes you invincible.

DEEP THINKER
Pause the game, hold Left Trigger and press Black, White, Y, Right, White, Y. This gives you unlimited concentration.

AWARE LIKE A FOX
Pause the game, hold Left Trigger and press Right, Right, X, White, Black, Right, White. This maxes out the alert meter.

NOBODY LOVES YOU
Pause the game, hold Left Trigger and press White, Right, White, Black, X, Right. This resets the alert meter.

FIND KEY TO ORTHOPOX'S LAB
On the Mothership, hold Left Trigger and press X, Y, Left, Left, Y, X. This gives you access to the Upgrades at Pox's Lab.

MMMM BRAINS!
On the Mothership, hold Left Trigger and press Black, Black, White, White, Left, Right, Left, Right, White, Black. This gives you extra DNA.

DESTROY ALL HUMANS! 2

SALAD DAYS WITH POX & CRYPTO MOVIE
Pause the game and select Archives. Hold Left Thumbstick and press A, X, Y, B, X, B, Y, A, A.

DIGIMON RUMBLE ARENA 2

ONE-HIT KILLS
At the Title screen, press Right, Up, Left, Down, A, Left Trigger + Right Trigger.

EVOLVE ENERGY ITEM
At the Title screen, press Y, Right, Down, B, Left Trigger, A, Right Trigger, A, Y.

EVOLVE METER ALWAYS FULL
At the Title screen, press X, Right, A, Y, Left, B, Left Trigger + Right Trigger.

DRAGON BALL Z: SAGAS

ALL UPGRADES
Pause the game, select Controller and press Up, Left, Down, Right, Back, Start, Y, X, A, B.

INVINCIBILITY
Pause the game, select Controller and press Down, A, Up, Y, Back, Start, Right, X, Left, B.

EA SPORTS ARENA FOOTBALL

BIG BALL
While at the line of scrimmage, press Left Trigger + Y, Up, Up.

SMALL BALL
While at the line of scrimmage, press Left Trigger + Y, Down, Down.

NORMAL SIZE BALL
While at the line of scrimmage, press Left Trigger + Y, Up, Down.

MAX STATS IN QUICK PLAY
Load a profile with the name **IronMen**. This will maximize all players' stats in Quick Play.

FANTASTIC 4

BARGE ARENA AND STAN LEE INTERVIEW #1
At the Main menu, press X, B, X, Down, Down, B, Up.

INFINITE COSMIC POWER
At the Main menu, press Up, X, X, X, Left, Right, B.

BONUS LEVEL
At the Main menu, press Right, Right, X, B, Left, Up, Down.

FLATOUT 2

ALL CARS AND 1,000,000 CREDITS
Select Enter Code from Extras and enter GIEVEPIX.

1,000,000 CREDITS
Select Enter Code from the Extras and enter GIVECASH.

PIMPSTER CAR
Select Enter Code from Extras and enter RUTTO.

FLATMOBILE CAR
Select Enter Code from Extras and enter WOTKINS.

MOB CAR
Select Enter Code from the Extras and enter BIGTRUCK.

SCHOOL BUS
Select Enter Code from Extras and enter GIEVCARPLZ.

ROCKET CAR
Select Enter Code from Extras and enter KALJAKOPPA.

TRUCK
Select Enter Code from the Extras and enter ELPUEBLO.

FORZA MOTORSPORT

START CAREER WITH 900,000,000 CREDITS
Start a new profile with the name **tEAm4za**.

ALL CARS
Start a new profile with the name **nOsLiW**.

FROGGER: ANCIENT SHADOW

UNLOCK LEVELS
To unlock various levels, select Cheat Codes and enter the following:

LEVEL	ENTER	LEVEL	ENTER
Level 4-1	Lily, Lumpy, Frogger, Finnius	Level 6-2	Lily, Lily, Wani, Lily
Level 4-2	Wani, Frogger, Lily, Berry	Level 6-3	Berry, Frogger, Lily, Lily
Level 5-1	Wani, Wani, Berry, Frogger	Level 7-1	Lumpy, Wani, Frogger, Frogger
Level 5-2	Frogger, Finnius, Lily, Lily	Level 7-2	Lumpy, Frogger, Lily, Berry
Level 6-1	Wani, Lily, Lily, Frogger		

UNLOCK LETTERS
To unlock various letters, select Cheat Codes and enter the following:

LEVEL	ENTER	LEVEL	ENTER
Hyacinth Letter	Berry, Frogger, Lumpy, Berry	Rose Letter	Frogger, Wani, Berry, Lumpy
Cosmos Letter	Lumpy, Frogger, Frogger, Lumpy	Pansy Letter	Finnius, Lumpy, Lily, Wani

UNLOCK WIGS
To unlock various wigs, select Cheat Codes and enter the following:

LEVEL	ENTER	LEVEL	ENTER
Lobster Wig	Finnius, Wani, Lumpy, Frogger	Sail Boat Wig	Lumpy, Lumpy, Lumpy, Lumpy
Bird Nest Wig	Lily, Lily, Lily, Lily	Skull Wig	Frogger, Lumpy, Lily, Frogger

UNLOCK ARTWORK
To unlock different kinds of artwork, select Cheat Codes and enter the following:

LEVEL	ENTER	LEVEL	ENTER
Programmer Art 1	Wani, Wani, Wani, Wani	Additional Art 1	Frogger, Frogger, Frogger, Frogger
Programmer Art 2	Lumpy, Frogger, Berry, Lily	Additional Art 2	Finnius, Finnius, Finnius, Finnius
Programmer Art 3	Wani, Frogger, Lily, Finnius	Additional Art 3	Berry, Berry, Berry, Berry

DEVELOPER PICTURE 1
Select Cheat Codes and enter Wani, Frogger, Wani, Frogger.

DEVELOPER PICTURE 2
Select Cheat Codes and enter Berry, Berry, Berry, Wani.

FUTURE TACTICS: THE UPRISING

LEVEL SKIP
At the Game Select screen, press Left Trigger, X, Right Trigger, Right Trigger, Black, X, Left Trigger, Right Trigger, Black.

UNLIMITED TURNS AND MOVEMENT
During a game, press Up, Up, Down, Down, Left, Right, Left, Left, Right Trigger, Left Trigger.

BIG HEADS
During a game, press Up, Left, Down, Left, Down, Up, Up, Left.

DISCO MODE
During a game, press Left Trigger, Left, Left Trigger, Left, Right Trigger, Right, Right Trigger, Right.

LOW GRAVITY
During a game, press Up (x6), Down, Right, Up.

GODZILLA: SAVE THE EARTH

CHEAT MENU

At the Main menu, press and hold Left Trigger, B, Right Trigger in that order, then release B, Right Trigger, Left Trigger. Now you can enter the following cheats.

ALL CITIES
Enter 659996.

ALL MONSTERS
Enter 525955.

UNLOCK CHALLENGES
Enter 975013.

HEALTH REGENERATES
Enter 536117.

ENERGY DOESN'T REGENERATE
Enter 122574.

INDESTRUCTIBLE BUILDINGS
Enter 812304.

100,000 POINTS
Enter 532459.

150,000 POINTS
Enter 667596.

200,000 POINTS
Enter 750330.

PLAYER 1: 4X DAMAGE
Enter 259565.

PLAYER 1: INFINITE ENERGY
Enter 819342.

PLAYER 1: INVISIBLE
Enter 531470.

PLAYER 1: INVULNERABLE
Enter 338592.

PLAYER 2: 4X DAMAGE
Enter 927281.

PLAYER 2: INFINITE ENERGY
Enter 324511.

PLAYER 2: INVISIBLE
Enter 118699.

PLAYER 2: INVULNERABLE
Enter 259333.

PLAYER 3: 4X DAMAGE
Enter 500494.

PLAYER 3: INFINITE ENERGY
Enter 651417.

PLAYER 3: INVISIBLE
Enter 507215.

PLAYER 3: INVULNERABLE
Enter 953598.

PLAYER 4: 4X DAMAGE
Enter 988551.

PLAYER 4: INFINITE ENERGY
Enter 456719.

PLAYER 4: INVISIBLE
Enter 198690.

PLAYER 4: INVULNERABLE
Enter 485542.

GALLERY
Enter 294206.

GODZILLA FINAL WARS
Enter 409014.

GREG HASTINGS' TOURNAMENT PAINTBALL

FLYING
During a game, hold Black + X + Right Trigger and press Up, Up, Down, Down, Right, Left, Down, Up.

GUN METAL

ALL MISSIONS
At the Mission Select screen, press Left Thumbstick, Black, Right Trigger, Right Thumbstick, White, Left Trigger.

MISSION SKIP
During a mission, press Left Thumbstick, White, White, Down, Right Thumbstick, White.

ALTERNATE MUSIC
At the Title screen, press Left Thumbstick, Left Thumbstick, Right Thumbstick, Right Thumbstick, Left Trigger, Right Trigger.

JOKE MISSION BREIFINGS
During Missions 1, 3, 6, 8, 9 or 14, press Left Trigger, Left Trigger, Right Trigger, Right Trigger, Left Thumbstick, Right Thumbstick.

HEROES OF THE PACIFIC

Note that the following cheats will disable game saving.

CHEAT MENU
At the Main menu, press Y, Left Trigger, Left on D-pad, Right Trigger, Right on D-pad, White.

UPGRADE PLANES
At the Main menu, press Left Trigger, Left on the Right Thumbstick, Right Trigger, Right on the Right Thumbstick, White, Y.

ALL PLANES AND MISSIONS
At the Main menu, press Up on the Right Thumbstick, Down on the Right Thumbstick, White, Black, Left on the Right Thumbstick, Right on the Right Thumbstick.

JAPANESE PLANES
At the Main menu, press White, Black, Left Trigger, Right Trigger, Up on the Right Thumbstick, Left on the Right Thumbstick.

ICE AGE 2: THE MELTDOWN

INFINITE PEBBLES
Pause the game and press Down, Down, Left, Up, Up, Right, Up, Down.

INFINITE ENERGY
Pause the game and press Down, Left, Right, Down, Down, Right, Left, Down.

INFINITE HEALTH
Pause the game and press Up, Right, Down, Up, Left, Down, Right, Left.

THE INCREDIBLE HULK: ULTIMATE DESTRUCTION

You must first collect a specific comic in the game to activate each code. After collecting the appropriate comic, you can enter the following. If you don't have the comic and enter the code, you get the following message: "That code cannot be activated...yet". You can access the cheats on the Code Input screen.

UNLOCKED: CABS GALORE
Select Code Input from the Extras menu and enter **CABBIES**.

UNLOCKED: GORILLA INVASION
Select Code Input from the Extras menu and enter **KINGKNG**.

UNLOCKED: MASS TRANSIT
Select Code Input from the Extras menu and enter **TRANSIT**.

UNLOCKED: 5000 SMASH POINTS
Select Code Input from the Extras menu and enter **SMASH5**.

UNLOCKED: 10000 SMASH POINTS

Select Code Input from the Extras menu and enter **SMASH10**.

UNLOCKED: 15000 SMASH POINTS

Select Code Input from the Extras menu and enter **SMASH15**.

UNLOCKED: AMERICAN FLAG SHORTS

Select Code Input from the Extras menu and enter **AMERICA**.

UNLOCKED: CANADIAN FLAG SHORTS

Select Code Input from the Extras menu and enter **OCANADA**.

UNLOCKED: FRENCH FLAG SHORTS

Select Code Input from the Extras menu and enter **Drapeau**.

UNLOCKED: GERMAN FLAG SHORTS

Select Code Input from the Extras menu and enter **DEUTSCH**.

UNLOCKED: ITALIAN FLAG SHORTS

Select Code Input from the Extras menu and enter **MUTANDA**.

UNLOCKED: JAPANESE FLAG SHORTS

Select Code Input from the Extras menu and enter **FURAGGU**.

UNLOCKED: SPANISH FLAG SHORTS

Select Code Input from the Extras menu and enter **BANDERA**.

UNLOCKED: UK FLAG SHORTS

Select Code Input from the Extras menu and enter **FSHNCHP**.

UNLOCKED: COW MISSILES

Select Code Input from the Extras menu and enter **CHZGUN**.

UNLOCKED: DOUBLE HULK'S DAMAGE

Select Code Input from the Extras menu and enter **DESTROY**.

UNLOCKED: DOUBLE POWER COLLECTABLES

Select Code Input from the Extras menu and enter **BRINGIT**.

UNLOCKED: BLACK AND WHITE

Select Code Input from the Extras menu and enter **RETRO**.

UNLOCKED: SEPIA

Select Code Input from the Extras menu and enter **HISTORY**.

UNLOCKED: ABOMINATION

Select Code Input from the Extras menu and enter **VILLAIN**.

UNLOCKED: GRAY HULK

Select Code Input from the Extras menu and enter **CLASSIC**.

UNLOCKED: JOE FIXIT SKIN

Select Code Input from the Extras menu and enter **SUITFIT**.

UNLOCKED: WILD TRAFFIC

Select Code Input from the Extras menu and enter **FROGGIE**.

UNLOCKED: LOW GRAVITY

Select Code Input from the Extras menu and enter **PILLOWS**.

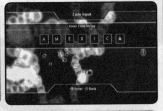

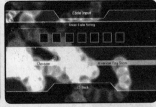

THE INCREDIBLES: RISE OF THE UNDERMINER

BIG HEADS
Pause the game and press B to access the Options screen. Choose Secrets and enter **EGOPROBLEM**. Re-enter the code to disable it.

MR. INCREDIBLE GAINS 1000 EXPERIENCE POINTS
Pause the game and press B to access the Options screen. Choose Secrets and enter **MRIPROF**.

FROZONE 1000 GAINS EXPERIENCE POINTS
Pause the game and press B to access the Options screen. Choose Secrets and enter **FROZPROF**.

MR. INCREDIBLE GAINS A SUPER-MOVE
Pause the game and press B to access the Options screen. Choose Secrets and enter **MRIBOOM**.

FROZONE GAINS A SUPER-MOVE
Pause the game and press B to access the Options screen. Choose Secrets and enter **FROZBOOM**.

SHOWS THE GAME CREDITS
Pause the game and press B to access the Options screen. Choose Secrets and enter **ROLLCALL**.

TOUGHER GAME
Pause the game and press B to access the Options screen. Choose Secrets and enter **THISISTOOEASY**. This code cuts damage done to enemies in half, doubles damage caused to the Supers, there is no health recovery, and Experience Points are halved.

EASIER GAME
Pause the game and press B to access the Options screen. Choose Secrets and enter **THISISTOOHARD**. This code causes double damage to enemies, halves damage done to the Supers, and doubles the amount of health recovery and Experience Points!

ALL GALLERY ITEMS
Pause the game and press B to access the Options screen. Choose Secrets and enter **SHOWME**.

DOUBLE EXPERIENCE POINTS
Pause the game and press B to access the Options screen. Choose Secrets and enter **MAXIMILLION**.

JUICED

ARCADE/CUSTOM MODE UNLOCKED
Select Cheats from the Extras menu and enter PINT.

JUSTICE LEAGUE HEROES

ALL COSTUMES
Pause the game, hold Left Trigger + Right Trigger and press Down, Left, Up, Right.

UNLIMITED ENERGY
Pause the game, hold Left Trigger + Right Trigger and press Down, Down, Right, Right, Up, Up, Left, Left.

20 SHIELDS
Pause the game, hold Left Trigger + Right Trigger and press Up, Up, Down, Down.

L.A. RUSH

$5,000
During a game, press Up, Down, Left, Right, B, Left, A, Up.

UNLIMITED N20
During a game, press Up, Down, Left, Right, X, Up, Down, B, Up.

ALL CARS IN GARAGE PIMPED
During a game, press Up, Down, Left, Right, B, X, A, Y, Up, Down, Left, Right.

DISABLE POLICE
During a game, press Up, Down, Left, Right, A, X, Right, Y, Left.

FAST TRAFFIC
During a game, press Up, Down, Left, Right, X, Right, B, Left.

NO CATCH UP
Use C-VHARD as a profile name.

SLOWER OPPONENTS
Use C-EASY as a profile name.

LEGO STAR WARS: THE VIDEO GAME

Extras
Pause the game and select Extras to toggle these cheats on and off.

INVINCIBILITY
At Dexter's Diner, select Enter Code and enter **4PR28U**.

BIG BLASTERS
At Dexter's Diner, select Enter Code and enter **IG72X4**.

CLASSIC BLASTERS
At Dexter's Diner, select Enter Code and enter **L449HD**.

SILLY BLASTERS
At Dexter's Diner, select Enter Code and enter **NR37W1**.

BRUSHES
At Dexter's Diner, select Enter Code and enter **SHRUB1**.

TEA CUPS
At Dexter's Diner, select Enter Code and enter **PUCEAT**.

MINIKIT DETECTOR
At Dexter's Diner, select Enter Code and enter **LD116B**.

MOUSTACHES
At Dexter's Diner, select Enter Code and enter **RP924W**.

PURPLE
At Depxter's Diner, select Enter Code and enter **YD77GC**.

SILHOUETTES
At Dexter's Diner, select Enter Code and enter **MS999Q**.

Character Codes
The following codes make each character available for purchase from Dexter's Diner.

BATTLE DROID
At Dexter's Diner, select Enter Code and enter **987UYR**.

BATTLE DROID (COMMANDER)
At Dexter's Diner, select Enter Code and enter **EN11K5**.

BATTLE DROID (GEONOSIS)
At Dexter's Diner, select Enter Code and enter **LK42U6**.

BATTLE DROID (SECURITY)
At Dexter's Diner, select Enter Code and enter **KF999A**.

BOBA FETT
At Dexter's Diner, select Enter Code and enter **LA811Y**.

CLONE
At Dexter's Diner, select Enter Code and enter **F8B4L6**.

CLONE (EPISODE III)
At Dexter's Diner, select Enter Code and enter **ER33JN**.

CLONE (EPISODE III, PILOT)
At Dexter's Diner, select Enter Code and enter **BHU72T**.

CLONE (EPISODE III, SWAMP)
At Dexter's Diner, select Enter Code and enter **N3T6P8**.

CLONE (EPISODE III, WALKER)
At Dexter's Diner, select Enter Code and enter **RS6E25**.

COUNT DOOKU
At Dexter's Diner, select Enter Code and enter **14PGMN**.

DARTH MAUL
At Dexter's Diner, select Enter Code and enter **H35TUX**.

DARTH SIDIOUS
At Dexter's Diner, select Enter Code and enter **A32CAM**.

DISGUISED CLONE
At Dexter's Diner, select Enter Code and enter **VR832U**.

DROIDEKA
At Dexter's Diner, select Enter Code and enter **DH382U**.

GENERAL GRIEVOUS
At Dexter's Diner, select Enter Code and enter **SF321Y**.

GEONOSIAN
At Dexter's Diner, select Enter Code and enter **19D7NB**.

GRIEVOUS' BODYGUARD
At Dexter's Diner, select Enter Code and enter **ZTY392**.

GONK DROID
At Dexter's Diner, select Enter Code and enter **U63B2A**.

JANGO FETT
At Dexter's Diner, select Enter Code and enter **PL47NH**.

KI-ADI MUNDI
At Dexter's Diner, select Enter Code and enter **DP55MV**.

LUMINARA
At Dexter's Diner, select Enter Code and enter **A725X4**.

MACE WINDU (EPISODE III)
At Dexter's Diner, select Enter Code and enter **MS952L**.

PADMÉ
At Dexter's Diner, select Enter Code and enter **92UJ7D**.

PK DROID
At Dexter's Diner, select Enter Code and enter **R840JU**.

PRINCESS LEIA
At Dexter's Diner, select Enter Code and enter **BEQ82H**.

REBEL TROOPER
At Dexter's Diner, select Enter Code and enter **L54YUK**.

ROYAL GUARD
At Dexter's Diner, select Enter Code and enter **PP43JX**.

SHAAK TI
At Dexter's Diner, select Enter Code and enter **EUW862**.

SUPER BATTLE DROID
At Dexter's Diner, select Enter Code and enter **XZNR21**

LEGO STAR WARS II: THE ORIGINAL TRILOGY

BEACH TROOPER
At Mos Eisley Canteena, select Enter Code and enter UCK868. You still need to select Characters and purchase this character for 20,000 studs.

BEN KENOBI (GHOST)
At Mos Eisley Canteena, select Enter Code and enter BEN917. You still need to select Characters and purchase this character for 1,100,000 studs.

BESPIN GUARD
At Mos Eisley Canteena, select Enter Code and enter VHY832. You still need to select Characters and purchase this character for 15,000 studs.

BIB FORTUNA
At Mos Eisley Canteena, select Enter Code and enter WTY721. You still need to select Characters and purchase this character for 16,000 studs.

BOBA FETT
At Mos Eisley Canteena, select Enter Code and enter HLP221. You still need to select Characters and purchase this character for 175,000 studs.

DEATH STAR TROOPER
At Mos Eisley Canteena, select Enter Code and enter BNC332. You still need to select Characters and purchase this character for 19,000 studs.

EWOK
At Mos Eisley Canteena, select Enter Code and enter TTT289. You still need to select Characters and purchase this character for 34,000 studs.

GAMORREAN GUARD
At Mos Eisley Canteena, select Enter Code and enter YZF999. You still need to select Characters and purchase this character for 40,000 studs.

GONK DROID
At Mos Eisley Canteena, select Enter Code and enter NFX582. You still need to select Characters and purchase this character for 1,550 studs.

GRAND MOFF TARKIN
At Mos Eisley Canteena, select Enter Code and enter SMG219. You still need to select Characters and purchase this character for 38,000 studs.

GREEDO
At Mos Eisley Canteena, select Enter Code and enter NAH118. You still need to select Characters and purchase this character for 60,000 studs.

HAN SOLO (HOOD)
At Mos Eisley Canteena, select Enter Code and enter YWM840. You still need to select Characters and purchase this character for 20,000 studs.

IG-88
At Mos Eisley Canteena, select Enter Code and enter NXL973. You still need to select Characters and purchase this character for 30,000 studs.

IMPERIAL GUARD
At Mos Eisley Canteena, select Enter Code and enter MMM111. You still need to select Characters and purchase this character for 45,000 studs.

IMPERIAL OFFICER
At Mos Eisley Canteena, select Enter Code and enter BBV889. You still need to select Characters and purchase this character for 28,000 studs.

IMPERIAL SHUTTLE PILOT
At Mos Eisley Canteena, select Enter Code and enter VAP664. You still need to select Characters and purchase this character for 29,000 studs.

IMPERIAL SPY
At Mos Eisley Canteena, select Enter Code and enter CVT125. You still need to select Characters and purchase this character for 13,500 studs.

JAWA
At Mos Eisley Canteena, select Enter Code and enter JAW499. You still need to select Characters and purchase this character for 24,000 studs.

LOBOT
At Mos Eisley Canteena, select Enter Code and enter UUB319. You still need to select Characters and purchase this character for 11,000 studs.

PALACE GUARD
At Mos Eisley Canteena, select Enter Code and enter SGE549. You still need to select Characters and purchase this character for 14,000 studs.

REBEL PILOT
At Mos Eisley Canteena, select Enter Code and enter CYG336. You still need to select Characters and purchase this character for 15,000 studs.

REBEL TROOPER (HOTH)
At Mos Eisley Canteena, select Enter Code and enter EKU849. You still need to select Characters and purchase this character for 16,000 studs.

SANDTROOPER
At Mos Eisley Canteena, select Enter Code and enter YDV451. You still need to select Characters and purchase this character for 14,000 studs.

SKIFF GUARD
At Mos Eisley Canteena, select Enter Code and enter GBU888. You still need to select Characters and purchase this character for 12,000 studs.

SNOWTROOPER
At Mos Eisley Canteena, select Enter Code and enter NYU989. You still need to select Characters and purchase this character for 16,000 studs.

STROMTROOPER
At Mos Eisley Canteena, select Enter Code and enter PTR345. You still need to select Characters and purchase this character for 10,000 studs.

THE EMPEROR
At Mos Eisley Canteena, select Enter Code and enter HHY382. You still need to select Characters and purchase this character for 275,000 studs.

TIE FIGHTER
At Mos Eisley Canteena, select Enter Code and enter HDY739. You still need to select Characters and purchase this character for 60,000 studs.

TIE FIGHTER PILOT

At Mos Eisley Canteena, select Enter Code and enter NNZ316. You still need to select Characters and purchase this character for 21,000 studs.

TIE INTERCEPTOR

At Mos Eisley Canteena, select Enter Code and enter QYA828. You still need to select Characters and purchase this character for 40,000 studs.

TUSKEN RAIDER

At Mos Eisley Canteena, select Enter Code and enter PEJ821. You still need to select Characters and purchase this character for 23,000 studs.

UGNAUGHT

At Mos Eisley Canteena, select Enter Code and enter UGN694. You still need to select Characters and purchase this character for 36,000 studs.

MADDEN NFL 06

Select Madden Cards from My Madden. Then select Madden Codes and enter the following:

PASSWORD	CARD	PASSWORD	CARD
6W5J6Z	#1 Rex Grossman Gold	7U6B3L	#31 LaDainian Tomlinson Gold
6X7W2O	#2 Thomas Jones Gold	8Q2J2R	#55 Donovan McNabb Bronze
6Y5Z6H	#3 Brian Urlacher Gold	8Q2J2X	#55 Donovan McNabb Gold
6Z9X5Y	#4 Olin Kreutz Gold	8V9Y3X	#62 Michael Vick Gold
7A7Z2G	#5 Tommie Harris Gold	8X2Y9G	#64 Alge Crumpler Gold
7C6U4H	#6 Carson Palmer Gold	2W4P9T	#188 First and Fifteen Bronze
7D1B2H	#7 Chad Johnson Gold	2W4P9G	#188 First and Fifteen Silver
7D1X8K	#8 Rudi Johnson Gold	2Y7L8B	#189 First and Five Bronze
7D5W8J	#9 Brian Simmons Gold	2Z2F4H	#190 Unforced Errors Bronze
7D8S6J	#10 J.P. Losman Gold	2Z2F4G	#190 Unforced Errors Silver
7E3G7Y	#11 Willis McGahee Gold	3D3Q3P	#191 Extra Credit Bronze
7F5B2Y	#12 Eric Moulds Gold	3D8X6Z	#191 Extra Credit Gold
7H3B2Y	#13 Takeo Spikes Gold	3D8X6T	#192 Tight Fit Bronze
7H9E8L	#14 Lawyer Milloy Gold	3E9R4V	#193 5th Down Bronze
7J3Y7F	#15 Jake Plummer Gold	3E9R4I	#193 5th Down Silver
7J8F4J	#16 Ashley Lelie Gold	3F9G4J	#194 3rd Down Bronze
7K5C8V	#17 Al Wilson Gold	3F9G4O	#194 3rd Down Silver
7L8C2W	#18 Champ Bailey Gold	3H3U7T	#194 3rd Down Gold
1A2D9F	#19 John Lynch Gold	3H3U7F	#195 Human Plow Bronze
7O1J3F	#20 D.J. Williams Gold	3H8M5U	#196 Super Dive Bronze
7P5G3N	#21 Lee Suggs Gold	3J3S9Y	#197 Da Boot Bronze
7Q2E45	#22 Kellen Winslow Jr. Gold	3J3S9E	#197 Da Boot Silver
7Q6F4G	#23 Simeon Rice Gold	3T4E3Y	#208 Pocket Protectors Gold
7Q6X4L	#24 Derrick Brooks Gold	3X1V2H	#210 QB on Target Gold
7R7V2E	#25 Ronde Barber Gold	4D1V2Y	#217 Ouch Gold
7S4C4D	#26 Anthony McFarland Gold	4F9D2B	#220 Super Bowl XL Gold
7T1G2Y	#27 Michael Clayton Gold	4F9D2H	#221 Super Bowl XLI Gold
7T3V5K	#28 Anquan Boldin Gold	4I1V6T	#222 Super Bowl XLII Gold
7T6B5N	#29 Larry Fitzgerald Gold	4F3D7E	#223 Super Bowl XLIII Gold
7U4M9B	#30 Bertrand Berry Gold	4I1V6K	#224 Aloha Stadium Gold

MADDEN NFL 07

#199 GOLD LAME DUCK CHEAT CARD

In My Madden, select Madden Codes from Madden Cards. Enter 5LAW00.

#200 GOLD MISTAKE FREE CHEAT CARD

In My Madden, select Madden Codes from Madden Cards. Enter XL7SP1.

#210 GOLD QB ON TARGET CHEAT CARD

In My Madden, select Madden Codes from Madden Cards. Enter WROA0R.

MAGIC: THE GATHERING—BATTLEGROUNDS

ALL QUESTS
At the Quest Select screen, press Left Trigger + Right Trigger, Down, Up, press the Left Thumbstick, White, Up, Right, Left, Down, Left Trigger + Right Trigger.

SECRET LEVEL
At the Arena Select screen, press Left Trigger + Right Trigger, Left, Up, X, Up, Right, Y, Left Trigger + Right Trigger.

ALL DUELISTS
At the Character Select screen, press Left Trigger + Right Trigger, Down, Up, X, White, Up, X, Black, Up, Left, Left Trigger + Right Trigger.

MAJOR LEAGUE BASEBALL 2K6

UNLOCK EVERYTHING
Select Enter Cheat Code from the My 2K6 menu and enter **Derek Jeter**.

TOPPS 2K STARS
Select Enter Cheat Code from the My 2K6 menu and enter **Dream Team**.

SUPER WALL CLIMB
Select Enter Cheat Code from the My 2K6 menu and enter **Last Chance**. Enable the cheats by selecting My Cheats or selecting Cheat Codes from the Options screen in-game.

SUPER PITCHES
Select Enter Cheat Code from the My 2K6 menu and enter **Unhittable**. Enable the cheats by selecting My Cheats or selecting Cheat Codes from the Options screen in-game.

ROCKET ARMS
Select Enter Cheat Code from the My 2K6 menu and enter **Gotcha**. Enable the cheats by selecting My Cheats or selecting Cheat Codes from the Options screen in-game.

BOUNCY BALL
Select Enter Cheat Code from the My 2K6 menu and enter **Crazy Hops**. Enable the cheats by selecting My Cheats or selecting Cheat Codes from the Options screen in-game.

MARVEL NEMESIS: RISE OF THE IMPERFECTS

UNLOCKS ALL FANTASTIC FOUR COMICS
Select Cheats from the Options screen and enter **SAVAGELAND**.

UNLOCKS ALL TOMORROW PEOPLE COMICS
Select Cheats from the Options screen and enter **NZONE**.

MARVEL ULTIMATE ALLIANCE

UNLOCK ALL SKINS
At the Team Menu, press Up, Down, Left, Right, Left, Right, Start.

UNLOCKS ALL HERO POWERS
At the Team Menu, press Left, Right, Up, Down, Up, Down, Start.

ALL HEROES TO LEVEL 99
At the Team Menu, press Up, Left, Up, Left, Down, Right, Down, Right, Start.

UNLOCK ALL HEROES
At the Team Menu, press Up, Up, Down, Down, Left, Left, Left, Start.

UNLOCK DAREDEVIL
At the Team Menu, press Left, Left, Right, Right, Up, Down, Up, Down, Start.

UNLOCK SILVER SURFER
At the Team Menu, press Down, Left, Left, Up, Right, Up, Down, Left, Start.

GOD MODE
During gameplay, press Up, Down, Up, Down, Up, Left, Down, Right, Start.

TOUCH OF DEATH
During gameplay, press Left, Right, Down, Down, Right, Left, Start.

SUPER SPEED
During gameplay, press Up, Left, Up, Right, Down, Right, Start.

FILL MOMENTUM
During gameplay, press Left, Right, Right, Left, Up, Down, Down, Up, Start.

UNLOCK ALL COMICS
At the Review menu, press Left, Right, Right, Left, Up, Up, Right, Start.

UNLOCK ALL CONCEPT ART
At the Review menu, press Down, Down, Down, Right, Right, Left, Down, Start.

UNLOCK ALL CINEMATICS
At the Review menu, press Up, Left, Left, Up, Right, Right, Up, Start.

UNLOCK ALL LOAD SCREENS
At the Review menu, press Up, Down, Right, Left, Up, Up Down, Start.

UNLOCK ALL COURSES
At the Comic Missions menu, press Up, Right, Left, Down, Up, Right, Left, Down, Start.

MIDNIGHT CLUB 3: DUB EDITION REMIX

ALL CITIES AND RACES IN ARCADE MODE
Select Cheat Codes from the Options screen and enter **urbansprawl**, **roadtrip** or **crosscountry**.

NO DAMAGE
Select Cheat Codes from the Options screen and enter **ontheroad**.

ARGO SPECIAL MOVE
Select Cheat Codes from the Options screen and enter **dfens**.

ROAR SPECIAL MOVE
Select Cheat Codes from the Options screen and enter **Rjnr**.

ZONE SPECIAL MOVE
Select Cheat Codes from the Options screen and enter **allin**.

ADD $1 TO CAREER MONEY
Select Cheat Codes from the Options screen and enter **kubmir**.

SUBTRACT $1 OF CAREER MONEY
Select Cheat Codes from the Options screen and enter **rimbuk**.

BUNNY HEAD
Select Cheat Codes from the Options screen and enter **getheadl**.

CHROME HEAD
Select Cheat Codes from the Options screen and enter **haveyouseenthisboy**.

FLAMING HEAD
Select Cheat Codes from the Options screen and enter **trythisathome**.

SNOWMAN HEAD
Select Cheat Codes from the Options screen and enter **getheadm**.

PUMPKIN HEAD
Select Cheat Codes from the Options screen and enter **getheadk**.

YELLOW SMILE HEAD
Select Cheat Codes from the Options screen and enter **getheadj**.

MIDWAY ARCADE TREASURES 3

HYDRO THUNDER

ALL TRACKS AND BOATS
Get a high score and enter ?PB as your initials.

Offroad Thunder

CLIFFHANGER TRACK
Select Rally and press Right at the Choose Track screen press Right to bring up the Secret Code option. Press Right, Up, Left, to unlock the Cliffhanger track.

CHIEFTAIN & GENERAL VEHICLES
Select Rally and press Right at the Choose Machine screen press Right to bring up the Secret Code option. Press Left (x3) to unlock Chieftain. Press Left (x3) again to unlock General.

DUST DEVIL & SILVER STREAK VEHICLES
Select Rally and press Right at the Choose Machine screen press Right to bring up the Secret Code option. Press Left, Up, Right to unlock Dust Devil. Press Left, Up, Right again to unlock Silver Streak.

HYENA & BAD OMEN VEHICLES
Select Rally and press Right at the Choose Machine screen press Right to bring up the Secret Code option. Press Right (x3) to unlock Hyena. Press Right (x3) again to unlock Bad Omen.

WILDCAT & THRASHER VEHICLES
Select Rally and press Right at the Choose Machine screen press Right to bring up the Secret Code option. Press Up (x3) to unlock Wildcat. Press Up (x3) again to unlock Thrasher.

MLB SLUGFEST 2006

ATLANTIS
Hit a Homer in AT&T Park.

COLISEUM
Hit a Homer in Fenway.

EMPIRE
Hit a Homer in Yankee Stadium.

FORBIDDEN CITY
Hit Homer in PetCo Park.

MONUMENT STADIUM
Hit homer in Citizens Bank Park.

ROCKET PARK
Hit a Homer in Minute Maid Park.

TEAM BOBBLE HEAD
Hit 10 homers in one game.

TEAM CASEY
Hit a Triple in Wrigley Field.

TEAM DOLPHINS
Hit a homer in Atlantis.

TEAM EAGLES
Walk 3 times in one game.

TEAM EVIL CLOWNS
Hit a homer in Empire Park with the Yankees.

TEAM GLADIATOR
Hit homer in The Coliseum.

TEAM HORSE
Steal 5 bases in one game.

TEAM LIONS
Hit a homer with the Tigers in Comerica Park.

TEAM MARTIANS
Hit a Triple in Rocket Park.

TEAM MINTAUR
Hit a homer in The Forbidden City.

TEAM PINTO
Hit an inside-the-park homer in Busch Stadium.

TEAM RODEO CLOWN
Perform a double play.

MLB SLUGFEST: LOADED

CHEATS
At the Match-Up screen, press X, Y, and B to enter the following codes, then press the appropriate direction. For example, for 16" Softball press X (x2), Y (x4), B (x2), then press Down.

CODE	ENTER	CODE	ENTER	CODE	ENTER
Bone Bat	0-0-1 Up	Tiny Head	2-0-0 Left	Olshan Team	2-2-2 Down
Blade Bat	0-0-2 Up	Big Head	2-0-0 Right	Pinto Team	2-1-0 Right
Ice Bat	0-0-3 Up	Alien Team	2-3-1 Down	Rivera Team	2-2-2 Up
Log Bat	0-0-4 Up	Bobblehead Team	1-3-3 Down	Rodeo Clown Team	1-3-2 Down
Spike Bat	0-0-5 Up	Casey team	2-3-3 Down	Scorpion Team	1-1-2 Down
Whiffle Bat	0-0-4 Right	Dolphin Team	1-0-2 Down	Terry Fitzgerald Team	3-3-3 Right
Max Batting	3-0-0 Left	Dwarf Team	1-0-3 Down	Todd McFarlane Team	2-2-2 Right
Max Power	0-3-0 Left	Eagle Team	2-1-2 Right	Atlantis Stadium	3-2-1 Left
Max Speed	0-0-3 Left	Evil Clown Team	2-1-1 Down	Coliseum Stadium	3-3-3 Up
Unlimited Turbo	4-4-4 Down	Gladiator Team	1-1-3 Down	Empire Park Stadium	3-2-1 Right
Extra Time After Plays	1-2-3 Left	Horse Team	2-1-1 Right	Forbidden City Stadium	3-3-3 Left
Little League Mode	1-0-1 Down	Lion Team	2-2-0 Right	Midway Park Stadium	3-2-1 Down
16" Softball	2-4-2 Down	Minotaur Team	1-1-0 Down	Monument Stadium	3-3-3 Down
Rubber Bball	2-4-2 Up	Napalitano Team	2-3-2 Down	Rocket Park Stadium	3-2-1 Up

MVP 06 NCAA BASEBALL

ALL CHALLENGE ITEMS
In Dynasty Mode, create a player with the name **Dee Jay Randall**.

LEVEL 1 CHALLENGE ITEMS
In Dynasty Mode, create a player with the name **Peter Trenouth**.

ALL LEVEL 2 CHALLENGE ITEMS
In Dynasty Mode, create a player with the name **Trey Smith**.

ALL LEVEL 3 CHALLENGE ITEMS
In Dynasty Mode, create a player with the name **Chris Chung**.

ALL LEVEL 4 CHALLENGE ITEMS
In Dynasty Mode, create a player with the name **Federico Rahal**.

BIG BAT
In Dynasty Mode, create a player with the name **Chris Deas**.

SHORT PLAYER WITH BIG BAT
In Dynasty Mode, create a player with the name **Alan Blouin**.

THICK BAT
In Dynasty Mode, create a player with the name **Melissa Shim**.

LARGE PLAYER WITH THIN BAT
In Dynasty Mode, create a player with the name **Neale Genereux**.

SHORT PLAYER WITH THIN BAT
In Dynasty Mode, create a player with the name **Julia Kwan**.

SUPER HITTER
In Dynasty Mode, create a player with the name **Tim Regel**.

MX vs. ATV UNLEASHED

UNLOCK EVERYTHING
Select Cheat Codes from the Options screen and enter **TOOLAZY**.

1,000,000 POINTS
Select Cheat Codes from the Options screen and enter **BROKEASAJOKE**. After entering the code, press Done multiple times for more points.

ALL PRO RIDERS
Select Cheat Codes from the Options screen and enter **WANNABE**.

ALL GEAR
Select Cheat Codes from the Options screen and enter **WARDROBE**.

50CC BIKE CLASS
Select Cheat Codes from the Options screen and enter **MINIMOTO**.

ALL MACHINES
Select Cheat Codes from the Options screen and enter **LEADFOOT**.

ALL FREESTYLE TRACKS
Select Cheat Codes from the Options screen and enter **HUCKIT**.

NASCAR 06: TOTAL TEAM CONTROL

UNLOCK EVERYTHING
In Fight to the Top mode, select Edit Driver. Enter **Gimme Gimme** as the first and last names.

$10,000,000
In Fight to the Top mode, select Edit Driver. Enter **Walmart Money** as the first and last names.

MAX FAN LEVEL
In Fight to the Top mode, select Edit Driver. Enter **Super Star** as the first and last names.

MAX PRESTIGE
In Fight to the Top mode, select Edit Driver. Enter **MeMyself AndI** as the first and last names.

MAX TEAM PRESTIGE
In Fight to the Top mode, select Edit Driver. Enter **All ForOne** as the first and last names.

WALMART TRACKS AND CARS
In Fight to the Top mode, select Edit Driver. Enter **Walmart Exclusive** as the first and last names.

OLD SPICE TRACKS AND CARS
In Fight to the Top mode, select Edit Driver. Enter **KeepCool SmellGreat** as the first and last names.

DALE EARNHARDT SR.
In Fight to the Top mode, select Edit Driver. Enter **The Intimidator** as the first and last names.

NASCAR 07

$10,000,000
In Fight to the Top mode, enter your name as **GiveMe More**.

10,000,000 FANS
In Fight to the Top mode, enter your name as **AllBow ToMe**.

PRESTIGE LEVEL 10 WITH 2,000,000 POINTS
In Fight to the Top mode, enter your name as **Outta MyWay**.

100% TEAM PRESTIGE
In Fight to the Top mode, enter your name as **MoMoney BlingBling**.

ALL CHASE PLATES
In Fight to the Top mode, enter your name as **ItsAll ForMe**.

OLD SPICE TRACKS AND CARS.
In Fight to the Top mode, enter your name as **KeepCool SmellGreat**.

WALMART TRACK AND CARS
In Fight to the Top mode, enter your name as **Walmart EveryDay**.

NBA 2K6

CELEBRITY STREET OPTION
Select Codes from the Features menu and enter **ballers**.

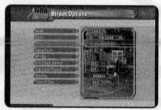

2KSPORTS TEAM
Select Codes from the Features menu and enter **2ksports**.

2K6 TEAM
Select Codes from the Features menu and enter **nba2k6**.

VC TEAM
Select Codes from the Features menu and enter **vcteam**.

NIKE SHOX MTX SHOES
Select Codes from the Features menu and enter **crazylift**.

NIKE ZOOM 20-5-5 SHOES
Select Codes from the Features menu and enter **lebronsummerkicks**.

NIKE ZOOM KOBE 1 SHOES
Select Codes from the Features menu and enter **kobe**.

NIKE ZOOM LEBRON III ALL-STAR COLORWAY SHOES
Select Codes from the Features menu and enter **lb allstar**.

NIKE ZOOM LEBRON III BLACK/CRIMSON SHOES
Select Codes from the Features menu and enter **lb crimsonblack**.

NIKE ZOOM LEBRON III SPECIAL BIRTHDAY EDITION SHOES
Select Codes from the Features menu and enter **lb bday**.

NIKE ZOOM LEBRON III WHITE/GOLD SHOES
Select Codes from the Features menu and enter **lb whitegold**.

NIKE UP TEMPO PRO SHOES

Select Codes from the Features menu and enter **anklebreakers**.

ALTERNATE UNIFORMS

To access various uniforms, select Codes from the Features menu and enter the following to unlock the different uniforms:

UNIFORM	ENTER	UNIFORM	ENTER	UNIFORM	ENTER
2006 All-Star	fanfavorites	Heat Retro	mia retro	2005-06 Pacers	31andonly
St. Patrick's Day	gogreen	Hornets Retro	no retro	Pistons Alternate	det 2nd
Bulls Retro	chi retro	Kings Alternate	sac 2nd	Rockets Retro	hou retro
Cavaliers Alternate	cle 2nd	Knicks Retro	ny retro	Sonics Retro	sea retro
Celtics Alternate	bos 2nd	Magic Retro	orl retro	Suns Retro	phx retro
Clippers Retro	lac retro	Nets Retro	nj retro	Wizards Retro	was retro
Grizzlies Retro	mem retro	Nuggets Alternate	den 2nd		

+10 BONUS FOR DEFENSIVE AWARENESS

Find the PowerBar vending machine in The Crib. Choose Enter Code and enter **lockdown**.

+10 BONUS FOR OFFENSIVE AWARENESS

Find the PowerBar vending machine in The Crib. Choose Enter Code and enter **getaclue**.

MAX DURABILITY

Find the PowerBar vending machine in The Crib. Choose Enter Code and enter **noinjury**.

UNLIMITED STAMINA

Find the PowerBar vending machine in The Crib. Choose Enter Code and enter **nrgmax**.

POWERBAR TATTOO

Find the PowerBar vending machine in The Crib. Choose Enter Code and enter **pbink**. You can now use this feature in the game's Create Player feature.

ALL ITEMS IN THE CRIB

Find the PowerBar vending machine in The Crib. Choose Enter Code and enter **criball**.

NBA 2K7

MAX DURABILITY

Select Codes from the Features menu and enter ironman.

UNLIMITED STAMINA

Select Codes from the Features menu and enter norest.

+10 DEFFENSIVE AWARENESS

Select Codes from the Features menu and enter getstops.

+10 OFFENSIVE AWARENESS

Select Codes from the Features menu and enter inthezone.

TOPPS 2K SPORTS ALL-STARS

Select Codes from the Features menu and enter topps2ksports.

ABA BALL

Select Codes from the Features menu and enter payrespect.

NBA BALLERS

VERSUS SCREEN CHEATS

You can enter the following codes at the Vs screen. The X button corresponds to the first number in the code, the Y is the second number, and the B button corresponds to the last number. Press the D-pad in any direction to enter the code.

CODE	ENTER	CODE	ENTER	CODE	ENTER
Tournament Mode	011	Kid Ballers	433	Alternate Gear	123
Big Head	134	Young Ballers1	443	Expanded Move Set	512
Baby Ballers	423	Paper Ballers	354	Super Push	315

CODE	ENTER	CODE	ENTER	CODE	ENTER
Super Block Ability	1 2 4	2x Juice Replenish	4 3 1	Play as Secretary	5 4 7
Great Handles	3 3 2	Stunt Ability	3 7 4	Play as BiznezMan-A	5 3 7
Unlimited Juice	7 6 3	Pass 2 Friend Ability	5 3 6	Play as BiznezMan-B	5 2 7
Super Steals	2 1 5	Alley-Oop Ability	7 2 5	Play as Afro Man	5 1 7
Perfect Free Throws	3 2 7	Put Back Ability	3 1 3	Super Back-Ins	2 3 5
Speedy Players	2 1 3	Legal Goal Tending	7 5 6	Half House	3 6 7
Better Free Throws	3 1 7	Show Shot Percentage	0 1 2	Random Moves	3 0 0
Fire Ability	7 2 2	R2R Mode	0 0 8	Pygmy	4 2 5
Hotspot Ability	6 2 7	Play as Coach	5 6 7		
Back-In Ability	1 2 2	Play as Agent	5 5 7		

PHRASE-OLOGY CODES/ALTERNATE GEAR

Select Phrase-ology from the Inside Stuff option and enter the following codes to unlock the Alternate Gear for the corresponding player.

PLAYER	PHRASE	PLAYER	PHRASE
Allan Houston	KNICKER BOCKER PLEASE	Latrell Sprewell	SPREE
Allen Iverson	KILLER CROSSOVER	Lebron James	KING JAMES
Alonzo Mourning	ZO	Magic Johnson	LAKER LEGENDS
Amare Stoudemire	RISING SUN	Michael Finley	STUDENT OF THE GAME
Antoine Walker	BALL HAWK	Mike Bibby	DREAMS & SCHEMES
Baron Davis	STYLIN' & PROFILIN'	Moses Malone	LOST FREESTYLE FILES
Ben Wallace	RADIO CONTROLLED CARS	Nate "Tiny" Archibald	NATE THE SKATE
Bill Russell	CELTICS DYNASTY	Nene Hilario	RAGS TO RICHES
Bill Walton	TOWERS OF POWER	Oscar Robertson	AINT NO THING
Carmelo Anthony	NEW TO THE GAME	Pau Gasol	POW POW POW
Chris Webber	24 SECONDS	Paul Pierce	CELTICS SUPREME
Clyde Drexler	CLYDE THE GLIDE	Pete Maravich	PISTOL PETE
Darko Milicic	NBA FASTBREAK	Rashard Lewis	FAST FORWARD
Darryl Dawkins	RIM WRECKER	Rasheed Wallace	BRING Down THE HOUSE
Dejaun Wagner	NBA HANGTIME	Ray Allen	ALL STAR
Dikembe Mutumbo	IN THE PAINT	Reggie Miller	FROM DownTOWN
Dominique Wilkins	DUNK FEST	Richard Hamilton	RIP
Eddie Jones	BALLER UPRISING	Robert Parish	THE CHIEF
Elton Brand	REBOUND	Scottie Pippen	PLAYMAKER
Emanuel Ginobili	MANU	Shaquille O'Neal	DIESEL RULES THE PAINT
Gary Payton	GLOVE IS IN LA	Shawn Marion	MAKE YOUR MARK
George Gervin	THE ICE MAN COMETH	Stephon Marbury	PLATINUM PLAYA
Grant Hill	GONE GOLD WITH IT	Steve Francis	ANKLE BREAKER
Isiah Thomas	TRUE BALLER	Steve Francis	RISING STAR
Jalen Rose	BRING IT	Steve Nash	HAIR CANADA
Jason Kidd	PASS THE ROCK	Tim Duncan	MAKE IT TAKE IT
Jason Terry	BALL ABOVE ALL	Tony Parker	RUN AND SHOOT
Jason Williams	GIVE AND GO	Tracy McGrady	LIVING LIKE A BALLER
Jerry Stackhouse	STOP DROP AND ROLL	Vince Carter	CHECK MY CRIB
John Stockton	COURT VISION	Wally Szczerbiak	WORLD
Julius Irving	ONE ON ONE	Walt Frazier	PENETRATE AND PERPETRATE
Karl Malone	SPECIAL DELIVERY		
Kenyon Martin	TO THE HOLE	Wes Unseld	OLD SCHOOL
Kevin Garnett	BOSS HOSS	Willis Reed	HALL OF FAME
Kevin McHale	HOLLA BACK	Wilt Chamberlain	WILT THE STILT
Kobe Bryant	JAPANESE STEAK	Yao Ming	CENTER OF ATTENTION
Larry Bird	HOOSIER		

CRIBS

Select Phrase-ology from the Inside Stuff option and enter the following to unlock player cribs.

CRIB	PHRASE	CRIB	PHRASE
Allen Iverson's Recording Studio	THE ANSWER	Scottie Pippen's Yacht	NICE YACHT
Karl Malone's Devonshire Estate	ICE HOUSE	Yao Ming's Childhood Grade School	PREP SCHOOL
Kobe Bryant's Italian Estate	EURO CRIB		

OTHER PHRASE-OLOGY CODES

Select Phrase-ology from the Inside Stuff option and enter the following to unlock that bonus.

BONUS	PHRASE	BONUS	PHRASE
All Players, Alternate Gear, and Cinemas	NBA BALLERS TRUE PLAYA	Special Movie #4	HATCHET MAN
Special Movie #1	JUICE HOUSE	Special Movie #5	SLAM IT
Special Movie #2	NBA SHOWTIME	Special Shoe #2	COLD STREAK
Special Movie #3	NBA BALLERS RULES	Special Shoe #3	LOST YA SHOES

NBA BALLERS: PHENOM

VERSUS SCREEN CHEATS

You can enter the following codes at the Vs screen. The X button corresponds to the first number in the code, the Y is the second number, and the B button corresponds to the last number. Press the D-pad in any direction to enter the code.

EFFECT	CODE	EFFECT	CODE
Tournament Mode	0 1 1	Unlimited Juice	7 6 3
Big Head	1 3 4	House meter half full at start	3 6 7
Baby Ballers	4 2 3	Super block ability	1-2-4
Kid Ballers	4 3 3	Show Shot Percentage	0 1 2
2D Ballers	3 5 4	Alternate Gear	1 2 3
Speedy Players	2 1 3		

NBA LIVE 06

EASTERN ALL-STARS 2005-06 AWAY JERSEYS
Select NBA Codes from My NBA Live and enter **XCVB5387EQ**.

EASTERN ALL-STARS 2005-06 HOME JERSEY
Select NBA Codes from My NBA Live and enter **234SDFGHMO**.

WESTERN ALL-STARS 2005-06 AWAY JERSEY
Select NBA Codes from My NBA Live and enter **39N56B679J**.

WESTERN ALL-STARS 2005-06 HOME JERSEY
Select NBA Codes from My NBA Live and enter **2J9UWABNP1**.

BOSTON CELTICS 2005-06 ALTERNATE JERSEY
Select NBA Codes from My NBA Live and enter **193KSHU88J**.

CLEVELAND CAVALIERS 2005-06 ALTERNATE JERSEY
Select NBA Codes from My NBA Live and enter **9922NVDKVT**.

DENVER NUGGETS 2005-06 ALTERNATE JERSEYS
Select NBA Codes from My NBA Live and enter **XWETJK72FC**.

DETROIT PISTONS 2005-06 ALTERNATE JERSEY
Select NBA Codes from My NBA Live and enter **JANTWIKBS6**.

INDIANA PACERS 2005-06 ALTERNATE AWAY JERSEY
Select NBA Codes from My NBA Live and enter **PSDF90PPJN**.

INDIANA PACERS 2005-06 ALTERNATE HOME JERSEY
Select NBA Codes from My NBA Live and enter **SDF786WSHW**.

SACRAMENTO KINGS 2005-06 ALTERNATE JERSEY
Select NBA Codes from My NBA Live and enter **654NNBFDWA**.

A3 GARNETT 3
Select NBA Codes from My NBA Live and enter **DRI239CZ49**.

JORDAN MELO V.5 WHITE & BLUE
Select NBA Codes from My NBA Live and enter **5223WERPII**.

JORDAN MELO V.5 WHITE & YELLOW
Select NBA Codes from My NBA Live and enter **ZXDR7362Q1**.

JORDAN XIV BLACK & RED
Select NBA Codes from My NBA Live and enter **144FVNHM35**.

JORDAN XIV WHITE & GREEN
Select NBA Codes from My NBA Live and enter **67YFH9839F**.

JORDAN XIV WHITE & RED
Select NBA Codes from My NBA Live and enter **743HFDRAU8**.

S. CARTER III LE
Select NBA Codes from My NBA Live and enter **JZ3SCARTVY**.

T-MAC 5 BLACK
Select NBA Codes from My NBA Live and enter **258SHQW95B**.

T-MAC 5 WHITE
Select NBA Codes from My NBA Live and enter **HGS83KP234P**.

ANSWER DMX 10
Select NBA Codes from My NBA Live and enter **RBKAIUSAB7**.

ANSWER IX AND THE RBK ANSWER IX VIDEO
Select NBA Codes from My NBA Live and enter **AI9BUBBA7T**.

THE QUESTION AND THE MESSAGE FROM ALLEN IVERSON VIDEO
Select NBA Codes from My NBA Live and enter **HOYAS3AI6L**.

NBA LIVE 07

ADIDAS ARTILLERY II BLACK AND THE RBK ANSWER 9 VIDEO
Select NBA Codes from My NBA Live and enter 99B6356HAN.

ADIDAS BTB LOW AND THE MESSAGE FROM ALLEN IVERSON VIDEO
Select NBA Codes and enter 7FB3KS9JQ0.

ADIDAS ARTILLERY II
Select NBA Codes and enter NTGNFUE87H.

ADIDAS C-BILLUPS
Select NBA Codes and enter BV6877HB9N.

ADIDAS C-BILLUPS BLACK
Select NBA Codes and enter 85NVLDMWS5.

ADIDAS CAMPUS LT
Select NBA Codes and enter CLT2983NC8.

ADIDAS CRAZY 8
Select NBA Codes and enter CC98KKL814.

ADIDAS EQUIPMENT BBALL
Select NBA Codes and enter 22OIUJKMDR.

ADIDAS GARNETT BOUNCE
Select NBA Codes and enter HYIOUHCAAN.

ADIDAS GARNETT BOUNCE BLACK
Select NBA Codes and enter KDZ2MQL17W.

ADIDAS GIL-ZERO
Select NBA Codes and enter 23DN1PPOG4.

ADIDAS GIL-ZERO BLACK
Select NBA Codes and enter QQQ3JCUYQ7.

ADIDAS GIL-ZERO MID
Select NBA Codes and enter 1GSJC8JWRL.

ADIDAS GIL-ZERO MID BLACK
Select NBA Codes and enter 369V6RVU3G.

ADIDAS STEALTH
Select NBA Codes and enter FE454DFJCC.

ADIDAS T-MAC 6
Select NBA Codes and enter MCJK843NNC.

ADIDAS T-MAC 6 WHITE
Select NBA Codes and enter 84GF7EJG8V.

CHARLOTTE BOBCATS 2006-07 ALTERNATE JERSEY
Select NBA Codes and enter WEDX671H7S.

UTAH JAZZ 2006-07 ALTERNATE JERSEY
Select NBA Codes and enter VCBI89FK83.

NEW JERSEY NETS 2006-07 ALTERNATE JERSEY
Select NBA Codes and enter D4SAA98U5H.

WASHINGTON WIZARDS 2006-07 ALTERNATE JERSEY
Select NBA Codes and enter QV93NLKXQC.

EASTERN ALL-STARS 2006-07 AWAY JERSEY
Select NBA Codes and enter WOCNW4KL7L.

EASTERN ALL-STARS 2006-07 HOME JERSEY
Select NBA Codes and enter 5654ND43N6.

WESTERN ALL-STARS 2006-07 AWAY JERSEY
Select NBA Codes and enter XX93BVL20U.

WESTERN ALL-STARS 2006-07 HOME JERSEY
Select NBA Codes and enter 993NSKL199.

NCAA FOOTBALL 06

PENNANT CODES
Select Pennant Collection from My NCAA. Press Select and enter the following codes:

CODE	ENTER	CODE	ENTER
Sic Em	#16 Baylor	Break Free	#213 Nike Free
Oskee Wow	#63 Illinois	Hand Picked	#214 Nike Magnigrip
Fight	#160 Texas Tech	No Sweat	#215 Nike Pro
Thanks	#200 First and Fifteen	Light Speed	#216 Nike Speed TD
For	#201 Blink	Elite 11	#219 QB Dud
Registering	#202 Boing	NCAA	#222 Stiffed
With EA	#204 Butter Fingers	Football	#224 Take Your Time
Tiburon	#205 Crossed The Line	06	#225 Thread & Needle
EA Sports	#206 Cuffed	Offense	#226 Tough As Nails
Touchdown	#207 Extra Credit	Defense	#227 Trip
In The Zone	#208 Helium	Blitz	#228 What a Hit!
Turnover	#209 Hurricane	Sideline	#229 Kicker Hex
Impact	#210 Instant Freplay	Fumble	#273 2004 All-Americans
Heisman	#211 Jumbalaya	Roll Tide	#274 All-Alabama
Game Time	#212 Molasses	Woopigsooie	#276 All-Arkansas

CODE	ENTER		CODE	ENTER
War Eagle	#277 All-Auburn		Big Orange	#300 All-Tennessee
Death Valley	#278 All-Clemson		Hook Em	#301 All-Texas
Glory	#279 All-Colorado		Gig Em	#302 All-Texas A&M
Great To Be	#280 All-Florida		Mighty	#303 All-UCLA
Uprising	#281 All-FSU		Fight On	#304 All-USC
Hunker Down	#282 All-Georgia		Wahoos	#305 All-Virginia
On Iowa	#283 All-Iowa		Tech Triumph	#306 All-Virginia Tech
Victory	#284 All-Kansas State		Bow Down	#307 All-Washington
Geaux Tigers	#285 All-LSU		U Rah Rah	#308 All-Wisconsin
Raising Cane	#286 All-Miami		Bear Down	#311 Ark Mascot
Go Blue	#287 All-Michigan		Red And Gold	#333 ISU Mascot
Hail State	#288 All-Mississippi State		Rock Chalk	#335 KU Mascot
Go Big Red	#289 All-Nebraska		Go Green	#346 Michigan State Mascot
Rah Rah	#290 All-North Carolina		Rah Rah Rah	#341 Minn Mascot
Golden Domer	#291 All-Notre Dame		Hotty Totty	#342 Miss Mascot
Killer Nuts	#292 All-Ohio State		Mizzou Rah	#344 Mizzou Mascot
Boomer	#293 All-Oklahoma		Go Pack	#349 NCSU Mascot
Go Pokes	#294 All-Oklahoma State		Go Cats	#352 NU Mascot
Quack Attack	#295 All-Oregeon		On On UK	#371 UK Mascot
We Are	#296 All-Penn State		Go Deacs Go	#382 Wake Mascot
Lets Go Pitt	#297 All-Pittsburgh		All Hail	#385 WSU Mascot
Boiler Up	#298 All-Purdue		Hail WV	#386 WVU Mascot
Orange Crush	#299 All-Syracuse			

NCAA FOOTBALL 07

#16 BAYLOR

Select Pennant Collection from My NCAA. Press Select and enter Sic Em.

#16 NIKE SPEED TD

Select Pennant Collection from My NCAA. Press Select and enter Light Speed.

#63 ILLINOIS

Select Pennant Collection from My NCAA. Press Select and enter Oskee Wow.

#160 TEXAS TECH

Select Pennant Collection from My NCAA. Press Select and enter Fight.

#200 FIRST AND FIFTEEN

Select Pennant Collection from My NCAA. Press Select and enter Thanks.

#201 BLINK

Select Pennant Collection from My NCAA. Press Select and enter For.

#202 BOING

Select Pennant Collection from My NCAA. Press Select and enter Registering.

#204 BUTTER FINGERS

Select Pennant Collection from My NCAA. Press Select and enter With EA.

#205 CROSSED THE LINE

Select Pennant Collection from My NCAA. Press Select and enter Tiburon.

#206 CUFFED

Select Pennant Collection from My NCAA. Press Select and enter EA Sports.

#207 EXTRA CREDIT

Select Pennant Collection from My NCAA. Press Select and enter Touchdown.

#208 HELIUM

Select Pennant Collection from My NCAA. Press Select and enter In The Zone.

#209 HURRICANE

Select Pennant Collection from My NCAA. Press Select and enter Turnover.

#210 INSTANT FREPLAY

Select Pennant Collection from My NCAA. Press Select and enter Impact.

#211 JUMBALAYA

Select Pennant Collection from My NCAA. Press Select and enter Heisman.

#212 MOLASSES

Select Pennant Collection from My NCAA. Press Select and enter Game Time.

#213 NIKE FREE

Select Pennant Collection from My NCAA. Press Select and enter Break Free.

#214 NIKE MAGNIGRIP
Select Pennant Collection from My NCAA. Press Select and enter Hand Picked.

#215 NIKE PRO
Select Pennant Collection from My NCAA. Press Select and enter No Sweat.

#219 QB DUD
Select Pennant Collection from My NCAA. Press Select and enter Elite 11.

#221 STEEL TOE
Select Pennant Collection from My NCAA. Press Select and enter Gridiron.

#222 STIFFED
Select Pennant Collection from My NCAA. Press Select and enter NCAA.

#223 SUPER DIVE
Select Pennant Collection from My NCAA. Press Select and enter Upset.

#224 TAKE YOUR TIME
Select Pennant Collection from My NCAA. Press Select and enter Football.

#225 THREAD & NEEDLE
Select Pennant Collection from My NCAA. Press Select and enter 06.

#226 TOUGH AS NAILS
Select Pennant Collection from My NCAA. Press Select and enter Offense.

#227 TRIP
Select Pennant Collection from My NCAA. Press Select and enter Defense.

#228 WHAT A HIT
Select Pennant Collection from My NCAA. Press Select and enter Blitz.

#229 KICKER HEX
Select Pennant Collection from My NCAA. Press Select and enter Sideline.

#273 2004 ALL-AMERICANS
Select Pennant Collection from My NCAA. Press Select and enter Fumble.

#274 ALL-ALABAMA
Select Pennant Collection from My NCAA. Press Select and enter Roll Tide.

#276 ALL-ARKANSAS
Select Pennant Collection from My NCAA. Press Select and enter Woopigsooie.

#277 ALL-AUBURN
Select Pennant Collection from My NCAA. Press Select and enter War Eagle.

#278 ALL-CLEMSON
Select Pennant Collection from My NCAA. Press Select and enter Death Valley.

#279 ALL-COLORADO
Select Pennant Collection from My NCAA. Press Select and enter Glory.

#280 ALL-FLORIDA
Select Pennant Collection from My NCAA. Press Select and enter Great To Be.

#281 ALL-FSU
Select Pennant Collection from My NCAA. Press Select and enter Uprising.

#282 ALL-GEORGIA
Select Pennant Collection from My NCAA. Press Select and enter Hunker Down.

#283 ALL-IOWA
Select Pennant Collection from My NCAA. Press Select and enter On Iowa.

#284 ALL-KANSAS STATE
Select Pennant Collection from My NCAA. Press Select and enter Victory.

#285 ALL-LSU
Select Pennant Collection from My NCAA. Press Select and enter Geaux Tigers.

#286 ALL-MIAMI
Select Pennant Collection from My NCAA. Press Select and enter Raising Cane.

#287 ALL-MICHIGAN
Select Pennant Collection from My NCAA. Press Select and enter Go Blue.

#288 ALL-MISSISSIPPI STATE
Select Pennant Collection from My NCAA. Press Select and enter Hail State.

#289 ALL-NEBRASKA
Select Pennant Collection from My NCAA. Press Select and enter Go Big Red.

#290 ALL-NORTH CAROLINA
Select Pennant Collection from My NCAA. Press Select and enter Rah Rah.

#291 ALL-NOTRE DAME
Select Pennant Collection from My NCAA. Press Select and enter Golden Domer.

#292 ALL-OHIO STATE
Select Pennant Collection from My NCAA. Press Select and enter Killer Nuts.

#293 ALL-OKLAHOMA
Select Pennant Collection from My NCAA. Press Select and enter Boomer.

#294 ALL-OKLAHOMA STATE
Select Pennant Collection from My NCAA. Press Select and enter Go Pokes.

#295 ALL-OREGON
Select Pennant Collection from My NCAA. Press Select and enter Quack Attack.

#296 ALL-PENN STATE
Select Pennant Collection from My NCAA. Press Select and enter We Are.

#297 ALL-PITTSBURGH
Select Pennant Collection from My NCAA. Press Select and enter Lets Go Pitt.

#298 ALL-PURDUE
Select Pennant Collection from My NCAA. Press Select and enter Boiler Up.

#299 ALL-SYRACUSE
Select Pennant Collection from My NCAA. Press Select and enter Orange Crush.

#300 ALL-TENNESSEE
Select Pennant Collection from My NCAA. Press Select and enter Big Orange.

#301 ALL-TEXAS
Select Pennant Collection from My NCAA. Press Select and enter Hook Em.

#302 ALL-TEXAS A&M
Select Pennant Collection from My NCAA. Press Select and enter Gig Em.

#303 ALL-UCLA
Select Pennant Collection from My NCAA. Press Select and enter MIGHTY.

#304 ALL-USC
Select Pennant Collection from My NCAA. Press Select and enter Fight On.

#305 ALL-VIRGINIA
Select Pennant Collection from My NCAA. Press Select and enter Wahoos.

#306 ALL-VIRGINIA TECH
Select Pennant Collection from My NCAA. Press Select and enter Tech Triumph.

#307 ALL-WASHINGTON
Select Pennant Collection from My NCAA. Press Select and enter Bow Down.

#308 ALL-WISCONSIN
Select Pennant Collection from My NCAA. Press Select and enter U Rah Rah.

#311 ARK MASCOT
Select Pennant Collection from My NCAA. Press Select and enter Bear Down.

#329 GT MASCOT
Select Pennant Collection from My NCAA. Press Select and enter RamblinWreck.

#333 ISU MASCOT
Select Pennant Collection from My NCAA. Press Select and enter Red And Gold.

#335 KU MASCOT
Select Pennant Collection from My NCAA. Press Select and enter Rock Chalk.

#341 MINN MASCOT
Select Pennant Collection from My NCAA. Press Select and enter Rah Rah Rah.

#344 MIZZOU MASCOT
Select Pennant Collection from My NCAA. Press Select and enter Mizzou Rah.

#346 MSU MASCOT
Select Pennant Collection from My NCAA. Press Select and enter Go Green.

#349 NCSU MASCOT
Select Pennant Collection from My NCAA. Press Select and enter Go Pack.

#352 NU MASCOT
Select Pennant Collection from My NCAA. Press Select and enter Go Cats.

#360 S CAR MASCOT
Select Pennant Collection from My NCAA. Press Select and enter Go Carolina.

#371 UK MASCOT
Select Pennant Collection from My NCAA. Press Select and enter On On UK.

#382 WAKE FOREST
Select Pennant Collection from My NCAA. Press Select and enter Go Deacs Go.

#385 WSU MASCOT
Select Pennant Collection from My NCAA. Press Select and enter All Hail.

#386 WVU MASCOT
Select Pennant Collection from My NCAA. Press Select and enter Hail WV.

NCAA MARCH MADNESS 06

ALL TEAMS
Select My NCAA, then Cheat Codes from the lounge. Enter **PSDF9078VT**.

AIR JORDAN III SHOES
Select My NCAA, then Cheat Codes from the lounge. Enter **39N56BXC4S**.

FIRST AIR JORDANS
Select My NCAA, then Cheat Codes from the lounge. Enter **2J9UWAS44L**.

NEED FOR SPEED CARBON

CASTROL CASH
At the main menu, press Down, Up, Left, Down, Right, Up, X, B. This will give you 10,000 extra cash.

INFINITE CREW CHARGE
At the main menu, press Down, Up, Up, Right, Left, Left, Right, X.

INFINITE NITROUS
At the main menu, press Left, Up, Left, Down, Left, Down, Right, X.

INFINITE SPEEDBREAKER
At the main menu, press Down, Right, Right, Left, Right, Up, Down, X.

NEED FOR SPEED CARBON LOGO VINYLS
At the main menu, press Right, Up, Down, Up, Down, Left, Right, X.

NEED FOR SPEED CARBON SPECIAL LOGO VINYLS
At the main menu, press Up, Up, Down, Down, Down, Down, Up, X.

NEED FOR SPEED MOST WANTED

BURGER KING CHALLENGE
At the Title screen, press Up, Down, Up, Down, Left, Right, Left, Right.

CASTROL SYNTEC VERSION OF THE FORD GT
At the Title screen, press Left, Right, Left, Right, Up, Down, Up, Down.

MARKER FOR BACKROOM OF ONE-STOP SHOP
At the Title screen, press Up, Up, Down, Down, Left, Right, Up, Down.

PORSCHE CAYMAN
At the Title screen, press Left Trigger, Right Trigger, Right Trigger, Right Trigger, Right, Left, Right, Down.

NEED FOR SPEED UNDERGROUND 2

ALL CIRCUIT TRACKS
At the Main menu, press Down, Right Trigger, Right Trigger, Right Trigger, Black, Black, Black, X.

BEST BUY VINYL
At the Main menu, press Up, Down, Up, Down, Down, Up, Right, Left.

BURGER KING VINYL
At the Main menu, press Up, Up, Up, Up, Down, Up, Up, Left.

H2 CAPONE
At the Main menu, press Up, Left, Up, Up, Down, Left, Down, Left.

NISSIAN SKYLINE
At the Main menu, press Down, Down, Left Trigger, White, Left Trigger, White, Left Trigger, Down.

LEVEL 1 PERFORMANCE PARTS
At the Main menu, press Left Trigger, Right Trigger, Left Trigger, Right Trigger, Left, Left, Right, Up.

LEVEL 2 PERFORMANCE PARTS
At the Main menu, press Right Trigger, Right Trigger, Left Trigger, Right Trigger, Left, Right, Up, Down.

LEVEL 1 VISUAL PARTS
At the Main menu, press Right Trigger, Right Trigger, Up, Down, Left Trigger, Left Trigger, Up, Down.

LEVEL 2 VISUAL PARTS
At the Main menu, press Left Trigger, Right Trigger, Up, Down, Left Trigger, Up, Up, Down.

NFL HEAD COACH

CLOWN
Name your coach Red Nose.

JOHN MADDEN
Name your coach John Madden.

SANTA CLAUS
Name your coach Merry Christmas.

SUPER BOWL ALWAYS AT HOMETOWN
Name your coach Hometown Hero.

NFL STREET 2

FUMBLE MODE IN QUICK GAME

Enter **GreasedPig** as a code.

MAX CATCH IN QUICK GAME

Enter **MagnetHands** as a code.

NO CHAINS MODE IN QUICK GAME

Enter **NoChains** as a code.

NO FUMBLE MODE IN QUICK GAME

Enter **GlueHands** as a code.

UNLIMITED TURBO IN QUICK GAME

Enter **NozBoost** as a code.

EA FIELD

Enter **EAField** as a code.

AFC EAST ALL-STARS

Enter **EAASFSCT** as a code.

AFC NORTH ALL-STARS

Enter **NAOFRCTH** as a code.

AFC SOUTH ALL-STARS

Enter **SAOFUCTH** as a code.

AFC WEST ALL-STARS

Enter **WAEFSCT** as a code.

NFC EAST ALL-STARS

Enter **NNOFRCTH** as a code.

NFC NORTH ALL-STARS

Enter **NNAS66784** as a code.

NFC SOUTH ALL-STARS

Enter **SNOFUCTH** as a code.

NFC WEST ALL-STARS

Enter **ENASFSCT** as a code.

TEAM REEBOK

Enter **Reebok** as a code.

TEAM XZIBIT

Enter **TeamXzibit** as a code.

NHL 2K6

UNLOCK EVERYTHING

Select Manage Profiles from the Options screen. Create a New Profile with the name **Turco813**.

ODDWORLD STRANGER'S WRATH

CHEAT MODE

During a game, insert a controller in port 2. Remove the controller and press X, X, Y, Y, B, B, A, A on controller 1.

INVINCIBILITY

After entering the Cheat Mode code, press X, Y, A, B, X, Y.

$1000

After entering the Cheat Mode code, press Left Thumbstick, Left Thumbstick, Right Thumbstick, Right Thumbstick, Left Thumbstick, Left Thumbstick, Right Thumbstick, Right Thumbstick. You can repeat this code multiple times.

OUTRUN 2

Select OutRun Challenge and go to the Gallery screen. Choose Enter Code and input the following:

ALL CARS
Enter **DREAMING**.

ALL MISSION STAGES
Enter **THEJOURNEY**.

BONUS TRACKS
Enter **TIMELESS**.

REVERSE TRACKS
Enter **DESREVER**.

ALL MUSIC
Enter **RADIOSEGA**.

ORIGINAL OUTRUN
Enter **NINETEEN86**.

ALL CARDS
Enter **BIRTHDAY**.

OUTRUN 2006: COAST 2 COAST

100% COMPLETE/UNLOCK EVERYTHING
Edit your license and change the name to **ENTIRETY**. Select Done, then back out of all menus.

1000000 OUTRUN MILES
Edit your license and change the name to **MILESANDMILES**. Select Done, then back out of all menus.

OVER THE HEDGE

COMPLETE LEVELS
Pause the game, hold Left Trigger + Right Trigger and press Y, B, Y, B, B, X.

ALL MINIGAMES
Pause the game, hold Left Trigger + Right Trigger and press Y, B, Y, Y, X, X.

ALL MOVES
Pause the game, hold Left Trigger + Right Trigger and press Y, B, Y, X, X, B.

EXTRA DAMAGE
Pause the game, hold Left Trigger + Right Trigger and press Y, B, Y, B, Y, X.

MORE HP FROM FOOD
Pause the game, hold Left Trigger + Right Trigger and press Y, B, Y, B, X, Y.

ALWAYS POWER PROJECTILE
Pause the game, hold Left Trigger + Right Trigger and press Y, B, Y, B, X, B.

BONUS COMIC 14
Pause the game, hold Left Trigger + Right Trigger and press Y, B, X, X, B, Y.

BONUS COMIC 15
Pause the game, hold Left Trigger + Right Trigger and press Y, Y, X, B, X, B.

PAC-MAN WORLD 3

ALL LEVELS AND MAZE GAMES
At the main menu, press Left, Right, Left, Right, B, Up.

PANZER DRAGOON ORTA

ORIGINAL PANZER DRAGOON CODES

The following codes are for the original Panzer Dragoon. Unlock it first by defeating the game or playing for five hours. After doing so, enter the following codes at the Main menu of the original Panzer Dragoon.

INVINCIBLE

Press Left Trigger, Left Trigger, Right Trigger, Right Trigger, Up, Down, Left, Right.

STAGE SELECT

Press Up, Up, Down, Down, Left, Right, Left, Right, X, Y, White.

PLAY STAGE 0

Press Up, Up, Up, Down, Down, Down, Left, Right, Left, Right, Left, Right, Left Trigger, Right Trigger.

ROLLING MODE

Press Up, Right, Down, Left, Up, Right, Down, Left, Up, Right, Down, Left, Up, Right, Down, Left.

WIZARD MODE (FASTER GAMEPLAY)

Press Left Trigger, Right Trigger, Left Trigger, Right Trigger, Up, Down, Up, Down, Left, Right.

WATCH ENDING

Press Up, Up, Down, Up, Right, Right, Left, Right, Down, Down, Up, Down, Left, Left, Right, Left.

PETER JACKSON'S KING KONG: THE OFFICIAL GAME OF THE MOVIE

At the Main menu, hold Left Trigger + Right Trigger and press Down, X, Up, Y, Down, Down, Up, Up. Release Left Trigger + Right Trigger to get the Cheat option on the menu. The Cheat option is also available on the pause menu.

GOD MODE
Select Cheat and enter **8wonder**

ALL CHAPTERS
Select Cheat and enter **KKst0ry**.

AMMO 999
Select Cheat and enter **KK 999 mun**.

MACHINE GUN
Select Cheat and enter **KKcapone**.

REVOLVER
Select Cheat and enter **KKtigun**.

SNIPER RIFLE
Select Cheat and enter **KKsn1per**.

INFINITE SPEARS
Select Cheat and enter **lance 1nf**.

ONE-HIT KILLS
Select Cheat and enter **GrosBras**.

EXTRAS
Select Cheat and enter **KKmuseum**.

PIRATES OF THE CARIBBEAN

100,000 GOLD
During a game, press A, X, Y, B, Y, B, X, B, B, A.

GOD MODE
During a game, press A, Y, X, X, Y, Y, B, Y, X, A.

50 SKILL POINTS
During a game, press A, B, Y, X, Y, B, B, Y, B, A.

RESET REPUTATION
During a game, press A, X, Y, X, Y, B, B, Y, B, A.

POWERDROME

TACHE TEPLAN XSU-K0CC RACER
At the vehicle select, hold Right Trigger + Left Trigger and press Black, White, X, X, Y. Release Right Trigger and Left Trigger.

PSYCHONAUTS

ALL POWERS
During a game, hold Left Trigger + Right Trigger and press B, B, Y, White, Left Thumbstick, Y.

9999 LIVES
During a game, hold Left Trigger + Right Trigger and press Left Thumbstick, White, White, B, A, Right Thumbstick.

9999 AMMO (BLAST, CONFUSION)
During a game, hold Left Trigger + Right Trigger and press Right Thumbstick, A, Left Thumbstick, Left Thumbstick, Y, B.

GLOBAL ITEMS (NO PSI-BALL COLORIZER, NO DREAM FLUFFS)
During a game, hold Left Trigger + Right Trigger and press Right Thumbstick, B, White, White, Left Thumbstick, Y.

ALL POWERS UPGRADED (MAX RANK)
During a game, hold Left Trigger + Right Trigger and press Left Thumbstick, Right Thumbstick, Left Thumbstick, White, B, White.

9999 ARROWHEADS
During a game, hold Left Trigger + Right Trigger and press A, Right Thumbstick, Right Thumbstick, White, Y, X.

INVINCIBILITY
During a game, hold Left Trigger + Right Trigger and press B, White, B, B, Y, Black.

WEIRD TEXT
During a game, hold Left Trigger + Right Trigger and press White, A, click Left Thumbstick, White, White, B.

RALLISPORT CHALLENGE 2

CARS AND TRACKS SET 1
Select Credits from the Options screen and press Down, Left, Down, Right, Up, Up.

CARS AND TRACKS SET 2
Select Credits from the Options screen and press Left, Left, Down, Down, Right, Right.

CARS AND TRACKS SET 3
Select Credits from the Options screen and press Down, Down, Left, Left, Up, Down.

CARS AND TRACKS SET 4
Select Credits from the Options and press Right, Down, Right, Down, Left, Up.

CARS AND TRACKS SET 5
Select Credits from the Options screen and press Left, Left, Right, Right, Down, Left.

CARS AND TRACKS SET 6
Select Credits from the Options screen and press Right, Up, Up, Up, Down, Left.

CARS AND TRACKS SET 7
Select Credits from the Options screen and press Left, Left, Left, Up, Up, Right.

CARS AND TRACKS SET 8
Select Credits from the Options screen and press Right, Up, Left, Up, Down, Right.

CARS AND TRACKS SET 9
Select Credits from the Options screen and press Down, Up, Down, Left, Left, Down.

CARS AND TRACKS SET 10
Select Credits from the Options screen and press Up, Up, Down, Down, Left, Right.

ROBOTS

BIG HEAD FOR RODNEY
Pause the game and press Up, Down, Down, Up, Right, Right, Left, Right.

UNLIMITED HEALTH
Pause the game and press Up, Right, Down, Up, Left, Down, Right, Left.

UNLIMITED SCRAP
Pause the game and press Down, Down, Left, Up, Up, Right, Up, Down.

ROGUE TROOPER

INFINITE HEALTH
At the Extra menu, press Left, Right, Up, Down, Left Thumbstick, X.

INFINITE SUPPLIES
At the Extra menu, press Back, R, L, Back, Right Thumbstick, L.

LOW GRAVITY RAGDOLL
At the Extra menu, press X, X, X, B, B, B, Up, Down.

EXTREME RAGDOLL
At the Extra menu, press Up, Up, Up, Black, Black, Black, Up.

HIPPY BLOOD
At the Extra menu, press White, Right, B, Down, R, Back.

RUGBY LEAGUE 2

UNLOCK EVERYTHING
Create a player with the name **Darren Unlockyer**.

BIG HANDS
Create a player with the name **Jumbo Mittens**.

BIG HEADS
Create a player with the name **Planetoid**.

SMALL HEADS
Create a player with the name **micro noggin**.

BIG MUSCLES
Create a player with the name **Dale P Pugh**.

FAT PLAYERS
Create a player with the name **Cakemaster 3000**.

SKINNY PLAYERS
Create a player with the name **Crash Diet**.

TIRE IN BODY
Create a player with the name **Junkinthetrunk**.

TOGGLE MATRIX KICKING OFF
Create a player with the name **There is no spoon**.

SCALER

FULL HEALTH
Pause the game, select Audio from the Options screen and press Right Trigger, Left Trigger, Right Trigger, Left Trigger, Y, Y, X, X, Right Trigger, X.

200,000 KLOKKIES
Pause the game, select Audio from the Options screen and press Left Trigger, Left Trigger, Right Trigger, Right Trigger, Y, X, Y.

INFINITE ELECTRIC BOMBS
Pause the game, select Audio from the Options screen and press Right Trigger, Right Trigger, Left Trigger, Left Trigger, Y, Y, X.

SECRET WEAPONS OVER NORMANDY

ALL PLANES, ENVIRONMENTS, GALLERY, & MISSIONS
At the Main menu, press Y, Y, Y, X, X, X, Left Trigger, Right Trigger, Black, Black, White White.

ALL ENVIRONMENTS IN INSTANT ACTION
At the Main menu, press Up, Down, Left, Right, Left Trigger, Right Trigger, Left Trigger, Right Trigger.

INVINCIBILITY
At the Main menu, press Up, Down, Left, Right, Left, Left, Right, Right, Left Trigger, Left Trigger, Right Trigger, Right Trigger, White, Black.

UNLIMITED AMMUNITION
At the Main menu, press Up, Right, Down, Left, Up, Right, Down, Left, Left Trigger, Right Trigger.

BIG HEADS
At the Main menu, press Right, Up, Left, Down, Right, Up, Left, Down, Right, Left Trigger, Right Trigger, Left Trigger, Right Trigger.

SHATTERED UNION

SKIP CURRENT WEEK IN CAMPAIGN MODE
At the US Map, press Start for the Options. Then select Cheat Menu and press X, Y, Y, X, B, A.

WIN CIVIL WAR IN CAMPAIGN MODE
At the US Map, press Start for the Options. Then select Cheat Menu and press X, B, A, B, Y.

$100,000
At the US Map, press Start for the Options. Then select Cheat Menu and press X, X, A, A, Y.

ARCADIA PLAINS
At the US Map, press Start for the Options. Then select Cheat Menu and press B, X, X, X, A.

ARIZONA TERRITORY
At the US Map, press Start for the Options. Then select Cheat Menu and press B, X, X, A, X.

CAROLINAS
At the US Map, press Start for the Options. Then select Cheat Menu and press B, X, Y, X, A.

CENTRAL CASCADES
At the US Map, press Start for the Options. Then select Cheat Menu and press B, X, X, X, Y.

CENTRAL HEARTLAND
At the US Map, press Start for the Options. Then select Cheat Menu and press B, X, X, B, Y.

CUMBERLANDS
At the US Map, press Start for the Options. Then select Cheat Menu and press B, X, Y, X, Y.

DAKOTAS
At the US Map, press Start for the Options. Then select Cheat Menu and press B, X, X, B, X.

EASTERN SHENANDOAH
At the US Map, press Start for the Options. Then select Cheat Menu and press B, X, Y, Y, B.

FLORIDA
At the US Map, press Start for the Options. Then select Cheat Menu and press B, X, Y, X, B.

GREAT BASIN
At the US Map, press Start for the Options. Then select Cheat Menu and press B, X, X, Y, A.

GREAT LAKES
At the US Map, press Start for the Options. Then select Cheat Menu and press B, X, X, B, A.

GREAT PLAINS
At the US Map, press Start for the Options. Then select Cheat Menu and press B, X, X, B, B.

MISSISSIPPI DELTA
At the US Map, press Start for the Options. Then select Cheat Menu and press B, X, Y, X, X.

NEW MEXICO
At the US Map, press Start for the Options. Then select Cheat Menu and press B, X, X, Y, B.

NEW YORK
At the US Map, press Start for the Options. Then select Cheat Menu and press B, X, Y, Y, Y.

NORTHERN CALIFORNIA
At the US Map, press Start for the Options. Then select Cheat Menu and press B, X, X, Y, X.

NORTHERN CASCADES
At the US Map, press Start for the Options. Then select Cheat Menu and press B, X, X, X, B.

NORTHERN NEW ENGLAND
At the US Map, press Start for the Options. Then select Cheat Menu and press B, X, Y, Y, A.

NORTHERN TEXAS
At the US Map, press Start for the Options. Then select Cheat Menu and press B, X, X, A, A.

OHIO VALLEY
At the US Map, press Start for the Options. Then select Cheat Menu and press B, X, Y, Y, X.

OKLAHOMA GRASSLANDS
At the US Map, press Start for the Options. Then select Cheat Menu and press B, X, X, A, Y.

SOUTHEASTERN CASCADES
At the US Map, press Start for the Options. Then select Cheat Menu and press B, X, X, X, X.

SOUTHERN CALIFORNIA
At the US Map, press Start for the Options. Then select Cheat Menu and press B, X, X, Y, Y.

SOUTHERN TEXAS
At the US Map, press Start for the Options. Then select Cheat Menu and press B, X, X, A, B.

SHREK 2

BONUS GAMES
Pause the game and select Scrapbook. Press Left, Up, A, B, Left, Up, A, B, Left, Up, A, B, X, B, X, B, X, B. Exit the level and select Bonus to access the games.

CHAPTER SELECT
Pause the game and select Scrapbook. Press Left, Up, A, B, Left, Up, A, B, Left, Up, A, B, Up (x5). Exit the level and choose Chapter Select to change chapters.

FULL HEALTH
Pause the game and select Scrapbook. Press Left, A, B, Circle, Left, A, B, Circle, Left, A, B, Up, Right, Down, Left, Up.

1,000 COINS
Pause the game and select Scrapbook. Press Left, Up, A, B, Left, Up, A, B, Left, Up, A, B (x6).

SID MEIER'S PIRATES!

FOOD NEVER DWINDLES
Name your character **Sweet Tooth**.

INVINCIBLE SHIP
Name your character **Bloody Bones Baz**.

JEFF BRIGGS AS ABBOTT
Name your character **Firaxis**.

SNAPPY DRESSER
Name your character **Bonus Frag**.

BEST SHIP AND FULL CREW
Name your character D.Gackey

YOUR FLEET IS TWICE AS FAST
Name your character Sprinkler.

HIGHEST MORALE
Name your character B.Caudizzle.

DUELING INVINCIBILITY
Name your character Dragon Ma.

SID MEIER AS MYSTERIOUS STRANGER
Name your character Max Remington.

THE SIMS 2

During gameplay, press Left Trigger, Right Trigger, Up on D-pad, A, Black. Now you can enter the following cheats:

ALL LOCATIONS
Press B, White, Left, B, Up, B.

ALL CLOTHES
Press X, Black, Down, Right, X.

ALL OBJECTS
Press White, B, Down, Left, Up.

ALL RECIPES
Press Black, X, Up, Down, Right, A.

MAX ALL MOTIVES
Press Up, B, Up, Right, White.

§10,000
Press Right Trigger, Left Trigger, Black, Right, Left.

CHANGES SIM'S SKILL
Press Y, B, X, Black, D-pad Left.

JUMP AHEAD SIX HOURS
Press B, X, Left Trigger, Up, Down.

REMOVE MESSAGES
Press Right, Up, Right, Down, Right, Up, Down, Right.

SONIC HEROES

METAL CHARACTERS IN 2-PLAYER
After selecting a level in 2-Player mode, hold A + Y.

SONIC MEGA COLLECTION PLUS

Comix Zone

INVINCIBILITY
Select the Jukebox from the Options screen and play the following tracks in order: 3, 12, 17, 2, 2, 10, 2, 7, 7, 11.

STAGE SELECT
Select the Jukebox from the Options screen and play the following tracks in order: 14, 15, 18, 5, 13, 1, 3, 18, 15, 6.

Dr. Robotnik's Mean Bean Machine

EASY PASSWORDS
Continue a game with the following passwords:

LEVEL	PASSWORD
2	Red Bean, Red Bean, Red Bean, Has Bean
3	Clear Bean, Purple Bean, Clear Bean, Green Bean
4	Red Bean, Clear Bean, Has Bean, Yellow Bean
5	Clear Bean, Blue Bean, Blue Bean, Purple Bean
6	Clear Bean, Red Bean, Clear Bean, Purple Bean
7	Purple Bean, Yellow Bean, Red Bean, Blue Bean
8	Yellow Bean, Green Bean, Purple Bean, Has Bean
9	Yellow Bean, Purple Bean, Has Bean, Blue Bean
10	Red Bean, Yellow Bean, Clear Bean, Has Bean
11	Green Bean, Purple Bean, Blue Bean, Clear Bean
12	Red Bean, Has Bean, Has Bean, Yellow Bean
13	Yellow Bean, Has Bean, Blue Bean, Blue Bean

NORMAL PASSWORDS

LEVEL	PASSWORD
2	Has Bean, Clear Bean, Yellow Bean, Yellow Bean
3	Blue Bean, Clear Bean, Red Bean, Yellow Bean
4	Yellow Bean, Blue Bean, Clear Bean, Purple Bean
5	Has Bean, Green Bean, Blue Bean, Yellow Bean
6	Green Bean, Purple Bean, Purple Bean, Yellow Bean
7	Purple Bean, Blue Bean, Green Bean, Has Bean
8	Green Bean, Has Bean, Clear Bean, Yellow Bean
9	Blue Bean, Purple Bean, Has Bean, Has Bean
10	Has Bean, Red Bean, Yellow Bean, Clear Bean
11	Clear Bean, Red Bean, Red Bean, Blue Bean
12	Green Bean, Green Bean, Clear Bean, Yellow Bean
13	Purple Bean, Yellow Bean, Has Bean, Clear Bean

HARD PASSWORDS

LEVEL	PASSWORD
2	Green Bean, Clear Bean, Yellow Bean, Yellow Bean
3	Yellow Bean, Clear Bean, Purple Bean, Clear Bean
4	Blue Bean, Green Bean, Clear Bean, Blue Bean
5	Red Bean, Purple Bean, Green Bean, Green Bean
6	Yellow Bean, Yellow Bean, Clear Bean, Green Bean
7	Purple Bean, Clear Bean, Blue Bean, Blue Bean
8	Clear Bean, Yellow Bean, Has Bean, Yellow Bean
9	Purple Bean, Blue Bean, Blue Bean, Green Bean
10	Clear Bean, Green Bean, Red Bean, Yellow Bean
11	Blue Bean, Yellow Bean, Yellow Bean, Has Bean
12	Green Bean, Clear Bean, Clear Bean, Blue bean
13	Has Bean, Clear Bean, Purple Bean, Has Bean

HARDEST PASSWORDS

LEVEL	PASSWORD
2	Blue Bean, Blue Bean, Green Bean, Yellow Bean
3	Green Bean, Yellow Bean, Green Bean, Clear Bean
4	Purple Bean, Purple Bean, Red Bean, Has Bean
5	Green Bean, Red Bean, Purple Bean, Blue Bean
6	Blue Bean, Purple Bean, Green Bean, Yellow Bean
7	Blue Bean, Purple Bean, Green Bean, Has Bean
8	Clear Bean, Purple Bean, Has Bean, Yellow Bean
9	Purple Bean, Green Bean, Has Bean, Clear Bean
10	Green Bean, Blue Bean, Yellow Bean, Has Bean
11	Green Bean, Purple Bean, Has Bean, Red Bean
12	Red Bean, Green Bean, Has Bean, Blue Bean
13	Red Bean, Red Bean, Clear Bean, Yellow Bean

RISTAR

LEVEL SELECT
Enter **ILOVEU** as a password.

FIGHT ONLY BOSSES
Enter **MUSEUM** as a password.

TIME ATTACK
Enter **DOFEEL** as a password.

TONE DEAF SOUNDS
Enter **MAGURO** as a password.

TRUE SIGHT
Enter **MIEMIE** as a password.

SUPER HARD
Enter **SUPER** as a password.

VERY HARD
Enter **SUPERB** as a password.

CANCEL CODES
Enter **XXXXXX** as a password.

SPIDER-MAN 2

TREYARCH PASSWORD
Start a New Game and enter **HCRAYERT** as your name. This starts the game at 44% complete, 201,000 Hero Points, some upgrades and more.

SPIKEOUT: BATTLE STREET

EASY MODE
Die twice and continue the game to unlock a new Easy Mode option.

SPONGEBOB SQUAREPANTS: BATTLE FOR BIKINI BOTTOM

The following codes must be entered quickly.

RESTORE HEALTH
Pause the game, hold Left Trigger + Right Trigger and press X, X, X, X, Y, X, Y, X, Y, Y, Y.

EXPERT MODE
Pause the game, hold Left Trigger + Right Trigger and press X, X, X, Y, Y, X, X, X, Y, X, Y, Y, Y, X, Y, X.

EARN 1,000 SHINY OBJECTS
Pause the game, hold Left Trigger + Right Trigger and press Y, X, X, Y, Y, X, X, Y.

EARN 10 GOLD SPATULAS
Pause the game, hold Left Trigger + Right Trigger and press X, Y, Y, X, X, Y, Y, X.

BUBBLE BOWL POWER-UP
Pause the game, hold Left Trigger + Right Trigger and press X, Y, X, Y, X, X, Y, Y. Press X to use.

CRUISE BUBBLE POWER-UP
Pause the game, hold Left Trigger + Right Trigger and press Y, X, Y, X, Y, Y, X, X. Press Left Trigger to use.

INCREASE VALUE OF SHINY OBJECTS
Pause the game, hold Left Trigger + Right Trigger and press Y, X, Y, X, X, Y, X, X, X, Y, Y, Y, Y, X, X, Y.

MODIFIED CRUISE BUBBLE CONTROLS

Pause the game, hold Left Trigger + Right Trigger and press X, X, X, X, Y, Y, X, X, Y, X, Y.

VILLAGERS GIVE SHINY OBJECTS WHEN HIT

Pause the game, hold Left Trigger + Right Trigger and press Y, Y, Y, Y, Y, X, Y, X, X, Y, X, Y.

VILLAGERS RESTORE HEALTH WHEN NEAR

Pause the game, hold Left Trigger + Right Trigger and press Y, Y, Y, Y, Y, X, Y, X, X, X, Y, Y.

NO PANTS

Pause the game, hold Left Trigger + Right Trigger and press X, X, X, X, Y, X, X, Y, X, Y, Y, X.

BIG PLANKTON

Pause the game, hold Left Trigger + Right Trigger and press Y, Y, Y, Y, X, Y, X, Y, X, X, X, X.

SMALL CHARACTERS

Pause the game, hold Left Trigger + Right Trigger and press Y, Y, Y, Y, X, Y, X, Y, Y, Y, Y, Y.

SMALL VILLAGERS

Pause the game, hold Left Trigger + Right Trigger and press Y, Y, Y, Y, Y, X, Y, X, Y, X, Y, X.

SPONGEBOB BREAKS APART WHEN DEFEATED

Pause the game, hold Left Trigger + Right Trigger and press X, X, X, X, Y, Y, X, Y, X, X, X, Y.

INVERT LEFT/RIGHT CAMERA CONTROLS

Pause the game, hold Left Trigger + Right Trigger and press Y, Y, X, X, X, X, Y, Y.

INVERT UP/DOWN CAMERA CONTROLS

Pause the game, hold Left Trigger + Right Trigger and press Y, X, X, X, X, X, X, Y.

SPONGEBOB SQUAREPANTS: LIGHTS, CAMERA, PANTS!

SILVER STORY MODE

Select Rewards from the Bonuses menu, then select Codes and enter **486739**.

ALL ACTION FIGURES

Select Rewards from the Bonuses menu, then select Codes and enter **977548**.

HOOK, LINE & CHEDDAR GAME

Select Rewards from the Bonuses menu, then select Codes and enter **893634**.

SPY HUNTER: NOWHERE TO RUN

SPY HUNTER ARCADE

This is a version of the old *Spy Hunter* arcade game, using the new 3D models, weapons, and enemies found in *Nowhere to Run*. As in the original game, you'll transform from a car to a boat and back again. You don't need to earn a certain ranking to unlock it; all you must do is activate the machine when you come across it in the safe house on Level 7 (Cleaning Up).

SPY VS SPY

ALL CLASSIC MAPS

Enter RETROSPY at the password screen.

ALL STORY MODE LEVELS

Enter ANTONIO at the password screen.

ALL LEVELS FOR SINGLE-PLAYER MODERN MODE

Enter PROHIAS at the password screen.

ALL MULTIPLAYER MAPS

Enter MADMAG at the password screen.

ALL OUTFITS

Enter DISGUISE at the password screen.

ALL WEAPONS

Enter WRKBENCH at the password screen.

INVULNERABILITY

Enter ARMOR at the password screen.

SUPER DAMAGE

Enter BIGGUNZ at the password screen.

PERMANENT FAIRY IN MODERN MODE

Enter FAIRY at the password screen.

NO DROPPED ITEMS WHEN KILLED

Enter NODROP at the password screen.

INVISIBLE HUD

Enter BLINK at the password screen.

ALL MOVIES

Enter SPYFLIX at the password screen.

CONCEPT ART

Enter SPYPICS at the password screen.

SSX ON TOUR

NEW THREADS

Select Cheats from the Extras menu and enter **FLYTHREADS**.

THE WORLD IS YOURS

Select Cheats from the Extras menu and enter **BACKSTAGEPASS**.

SHOW TIME (ALL MOVIES)

Select Cheats from the Extras menu and enter **THEBIGPICTURE**.

BLING BLING (INFINITE CASH)

Select Cheats from the Extras menu and enter **LOOTSNOOT**.

FULL BOOST, FULL TIME

Select Cheats from the Extras menu and enter **ZOOMJUICE**.

MONSTERS ARE LOOSE (MONSTER TRICKS)

Select Cheats from the Extras menu and enter **JACKALOPESTYLE**.

SNOWBALL FIGHT

Select Cheats from the Extras menu and enter **LETSPARTY**.

FEEL THE POWER (STAT BOOST)

Select Cheats from the Extras menu and enter **POWERPLAY**.

CHARACTERS ARE LOOSE

Select Cheats from the Extras menu and enter **ROADIEROUNDUp**.

UNLOCK CONRAD

Select Cheats from the Extras menu and enter **BIGPARTYTIME**.

UNLOCK MITCH KOOBSKI

Select Cheats from the Extras menu and enter **MOREFUNTHANONE**.

UNLOCK NIGEL

Select Cheats from the Extras menu and enter **THREEISACROWD**.

UNLOCK SKI PATROL

Select Cheats from the Extras menu and enter **FOURSOME**.

STAR WARS: BATTLEFRONT II

INFINITE AMMO
Pause the game and press Up, Down, Left, Down, Down, Left, Down, Down, Left, Down, Down, Down, Left, Right.

INVINCIBILITY
Pause the game and press Up, Up, Up, Left, Down, Down, Down, Left, Up, Up, Up, Left, Right.

NO HUD
Pause the game and press Up, Up, Up, Up, Left, Up, Up, Down, Left, Down, Up, Up, Left, Right. Re-enter the code to enable HUD again.

ALTERNATE SOLDIERS
Pause the game and press Down, Down, Down, Up, Up, Left, Down, Down, Down, Down, Left, Up, Up, Up, Left.

ALTERNATE SOUNDS
Pause the game and press Up, Up, Up, Left, Up, Down, Up, Up, Left, Down, Down, Down, Left, Up, Down, Down, Left, Right.

FUNNY MESSAGES WHEN REBELS DEFEATED
Pause the game and press Up, Down, Left, Down, Left, Right.

STAR WARS EPISODE III: REVENGE OF THE SITH

INFINITE FORCE
Select Codes from the Settings menu and enter **KAIBURR**.

INFINITE HEALTH
Select Codes from the Settings menu and enter **XUCPHRA**.

QUICK HEALTH & FORCE RESTORATION
Select Codes from the Settings menu and enter **BELSAVIS**.

ALL STORY, BONUS & CO-OP MISSIONS AND DUELISTS
Select Codes from the Settings menu and enter **021282**.

ALL STORY MISSIONS
Select Codes from the Settings menu and enter **KORRIBAN**.

ALL BONUS MISSIONS
Select Codes from the Settings menu and enter **NARSHADDAA**.

ALL DUEL ARENAS
Select Codes from the Settings menu and enter **TANTIVIEV**.

ALL DUELISTS
Select Codes from the Settings menu and enter
ZABRAK.

ALL POWERS & MOVES
Select Codes from the Settings menu and enter
JAINA.

SUPER LIGHTSABER MODE
Select Codes from the Settings menu and enter
SUPERSABERS.

TINY DRIOD MODE
Select Codes from the Settings menu and enter **071779**.

ALL REPLAY MOVIES
Select Codes from the Settings menu and enter **COMLINK**.

ALL CONCEPT ART
Select Codes from the Settings menu and enter **AAYLASECURA**.

STAR WARS KNIGHTS OF THE OLD REPUBLIC II: THE SITH LORDS

CHANGE VOICES
Add a controller to the fourth port and press Black or White to raise and lower character voices.

STOLEN

LEVEL SKIP
At the Title screen, press Right Trigger, Left Trigger, Start + Down.

99 OF ALL ITEMS
During gameplay, go to Equipment and press Right Trigger, Left Trigger, Right.

TAK: THE GREAT JUJU CHALLENGE

BONUS SOUND EFFECTS
In Juju's Potions, select Universal Card and enter the following numbers for Bugs, Crystals and Fruits: 20, 17, 5.

BONUS SOUND EFFECTS 2
In Juju's Potions, select Universal Card and enter the following numbers for Bugs, Crystals and Fruits: 50, 84, 92.

BONUS MUSIC TRACK 1
In Juju's Potions, select Universal Card and enter the following numbers for Bugs, Crystals and Fruits: 67, 8, 20.

BONUS MUSIC TRACK 2
In Juju's Potions, select Universal Card and enter the following numbers for Bugs, Crystals and Fruits: 6, 18, 3.

MAGIC PARTICLES
In Juju's Potions, select Universal Card and enter the following numbers for Bugs, Crystals and Fruits: 24, 40, 11.

MORE MAGIC PARTICLES
In Juju's Potions, select Universal Card and enter the following numbers for Bugs, Crystals and Fruits: 48, 57, 57.

VIEW JUJU CONCEPT ART
In Juju's Potions, select Universal Card and enter the following numbers for Bugs, Crystals and Fruits: Art 33, 22, 28.

VIEW VEHICLE ART
In Juju's Potions, select Universal Card and enter the following numbers for Bugs, Crystals and Fruits: 11, 55, 44.

VIEW WORLD ART
In Juju's Potions, select Universal Card and enter the following numbers for Bugs, Crystals and Fruits: 83, 49, 34.

TAK 2: THE STAFF OF DREAMS

BALLOON HEAD SHOWDOWN MINI-GAME
Select Universal Card from Juju Potions and enter the following numbers for Bugs, Crystals and Fruit: 48, 62, 19.

BARREL BLITZ MINI-GAME
Select Universal Card from Juju Potions and enter the following numbers for Bugs, Crystals and Fruit: 1, 105, 81.

CATAPULT CHAOS MINI-GAME
Select Universal Card from Juju Potions and enter the following numbers for Bugs, Crystals and Fruit: 103, 33, 20.

CHICKEN TENNIS MINI-GAME
Select Universal Card from Juju Potions and enter the following numbers for Bugs, Crystals and Fruit: 202, 17, 203.

CHUCKIN' CHICKENS MINI-GAME
Select Universal Card from Juju Potions and enter the following numbers for Bugs, Crystals and Fruit: 18, 71, 50.

DART TOOM DODGEM MINI-GAME
Select Universal Card from Juju Potions and enter the following numbers for Bugs, Crystals and Fruit: 83, 43, 142.

DINKY SNOWBOARD BIG AIR MINI-GAME
Select Universal Card from Juju Potions and enter the following numbers for Bugs, Crystals and Fruit: 233, 127, 204.

FLEA FLYER MINI-GAME
Select Universal Card from Juju Potions and enter the following numbers for Bugs, Crystals and Fruit: 22, 6, 17.

FROG DERBY MINI-GAME
Select Universal Card from Juju Potions and enter the following numbers for Bugs, Crystals and Fruit: 281, 62, 149.

GLIDE RIDE MINI-GAME
Select Universal Card from Juju Potions and enter the following numbers for Bugs, Crystals and Fruit: 131, 61, 179.

GLOOMLEAF ARENA MINI-GAME
Select Universal Card from Juju Potions and enter the following numbers for Bugs, Crystals and Fruit: 68, 13, 8.

KRASH KOURSE MINI-GAME
Select Universal Card from Juju Potions and enter the following numbers for Bugs, Crystals and Fruit: 5, 41, 41.

VINE CLIMB MINI-GAME
Select Universal Card from Juju Potions and enter the following numbers for Bugs, Crystals and Fruit: 8, 1, 3.

FAUNA IN MULTIPLAYER
Select Universal Card from Juju Potions and enter the following numbers for Bugs, Crystals and Fruit: 44, 13, 0.

JB IN MULTIPLAYER
Select Universal Card from Juju Potions and enter the following numbers for Bugs, Crystals and Fruit: 16, 19, 38.

LOK IN MULTIPLAYER
Select Universal Card from Juju Potions and enter the following numbers for Bugs, Crystals and Fruit: 2, 2, 5.

SKELETON JUJU SPIRIT IN MULTIPLAYER
Select Universal Card from Juju Potions and enter the following numbers for Bugs, Crystals and Fruit: 55, 171, 35.

TAK'S FEATHER COLOR
Select Universal Card from Juju Potions and enter the following numbers for Bugs, Crystals and Fruit: 4, 9, 23.

BETTER MANA MAGNET
Select Universal Card from Juju Potions and enter the following numbers for Bugs, Crystals and Fruit: 3, 27, 31.

TAK 1 GAME CINEMATIC SEQUENCE
Select Universal Card from Juju Potions and enter the following numbers for Bugs, Crystals and Fruit: 30, 21, 88.

CONCEPT ART
Select Universal Card from Juju Potions and enter the following numbers for Bugs, Crystals and Fruit: 30, 37, 51.

PICTURES OF THE TAK SUIT
Select Universal Card from Juju Potions and enter the following numbers for Bugs, Crystals and Fruit: 11, 4, 17.

SOUND EFFECTS SET ONE
Select Universal Card from Juju Potions and enter the following numbers for Bugs, Crystals and Fruit: 4, 55, 36.

VIEW COMMERICIALS
Select Universal Card from Juju Potions and enter the following numbers for Bugs, Crystals and Fruit: 6, 16, 6.

TAZ WANTED

ALL LEVELS
At the Start Game screen, select Marvin the Martian and enter **#OP**.

ALL BONUS GAMES
At the Start Game screen, select Daffy Duck and enter **?BN**.

2-PLAYER BOSS GAMES
At the Start Game screen, select Big red and enter ***JC**.

ART GALLERY
At the Start Game screen, select Tweety and enter **.RT**.

DISABLE WHACK IN THE BOXES
At the Start Game screen, select Taz and enter **!WB**.

TEENAGE MUTANT NINJA TURTLES 3: MUTANT NIGHTMARE

INVINCIBILITY
Select Passwords from the Options menu and enter MDLDSSLR.

HEALTH POWER-UPS TURN INTO SUSHI
Select Passwords from the Options menu and enter SLLMRSLD.

NO HEALTH POWER-UPS
Select Passwords from the Options menu and enter DMLDMRLD.

ONE-HIT DEFEATS TURTLE
Select Passwords from the Options menu and enter LDMSLRDD.

MAX OUGI
Select Passwords from the Options menu and enter RRDMLSDL.

UNLIMTED SHURIKEN
Select Passwords from the Options menu and enter LMDRRMSR.

NO SHURIKEN
Select Passwords from the Options menu and enter LLMSRDMS.

DOUBLE ENEMY ATTACK
Select Passwords from the Options menu and enter MSRLSMML.

DOUBLE ENEMY DEFENSE
Select Passwords from the Options menu and enter SLRMLSSM.

TOMB RAIDER: LEGEND

The following codes must be unlocked in the game before using them.

BULLETPROOF
During gameplay, hold Left Trigger and press A, Right Trigger, Y, Right Trigger, X, Black.

DRAIN ENEMY HEALTH
During gameplay, hold Left Trigger and press X, B, A, Black, Right Trigger, Y.

INFINITE ASSAULT RIFLE AMMO

During gameplay, hold Black and press A, B, A, Left Trigger, X, Y.

INFINITE GRENADE LAUNCHER AMMO

During gameplay, hold Black and press Left Trigger, Y, Right Trigger, B, Left Trigger, X.

INFINITE SHOTGUN AMMO

During gameplay, hold Black and press Right Trigger, B, X, Left Trigger, X, A.

INFINITE SMG AMMO

During gameplay, hold Black and press B, Y, Left Trigger, Right Trigger, A, B.

EXCALIBUR

During gameplay, hold Black and press Y, A, B, Right Trigger, Y, Left Trigger.

SOUL REAVER

During gameplay, hold Black and press A, Right Trigger, B, Right Trigger, Left Trigger, X.

NO TEXTURE MODE

During gameplay, hold Left Trigger and press Black, A, B, A, Y, Right Trigger.

TIGER WOODS PGA TOUR 06

ALL GOLFERS

Select Password from the Options screen and enter **WOOGLIN**.

ALL CLUBS

Select Password from the Options screen and enter **CLUB11**.

LEVEL 2 NIKE ITEMS

Select Password from the Options screen and enter **JUSTDOIT**.

ALL COURSES

Select Password from the Options screen and enter **ITSINTHEHOLE**.

TIGER WOODS IN HAT AND TIE

Select Password from the Options screen and enter **GOLDENAGE**.

TIGER WOODS IN STRIPED PANTS

Select Password from the Options screen and enter **TECHNICOLOR**.

TIGER WOODS IN OLD GOLF OUTFIT

Select Password from the Options screen and enter **OLDSKOOL**.

TIGER WOODS IN ALTERNATE OLD GOLF OUTFIT

Select Password from the Options screen and enter **THROWBACK**.

ARNOLD PALMER

Select Password from the Options screen and enter **ARNIESARMY**.

BEN HOGAN

Select Password from the Options screen and enter **THEHAWK**.

JACK NICKLAUS

Select Password from the Options screen and enter **GOLDENBEAR**.

OLD TOM MORRIS

Select Password from the Options screen and enter **FEATHERIE**.

TOMMY BLACK

Select Password from the Options screen and enter **IDONTHAVEAPROBLEM**.

WESLEY ROUNDER

Select Password from the Options screen and enter **POCKETPAIR**.

TIGER WOODS PGA TOUR 07

NIKE ITEMS

Select the Password option and enter JUSTDOIT.

TIM BURTON'S THE NIGHTMARE BEFORE CHRISTMAS: OOGIE'S REVENGE

PUMPKIN KING AND SANTA JACK COSTUMES
During gameplay, press Down, Up, Right, Left, Left Thumbstick, Right Thumbstick.

TONY HAWK'S AMERICAN WASTELAND

ALWAYS SPECIAL
Select Cheat Codes from the Options screen and enter **uronfire**. Pause the game and select Cheats from the Game Options to enable the cheat.

PERFECT RAIL
Select Cheat Codes from the Options screen and enter **grindxpert**. Pause the game and select Cheats from the Game Options to enable the cheat.

PERFECT SKITCH
Select Cheat Codes from the Options screen and enter **h!tchar!de**. Pause the game and select Cheats from the Game Options to enable the cheat.

PERFECT MANUAL
Select Cheat Codes from the Options screen and enter **2wheels!**. Pause the game and select Cheats from the Game Options to enable the cheat.

MOON GRAVITY
Select Cheat Codes from the Options screen and enter **2them00n**. Pause the game and select Cheats from the Game Options to enable the cheat.

MAT HOFFMAN
Select Cheat Codes from the Options screen and enter **the_condor**.

JASON ELLIS
Select Cheat Codes from the Options screen and enter **sirius-dj**.

TONY HAWK'S PROJECT 8

SPONSOR ITEMS
As you progress through Career mode and move up the rankings, you gain sponsors and each comes with its own Create-a-skater item.

RANK REQUIRED	CAS ITEM UNLOCKED	RANK REQUIRED	CAS ITEM UNLOCKED
Rank 040	Adio Kenny V2 Shoes	Rank 120	Almost Watch What You Say Deck
Rank 050	Quiksilver_Hoody_3	Rank 140	DVS Adage Shoe
Rank 060	Birdhouse Tony Hawk Deck	Rank 150	Element Illuminate Deck
Rank 080	Vans No Skool Gothic Shoes	Rank 160	Etnies Sheckler White Lavender Shoes
Rank 100	Volcom Scallero Jacket	Complete Skateshop Goal	Stereo Soundwave Deck
Rank 110	eS Square One Shoes		

SKATERS
All of the skaters, except for Tony Hawk, must be unlocked by completing challenges in the Career Mode. They are useable in Free Skate and 2 Player modes.

SKATER	HOW THEY ARE UNLOCKED	SKATER	HOW THEY ARE UNLOCKED
Tony Hawk	Always Unlocked	Paul Rodriguez	Complete Pro Challenge
Lyn-z Adams Hawkins	Complete Pro Challenge	Ryan Sheckler	Complete Pro Challenge
Bob Burquist	Complete Pro Challenge	Daewon Song	Complete Pro Challenge
Dustin Dollin	Complete Pro Challenge	Mike Vallely	Complete Pro Challenge
Nyjah Huston	Complete Pro Challenge	Stevie Willams	Complete Pro Challenge
Bam Margera	Complete Pro Challenge	Travis Barker	Complete Pro Challenge
Rodney Mullen	Complete Pro Challenge	Kevin Staab	Complete Pro Challenge

SKATER	HOW THEY ARE UNLOCKED
Zombie	Complete Pro Challenge
Christaian Hosoi	Animal Chin Challenge
Jason Lee	Complete Final Tony Hawk Goal
Photographer	Unlock Shops
Security Guard	Unlock School
Bum	Unlock Car Factory
Beaver Mascot	Unlock High School

SKATER	HOW THEY ARE UNLOCKED
Real Estate Agent	Unlock Downtown
Filmer	Unlock High School
Skate Jam Kid	Rank #4
Dad	Rank #1
Colonel	All Gaps
Nerd	Complete School Spirit Goal

CHEAT CODES

Select Cheat Codes from the Options and enter the following codes. In game you can access some codes from the Options menu.

CHEAT CODE	RESULTS
plus44	Unlocks Travis Barker
hohohosoi	Unlocks Christian Hosoi
notmono	Unlocks Jason Lee
mixitup	Unlocks Kevin Staab
strangefellows	Unlocks Dad & Skater Jam Kid
themedia	Unlocks Photog Girl & Filmer
militarymen	Unlocks Colonel & Security Guard
jammypack	Unlocks Always Special
balancegalore	Unlocks Perfect Rail
frontandback	Unlocks Perect Manual
shellshock	Unlocks Unlimited Focus
shescaresme	Unlocks Big Realtor
birdhouse	Unlocks Inkblot deck
allthebest	Full Stats
needaride	All Decks unlocked and free, except for inkblot deck and gamestop deck
yougotitall	All specials unlocked and in player's special list and set as owned in skate shop
enterandwin	Unlocks Bum
wearelosers	Unlocks Nerd
manineedadate	Unlocks Mascot
suckstobedead	Unlocks Zombie
sellsellsell	Unlocks Skinny real estate agent
newshound	Unlocks Anchor man
badverybad	Unlocks Twin

TY THE TASMANIAN TIGER 2: BUSH RESCUE

ALL BUNYIP KEYS
During a game, press Start, Y, Start, Start, Y, X, B, X, A.

ALL FIRST-LEVEL RANGS
During a game, press Start, Y, Start, Start, Y, B, X, B, X.

ALL SECOND-LEVEL RANGS
During a game, press Start, Y, Start, Start, Y, X, B, X, Y.

GET 100,000 OPALS
During a game, press Start, Y, Start, Start, Y, B, A, B, A.

CHEAT GNOME
During a game, press Left + Y + Down + A + X. Now you can enter the following cheats.

MAX ARTISTIC
Press Y, Down, Black, A, B.

MAX MENTAL
Press Left Trigger, B, A, Black, Down.

MAX PHYSTICAL
Press Left Trigger, Right Trigger, A, Down, Black.

ACQUIRE SKILL
Press Left Trigger, Black, Right, X, Left.

POWER SOCIAL
Press Down, Black, Right, X, Left.

TEAM PHOTO
At the Credits screen, press Up, Down, X, Up, Down.

GOD MODE
Pause the game and press Down, Up, Down, Up, Right, Down, Right, Left, Start.

MOVE FASTER

Pause the game and press Up, Up, Up, Down, Up, Down, Start.

UNLIMITED XTREME TOKENS

Pause the game and press Left, Down, Right, Down, Up, Up, Down, Up, Start.

TOUCH OF DEATH

During a game, press Left, Left, Right, Left, Right, Up, Start.

100,000 TECH-BITS

At Forge or Beast's store, press Up, Up, Down, Right, Right, Start.

ALL DANGER ROOM COURSES

At the Danger Room Course menu, press Right, Right, Left, Left, Up, Down, Up, Down, Start.

ALL COMICS

Select Review from the Main menu and press Right, Left, Left, Right, Up, Up, Right, Start.

ALL CINEMATICS

Select Review from the Main menu and press Left, Right, Right, Left, Down, Down, Left, Start.

ALL CONCEPTS

Select Review from the Main menu and press Left, Right, Left, Right, Up, Up, Down, Start.

ALL SCREENS

Select Review from the Main menu and press Right, Left, Right, Left, Up, Up, Down, Start.

TY THE TASMANIAN TIGER 3: NIGHT OF THE QUINKAN

100,000 OPALS

During a game, press Start, Start, Y, Start, Start, Y, B, A, B, A.

ALL RINGS

During a game, press Start, Start, Y, Start, Start, Y, B, X, B, X.

ULTIMATE SPIDER-MAN

ALL CHARACTERS

Pause the game and select Controller Setup from the Options screen. Press Right, Down, Right, Down, Left, Up, Left, Right.

ALL COVERS

Pause the game and select Controller Setup from the Options screen. Press Left, Left, Right, Left, Up, Left, Left, Down.

ALL CONCEPT ART

Pause the game and select Controller Setup from the Options screen. Press Down, Down, Down, Up, Down, Up, Left, Left.

ALL LANDMARKS

Pause the game and select Controller Setup from the Options screen. Press Up, Right, Down, Left, Down, Up, Right, Left.

WARPATH

ALL AMMO

Select Cheat Codes from the Options and enter Down, Up, Down, Y. You can also enter this code during a game, by pausing the game and selecting Cheat Codes from the Settings.

GOD MODE

Select Cheat Codes from the Options and enter Up, L-Trigger, X, L-Trigger. You can also enter this code during a game, by pausing the game and selecting Cheat Codes from the Settings.

WIN CURRENT MATCH

Select Cheat Codes from the Options and enter L-Trigger, L-Trigger, L-Trigger, Y. You can also enter this code during a game, by pausing the game and selecting Cheat Codes from the Settings.

LOSE CURRENT MATCH

Select Cheat Codes from the Options and enter L-Trigger, L-Trigger, L-Trigger, A. You can also enter this code during a game, by pausing the game and selecting Cheat Codes from the Settings.

SINGLE PLAYER

Select Cheat Codes from the Options and enter Y, Down, R-Trigger, Down. You can also enter this code during a game, by pausing the game and selecting Cheat Codes from the Settings.

LOCATION STAT

Select Cheat Codes from the Options and enter X, Right, L-Trigger, Left. You can also enter this code during a game, by pausing the game and selecting Cheat Codes from the Settings.

WORLD RACING 2

The following codes are case sensitive. You can enter them as many times as you want while creating a profile.

100 SPEEDBUCKS
Create a new profile with the name EC.

1,000 SPEEDBUCKS
Create a new profile with the name Visa.

10,000 SPEEDBUCKS
Create a new profile with the name MASTERCARD.

100,000 SPEEDBUCKS
Create a new profile with the name AmEx.

X-MEN LEGENDS II: RISE OF APOCALYPSE

ALL CHARACTERS
At the Team Management screen, press Right, Left, Left, Right, Up, Up, Up, Start.

ALL SKINS
At the Team Management screen, press Down, Up, Left, Right, Up, Up, Start.

ALL SKILLS
At the Team Management screen, press Left, Right, Left, Right, Down, Up, Start.

LEVEL 99
At the Team Management screen, press Up, Down, Up, Down, Left, Up, Left, Right, Start.

X-MEN: THE OFFICIAL GAME

DANGER ROOM ICEMAN
At the Cerebro Files menu, press Right, Right, Left, Left, Down, Up, Down, Up, Start.

DANGER ROOM NIGHTCRAWLER
At the Cerebro Files menu, press Up, Up, Down, Down, Left, Right, Left, Right, Start.

DANGER ROOM WOLVERINE
At the Cerebro Files menu, press Down, Down, Up, Up, Right, Left, Right, Left, Start.

XGRA: EXTREME-G RACING ASSOCIATION

ALL LEVELS OF RACING
Enter **FREEPLAY** at the Cheat menu.

ALL TRACKS
Enter **WIBBLE** at the Cheat menu.

O2 LIVERIED
Enter **UCANDO** at the Cheat menu.

MESSAGE IN CREDITS
Enter **MUNCHKIN**, **EDDROOLZ** or **EDDIEPOO** at the Cheat menu.

YAGER

ALL LEVELS
Enter **lvl.activate 1** as a profile name.

9 CONTINUES
Enter set **MAXCNT 9** as a profile name.

COMPLETE DATABASE
Enter **data.setvis 1** as a profile name.

YU-GI-OH! THE DAWN OF DESTINY

COSMO QUEEN CARD IN DECK
Enter your name as **KONAMI**.

TRI-HORN DRAGON CARD IN DECK
Enter your name as **HEARTOFCARDS**.

ZERA THE MANT CARD IN DECK
Enter your name as **XBOX**.

ZAPPER

UNLIMITED LIVES
Pause the game, hold Left Trigger and press Up, Up, Up, Left, Left, Right, Left, Right.

UNLIMITED SHIELD
Pause the game, hold Left Trigger and press Up, Down, Up, Left, Right, Down, Up.

XBOX™ 360

EVERYONE

CARS

FROGGER

LEGO STAR WARS II: THE ORIGINAL TRILOGY

MAJOR LEAGUE BASEBALL 2K6

MOTOGP 06

NBA 2K6

NBA 2K7

NBA LIVE 06

NBA LIVE 07

NCAA FOOTBALL 07

NEED FOR SPEED CARBON

NHL 2K6

TIGER WOODS PGA TOUR 06

TEEN

AMPED 3

BATTLEFIELD 2: MODERN COMBAT

BLAZING ANGELS: SQUADRONS OF WWII

FIGHT NIGHT ROUND 3

FULL AUTO

MARVEL ULTIMATE ALLIANCE

NEED FOR SPEED MOST WANTED

PETER JACKSON'S KING KONG: THE OFFICIAL GAME OF THE MOVIE

TOMB RAIDER: LEGEND

TOM CLANCY'S GHOST RECON ADVANCED WARFIGHTER

TONY HAWK'S AMERICAN WASTELAND

TONY HAWK'S PROJECT 8

Xbox 360™ Table of Contents

AMPED 3

ALL SLEDS

Select Cheat Codes from the Options screen and press Right Trigger, X, Left Trigger, Down, Right, Left Bumper, Left Trigger, Right Trigger, Y, X.

ALL GEAR

Select Cheat Codes from the Options and press Y, Down, Up, Left, Right, Left Bumper, Right, Right Trigger, Right Trigger, Right Bumper.

ALL TRICKS
Select Cheat Codes from the Options screen and press Left Bumper, Right Trigger, Y, Up, Down, X, Left Trigger, Left, Right Bumper, Right Trigger.

ALL LEVELS
Select Cheat Codes from the Options screen and press X, Y, Up, Left, Left Bumper, Left Bumper, Right Trigger, X, Y, Left Trigger.

ALL CONFIGS
Select Cheat Codes from the Options screen and press Down, X, Right, Left Bumper, Right, Right Bumper, X, Right Trigger, Left Trigger, Y.

SUPER SPINS
Select Cheat Codes from the Options screen and press X (x4), Y (x3), X.

AWESOME METER ALWAYS FULL
Select Cheat Codes from the Options screen and press Up, Right Trigger, X, Y, Left Bumper, X, Down, Left Bumper, Right Trigger, Right Bumper.

ALL AWESOMENESS
Select Cheat Codes from the Options screen and press Right Bumper, Right Bumper, Down, Left, Up, Right Trigger, X, Right Bumper, X, X.

ALL BUILD LICENSES
Select Cheat Codes from the Options screen and press Left, Right Trigger, Left Bumper, Right Trigger, X, X, Y, Down, Up, X.

ALL BUILD OBJECTS
Select Cheat Codes from the Options screen and press Left Trigger, Right Trigger, Up, Up, Right Bumper, Left, Right, X, Y, Left Bumper.

ALL CHALLENGES
Select Cheat Codes from the Options screen and press Right, Left Bumper, Left Trigger, X, Left, Right Bumper, Right Trigger, Y, Left Trigger, X.

LOUD SPEAKERS
Select Cheat Codes from the Options screen and press Y, Right Trigger, Right Trigger, Left Bumper, Down, Down, Left, Left, Right, Left Bumper.

LOW GRAVITY BOARDERS
Select Cheat Codes from the Options screen and press Right Trigger, Down, Down, Up, X, Left Bumper, Y, Right Trigger, Y, Down.

NO AI
Select Cheat Codes from the Options screen and press X, X, Left Bumper, Down, Right, Right, Up, Y, Y, Left Trigger.

ALL MUSIC
Select Cheat Codes from the Options screen and press Up, Left, Right Trigger, Right Bumper, Right Trigger, Up, Down, Left, Y, Left Trigger.

BATTLEFIELD 2: MODERN COMBAT

ALL WEAPONS
During a game, hold Right Bumper + Left Bumper and quickly press Right, Right, Down, Up, Left, Left.

BLAZING ANGELS: SQUADRONS OF WWII

ALL MISSIONS, MEDALS, & PLANES
At the Main menu hold Left Trigger + Right Trigger and press X, Left Bumper, Right Bumper, Y, Y, Right Bumper, Left Bumper, X.

GOD MODE
Pause the game, hold Left Trigger and press X, Y, Y, X. Release Left Trigger, hold Right Trigger and press Y, X, X, Y. Re-enter the code to disable it.

INCREASED DAMAGE
Pause the game, hold Left Trigger and press Left Bumper, Left Bumper, Right Bumper. Release Left Trigger, hold Right Trigger and press Right Bumper, Right Bumper, Left Bumper. Re-enter the code to disable it.

CARS

UNLOCK EVERYTHING
Select Cheat Codes from the Options and enter IF900HP.

ALL CHARACTERS
Select Cheat Codes from the Options and enter YAYCARS.

ALL CHARACTER SKINS
Select Cheat Codes from the Options and enter R4MONE.

ALL MINI-GAMES AND COURSES
Select Cheat Codes from the Options and enter MATTL66.

MATER'S COUNTDOWN CLEAN-UP MINI-GAME AND MATER'S SPEEDY CIRCUIT
Select Cheat Codes from the Options and enter TRGTEXC.

FAST START
Select Cheat Codes from the Options and enter IMSPEED.

INFINITE BOOST
Select Cheat Codes from the Options and enter VROOOOM.

ART
Select Cheat Codes from the Options and enter CONC3PT.

VIDEOS
Select Cheat Codes from the Options and enter WATCHIT.

FIGHT NIGHT ROUND 3

ALL VENUES
Create a champ with a first name of **NEWVIEW**.

FROGGER

BIG FROGGER
At the one/two player screen, press Up, Up, Down, Down, Left, Right, Left, Right, B, A.

FULL AUTO

ALL TRACKS, VEHICLES, & WEAPONS
Create a new profile with the name **magicman**.

LEGO STAR WARS II: THE ORIGINAL TRILOGY

BEACH TROOPER
At Mos Eisley Canteena, select Enter Code and enter UCK868. You still need to select Characters and purchase this character for 20,000 studs.

BEN KENOBI (GHOST)
At Mos Eisley Canteena, select Enter Code and enter BEN917. You still need to select Characters and purchase this character for 1,100,000 studs.

BESPIN GUARD
At Mos Eisley Canteena, select Enter Code and enter VHY832. You still need to select Characters and purchase this character for 15,000 studs.

BIB FORTUNA
At Mos Eisley Canteena, select Enter Code and enter WTY721. You still need to select Characters and purchase this character for 16,000 studs.

BOBA FETT

At Mos Eisley Canteena, select Enter Code and enter HLP221. You still need to select Characters and purchase this character for 175,000 studs.

DEATH STAR TROOPER

At Mos Eisley Canteena, select Enter Code and enter BNC332. You still need to select Characters and purchase this character for 19,000 studs.

EWOK

At Mos Eisley Canteena, select Enter Code and enter TTT289. You still need to select Characters and purchase this character for 34,000 studs.

GAMORREAN GUARD

At Mos Eisley Canteena, select Enter Code and enter YZF999. You still need to select Characters and purchase this character for 40,000 studs.

GONK DROID

At Mos Eisley Canteena, select Enter Code and enter NFX582. You still need to select Characters and purchase this character for 1,550 studs.

GRAND MOFF TARKIN

At Mos Eisley Canteena, select Enter Code and enter SMG219. You still need to select Characters and purchase this character for 38,000 studs.

GREEDO

At Mos Eisley Canteena, select Enter Code and enter NAH118. You still need to select Characters and purchase this character for 60,000 studs.

HAN SOLO (HOOD)

At Mos Eisley Canteena, select Enter Code and enter YWM840. You still need to select Characters and purchase this character for 20,000 studs.

IG-88

At Mos Eisley Canteena, select Enter Code and enter NXL973. You still need to select Characters and purchase this character for 30,000 studs.

IMPERIAL GUARD

At Mos Eisley Canteena, select Enter Code and enter MMM111. You still need to select Characters and purchase this character for 45,000 studs.

IMPERIAL OFFICER

At Mos Eisley Canteena, select Enter Code and enter BBV889. You still need to select Characters and purchase this character for 28,000 studs.

IMPERIAL SHUTTLE PILOT

At Mos Eisley Canteena, select Enter Code and enter VAP664. You still need to select Characters and purchase this character for 29,000 studs.

IMPERIAL SPY

At Mos Eisley Canteena, select Enter Code and enter CVT125. You still need to select Characters and purchase this character for 13,500 studs.

JAWA

At Mos Eisley Canteena, select Enter Code and enter JAW499. You still need to select Characters and purchase this character for 24,000 studs.

LOBOT

At Mos Eisley Canteena, select Enter Code and enter UUB319. You still need to select Characters and purchase this character for 11,000 studs.

PALACE GUARD

At Mos Eisley Canteena, select Enter Code and enter SGE549. You still need to select Characters and purchase this character for 14,000 studs.

REBEL PILOT

At Mos Eisley Canteena, select Enter Code and enter CYG336. You still need to select Characters and purchase this character for 15,000 studs.

REBEL TROOPER (HOTH)

At Mos Eisley Canteena, select Enter Code and enter EKU849. You still need to select Characters and purchase this character for 16,000 studs.

SANDTROOPER

At Mos Eisley Canteena, select Enter Code and enter YDV451. You still need to select Characters and purchase this character for 14,000 studs.

SKIFF GUARD

At Mos Eisley Canteena, select Enter Code and enter GBU888. You still need to select Characters and purchase this character for 12,000 studs.

SNOWTROOPER

At Mos Eisley Canteena, select Enter Code and enter NYU989. You still need to select Characters and purchase this character for 16,000 studs.

STROMTROOPER

At Mos Eisley Canteena, select Enter Code and enter PTR345. You still need to select Characters and purchase this character for 10,000 studs.

THE EMPEROR

At Mos Eisley Canteena, select Enter Code and enter HHY382. You still need to select Characters and purchase this character for 275,000 studs.

TIE FIGHTER

At Mos Eisley Canteena, select Enter Code and enter HDY739. You still need to select Characters and purchase this character for 60,000 studs.

TIE FIGHTER PILOT

At Mos Eisley Canteena, select Enter Code and enter NNZ316. You still need to select Characters and purchase this character for 21,000 studs.

TIE INTERCEPTOR

At Mos Eisley Canteena, select Enter Code and enter QYA828. You still need to select Characters and purchase this character for 40,000 studs.

TUSKEN RAIDER

At Mos Eisley Canteena, select Enter Code and enter PEJ821. You still need to select Characters and purchase this character for 23,000 studs.

UGNAUGHT

At Mos Eisley Canteena, select Enter Code and enter UGN694. You still need to select Characters and purchase this character for 36,000 studs.

MAJOR LEAGUE BASEBALL 2K6

UNLOCK EVERYTHING
Select Enter Cheat Code from the My 2K6 menu and enter **Derek Jeter**.

TOPPS 2K STARS
Select Enter Cheat Code from the My 2K6 menu and enter **Dream Team**.

SUPER WALL CLIMB
Select Enter Cheat Code from the My 2K6 menu and enter **Last Chance**. Enable the cheats by selecting My Cheats or selecting Cheat Codes from the in-game Options screen.

SUPER PITCHES
Select Enter Cheat Code from the My 2K6 menu and enter **Unhittable**. Enable the cheats by selecting My Cheats or selecting Cheat Codes from the in-game Options screen.

ROCKET ARMS
Select Enter Cheat Code from the My 2K6 menu and enter **Gotcha**. Enable the cheats by selecting My Cheats or selecting Cheat Codes from the in-game Options screen.

BOUNCY BALL
Select Enter Cheat Code from the My 2K6 menu and enter **Crazy Hops**. Enable the cheats by selecting My Cheats or selecting Cheat Codes from the in-game Options.

MARVEL ULTIMATE ALLIANCE

UNLOCK ALL SKINS
At the Team Menu, press Up, Down, Left, Right, Left, Right, Start.

UNLOCKS ALL HERO POWERS
At the Team Menu, press Left, Right, Up, Down, Up, Down, Start.

ALL HEROES TO LEVEL 99
At the Team Menu, press Up, Left, Up, Left, Down, Right, Down, Right, Start.

UNLOCK ALL HEROES
At the Team Menu, press Up, Up, Down, Down, Left, Left, Left, Start.

UNLOCK DAREDEVIL
At the Team Menu, press Left, Left, Right, Right, Up, Down, Up, Down, Start.

UNLOCK SILVER SURFER
At the Team Menu, press Down, Left, Left, Up, Right, Up, Down, Left, Start.

GOD MODE
During gameplay, press Up, Down, Up, Down, Up, Left, Down, Right, Start.

TOUCH OF DEATH
During gameplay, press Left, Right, Down, Down, Right, Left, Start.

SUPER SPEED
During gameplay, press Up, Left, Up, Right, Down, Right, Start.

FILL MOMENTUM
During gameplay, press Left, Right, Right, Left, Up, Down, Down, Up, Start.

UNLOCK ALL COMICS
At the Review menu, press Left, Right, Right, Left, Up, Up, Right, Start.

UNLOCK ALL CONCEPT ART
At the Review menu, press Down, Down, Down, Right, Right, Left, Down, Start.

UNLOCK ALL CINEMATICS
At the Review menu, press Up, Left, Left, Up, Right, Right, Up, Start.

UNLOCK ALL LOAD SCREENS
At the Review menu, press Up, Down, Right, Left, Up, Up Down, Start.

UNLOCK ALL COURSES
At the Comic Missions menu, press Up, Right, Left, Down, Up, Right, Left, Down, Start.

MOTOGP 06

USA EXTREME BIKE
At the game mode screen, press Right, Up, B, B, A, B, Up, B, B, A.

NBA 2K6

CELEBRITY STREET OPTION

Select Codes from the Features menu and enter

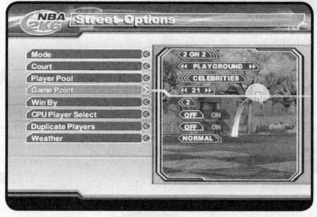

2KSPORTS TEAM

Select Codes from the Features menu and enter **2ksports. ballers**.

2K6 TEAM

Select Codes from the Features menu and enter **nba2k6**.

VC TEAM

Select Codes from the Features menu and enter **vcteam**.

NIKE SHOX MTX SHOES

Select Codes from the Features menu and enter **crazylift**.

NIKE ZOOM 20-5-5 SHOES

Select Codes from the Features menu and enter **lebronsummerkicks**.

NIKE ZOOM KOBE 1 SHOES

Select Codes from the Features menu and enter **kobe**.

NIKE ZOOM LEBRON III ALL-STAR COLORWAY SHOES

Select Codes from the Features menu and enter **lb allstar**.

NIKE ZOOM LEBRON III BLACK/CRIMSON SHOES

Select Codes from the Features menu and enter **lb crimsonblack**.

NIKE ZOOM LEBRON III SPECIAL BIRTHDAY EDITION SHOES

Select Codes from the Features menu and enter **lb bday**.

NIKE ZOOM LEBRON III WHITE/GOLD SHOES

Select Codes from the Features menu and enter **lb whitegold**.

NIKE UP TEMPO PRO SHOES

Select Codes from the Features menu and enter **anklebreakers**.

2006 ALL-STAR UNIFORMS

Select Codes from the Features menu and enter **fanfavorites**.

ST. PATRICK'S DAY UNIFORMS

Select Codes from the Features menu and enter **gogreen**.

BULLS RETRO UNIFORM

Select Codes from the Features menu and enter **chi retro**.

CAVALIERS ALTERNATE UNIFORM

Select Codes from the Features menu and enter **cle 2nd**.

CELTICS ALTERNATE UNIFORM

Select Codes from the Features menu and enter **bos 2nd**.

CLIPPERS RETRO UNIFORM

Select Codes from the Features menu and enter **lac retro**.

GRIZZLIES RETRO UNIFORM

Select Codes from the Features menu and enter **mem retro**.

HEAT RETRO UNIFORM

Select Codes from the Features menu and enter **mia retro**.

HORNETS RETRO UNIFORM

Select Codes from the Features menu and enter **no retro**.

KINGS ALTERNATE UNIFORM

Select Codes from the Features menu and enter **sac 2nd**.

KNICKS RETRO UNIFORM

Select Codes from the Features menu and enter **ny retro**.

MAGIC RETRO UNIFORM

Select Codes from the Features menu and enter **orl retro**.

NETS RETRO UNIFORM

Select Codes from the Features menu and enter **nj retro**.

NUGGETS ALTERNATE UNIFORM

Select Codes from the Features menu and enter **den 2nd**.

2005-06 PACERS UNIFORM

Select Codes from the Features menu and enter **31andonly**.

PISTONS ALTERNATE UNIFORM

Select Codes from the Features menu and enter **det 2nd**.

ROCKETS RETRO UNIFORM

Select Codes from the Features menu and enter **hou retro**.

SONICS RETRO UNIFORM

Select Codes from the Features menu and enter **sea retro**.

SUNS RETRO UNIFORM

Select Codes from the Features menu and enter **phx retro**.

WIZARDS RETRO UNIFORM

Select Codes from the Features menu and enter **was retro**.

+10 BONUS FOR DEFENSIVE AWARENESS

Find the PowerBar vending machine in The Crib. Select Enter Code and enter **lockdown**.

+10 BONUS FOR OFFENSIVE AWARENESS

Find the PowerBar vending machine in The Crib. Select Enter Code and enter **getaclue**.

MAX DURABILITY

Find the PowerBar vending machine in The Crib. Select Enter Code and enter **noinjury**.

UNLIMITED STAMINA

Find the PowerBar vending machine in The Crib. Select Enter Code and enter **nrgmax**.

POWERBAR TATTOO

Find the PowerBar vending machine in The Crib. Select Enter Code and enter **pbink**. You can now use it in the game's Create Player feature.

NBA 2K7

MAX DURABILITY

Select Codes from the Features menu and enter ironman.

UNLIMITED STAMINA

Select Codes from the Features menu and enter norest.

+10 DEFFENSIVE AWARENESS

Select Codes from the Features menu and enter getstops.

+10 OFFENSIVE AWARENESS

Select Codes from the Features menu and enter inthezone.

TOPPS 2K SPORTS ALL-STARS

Select Codes from the Features menu and enter topps2ksports.

ABA BALL

Select Codes from the Features menu and enter payrespect.

NBA LIVE 06

EASTERN ALL-STARS 2005-06 AWAY JERSEYS
Select NBA Codes from My NBA Live and enter XCVB5387EQ.

EASTERN ALL-STARS 2005-06 HOME JERSEY
Select NBA Codes from My NBA Live and enter 234SDFGHMO.

WESTERN ALL-STARS 2005-06 AWAY JERSEY
Select NBA Codes from My NBA Live and enter 39N56B679J.

WESTERN ALL-STARS 2005-06 HOME JERSEY
Select NBA Codes from My NBA Live and enter 2J9UWABNP1.

BOSTON CELTICS 2005-06 ALTERNATE JERSEY
Select NBA Codes from My NBA Live and enter 193KSHU88J.

CLEVELAND CAVALIERS 2005-06 ALTERNATE JERSEY
Select NBA Codes from My NBA Live and enter 9922NVDKVT.

DENVER NUGGETS 2005-06 ALTERNATE JERSEYS
Select NBA Codes from My NBA Live and enter XWETJK72FC.

DETROIT PISTONS 2005-06 ALTERNATE JERSEY
Select NBA Codes from My NBA Live and enter JANTWIKBS6.

INDIANA PACERS 2005-06 ALTERNATE AWAY JERSEY
Select NBA Codes from My NBA Live and enter PSDF90PPJN.

INDIANA PACERS 2005-06 ALTERNATE HOME JERSEY
Select NBA Codes from My NBA Live and enter SDF786WSHW.

SACRAMENTO KINGS 2005-06 ALTERNATE JERSEY
Select NBA Codes from My NBA Live and enter **654NNBFDWA**.

A3 GARNETT 3
Select NBA Codes from My NBA Live and enter **DRI239CZ49**.

JORDAN MELO V.5 WHITE & BLUE
Select NBA Codes from My NBA Live and enter **5223WERPII**.

JORDAN MELO V.5 WHITE & YELLOW
Select NBA Codes from My NBA Live and enter **ZXDR7362Q1**.

JORDAN XIV BLACK & RED
Select NBA Codes from My NBA Live and enter **144FVNHM35**.

JORDAN XIV WHITE & GREEN
Select NBA Codes from My NBA Live and enter **67YFH9839F**.

JORDAN XIV WHITE & RED
Select NBA Codes from My NBA Live and enter **743HFDRAU8**.

S. CARTER III LE
Select NBA Codes from My NBA Live and enter **JZ3SCARTVY**.

T-MAC 5 BLACK
Select NBA Codes from My NBA Live and enter **258SHQW95B**.

T-MAC 5 WHITE
Select NBA Codes from My NBA Live and enter **HGS83KP234P**.

ANSWER DMX 10
Select NBA Codes from My NBA Live and enter **RBKAIUSAB7**.

ANSWER IX AND THE RBK ANSWER IX VIDEO
Select NBA Codes from My NBA Live and enter **AI9BUBBA7T**.

THE QUESTION AND THE MESSAGE FROM ALLEN IVERSON VIDEO
Select NBA Codes from My NBA Live and enter **HOYAS3AI6L**.

NBA LIVE 07

ADIDAS ARTILLERY II BLACK AND THE RBK ANSWER 9 VIDEO
Select NBA Codes from My NBA Live and enter 99B6356HAN.

ADIDAS ARTILLERY II
Select NBA Codes and enter NTGNFUE87H.

ADIDAS BTB LOW AND THE MESSAGE FROM ALLEN IVERSON VIDEO
Select NBA Codes and enter 7FB3KS9JQ0.

ADIDAS C-BILLUPS
Select NBA Codes and enter BV6877HB9N.

ADIDAS C-BILLUPS BLACK
Select NBA Codes and enter 85NVLDMWS5.

ADIDAS CAMPUS LT
Select NBA Codes and enter CLT2983NC8.

ADIDAS CRAZY 8
Select NBA Codes and enter CC98KKL814.

ADIDAS EQUIPMENT BBALL
Select NBA Codes and enter 220IUJKMDR.

ADIDAS GARNETT BOUNCE
Select NBA Codes and enter HYIOUHCAAN.

ADIDAS GARNETT BOUNCE BLACK
Select NBA Codes and enter KDZ2MQL17W.

ADIDAS GIL-ZERO
Select NBA Codes and enter 23DN1PPOG4.

ADIDAS GIL-ZERO BLACK
Select NBA Codes and enter QQQ3JCUYQ7.

ADIDAS GIL-ZERO MID
Select NBA Codes and enter 1GSJC8JWRL.

ADIDAS GIL-ZERO MID BLACK
Select NBA Codes and enter 369V6RVU3G.

ADIDAS STEALTH
Select NBA Codes and enter FE454DFJCC.

ADIDAS T-MAC 6
Select NBA Codes and enter MCJK843NNC.

ADIDAS T-MAC 6 WHITE
Select NBA Codes and enter 84GF7EJG8V.

CHARLOTTE BOBCATS 2006-07 ALTERNATE JERSEY
Select NBA Codes and enter WEDX671H7S.

UTAH JAZZ 2006-07 ALTERNATE JERSEY
Select NBA Codes and enter VCBI89FK83.

NEW JERSEY NETS 2006-07 ALTERNATE JERSEY
Select NBA Codes and enter D4SAA98U5H.

WASHINGTON WIZARDS 2006-07 ALTERNATE JERSEY
Select NBA Codes and enter QV93NLKXQC.

EASTERN ALL-STARS 2006-07 AWAY JERSEY
Select NBA Codes and enter WOCNW4KL7L.

EASTERN ALL-STARS 2006-07 HOME JERSEY
Select NBA Codes and enter 5654ND43N6.

WESTERN ALL-STARS 2006-07 AWAY JERSEY
Select NBA Codes and enter XX93BVL20U.

WESTERN ALL-STARS 2006-07 HOME JERSEY
Select NBA Codes and enter 993NSKL199.

NCAA FOOTBALL 07

#16 BAYLOR
Select Pennant Collection from My NCAA. Press Select and enter Sic Em.

#16 NIKE SPEED TD
Select Pennant Collection from My NCAA. Press Select and enter Light Speed.

#63 ILLINOIS
Select Pennant Collection from My NCAA. Press Select and enter Oskee Wow.

#160 TEXAS TECH
Select Pennant Collection from My NCAA. Press Select and enter Fight.

#200 FIRST AND FIFTEEN
Select Pennant Collection from My NCAA. Press Select and enter Thanks.

#201 BLINK
Select Pennant Collection from My NCAA. Press Select and enter For.

#202 BOING
Select Pennant Collection from My NCAA. Press Select and enter Registering.

#204 BUTTER FINGERS
Select Pennant Collection from My NCAA. Press Select and enter With EA.

#205 CROSSED THE LINE
Select Pennant Collection from My NCAA. Press Select and enter Tiburon.

#206 CUFFED
Select Pennant Collection from My NCAA. Press Select and enter EA Sports.

#207 EXTRA CREDIT
Select Pennant Collection from My NCAA. Press Select and enter Touchdown.

#208 HELIUM
Select Pennant Collection from My NCAA. Press Select and enter In The Zone.

#209 HURRICANE
Select Pennant Collection from My NCAA. Press Select and enter Turnover.

#210 INSTANT FREPLAY
Select Pennant Collection from My NCAA. Press Select and enter Impact.

#211 JUMBALAYA
Select Pennant Collection from My NCAA. Press Select and enter Heisman.

#212 MOLASSES
Select Pennant Collection from My NCAA. Press Select and enter Game Time.

#213 NIKE FREE
Select Pennant Collection from My NCAA. Press Select and enter Break Free.

#214 NIKE MAGNIGRIP
Select Pennant Collection from My NCAA. Press Select and enter Hand Picked.

#215 NIKE PRO
Select Pennant Collection from My NCAA. Press Select and enter No Sweat.

#219 QB DUD
Select Pennant Collection from My NCAA. Press Select and enter Elite 11.

#221 STEEL TOE
Select Pennant Collection from My NCAA. Press Select and enter Gridiron.

#222 STIFFED
Select Pennant Collection from My NCAA. Press Select and enter NCAA.

#223 SUPER DIVE
Select Pennant Collection from My NCAA. Press Select and enter Upset.

#224 TAKE YOUR TIME
Select Pennant Collection from My NCAA. Press Select and enter Football.

#225 THREAD & NEEDLE
Select Pennant Collection from My NCAA. Press Select and enter 06.

#226 TOUGH AS NAILS
Select Pennant Collection from My NCAA. Press Select and enter Offense.

#227 TRIP
Select Pennant Collection from My NCAA. Press Select and enter Defense.

#228 WHAT A HIT
Select Pennant Collection from My NCAA. Press Select and enter Blitz.

#229 KICKER HEX
Select Pennant Collection from My NCAA. Press Select and enter Sideline.

#273 2004 ALL-AMERICANS
Select Pennant Collection from My NCAA. Press Select and enter Fumble.

#274 ALL-ALABAMA
Select Pennant Collection from My NCAA. Press Select and enter Roll Tide.

#276 ALL-ARKANSAS
Select Pennant Collection from My NCAA. Press Select and enter Woopigsooie.

#277 ALL-AUBURN
Select Pennant Collection from My NCAA. Press Select and enter War Eagle.

#278 ALL-CLEMSON
Select Pennant Collection from My NCAA. Press Select and enter Death Valley.

#279 ALL-COLORADO
Select Pennant Collection from My NCAA. Press Select and enter Glory.

#280 ALL-FLORIDA
Select Pennant Collection from My NCAA. Press Select and enter Great To Be.

#281 ALL-FSU
Select Pennant Collection from My NCAA. Press Select and enter Uprising.

#282 ALL-GEORGIA
Select Pennant Collection from My NCAA. Press Select and enter Hunker Down.

#283 ALL-IOWA
Select Pennant Collection from My NCAA. Press Select and enter On Iowa.

#284 ALL-KANSAS STATE
Select Pennant Collection from My NCAA. Press Select and enter Victory.

#285 ALL-LSU
Select Pennant Collection from My NCAA. Press Select and enter Geaux Tigers.

#286 ALL-MIAMI
Select Pennant Collection from My NCAA. Press Select and enter Raising Cane.

#287 ALL-MICHIGAN
Select Pennant Collection from My NCAA. Press Select and enter Go Blue.

#288 ALL-MISSISSIPPI STATE
Select Pennant Collection from My NCAA. Press Select and enter Hail State.

#289 ALL-NEBRASKA
Select Pennant Collection from My NCAA. Press Select and enter Go Big Red.

#290 ALL-NORTH CAROLINA
Select Pennant Collection from My NCAA. Press Select and enter Rah Rah.

#291 ALL-NOTRE DAME
Select Pennant Collection from My NCAA. Press Select and enter Golden Domer.

#292 ALL-OHIO STATE
Select Pennant Collection from My NCAA. Press Select and enter Killer Nuts.

#293 ALL-OKLAHOMA
Select Pennant Collection from My NCAA. Press Select and enter Boomer.

#294 ALL-OKLAHOMA STATE
Select Pennant Collection from My NCAA. Press Select and enter Go Pokes.

#295 ALL-OREGON
Select Pennant Collection from My NCAA. Press Select and enter Quack Attack.

#296 ALL-PENN STATE
Select Pennant Collection from My NCAA. Press Select and enter We Are.

#297 ALL-PITTSBURGH
Select Pennant Collection from My NCAA. Press Select and enter Lets Go Pitt.

#298 ALL-PURDUE
Select Pennant Collection from My NCAA. Press Select and enter Boiler Up.

#299 ALL-SYRACUSE
Select Pennant Collection from My NCAA. Press Select and enter Orange Crush.

#300 ALL-TENNESSEE
Select Pennant Collection from My NCAA. Press Select and enter Big Orange.

#301 ALL-TEXAS
Select Pennant Collection from My NCAA. Press Select and enter Hook Em.

#302 ALL-TEXAS A&M
Select Pennant Collection from My NCAA. Press Select and enter Gig Em.

#303 ALL-UCLA
Select Pennant Collection from My NCAA. Press Select and enter MIGHTY.

#304 ALL-USC
Select Pennant Collection from My NCAA. Press Select and enter Fight On.

#305 ALL-VIRGINIA
Select Pennant Collection from My NCAA. Press Select and enter Wahoos.

#306 ALL-VIRGINIA TECH
Select Pennant Collection from My NCAA. Press Select and enter Tech Triumph.

#307 ALL-WASHINGTON
Select Pennant Collection from My NCAA. Press Select and enter Bow Down.

#308 ALL-WISCONSIN
Select Pennant Collection from My NCAA. Press Select and enter U Rah Rah.

#311 ARK MASCOT
Select Pennant Collection from My NCAA. Press Select and enter Bear Down.

#329 GT MASCOT
Select Pennant Collection from My NCAA. Press Select and enter RamblinWreck.

#333 ISU MASCOT
Select Pennant Collection from My NCAA. Press Select and enter Red And Gold.

#335 KU MASCOT
Select Pennant Collection from My NCAA. Press Select and enter Rock Chalk.

#341 MINN MASCOT
Select Pennant Collection from My NCAA. Press Select and enter Rah Rah Rah.

#344 MIZZOU MASCOT
Select Pennant Collection from My NCAA. Press Select and enter Mizzou Rah.

#346 MSU MASCOT
Select Pennant Collection from My NCAA. Press Select and enter Go Green.

#349 NCSU MASCOT
Select Pennant Collection from My NCAA. Press Select and enter Go Pack.

#352 NU MASCOT
Select Pennant Collection from My NCAA. Press Select and enter Go Cats.

#360 S CAR MASCOT
Select Pennant Collection from My NCAA. Press Select and enter Go Carolina.

#371 UK MASCOT
Select Pennant Collection from My NCAA. Press Select and enter On On UK.

#382 WAKE FOREST
Select Pennant Collection from My NCAA. Press Select and enter Go Deacs Go.

#385 WSU MASCOT
Select Pennant Collection from My NCAA. Press Select and enter All Hail.

#386 WVU MASCOT
Select Pennant Collection from My NCAA. Press Select and enter Hail WV.

NEED FOR SPEED CARBON

CASTROL CASH
At the main menu, press Down, Up, Left, Down, Right, Up, X, B. This will give you 10,000 extra cash.

INFINITE CREW CHARGE
At the main menu, press Down, Up, Up, Right, Left, Left, Right, X.

INFINITE NITROUS
At the main menu, press Left, Up, Left, Down, Left, Down, Right, X.

INFINITE SPEEDBREAKER
At the main menu, press Down, Right, Right, Left, Right, Up, Down, X.

NEED FOR SPEED CARBON LOGO VINYLS
At the main menu, press Right, Up, Down, Up, Down, Left, Right, X.

NEED FOR SPEED CARBON SPECIAL LOGO VINYLS
At the main menu, press Up, Up, Down, Down, Down, Down, Up, X.

NEED FOR SPEED MOST WANTED

BURGER KING CHALLENGE
At the Title screen, press Up, Down, Up, Down, Left, Right, Left, Right.

CASTROL SYNTEC VERSION OF THE FORD GT
At the Title screen, press Left, Right, Left, Right, Up, Down, Up, Down.

MARKER FOR BACKROOM OF THE ONE-STOP SHOP
At the Title screen, press Up, Up, Down, Down, Left, Right, Up, Down.

JUNKMAN ENGINE
At the Title screen, press Up, Up, Down, Down, Left, Right, Up, Down.

PORSCHE CAYMAN
At the Title screen, press L, R, R, R, Right, Left, Right, Down.

NHL 2K6

CHEAT MODE
Select Manage Profiles from the Options menu. Create a new profile with the name **Turco813**.

PETER JACKSON'S KING KONG: THE OFFICIAL GAME OF THE MOVIE

At the Main menu hold Left Bumper + Right Bumper + Left Trigger + Right Trigger and press Down, Up, Y, X, Down, Down, Y, Y. Release the buttons to access the Cheat option. The Cheat option will also be available on the pause menu. You cannot record your scores using cheat codes.

GOD MODE
Select Cheat and enter **8wonder**.

ALL CHAPTERS
Select Cheat and enter **KKst0ry**.

AMMO 999
Select Cheat and enter **KK 999 mun**.

MACHINE GUN
Select Cheat and enter **KKcapone**.

REVOLVER
Select Cheat and enter **KKtigun**.

SNIPER RIFLE
Select Cheat and enter **KKsn1per**.

INFINITE SPEARS
Select Cheat and enter **lance 1nf**.

ONE-HIT KILLS
Select Cheat and enter **GrosBras**.

EXTRAS
Select Cheat and enter **KKmuseum**.

TIGER WOODS PGA TOUR 06

ALL GOLFERS
Select Password from the Options screen and enter **itsinthegame**.

ALL CLUBS
Select Password from the Options screen and enter **clubs11**.

GOLD COLLECTION EA SPORTS BALL
Select Password from the Options screen and enter **golfisfun**.

NICKLAUS ITEMS
Select Password from the Options screen and enter **goldenbear**.

ALL COURSES
Select Password from the Options screen and enter **eyecandy**.

VIJAY SINGH
Select Password from the Options screen and enter **victory**.

TOMB RAIDER: LEGEND

The following codes must be unlocked in the game before using them.

BULLETPROOF
During a game, hold Left Trigger and press A, Right Trigger, Y, Right Trigger, X, Left Bumper.

DRAIN ENEMY HEALTH
During a game, hold Left Trigger and press X, B, A, Left Bumper, Right Trigger, Y.

INFINITE ASSAULT RIFLE AMMO
During a game, hold Left Bumper and press A, B, A, Left Trigger, X, Y.

INFINITE GRENADE LAUNCHER AMMO
During a game, hold Left Bumper and press Left Trigger, Y, Right Trigger, B, Left Trigger, X.

INFINITE SHOTGUN AMMO
During a game, hold Left Bumper and press Right Trigger, B, X, Left Trigger, X, A.

INFINITE SMG AMMO
During a game, hold Left Bumper and press B, Y, Left Trigger, Right Trigger, A, B.

EXCALIBUR
During a game, hold Left Bumper and press Y, A, B, Right Trigger, Y, Left Trigger.

SOUL REAVER
During a game, hold Left Bumper and press A, Right Trigger, B, Right Trigger, Left Trigger, X.

ONE-SHOT KILL
During a game, hold Left Trigger and press Y, A, Y, X, Left Bumper, B.

TEXTURELESS MODE
During a game, hold Left Trigger and press Left Bumper, A, B, A, Y, Right Trigger.

TOM CLANCY'S GHOST RECON ADVANCED WARFIGHTER

ALL MISSIONS
At the Mission Select screen, hold Back + Left Trigger + Right Trigger and press Y, Right Bumper, Y, Right Bumper, X.

FULL HEALTH
Pause the game, hold Back + Left Trigger + Right Trigger and press Left Bumper, Left Bumper, Right Bumper, X, Right Bumper, Y.

INVINCIBLE
Pause the game, hold Back + Left Trigger + Right Trigger and press Y, Y, X, Right Bumper, X, Left Bumper.

TEAM INVINCIBLE
Pause the game, hold Back + Left Trigger + Right Trigger and press X, X, Y, Right Bumper, Y, Left Bumper.

UNLIMITED AMMO
Pause the game, hold Back + Left Trigger + Right Trigger and press Right Bumper, Right Bumper, Left Bumper, X, Left Bumper, Y.

TONY HAWK'S AMERICAN WASTELAND

ALWAYS SPECIAL
Select Cheat Codes from the Options screen and enter **uronfire**. Pause the game and select Cheats from the Game Options to enable the code.

PERFECT RAIL
Select Cheat Codes from the Options screen and enter **grindxpert**. Pause the game and select Cheats from the Game Options to enable the code.

PERFECT SKITCH
Select Cheat Codes from the Options screen and enter **h!tchar!de**. Pause the game and select Cheats from the Game Options to enable the code.

PERFECT MANUAL
Select Cheat Codes from the Options and enter **2wheels!**. Pause the game and select Cheats from the Game Options to enable the code.

MOON GRAVITY
Select Cheat Codes from the Options and enter **2them00n**. Pause the game and select Cheats from the Game Options to enable the code.

MAT HOFFMAN
Select Cheat Codes from the Options screen and enter **the_condor**.

TONY HAWK'S PROJECT 8

SPONSOR ITEMS
As you progress through Career mode and move up the rankings, you gain sponsors and each comes with its own Create-a-skater item.

RANK REQUIRED	CAS ITEM UNLOCKED
Rank 040	Adio Kenny V2 Shoes
Rank 050	Quiksilver_Hoody_3
Rank 060	Birdhouse Tony Hawk Deck
Rank 080	Vans No Skool Gothic Shoes
Rank 100	Volcom Scallero Jacket
Rank 110	eS Square One Shoes
Rank 120	Almost Watch What You Say Deck
Rank 140	DVS Adage Shoe
Rank 150	Element Illuminate Deck
Rank 160	Etnies Sheckler White Lavender Shoes
Complete Skateshop Goal	Stereo Soundwave Deck

SKATERS
All of the skaters, except for Tony Hawk, must be unlocked by completing challenges in the Career Mode. They are useable in Free Skate and 2 Player modes.

SKATER	HOW THEY ARE UNLOCKED
Tony Hawk	Always Unlocked
Lyn-z Adams Hawkins	Complete Pro Challenge